'Everything you would expect of a James Naughtie book – droll, absorbing and wonderfully perceptive.'
Bill Bryson

'Naughtie has been there, done that and got the bumper sticker. Now 50 years of adventuring is distilled into a revealing and at times spellbinding tapestry of a nation in all its glories and complexities ... This is the rarest of reads, a book that makes you ache to hop on a plane and sample this extraordinary country for yourself. It is thought-provoking, constantly surprising and hugely entertaining. Sublime stuff.'
Michael Simkins, *The Mail on Sunday*

'This book is first a memoir of his experiences which have included covering every Presidential election from Reagan to Trump ... There are lively descriptions and acute observations of politicians in action ... Delightful and always informative ... This is an illuminating and thoroughly enjoyable book.'
Allan Massie, *Scotland on Sunday*

'Naughtie's longstanding experience with and love for this wonderful, frustrating, perplexing country produces brilliant insights about our wonders and acute analyses of our frustrations. Yet – outsider though Naughtie may be – there is something almost American in his observations. That is, Jim admits to remaining perplexed by America, just like a true American.'
P.J. O'Rourke

'An insightful account of living through momentous times ... much to enjoy in Naughtie's astute memoir.'
Martin Chilton, *The Independent*

ON THE ROAD

*American Adventures
from Nixon to Trump*

JAMES NAUGHTIE

**SIMON &
SCHUSTER**

London · New York · Sydney · Toronto · New Delhi

First published in Great Britain by Simon & Schuster UK Ltd, 2020
This edition published in Great Britain by Simon & Schuster UK Ltd, 2021

1 3 5 7 9 10 8 6 4 2

Simon & Schuster UK Ltd
1st Floor
222 Gray's Inn Road
London WC1X 8HB

www.simonandschuster.co.uk
www.simonandschuster.com.au
www.simonandschuster.co.in

Simon & Schuster Australia, Sydney
Simon & Schuster India, New Delhi

A CIP catalogue record for this book
is available from the British Library

Paperback ISBN: 978-1-4711-7744-6
eBook ISBN: 978-1-4711-7743-9

Typeset in Sabon by M Rules
Printed in the UK by CPI Group (UK) Ltd, Croydon, CR0 4YY

In memory of Felicity Bryan (1945 - 2020)

and for

Helen Hershkoff and Stephen Loffredo,
true Americans friends

'In this land of the most persistent idealism and the blandest cynicism, the race is on between its decadence and its vitality.'

ALISTAIR COOKE, *America*,
BBC Television 1972

CONTENTS

Introduction: Journeying   1

1. Into the Pickle Barrel   9

2. Floodtide   34

3. The Pursuit of Happiness   60

4. The Genial Revolution   78

5. The Roaring Nineties   101

6. Wartime   129

7. Two Races of a Lifetime   157

8. A Culture of Contempt   193

9. 'Don't You Know Me, I'm Your Native Son'   221

10. From Venus to Mars   253

11. Decadence and Vitality   282

12. Alone   299

13. Afterwards   327

Acknowledgements   331

Index   333

Journeying

Flying from a near-empty airport and a boarded-up, buttoned-down New York a few days after the presidential election of 2020 was to leave behind an embattled country. Fear of the pandemic was visible on the streets, and the four days that had passed before the result became clear spawned exuberance that was matched by bitter anger. Joe Biden's supporters were gleeful at the coming end of the Donald Trump era, but the president himself was leading a charge against perhaps the last of the enemies he'd confront from the White House, the American democratic process itself.

Having claimed premature victory on election night, knowing that the proper counting of mail-in ballots had yet to begin in some of the most closely contested states, he was fulfilling a promise he'd made in the summer of a tumultuous year – that if he lost, he would not feel obliged to accept the result. As an emblem of national division, that challenge was the natural climax to his four years in office. He had never planned to go quietly. Instead, there would be one last fight.

For someone who first experienced America when it was troubled to its core by the Vietnam war, the tumult surrounding Trump's defeat was like an echo of distant thunder in the memory. In the intervening decades, the country had never been so divided as it now found itself again. Anger was everywhere: from Trump's opponents in despair at his behaviour, and among his own supporters for whom defeat of their hero could only be explained by fraud perpetrated by malevolent forces. Those millions who just wanted some relief and some quiet – an end to an angry time – could only listen to the rage.

Somewhere in that noise, I recognised the America I first experienced as a teenager, and the experiences and travels afterwards seemed more than ever to take the shape of one journey. That is the story of this book, which was partly conceived as a result of the shock in realising that in mid-summer of election year, fifty years would have passed since I first set foot in the country. The best American journeys are long, and they take time to reveal their secrets.

But the story in these pages is not history, nor polemic – just the contents of a reporter's notebook and a tumbledown release of memories of people, places and events. It's a tale of personal experience, no more, with observations that spring naturally from a fascination with the United States. These reflections are both sunny and dark, and the fun is just as important. Public events, happy and melancholy, obviously shape this account – presidential elections, the rise and fall of political fortunes, lightning strikes and wars – but I hope a light breeze zips through it all, and brings brightness. Looking back to first experiences in America, with the 1960s just behind, the thrill in my memory comes from the characters. Encountering for the first time New Yorkers leaping straight out of Damon Runyan's pages, hearing the music of the South in black bars and Appalachian hamlets, encountering that indomitable frontier spirit, was to be taken away; just as the open road to the prairies or along the seashore pulled the curtain up on a different landscape.

The intoxication is easily described, yet it's touched by an old shadow cast by every empire that has seen its power and assurance wax and wane. The heart of America, although it beats with precious self-confidence, is trembling.

Donald Trump was the emblem of that pain for four years, but the story he told stretched back a long way. Anyone who first came to America in the age of Vietnam, like me, and then watched Watergate drain politics of so many illusions, has watched the struggle between America's view of itself and, set against it, the judgement of an often-sceptical world. A crisis of identity now runs deep. For more than a century, Americans have been reared to accept with certainty the idea that progress is in their gift – that each generation will pass on more to its children that it inherited itself, and that the world will benefit. Perhaps even be grateful. But the questioning is louder now, and the doubt gnaws away.

Nowhere talks about itself with more enthusiasm and feeling, and like all obsessions it has an undulating fear underneath: can this survive?

Not long ago it was routine for American schoolchildren to have to memorise Abraham Lincoln's Gettysburg address, admittedly quite a manageable task because that glittering piece of oratory does its work in only 272 words. The effect was to remind them how young the country was, because the words hark back to a time when national survival was in question, thanks to the wounds of a Civil War that eventually killed one in fifty of the population – 620,000, a number that was only surpassed in all foreign wars put together in Vietnam a century later. Lincoln's words at the graves on the Gettysburg battlefield in 1863 were about the childhood of a country and its fragility.

'Four score and seven years ago our fathers brought forth on this continent a new nation, conceived in Liberty, and dedicated to the proposition that all men are created equal. Now we are engaged in a great civil war, testing whether that nation, or any nation so conceived and so dedicated, can long endure.'

Most Americans wouldn't talk today about the capacity of the Republic to endure, but they certainly wonder what kind of country it will be for their successors, and sense a modern version of that fragility. The current generation has split on ideological lines that once seemed fuzzy, and people talk of the future as a series of decisions that are like turning points with consequences far beyond day-to-day policy, each forcing a choice between radically different options. So the most important political arguments – about citizens' rights, equality between the races, fairness in economic and social life, the very power of national government and the law, the balance between corporate and individual economic interests, the posture to the rest of the world – are always distilled into an argument about what the promise of America was meant to be. Think of the last words of Nick Carraway, F. Scott Fitzgerald's narrator in *The Great*

Gatsby, ruminating even at a time of 1920s wild optimism when he tires of the emptiness he's found in New York and turns to home in the midwest. They ring true today. 'So we beat on, boats against the current, borne back ceaselessly into the past.'

Americans still feel the grip of their national story, and all the contradictions it throws up. A country of different traditions and different peoples; cultures that have gone their separate ways and find it hard to keep in touch. Races that were separated in a country refusing to live out its creed, and who therefore think so differently about it in our time. Yet against that background there is a history of innovation and success, mingled with introspective alarm, that means that light and shade in America becomes a blazing brightness, fighting the dark. The attractiveness of that fire is obvious. Who can ignore it?

Then you face the truth that the country that became the powerhouse of the industrialised world, and the home of adaptability, inventiveness and wealth, was one where such success has bred unrest, social division and where a love of excess in all things has sometimes come to overshadow the original idea at the its heart.

No wonder the place is irresistible. Thinking back to political campaigns and holidays, wanderings into the wild, dozens of small towns and happy valleys, cities that sketch out the twentieth century in their streets, these contrasts are sharp – a vigorous optimism set against urban despair and violence, and an unmistakable anxiety about the future. It explains many of the upheavals of our time, and Donald Trump, too. This book is not about him – emphatically not, because he would take it over – but about the urge that he recognised and to which he gave voice for his own purposes, turning the anger and sense of loss that he identified into an electric current to shock politics. Anyone who has enjoyed America over the last few decades, in melodramatic moments, in crises and at times of hope, will recognise the feelings that are now on the loose in the era that follows Trump.

A storm has passed, but the calm won't last long.

The years covered in these pages catch the modern American paradox. The country that dominated the democratic world in the twentieth century, and claimed victory in the Cold War, found itself at the beginning of the twenty-first at least as divided as it had been when Vietnam wormed into its soul in the 1960s, as if half a century of rampant progress had got it nowhere. Brought up in the belief that no one was stronger, Americans are asking now whether they have become too weak, about the principles of their democracy, why race still matters, and about how they should face the world. It was maybe inevitable that this would come about under a president who, beyond any reasonable argument, had the lowest level of literacy and historical knowledge of any occupant of the White House in his lifetime (as a compendium of his Tweets alone will attest to any doubter, who might note the post-election preferences for messages written in child-like capital letters), and for whom the cry 'America First!' on the day of his inauguration was code for the primacy of self in both politics and the exercise of government.

This is a story about people, some famous and most not, who help to reveal the texture of that history and argument, because they have lived through it, with all the enthusiasm that they're brought up to throw at life. It meanders through corridors in Washington, along country roads, in the canyons of New York, and takes in many of the public events that have shaped the America we know now. But I hope I have balanced them with out-of-the-way experiences, the ones that reveal how people are thinking, and maybe how they have changed in the last few decades. Naturally, voting seasons give the story much of its shape – the four-year cycles of presidential elections, preceded by the spring primaries to weed out candidates and the summer conventions to anoint the two protagonists for a November fight – but there are many digressions on the way

I saw the country for the first time in the summer of 1970, as a young student looking for adventure. A few months of work and travel, which let me wander by bus from coast to coast and absorb some of the bewildering contradictions of America, filled me with the certainty that I would be back soon.

Three years later, I studied there during a year that framed the last act of the Watergate saga, and from the mid-1970s began to come and go as an exhilarating part of a journalistic life. That began as a newspaper reporter on the *Scotsman* and then the *Guardian*, from 1977 until 1988, when I joined the BBC full-time and became presenter of the *World at One* on Radio 4. After six years, I joined the *Today* programme as a presenter, and stayed in the role for twenty-one years before loosening the straps and becoming special correspondent. Throughout, I have been a regular traveller to the United States, sometimes anchoring programmes – on election nights, for example, or in writing and narrating documentaries – but more often simply following the scent that any reporter picks up on the road. I have never been a resident correspondent in Washington – although there was an unforgettable period on the *Washington Post* in 1981 – but I was lucky enough, because of a life that allowed an American interest to grow, to be a regular visitor for work and for pleasure.

My bookshelves are crammed with American history, politics, literature and storytelling of all kinds. Whether at sea on the Pequod with Ishmael and Captain Ahab, following the historian James McPherson on the Civil War trail all the way from Fort Sumter to Appomattox, letting James Lee Burke open up the underworld of New Orleans, walking with Ed McBain through the 87th precinct of New York, or with Robert Frost and Robert Lowell in the poetry that captures the New England spirit at its best, at a political convention with Norman Mailer, or following LBJ from Texas with Robert A. Caro as biographer, all of it is part of the same kaleidoscope, ever changing and never losing its sparkle.

Of course, there is among the jumble of books on those shelves a novel called *On the Road*. But it is important to say that Jack Kerouac's hedonistic insights from the 1950s, which, obviously, I could never match for their originality, were not the inspiration for this book. For example, Gore Vidal once told me in unfortunate detail the tale of his own sexual experience with Kerouac (unsatisfactory), which I have no interest in recalling, describing nor certainly replicating. I'm simply calling on the phrase that those in my trade use when you escape from the office, or the studio, and head away with a tingle of excitement in your bones. There is nothing like being on the road.

I remember clearly how it began, when I already knew in my teens that I was hooked on journalism. In the 1960s, the British Universities North America Club was a gateway to America for a generation of students. For a modest sum we could get a return flight, a student visa (the treasured B1), the promise of a temporary job, and a Greyhound Bus pass, which let us travel anywhere, day or night, for $99 a month. Despite all this, we were jealous of students only a year or two older, because their passes had let them travel for $99 for 99 days (at that time around £40). Bliss. I assume Greyhound stopped it when they realised what was going on. Even in my year, you could hardly stop off for a wash at a Greyhound station on some dingy downtown corner – having spent the night on the bus, because that saved you paying for a motel room – without finding students from home travelling on the same circuit round the country, clockwise or anticlockwise according to whim.

I once met unexpectedly a bunch of medical students from Aberdeen whom I knew, splashing around in a grotty bathroom in New Orleans – truthfully, most of us were at least as scruffy as the people who had slept all night there – but none of us was surprised. On one summer morning in June 1970, I turned up at Gatwick. It will surprise no one born in the 1950s to know that it was my first flight. A long delay meant we landed at JFK in New York late in the evening, in the dark. My first encounter with American officialdom was with an intimidating, uniformed immigration official who insisted on rifling through a thick thriller I had taken on the plane, presumably in search of pornography or any reference to drugs, or both. Silence for a minute or two, while he turned the pages. Then, unsmiling, he asked if I had liked the book.

Pleased to have my first conversation on American soil, I said cheerily that I had enjoyed it and looked forward to an encounter with the legendary hospitality we'd been told to expect.

'Da movie stinks!' he said, and waved me through.

We continued by bus, from which I had my first sight as we approached the East River of the magical outline of night-time Manhattan, and decamped into the student-occupied lobby of the long-gone McAlpin Hotel, on the corner of 34th Street and Herald Square, a block from the Empire State Building. I got a brief flavour of the city – its noise and its smells, the perpetual race on its streets.

We were sleeping three or four to a room. I knew nothing except that I had to find my way to the Port Authority Bus Terminal a short walk away on 8th Avenue and head for the Catskill Mountains, where, so my crumpled piece of paper told me, a job was waiting.

It was past midnight. I looked from the window to Broadway far below and the lights illuminating the crowds that wouldn't disperse, watched the steam rising from the subway, heard the taxis honking at each other on the corner. Making sure I still had my passport, I lay down, wondering just before I slept what lay in store in America.

CHAPTER 1

INTO THE PICKLE BARREL

South Fallsburg lies about 90 miles north-west of New York City. It is a sprawling community surrounded by hills wreathed in thick woods with a rim of mountains just beyond, marking the northern end of the Appalachians. There are peaceful lakes, and a wide river called the Neversink. When I arrived there early that summer afternoon in 1970, the embrace of that landscape and its intimacy – the one-man gas stations, clapperboard all-you-need stores on Main Street, makeshift stalls at the roadside weighed down by piles of gleaming vegetables – made it seem warm, even familiar. It turned out to be the strangest place I'd ever known.

For more than 25 miles in every direction, in every town and village and along the fringes of the lakes, there squatted great white buildings that looked like ocean liners come into harbour and moored together for company. Most of them were old and creaky-looking, certainly in need of regular patching up, some with wooden towers that harked back to an earlier time and others with clunky extensions stuck on for the new season. A few – the grander ones, with longer outdoor pools, jetties on a private lakeside and obvious glamorous pretensions – seemed glassy and modern. But even they were meant to remind people how it had always been. The world I'd stepped into was one of which I knew nothing, but which inspired great loyalty because it valued tradition above all. These were the hotels of the Borscht Belt, where every summer many tens of thousands of New Yorkers came to play, and where they held jealously to old ways, because even as they celebrated assimilation with everyone else in the great American melting pot, they cherished even more their own identity and wanted to hold it close.

Nothing could introduce you more quickly into the byways of the American story.

For many Jewish families, the short trek to the Catskill Mountains was the never-changing story of summer. Loyal adherents came back year after year to Grossinger's and The Concord, Kutsher's, The Aladdin and The Evergreen, and lesser imitators like the Shady Nook and The Pines. More than 200 resort hotels sent out their message that guests could know for certain that not much would have changed when they came back. In South Fallsburg itself there were The Olympic and The Irvington, among others, and the place where I was due to present myself at the back door, The Flagler. Within a few hours of arriving, announcing myself as the last of the British students to sign up for that season, as a hired hand in exchange for something well under the New York state minimum wage, I realised that I had a great deal to learn. The feeling was sharpened when I was told, at the end of that first day, that they had assigned me the perfect position. I was expected to be grateful, but in truth I paid the penalty for being among the last students to arrive for the summer and landed the job no one else wanted. Dogsbody in the kitchen. Or, as they insisted on putting it, assistant salad chef.

Apart from the shock, I knew on the spot that this was going to be a taxing business. Not for me the soft option of some front-of-house duty where I might even converse with an interesting guest, or a spot of gentle gardening on the wide lawns that spread towards the forest from the front door. No straightforward folding of bed linen. I had pointed out, hopefully, that I could drive, and had taken the trouble to get a piece of paper from the AA that announced me as the holder of an international licence, but any job that involved the chance to tour around the neighbourhood had long gone, snapped up by the first of my student colleagues to arrive, a week or two before. So I was stuck, and facing quite a serious problem of which I had no warning.

All I knew when I left home was that BUNAC's best efforts had placed me at The Flagler, and nothing more. My piece of paper told me to take a Greyhound to South Fallsburg, then find the hotel (at 5538 Main Street, confusingly surrounded by countryside) and all would be well. No one had warned me that the hotel was strictly kosher, since guests had to be reassured that the kitchen would observe dietary laws at every meal. Unfortunately, the whole business was a mystery to me, one that I had never confronted before.

Strange though it is to admit it now, I didn't even know that lox were smoked salmon. I had heard of bagels, only just, and that was about all. When it came to the difference between a knish and a kugel, the preparation of matzo balls, which would be floated on bowls of chicken soup, gefilte fish, kishkes and bialys or a mandel-brot cookie, I was adrift in ignorance. Salads would surely be easier, I thought. But as for how the dietary laws applied to the cold plate, how was I supposed to know? The steward whom I met very early the next morning, and who ran the place with a rod of iron, told me that this inadequacy would be dealt with, somehow. He pointed out that I was ignorant, but needed only to listen carefully to John, the salad chef, and do what I was told. Nothing else was required of me, except hard work and the avoidance of trouble of any kind. Trouble, of course, was the last thing I was thinking of stirring up, because I was terrified.

But my dutiful listening to the chatter of John the salad chef turned out to be the second problem. He was Chinese American, an adopted New Yorker, who – I discovered eventually – had sailed the seven seas in some mysterious capacity for many years. And trying to tune in to him didn't do me much good. The reason it took me so long to establish his simple biography was that I couldn't understand him at all, nor he me. Our accents were incomprehensible to each other. His seagoing days had clearly never taken him to northern Scotland. He had one exclamation that peppered every sentence, and was contained in his first greeting. It took me a day or two to work out that he was saying, 'Fulla shit!'

Apparently, this applied not only to me, but to the kitchen steward above all, most of the other chefs, and certainly all the unseen guests who waited in their hundreds behind the big swing doors for food. It was delivered by waiters who were mostly quite elderly and fearsome, and the remains on their plates were removed on large trays by busboys of roughly my own age, whose company I enjoyed because they seemed perpetually cheerful, came generally from Brooklyn, talked about baseball and all looked like Jerry Lewis, which gave the place a certain joie de vivre despite everything. But as is customary among New Yorkers, John's bark was as much a matter of showmanship as anything else, albeit in his case without an obvious smile. This still didn't help my first tour of the salad station, which was a knotty affair. I could make a reasonable stab at quartering a lemon, which was a start, but the chicken livers, gefilte fish, the bewildering salad ingredients and sauces demanded some study, and took me about a week of heavy going to understand and get into some order. One introduction, however, was made early on the first day, and from that moment it cemented my awkward relationship with the kitchen.

John swung back the heavy door of a cold room and gestured to a pair of wide barrels standing side by side, each with a wooden lid hinged across the middle. They were about the same height as me, and even when you stood well back they stank. At his direction, I stepped onto a little stool so as to be able to get a look inside, and folded back one of the lids to explore. The barrel was full of pickles, floating in brine, which I thought were among the most disgusting things I had ever seen.

They were proper dill pickles, of course, not the long summer cucumbers of home. Shorter, chunky jobs pockmarked with scaly nodules that made the inside of the barrel look like a bathtub brimming with baby iguanas. Both the barrels were full, and I guessed that the brew had been fermenting for months in preparation for the summer season. By sign language, John made it clear that my first job each morning – I had to be in the kitchen by 6.30, while most of my student colleagues were still asleep – was to delve alone into this hellish soup and fish for pickles.

The first few days were miserable, while I tried to develop a technique with a long wooden ladle to avoid soaking myself with the pungent brine every time I tried to lift a consignment of pickles into the basin where they would wait to be sliced up as neatly as I could manage, ready for hundreds of plates later in the day. Not surprisingly, I couldn't bear to eat one. I would hear stories from student colleagues – most of us were British but there was a happy contingent from rural Ireland that greatly enlivened proceedings – about how they could knock off before lunch and spend some time swimming in a pool we were allowed to use, down the hill at the back of the hotel, before returning for a light afternoon's work. The laundry seemed to be a particularly easy number. Meanwhile, I was swimming in foul pickle juice just after dawn, with a working day that included a mere hour and a half off in the afternoon before the interminable dinner service, and a seven-day week that permitted me only half a day to myself. The best that could allow was a ride into the small town of Monticello not far away for an evening at the Raceway, where a few of us would place modest wagers on the sulky races (they called it harness racing), an unsatisfactory sport that I'd never observed before, and have never had the inclination to watch again.

In the course of this I had some bad days, as when my attention lapsed and I laid out at least 150 portions of chopped chicken livers on plates with blue rims. This sounds less than dangerous, but because of the required separation of meat and dairy meals under kosher rules, the colour of the plates was a vital affair. Blue rims for lunch (dairy) and brown for dinner (meat). Never the twain could meet. I was in serious trouble for a while, the steward warning me that all the plates would have to be destroyed, being contaminated. He said my pay might be reduced for a while to make up for it. I didn't believe him for a moment, and pointed out that there was an army of dishwashers (mostly busboys who'd been demoted for unmentionable misdemeanours), a remark that didn't go down well. I'm sure, however, that they were never destroyed. My meagre pay was waiting as usual the next day at the little window where we collected it in a long line, and I assume the guests were kept in happy ignorance.

Most of the time it was reasonably calm, although one evening two chefs let their bubbling emotions get the better of them, and had a fine fight that involved each trying to scald the other with ladlefuls of hot soup. One lunchtime a troubled guest burst through the swing doors and tipped an enormous plate of food over one of the junior chefs, who could be heard screaming that it wasn't even a dish he had prepared. And one of the biggest rows was about whether we could accommodate a valued guest who had demanded steak drenched in chocolate sauce – most of the cooks, even at The Flagler, refused to contemplate such an insult. It was the only case in which the dietary laws came to the rescue. I watched in wonder, and as a consequence I have never felt any surprise at the revelations of the tantrums of celebrity chefs or other kitchen capers. They're as old as the hills. But John and I, despite our verbal obstacles, rubbed along surprisingly amicably in the end. After a week or two, if there were complaints about an ugly-looking salad, or a deformed pickle, he would take the blame and tell the complainant that he was 'fulla shit', unlike his Scottish friend. I remain grateful and, with the passing years, have even become something of a pickle aficionado, perhaps in his memory.

The origins of the Catskills resort hotels are intriguing and instructive. In the interwar years there were many Jewish families in New York who found that, even if they were able to afford to travel to a resort in the summer, there were many hotels that wouldn't take them. There was more discrimination, even segregation, than many cared afterwards to admit. A wrong-sounding name on the phone was frequently enough to make it certain that the hotel was booked up. The consequence was that safe territory was staked out in those villages in the hills that roll into Pennsylvania and become the Appalachians when they rise and ripple southwards. The area is alluring, and has always inspired affection. The young British painter Thomas Cole produced a famous dreamy picture, *Falls of the Kaaterskill*, in the 1820s; Washington Irving imagined his fairy tale Rip Van Winkle after looking into the hills from a boat heading up the Hudson River. But it was in the 1920s and '30s that the Borscht Belt was born.

Jewish families in the city with incomes that were on the rise, but who couldn't afford an exotic distant adventure or found many hotels unwelcoming, discovered a ready-made playground. Hotels sprang up in their dozens – many calling themselves resorts, and offering sport and recreation as well as familiar food and comfort. Postcards from The Flagler just before the Second World War even advertised new ski slopes for guests, and were covered in drawings of golf clubs and fishing rods. As a result, a rolling summer community was established. It grew and grew. The railroad that connected the city to the Catskills until the 1950s was thronged all summer.

For those who went there was never a contradiction in wanting to assimilate, to demonstrate that they might share an American Dream that was said to guarantee more stability for the next generation, and at the same time to treasure the ties of a European and Russian Jewish heritage that consisted of food and family customs, old tales and a rich stream of Yiddish, together with bits of religion handled with varying degrees of orthodoxy. What could be more natural than to want it both ways? The promise of America, after all, was not that you were expected to abandon the identity of the old country – the one that tyrants of various kinds had tried to take away from you by force – but that you could fuse it happily with your growth as an American citizen, deep inside, and be proud of it to your dying day. Part of the deal was the perpetual right to boast about it.

A useful early lesson for any outsider.

In the post-war era, that kind of cultural confidence was epitomised in the Catskills summers and reached its peak in the two decades before I briefly experienced it. Only a tiny number of Americans outside the very well-heeled classes wanted to consider a foreign holiday at that time – according to the State Department, it was only in the mid-1990s that the passport-holding proportion of the US population reached 10 per cent – and this upstate Shangri-La offered predictability and comfort (if you could afford the more luxurious hotels) and a guarantee of entertainment. The show, in some ways, was the best of it.

If you didn't want to join the kids on a trek or in a kayak, and didn't want to stray far from the wooden sunlounger, the bigger hotels all had some kind of nightclub, called a theatre if you were lucky. There you could be sure that you would be teased to distraction, forced to laugh, and then have the privilege of being insulted by the best in the business. These were the happy hunting grounds for three generations of Jewish comedians who made the Borscht Belt their stage, and repelled all invaders. Milton Berle, Mel Brooks and Jerry Lewis, Jackie Mason and Jerry Seinfeld later, were all stars of the circuit. You might have heard the young Streisand sing, or risked being in the audience for the toxic Joan Rivers or Don Rickles, famous for being the rudest of them all. He was said to be the only comic who'd dare to insult Frank Sinatra if he came to one of his Las Vegas shows with his Rat Pack in tow. 'What do we need the Italians for? All they do is keep the flies off our fish.' They specialised in the red-raw, self-deprecatory, put-down humour that became as near to an all-American style as you could imagine, spinning a never-ending riff on the question – why are we like this?

Wives and mothers took a special bashing, and the Jewish experience was sent up in a way that only the home team would dare. Always, stretching far beyond the one-liners and the pained storytelling of some social disaster with the children or a sullen grandma, a familiar landscape of shared experience was sketched out, with an inherited folklore and the confidence that a punchline delivered in Yiddish would be understood by everyone.

So this was a community gathered round the campfire, sharing what they had in common. The young Woody Allen used to turn up in the Catskills to take his chance. I have a fantasy that it was there that he told his surreal moose story for the first time, the one that begins, without any explanation and no whys or wherefores, 'I shot a moose once.' The animal turns out to be wounded, not dead, so he ties it to the front of his car as a living trophy and, facing the tricky problem of disposal, comes up with the idea of ditching it at a fancy dress party in the city, pretending that it's a costume – so realistic! – being worn by an ingenious couple (introduced to the other guests as 'the Solomons') who are hidden inside. Why not? But at the party, Mr and Mrs Berkowitz do better. They've hired a fancy moose suit, into which they can fit snugly together, and they win first prize. The real moose comes second. But that's not all. The story ends with the unfortunate Mr Berkowitz turning out to be a little too convincing in his moose costume, and being shot, stuffed and mounted at the New York City Golf Club. The pay-off is per-fection. 'The joke's on them – 'cause it's restricted.' No Jews were allowed on the fairways, let alone in the clubhouse.

Ruthless introspection and wild absurdity all at once.

Along with the borscht, this was sustenance for the people who came to the hotels, rented the bungalows, packed the children off to summer camps – a million of them in the course of every summer, so some will tell you. They came in campers and gas-guzzlers, some hired bungalows or stayed in boarding houses, the rest filled up the hotels, and the lucky ones made it to Grossinger's in Ferndale, with thirty-five buildings, its own post office and an airstrip.

In my summer at The Flagler, which I thought of as just outside the premier league, there was an appearance for a week or two by one of the Catskills' most famous characters. Murray Waxman enjoyed the title of 'The Last of the Tumlers', tumler being a Yiddish word for someone who creates a tumult. He was resident at The Aladdin in Woodbourne not far away, but had somehow been nabbed for a stint by The Flagler (either that, or The Aladdin wanted a break). He was in charge of the nightclub – the Starlit Room, as I recall – and sometimes we were able to slip in to watch the show – not that you would want to see it too often. He had a jet-black pencil-thin moustache, hair that shone so brightly that you would never forget his surname, and a selection of garish velvet bow ties. His appearance would always be signalled by the band leader calling 'Heee-eerrre-'sss Muuu-rrrr-aaaaa-yyyyyy', spinning out his name for so long that we used to say it was intended to give people time to leave if they wanted. Then there would be a fusillade of one-liners, some of them very funny, but the overall effect being to leave you thinking you had been caught in a hailstorm and had to find somewhere to dry off quickly. The type of thing that, once heard, is never forgotten. 'I answered the doorbell. It was the Boston Strangler. I called my wife. "It's for you!"'

But on one terrible night in the Starlit Room, amid this storm of harmless hokum, I came a cropper.

One of our student number had got a job – lucky him, I thought innocently – to be the stage lighting assistant. He asked me if I could fill in for him for an evening show, because he was off on some escapade. Not to worry, he assured me, it was a piece of cake. Fortunately, as it turned out, this happened in my last week at The Flagler. I accompanied him for a night or two to learn the ropes, particularly the programming of two or three switches with intimidating handles that allowed you to pre-set the lights and change the stage appearance with one well-timed downward pull at the right moment. I was connected by headphones to another British student, Jeff, who was in a box at the back of the auditorium, watching the stage. (Better than being an assistant salad chef, certainly. A doddle.) He was a friend whom I trusted.

On the night in question, the visiting crooner – whose name I have long since wiped from my memory – arrived, beaming, for his rehearsal, and was pleasantness itself. I asked him how he wanted the lighting for his act, hoping he didn't want special effects. 'Keep 'em all on. I wanna see these lovely people. Bright, bright, bright.' Okay, my pleasure. I think I managed to sound competent. But then he said he did want something particular at the end. For the climax, the stage should be darkened for the first time, except for a spot-light trained on his face, just at the moment when he reached the end of Al Jolson's 'My Mammy', which bizarrely seemed to be his signature tune. It was a relief, even in 1970, to learn that he wasn't proposing to black up for the occasion. After a discussion about the technicalities, Jeff and I marked his position on the stage, set the spotlight out front to catch him kneeling in all his splendour, and everything was ready. We then passed a happy half-hour while he told us about his latest success in Vegas. I wanted to ask, but didn't, why in that case he was at The Flagler. No matter. He was.

Most of the show passed uneventfully. Murray Waxman did his stuff – when he slid onto the stage he seemed to become a man possessed – and the patrons loved it. Then came the singer, with an audience spread out on his lap. All was well, and they purred. The lights shone out so that he could see his people, as advertised. Then, 'My Mammy'. I prepared for his big finish.

'The sun shines east, the sun shines west, / I know where the sun shines best / . . . I'd walk a million miles / For one of your smiles . . .'

In my ear, Jeff whispered from his box out front that all seemed set fair. The crooner had manoeuvred himself onto his allo-cated spot.

I got into position. The music slowed, announcing his last chorus, and from behind the back curtain I could picture him getting down on one knee. I waited for the band, and my musical cues.

On the beat, I pulled down the switch.

And I heard Jeff's voice in my ear, sounding louder. 'Oh my God.'

With a shaking hand I pulled aside the back curtain to look onto the stage. It was as black as night.

I'd pulled down the master switch by mistake, and plunged the whole building into darkness.

He was still singing, somewhere deep in the night that had descended, but I could hear people squawking and getting up to leave, presumably from alarm. In panic, I pulled all the switches up again and the whole room was filled with a dazzling light, just as he approached his tearful climax, with people starting to blunder towards the doors in alarm. The required reverential hush was missing.

A few moments later, as he acknowledged the cheers, I realised he was also contemplating the ruin of his act.

The next few minutes were difficult. Waxman did his best, at least with the singer, to calm things down. But from behind my curtain I could also hear them asking each other where the guy who'd been handling the lights had gone.

I muttered apologies to the stage manager, said I had to check what had happened with Jeff out front, and fled.

The next morning I was glad for the first time to be tucked away with the pickle barrels, out of sight of everyone but John, who said that if I'd been working in the nightclub last night I must know now that it was 'fulla shit'. Who was I to disagree?

Jeff covered for me manfully, and I looked forward to my departure a couple of days later. I picked up my last pay envelope with relief, but aware of what I'd learned.

America in 1970 was on the turn, reflected in the life of that little corner of New York state, deep in the wooded hills. While we were there, the first anniversary of Woodstock was celebrated in the fields of Max Yasgur's farm, which was only about 15 miles away. Richie Havens came back – he was the first act that the half-million people heard on those fabled fields a year before, performing for three hours straight – and the cast of *Hair* was driven up from Broadway for the night. There would never be another weekend like the first, but everyone knew, I dare say even in the best suites in Grossinger's, that the mood it caught in those three days – freewheeling, joyous and angry all at once – announced the coming of a different time. The loss of innocence in the 1960s turbulence promised change and uncertainty. There was no going back.

Even in the Catskills haven, the sense of an ordered world – hotels that catered for one generation and then the next in the same way, a pattern for the summer that valued continuity and reassurance – was disappearing. People were travelling more freely, at least some old prejudices were dying out, the world was opening up, and there seemed more to life than the old borscht comics' routines. Even by the time I left South Fallsburg, after a summer of rapid learning, we all recognised that this was a country in transition.

The old footholds seemed looser, which may be one of the reasons that even as the holiday market began to operate cruelly against the Catskills resorts, there was a greater desperation to hold onto the old ways. But it was too late. Within a mere five years, the big hotels had started to close or to find new ways to make a living. The Flagler became a chess centre for a while, and later had a brief incarnation as 'the Fountains of Rome', of all things. Then, like most of its neighbours, it closed its doors for the last time, before everything got too embarrassing. Some of the ruins of these old palaces can still be seen. Through the trees you can spot skeletal balconies and discarded furniture jutting out of rubbish heaps, along with a few sad relics of vacation frolics, perhaps some cracked stones from walkways that no one can take to the lakeside any more. Children's summer camps have colonised the golf courses. There are fences around the old sites to warn you of the presence of asbestos, almost certainly in vast amounts. A few hotels did survive their reinvention. The Concord has expanded. But they are a handful, compared to the scene in the glory days. Tourists still come, because the lure of the woods and the hills survives, but the real Borscht Belt is a piece of nostalgia. Of The Flagler, its white pillars and high windows and the rickety rooms in the outhouses where we lived behind the hotel, not a stick or stone remains. It has been razed from the landscape.

First memories won't go away, however. The pinpricks from that summer can still sting.

I remember Lou well. He was the handyman around the hotel,

a tall and broad-shouldered, red-headed guy, probably in his early thirties, covered in hair and a few modest tattoos. Irish lineage, we decided correctly on the first day. He was fun in his rough way, but liked to play the knowing fixer and to set his bruising life experience against the precocious confidence that he associated with all students. You couldn't blame him for that, although he did greatly underestimate our innocence. Never mind, he was always up for adventure and we listened to his stories. He was the first Vietnam veteran I knew.

In that year, the official figures for the number of American troops deployed in the war was about 335,000, down from a peak of more than half a million in 1968, the year that began with the Tet Offensive by the North Vietnamese, which did more than any other engagement in the war to turn American public opinion against it. That sentiment was not shared by Lou. Peaceniks weren't his cup of tea.

Most of the time, we'd see him wandering around the back premises of the hotel doing this and that with his bag of tools, on some mission of his own. He was always somewhere close by, mostly near the rough wooden buildings where we lived with a large colony of rodents and bugs that always seemed to start marching in formation up the white walls just as you were trying to get to sleep. (I shared a room with a student from Taiwan who fled from the hotel after two weeks, largely on account of the bugs, leaving a sad letter asking if I'd pick up his wages for him and forward them to a post office box in New York.) Although Lou could have an intimidating presence, he laughed quite a lot, and we had amiable conversations. He talked about how he had enjoyed the war, and for students from across the pond like us who'd imbibed over the previous two years or so a heady anti-war sentiment, it was arresting. Like most men who fought in Vietnam, he had volunteered (about 10 per cent of his generation were also called up through the hated draft) and sometimes he spoke of friends he had lost. In the whole course of the war, more than 60 per cent of the Americans killed were under twenty-two.

Lou would tell stories about jungle fighting, and it was always hard to know how much was true and how much of it the kind of exaggeration that must be hard to avoid when you have a young and captive audience who know so little. We could hardly challenge him about the truth concerning some helicopter foray against the Viet Cong on a rainy night nearly 9,000 miles away. Although friendly to us all, he certainly appeared to have a penchant for violence, and we knew he had guns – one of them was often visible – that he enjoyed taking into the woods. Black bears lived there, and porcupines and bobcats, as well as white-tailed deer that got everywhere. Whether he was a serious hunter or just enjoyed the shooting, I was never sure. He never brought back a carcass.

Once, though, he called some of us to a shallow creek at the edge of the woods to see a snake that he wanted us to believe he had killed with his bare hands, and then chopped up. He didn't argue when someone suggested it was a timber rattlesnake, which we'd been warned about for their nastiness, but the consensus afterwards was that it was a mere garter snake. Still horrible in my view, but harmless and therefore no great prize.

But more than once I found Lou alone, stripped of bravado and sunk deep in a melancholy mood, usually with a few cans of beer, when he would find it difficult to talk and wanted to drift away. I fancied that there was a good deal of darkness around him, although I couldn't know whether it sprang from experiences he didn't want to discuss or from some kind of anger. Both, probably. It seemed unfair to try to dig down too far. All of us, aware that we were outside observers of the trauma that had gripped America in the previous four years or so, were marked by having known him. When we left, we all remembered his tall and heavy frame, the camouflage gear he always wore, and his friendship. But we all wondered, too, what stories he could really tell if the mask were finally to fall away. It struck me much later that we never found out exactly why he wasn't still fighting, and what had brought him to our corner of the Catskills.

I can hear him now, talking about going into the woods with a gun. I have often wondered what became of Lou.

That summer, the war had five more years to run. The number of American dead was already approaching 40,000, and would rise to more than 58,000 by the time of the fall of Saigon in 1975. The number of severely injured is put officially at around 75,000, and even by 1970 it was common to see young men in wheelchairs who were living evidence of the cost. The first televised war was also visible on the streets of small-town America.

Our Flagler time came to an end as the long days began to wane and the visitors began to look towards Labor Day and the formal end of summer. We turned to the bus timetables, and the four of us planned our route together.

The journey that followed felt as if we were watching an old newsreel. A magical summer ended as it had begun, thanks to our $99 freedom pass, on dozens of Greyhound buses that carried the four of us on an epic meander into the Deep South, then westwards all the way to the Pacific, north again to the Canadian border and then back across the northern plains and Badlands to Chicago and eventually New York. It was the standard itinerary for many British students each summer. Of all the strange camaraderies I have known, this was one of the most unexpected. Entering a grim men's room in Mobile, Alabama, or Laramie, Wyoming, and finding an acquaintance who was a first-year law student from Aberdeen was always going to be a surprise. But we got used to the experience. Typically, we'd all slept through the night on a bus from somewhere far away, because that was the cheapest way to do it. A darkened Greyhound on the freeway, with the lights down and a soundtrack of gentle snoring, was better than many of the motels we could afford. The buses became a kind of mobile home, the seating layout familiar and welcoming, the sound of the engine and the hiss of the opening door a reminder that each bus, whether leaving Atlanta, New Orleans, Flagstaff or Spokane, was the same. Our own little cocoon. We also became used to the passengers. Many were elderly, the quotient of African Americans was high because a long-distance bus was so much cheaper than a flight, and there were always at least two people reading a thick, black Bible. The old travellers gave the company a richness, some of them as near to the train-hopping hobo of long ago as I could have hoped to know. Wiry men with bulging backpacks and heavy boots who seemed to fall into two categories – those who spoke to no one and kept their silence, and those who couldn't stop talking. They'd talk about the city they'd just left and where they were going, but often without explanation. It was all about the travelling, and nothing more.

The four of us were together for most of the journey – Andy, Dave, John and me – which must have amounted to about 4,000 miles through the weeks. It was a revelation, like our time at The Flagler, and taught me the first things I needed to know. Even on a long overnight run across the plains, or hour after hour on freeways fringed by acres of bright-green kudzu foliage in the South, it felt as if every day was a discovery. We trekked into the Grand Canyon on mules, walked across the border into Mexico, lost a few dollars in Las Vegas, and discovered San Francisco.

It was a surprise to inhale the first sultry scent of the South not in a tobacco field or some sleepy township in Georgia, but in the streets of Washington. Even at the start of the 1970s, the capital retained the unmistakable flavour of a southern city. Despite the business of government, it was slower than you might expect. Its wide streets had none of the frenzy of New York. It was hot, the notorious humidity of the summer months draining everyone's energy. So it always seemed to be taking its time. And because, at the beginning of the 1970s, seven out of ten residents of the District of Columbia were African Americans, the vast majority of them still speaking in the languid voices of the South, it felt like the gateway to a different country. There were grits at breakfast, the clincher. For those of us who had watched through our teenage years the progress of the civil rights movement, and who remembered news of the bus boycotts, the Selma marches, the street battles over segregation and the shooting of Martin Luther King, it was extraordinary to walk past Union Station on Capitol Hill and remember that a mere decade before, trains had had to be segregated before they could proceed across the Potomac River to enter Virginia. Everyone had to get off, and then the black passengers – or those who hadn't accepted the inevitable when they'd climbed on board in Baltimore or Newark or somewhere else – were herded towards the back (where, just as you would expect, the seats were much less comfortable).

In the South in that summer of 1970, you couldn't leave the northern cities behind without the feeling that you were stepping back in time. We four travelled through the Carolinas and into

Georgia, and one incident that lodged in my mind has stayed there ever since. There was nothing spectacular about what happened, but maybe because of its raw banality it cut deep.

I was on my own one morning, in Atlanta, and sitting at the counter of a diner in a fairly run-down part of town. There was only one other customer at the counter, on the high stool at the end, slouched against the wall – a big, middle-aged white man in a loud-check sports jacket, smoking one of the long greenish, loosely rolled and pungent cigars that used to be everywhere. He was reading the sports pages of his newspaper, and I remember he wore a garish fraternity ring that looked as if it was the remnant of a knuckleduster. The waiter behind the bar was black. He was probably in his late fifties, and the older of the two by some way. This did not stop the other customer calling him 'boy', and putting on an almost theatrical scowl whenever he looked at him. Neither voice was raised, and there was no violence of any kind. But I remember vividly the experience of watching the operation of utter disdain, verging on contempt, that was clearly the relationship that both of them expected, and lived with every day.

Each of them had known it all their lives, and I had never seen anything like it.

It was as if the man serving us breakfast didn't exist. He might have been a robot, for all the other customers cared. When the coffee didn't come immediately, there was a rap on the counter and the cry of 'Boy!', as if the customer was a military officer dealing with some first-day recalcitrant recruit. The waiter went along meekly with the humiliation, as he was obliged to. In part of America where the white population prided themselves on politeness, and boasted about the graciousness of the Old South, this was the truth about daily life.

For some reason, this particular incident – undramatic, commonplace across the South, involving nothing that would be remarked upon by a local – stayed with me, stubbornly. We had many adventures on that trip, listening to jazz in the French Quarter in New Orleans, hiking into the Grand Canyon, experiencing the drive up the California coast on Highway 1 to San Francisco, where Haight-Ashbury was still pretending it was 1967, 'the summer of love'. Breathing the exhilarating air of the Pacific north-west. Traversing the moonscape of the Badlands in the Dakotas. But the South had the greatest effect, and for a reason that I understood. I was tormented by the feeling that it was a familiar place, despite its troubles, peopled by characters whom I knew.

Their often gracious speech, decorated with old cadences, and the formalities of meeting and greeting, were an echo of home and the social habits with which I'd grown up. Many of their conventions I understood. I could enjoy the way people talked, and it was precisely because this was also the anchor of social attitudes that were unforgiving and cruel that it was so disturbing. On many occasions since, I've experienced generosity and kindness from people who, a generation ago, would have given no thought to the well-being of the dispossessed around them, simply because they were black and that was the way things were. When, throughout the 1950s and early '60s, the elderly southern members of the Senate in Washington lined up, month after month, to filibuster and strangle any civil rights bill, however mild, they would talk about 'the traditional values of the South'. But what mattered most to them about the tradition, and had to be defended at all costs, was not the gentle pace of life and the formal courtesies, nor the church-going stability of small-town life, it was the fixed relationship between the races, which must never be disturbed.

The surprise wasn't in seeing the elected demagogues at work (echoing Governor George Wallace in his inaugural address as Governor of Alabama in 1963 – 'Segregation now! Segregation tomorrow! Segregation for ever!') because they had long been notorious and to outsiders had become almost comic characters. Unstinting and routine discrimination – in shops and restaurants, parks and movie theatres and bus stations, schools, courts and, of course, at election polling stations – was so much part of normal life that for many people it was not a subject for discussion. For an outsider like me the sharp images, startling and exciting all at once, created an indelible tableau.

Nearly four decades later, I made a film about the master observer Alistair Cooke after his death, using home movies he had shot in his first explorations of America in the year or two after he arrived as a student at Yale in the early 1930s, and then drove across the country. His family had found them in boxes tucked away in the basement of his New York apartment block, long-since forgotten but containing a treasure trove. They were jerky films, sometimes blurred, but diamond-sharp in their observation. New England in the fall and a tour of the physical footprints left by the Pilgrim settlers, New York streets and the buildings rising to the sky in an era of wild expansion, jazz in the South and the cotton fields, straight roads that seemed to have no end across the prairies, canyons and redwoods and Rockies, the Chicago cityscape, San Francisco Bay. Hollywood. Long afterwards, for countless young travellers on their first American road trip, the experience replicated the kaleidoscopic excitement in those black-and-white images jumping across the screen. A country that could never be at rest, with different regions and cultures drawn together by a stubborn idealism, then divided so often by misunderstanding and conflict. It is a picture replicated by all young travellers who take that road for the first time.

On the last leg of the bus journey back to New York, the image of the country that I carried in my mind looked like a ragged continental map showing a time of turmoil rather than the 'perfect union' of its founding dream. The fascination didn't lie in the triumph of bringing so many different influences together, but in watching how their differences were still playing out. Between black and white, most painfully of all. And also among ethnic communities balancing their identities with their desire to become all-American, between generations pulled apart by the arrival of the first youth culture they had ever known, and among those who believed in the war and those who never would. The battles of the 1960s meant that no one could preserve the illusion of peaceful unity, for all the relentless progress in the most prosperous country the world had ever seen. From the social maelstrom stirred up in the previous decade came an electric feeling of alarm – because the question of identity, which so many had been brought up to believe was simply solved by a belief in America, seemed to be gnawing at everyone as painfully as it ever had in the past. What should it mean to be an American? The country was tumbling into a time of brutal introspection, and knew it.

The New York gateway has always promised everyone that it will let them be who they want to be, as if it had found the formula that no one else could crack. Its essence is what E. B. White, in his love-letter essay to the city, called its 'tidal restlessness' – among natives who accepted its turbulence as inevitable, commuters who arrived like locusts each day and then spat the city out at night, and those from elsewhere who were drawn to it on a quest for something.

Leave the commuter out of it for the moment, and that early-evening train from Grand Central to Greenwich or Stamford, and think instead about the hometown New Yorker. Most big cities claim a unique character that's understood by each generation that grows up there, and then passed on to the next with love. None, though, infuses the process with more excitement – perhaps shaken into a cocktail of exhilaration and anger – than New York. Turbulence is precisely the right word. Nothing stays the same for a moment. Buildings rise and fall in what seems to be a few weeks, fashions take a grip and new stars cast their spell, then move on, yet the city gets its flavour not from the constant shock of the new, but from the rich and nourishing engagement with the old. Hypnotic and undeniable.

Working like a microcosm of the whole American story, New York dramatises its past even as it races to find ways of changing. The city's story is told not only in the many fine buildings that survive in the skyscraper canyons, nor in its galleries or museums, but most of all by people on the street. Their voices are part of the cacophony that everyone loves. They are the reason the city has managed to preserve enough of a flavour of the past to let its identity flourish, and not to wane. You have to be dull indeed not to savour it.

Visit, for instance, McSorley's Old Ale House on East 7th Street near 3rd Avenue on the Lower East Side. That area, south of 14th Street and west for a few blocks in from the East River, was the destination for hundreds of thousands of European immigrants from the mid-nineteenth century onwards. Russians, Poles and Ukrainians, Germans and Italians, and, of course, the Irish. Much of the sound of America for the first half of the twentieth century came from there. Its language, its music, its rhythm. George and Ira Gershwin grew up there. Its smells came from Russian bakeries,

Italian pizza ovens, and I dare say Polish pickle barrels. The polyglot streets turned it into an urban Tower of Babel.

McSorley's claims to have opened in 1854, and if you believe what its proprietors still say, a barrel of salt to hand, almost no one of any note in American history since that date has failed to come through its doors. It remains a monument to old New York, though now flirting dangerously with heritage status. Even in 2019 sawdust was still spread on the floor, and the barman would tell innocent newcomers that he sold neither liquor nor wine and only two kinds of beer, light and dark, which came in two separate glasses (they only serve one size) if you wanted something approximating a pint. The bar can certainly claim that throughout its life it has held out against any tide of progress. It was only in August 1970, in the same summer as I first encountered the city, that it accepted that it could no longer exclude women – whom it had once put in the same bracket as 'raw onions' on the list of things it wouldn't allow – after a famous demonstration against its refusal to acknowledge that the law in New York had changed. So it has always harked back, and perhaps the best description of what it was once like in the late 1930s was written by Joseph Mitchell, a poet of the streets who wrote portraits of the city for the *New Yorker* from the era of Dorothy Parker into the 1960s, many of whose magical pieces appear in his collection *Up in the Old Hotel*.

It is equipped with electricity, but the bar is stubbornly illuminated with a pair of gas lamps, which flicker fitfully and throw shadows on the low, cobwebby ceiling each time someone opens the street door. There is no cash register. Coins are dropped in soup bowls – one for nickels, one for dimes, one for quarters, and one for halves – and bills are kept in a rosewood cashbox. It is a drowsy place; the bartenders never make a needless move, the customers nurse their mugs of ale and the three clocks on the wall have not been in agreement for many years. The clientele is motley.

Motley indeed. Mitchell, whose favourite subjects were New Yorkers who were loners or eccentrics or secret obsessives, knew

by instinct that the city could be best understood by looking at the
people who lived on the edge. It was as if the city was unbelievable,
making no sense because no one had built a place like that before,
and therefore you needed to see it from an odd angle. Mitchell
arrived in the city in October 1929, on the very day usually identified as the most cataclysmic in the Wall Street Crash, and in a
decade or so of reporting on *The World*, the *Herald Tribune* and
the *World-Telegram*, before he was lured to join the *New Yorker*,
he began to tell the story of the place from the bottom up, through
the people who fascinated him. They weren't in politics or business
but were longshoremen or hotel porters, gamblers and hustlers who
strolled in the street, men who gathered the clams and oysters from
the beds off Long Island, or just drifted among the Irish bars of
Lower Manhattan, never even making it as far north as Midtown.
One memorable piece simply told the story of rats that once nearly
brought plague to the city, an episode that was hushed up for years
to prevent panic. In 1942, he wrote a profile of a man called Joe
Gould, to whom he returned in 1964, with two pieces entitled *Joe
Gould's Secret*. This is how the first profile began: 'Joe Gould is a
blithe and emaciated little man who has been a notable in the cafes,
diners, barrooms and dumps of Greenwich Village for a quarter of
a century. He sometimes brags rather wryly that he is the last of the
bohemians. "All the others fell by the wayside," he says. "Some are
in the grave, some are in the loony bin, and some are in the advertising business."'

A story of survival, and in those three pieces he contrived to
write a beguiling biography of a man who left little mark but whose
experience was a tour of the city through the back door. Mitchell's
own story became an echo of the theme that he had teased out from
the characters he knew. Without warning, in 1964, he stopped producing copy for his editors. He continued to come to the magazine's
office each day and, from behind the glass door of his office, his
colleagues would sometimes hear typing. But there were no more
stories. He remained on the staff of the *New Yorker* until his death
in 1996, having written nothing for publication for more than thirty
years. A spectacular swan song. Friends who thought they might
find some magnum opus stuffed away in the bottom of his desk

after he'd gone were disappointed. It appeared that he had simply paused, and never got going again. He involved himself in many causes dear to the heart of the city – including the rescue of Grand Central Station (and its treasured oyster bar, one of the jewels of the city, which he loved) from the unbelievable threat of the developers' bulldozers – but, as a writer, he dried up. His friend Roger Angell, a poet of the sports field who reached his centenary in 2020, knew him through much of that time, and still can't explain it. Mitchell would leave for lunch each day wearing his fedora – brown in the winter months, swapped for a straw replacement for the summer – and say very little. Everyone knew he was going to walk the streets, which was the thrill of his life. 'When the end of the day came,' Angell wrote, 'he went home. Sometimes, in the evening elevator, I heard him emit a small sigh, but he never complained, never explained.'

The city has always celebrated the outsider and the oddball, with a brashness that almost nowhere else can summon up, yet keeps to itself some secrets that it won't give up and will never share. Many other cities try to do the same, but none does it with such style. These stories, and so many others like them, sustain its identity, which is why they are as important to the city – to its heart – as the next new tower or subway line. Or the next Trumpish figure wanting to become a new Master of the Universe.

In 1970, so much of that old New York was still on display. The gentrification of Lower Manhattan had hardly begun. The Lower East Side, around McSorley's Old Ale House, would have been familiar to someone who had lived there in the later 1940s. The neighbourhoods of the city were still living in their own ways. Little Italy, for example, wasn't yet the tourist trap it became, and the Upper West Side was still the place where the Sharks and Jets might have battled in the street, to Leonard Bernstein's score. Donald Trump hadn't yet demolished the art deco sculptures on the Bonwit Teller store at 56th Street and 5th Avenue to build Trump Tower. Having promised that he would preserve them, he subsequently professed innocence about what his builders had got up to with their wrecking balls one night in 1979.

Yet for all the resilience of the city, the ferment of that year was taking its toll and in New York, as in regions of the country far away to whom the city was a place of strange habits and too many foreigners, as well as being too loud, the decade that beckoned was going to be grim. The violence on the streets was increasing, the scars of poverty were all around, and before long the mayor would have to send ambassadors around the world to tell prospective visitors that it really was safe to ride the subway (although at that time, to be honest, it wasn't).

A history of neglect was catching up. Bedford-Stuyvesant is a 9-square-mile area of Brooklyn, across the East River. By the end of the 1960s it was home to about half a million people, and the second highest concentration of African Americans in the country, most of them living in deep poverty. The housing was terrible, violent crime and drug abuse were rampant, the schools were failing and falling apart. Robert F. Kennedy was elected to the Senate from New York in 1964, and became convinced that poverty and hopelessness were bound to produce race riots, and a decline that might be irreversible. He began to develop an anti-poverty programme directed at Bedford-Stuyvesant, helping to found a Renewal and Rehabilitation Corporation, using public and private money, the first of its kind in the United States. When he was killed in 1968 a little progress had been made, but even by 1970 not much had changed for the residents. It was a long haul.

Street violence was obvious to everyone. The mob controlled the docks, many restaurants and bars, and terrorised small businesses for protection money. The police department was weighed down by corruption – the famous whistle-blower Frank Serpico began to tell his story in 1967, but it took years for the scale of the scandal to emerge – and the national economic performance meant that the city finances were taking a pounding. By 1975, it was effectively broke, and the mayor – the ineffective Democrat Abe Beame – needed a bailout. In Washington, President Gerald Ford said no, producing a famous *New York Post* headline: 'Ford to City: Drop Dead'. For New York, thoroughly uncharacteristically, they were years of retreat.

All this was beginning to bubble up at the start of the 1970s. Like the whole country, the city was feeling the consequences of the troubled 1960s, which exposed the divisions between the races, between rich and poor, between the young and the old, in a way that shook the country more deeply than anything since the trauma of the Great Depression in the early 1930s. In a country more conscious of itself than many others, that meant that Americans' sense of themselves – which they considered their most precious inheritance – was being challenged. Most of them had been raised to believe that they were on a path of perpetual progress, and to treasure a citizen's identity that was said to be the envy of the world. But in the course of a few years that confidence had been shaken. The moon landing, in 1969, was a brief moment of national celebration. But as they looked around, there seemed to be trouble everywhere else on earth.

Therefore, even to a first-time visitor, dazzled by new experiences and the sheer power of the American idea, the political and social fissures were obvious. Americans were being challenged head-on. In a country with a determined individuality, celebrated more rigorously than anywhere else in the Western world, they were confronting social divisions that had been papered over for too long, and, as so often in their history, they were being asked again what it meant to be an American.

When I left, I had a photograph in my camera that I was happy to show to friends when I got home. It seemed to catch that endless spirit of adventure. Times might be bad, New York could say to itself, but we can still run faster, play harder, build higher. It was a picture taken by one of my student friends on the Staten Island ferry chugging back across the harbour towards Lower Manhattan. Behind me, as I look into the camera, only about two-thirds complete with cranes sticking out from the top, rising with confidence to the sky, are two symbols of optimism. The twin towers of the World Trade Center.

CHAPTER 2

FLOODTIDE

By the time I went back, the bubbling cauldron of discontent had boiled over. The war wouldn't end, and Richard Nixon had managed to turn the presidency, despite the political dominance he'd cemented with his 1972 re-election, into a byword for chicanery.

As a student in the United States during the climactic phase of Watergate, I was fortunate to experience that crisis at first hand, and feel the force with which it disturbed Americans, and the extent to which it reinforced the feeling, born in the '60s, that all innocence had gone. During that year, I was preparing for a job in journalism back home and, therefore, with fellow students who were bent on the same path, I spent as much time in Washington as I could. A group of us – in the useful guise of a research project on political reporting – got stuck into the story. We were students at Syracuse University in upstate New York, but for much of that year we were using my old friend the Greyhound bus as a shuttle to Washington.

One of our interviews affected me particularly, and has stayed in my mind. Close to the climax of Watergate, with the president flailing ever more wildly at his enemies from the White House and his own party bracing itself for his looming impeachment, I met one of the sharpest political reporters in Washington, and heard him explain why the political drama that had been rolling on for nearly two years was, for him, much more than a journalist's dream story. It touched the heart of his American identity.

He was Carl Leubsdorf, then working for the Associated Press, and he told a story of the Saturday Night Massacre, a few months earlier in October 1973, when Nixon summarily fired the Watergate special prosecutor, Archibald Cox, losing in the process his attorney general, Elliot Richardson, and his solicitor general too, who both resigned in direct defiance of a presidential order to dismiss Cox.

It had been assumed that a president mired in scandal with so many legitimate questions to answer wouldn't risk removing Cox at a stroke. Everyone knew he wanted to, because his determination to uncover the Watergate story threatened Nixon's survival, but few thought he'd dare. Like nearly everyone else in town, Leubsdorf was unprepared for the news that flashed up on TV screens on mid-evening that Saturday, in the middle of the sixth game in the baseball World Series between the Oakland As and the New York Mets, which I happened to be watching in a student house in upstate New York. Leubsdorf, with the necessary agility of the wire service reporter, raced to the White House to get on top of the story and started to file hours of bulletins that set off bells on teletype machines around the world.

The most arresting element of his recollection, however, didn't concern that frenzy, but the aftermath. He was driving home in the early hours of the morning, his reams of copy filed, heading east along Pennsylvania Avenue and up the slope towards Capitol Hill. As he passed one of the Senate office buildings he saw lights shining from a few windows: staff, perhaps even some senators, were working. He said that the sight moved him deeply, because of his own background.

His parents were Jewish refugees from Nazi Germany in the 1930s, and cherished the democracy of their new American home, which had removed the overwhelming threat to their lives. For Carl, born just before the Second World War, the idea of freedom wasn't nebulous, but a tangible gift. Now, he said, he felt for the first time that it might be taken away. When he saw the lights burning on Capitol Hill he experienced a physical rush of reassurance: people who cared about their democracy were at their desks in the middle of the night. They would not let a president act with impunity.

It would be easy to be sceptical about this – especially for a European like me for whom these events seemed settled, and long since folded up in history – but it was an arresting story, told by someone who had never doubted until that moment the strength of the democratic institutions that he had grown up to revere in his parents' place of safety. On that night he realised that the battle was truly joined.

Of many conversations in Washington around that time, it was the one that struck home with the greatest force. This wasn't an everyday political struggle, albeit one with lashings of delicious melodrama on top, but an argument about power with consequences for the integrity of government itself. I was talking to Leubsdorf with student colleagues, and none of us thought for a moment that he was exaggerating or overdramatising. He meant every word, and we were moved.

We had gone to Washington on our project to write about the coverage of Watergate, because all of us were heading for jobs in journalism and found ourselves, in our early twenties, in a position to look in on the most gripping political drama of which any of us had been closely aware. How could we resist the chance? If we'd had any doubts about the trade we had chosen, those days in Washington would have dispelled them. We were smitten, and as a result engineered with our university the chance to talk to as many journalists as we could, to get a smell of the story. We dressed it up as a research project, but in truth we just wanted to get a taste of the action.

I had fetched up at Syracuse, 250 miles north-west of New York, to study for a master's degree. I had the St Andrew's Society of New York to thank for the experience. It was, and remains, an enlightened outfit that began life in the eighteenth century as a charitable source of funds for the many wandering Scots who arrived in the US and needed a first helping hand, and then it benefited from the philanthropic impulses of those who had prospered. That charitable work continues, and it has long been a serious cultural institution, fostering healthy and creative links with the old country. In 1956, the society established a scholarship to celebrate the bicentenary of its foundation, which would allow one student from the four ancient Scottish universities (the only ones around in the 1950s), or a Scot at Oxford or Cambridge, to study for a year in the United States. There is an equivalent award each year to an American student to come the other way to Scotland. Sitting in Aberdeen, I was impatient to get back to America to continue on the journey I'd begun three years before, and with the encouragement of my tutors (especially the Dickensian scholar Paul Schlicke, who had come to teach in Aberdeen from California, and became a close friend) I applied, and to my surprise was chosen to go.

This was awkward, because I had already been offered and had accepted a place on the Thomson Regional Newspapers training scheme, which was then one of the best routes into newspapers. Among other publications, they owned the morning and evening titles in Aberdeen, Edinburgh, Newcastle and Cardiff and were linked through the parent company to *The Times* and the *Sunday Times*. I prepared for the tricky task of asking them if I could take up my place the following year, because of this unexpected American offer and because I didn't want the job to slip away. They were generous enough to agree. But the whole business was also wreathed in personal sadness, because my father, whom I adored, died of a heart attack, without warning, in March 1973. He was only sixty-two. The interview with the St Andrew's Society's trustees in Edinburgh was scheduled for the day of his funeral, and I had to postpone. I was therefore not in the best frame of mind when I did meet them, not least because I was concerned – as an only child – about going abroad for a year and leaving my widowed mother alone. When the offer came two days later, however, she was insistent that I should go, and refused, with her unfailing generosity, to think of herself. She was still teaching, as my father had been until the end, and resilient. I was off.

I still had final exams to take in Aberdeen, but Shakespeare and Pope, Dickens and the Romantic poets were rather relegated in my mind because I was already looking westwards. I was fortunate, though, in having the excitement of immersion in American literature of the 1920s (thanks to the enthusiasm and scholarship of my tutor Andrew Hook) and there also came along, by chance, a political primer for my American year, which unfolded at the perfect moment, an irresistible drama that could be followed in detail, scene by scene, and which provided rich entertainment in the long days of summer after my last exam paper had been written.

It happened to be an essay on censorship, which I remember entitling, on a front page covered with ink blots and scorings-out, after three hours of scribbling, 'Wordsworth, Pornography and Mr Nixon'. We had been asked to write about an entry in Dorothy Wordsworth's diary in which she described sitting by the fire at Grasmere and reading aloud to her brother Chaucer's bawdy 'Miller's Tale'. Something took me straight from Lakeland to the cultural arguments about censorship that were boiling up in the United States.

Nixon was on my mind because in that same month, May 1973, the Senate Watergate Committee began its televised hearings in the Senate Caucus Room on Capitol Hill. This was my primer. The room itself had been the pillared stage set for many dramas over the years – Joe McCarthy's anti-communist hearings in the 1950s, which fuelled a notorious witch-hunt, the launch of both the Kennedys' presidential campaigns in the 1960s – and now it was where the story behind the 'third-rate burglary attempt' and the subsequent White House cover-up began to be stripped of its flimsy garb. The three American networks and the viewer-subscribed Public Broadcasting Service – there being no cable news in those days – began to cover them live, gavel-to-gavel as they liked to put it, and we watched long extracts back home, with the incomparable Charles Wheeler, one of the BBC's most eloquent foreign correspondents, as a guide through the complexities of the story.

After the botched burglary of the offices of the Democratic National Committee in the Watergate building in the summer of 1972 by associates of the Nixon campaign who were ex-CIA operatives and shady hangers-on, the story turned into a struggle by the press to follow the trail into the White House and the Oval Office, and an effort by Nixon's men to make sure that the cover-up held. It took two years for them to lose that fight.

Gradually, but with devastating force, Nixon's defences were breached in the Senate hearings and then pulled down. The blanket denials of the stream of stories that Bob Woodward and Carl Bernstein had been producing in the *Washington Post* since the summer of 1972 (with Seymour Hersh and others in the *New York Times* competing at every turn) – which at first had been almost completely ignored by the papers in small-town America – were exploded. The burglary was shown to be only one melodramatic element of a campaign fuelled from inside by dirty tricks, illegal funds and a stream of cynicism, and the president himself revealed as something suspiciously close to the caricature his opponents had always painted of him – petty, shifty, duplicitous. A dark man, and getting darker. Most Americans had never seen a transformation like it. The statesman who'd built a bridge to China in a dazzling diplomatic coup the previous year was, all of a sudden, being eviscerated before their eyes.

A few months later, he'd be bumbling through a sweaty speech to newspaper editors in Florida, saying this: 'People have got to know whether their president is a crook. Well, I'm not a crook.'

By then, with those words making it inescapable, the descent to disgrace had begun. The White House counsel John Dean admitted to the Senate committee, in electrifying fashion, to his role in advising Nixon how to lie his way out of trouble (thirty-five times, as it turned out), a host of minor players painted the picture of a president plunging into something that looked close to paranoia and, most startlingly of all, an aide of whom almost no one had heard, Alexander Butterfield, revealed the secret whose existence Nixon must have wanted to conceal most of all – that his conversations in the Oval Office and elsewhere around the White House had all been recorded on tape, and were crying out to be heard. As in the best courtroom dramas, this was the game-changing revelation that came from nowhere and set in train an accelerating series of events – the appointment of the special prosecutor and his subsequent firing, the struggles with judges all the way up to the Supreme Court itself, the publication of the tapes, the impeachment hearings in the House of Representatives, the desperate and eventually pathetic battle for public support and, finally, almost exactly fifteen months after the committee was appointed, Nixon's lachrymose departure when he realised that all but a miserable rump of his Republican friends had deserted him, and even the humiliation of resignation was preferable to conviction after a trial in the Senate.

For anyone with even the faintest interest in the psychology of power, this was a performance to be savoured from start to finish.

The committee hearings were also an introduction to the strange ways of the US Senate, its habits and its character. As a result, even before I set off in mid-summer, I felt that because of this glimpse I had an idea of the way this place worked and how it regarded itself. Later, when I finally got inside, saw the brass spittoons and the glassy marble floors, watched senators who'd dealt with Truman, Eisenhower and Kennedy take their places at their dark wooden desks, heard the 'yeas and nays' summoned for a roll-call vote, imagined LBJ strong-arming a wobbling senator in the cloakroom, it was immediately and absurdly familiar.

Presiding in the Caucus Room when the committee assembled in that May, under a pair of elaborate chandeliers, in front of an imposing marble backdrop and the inevitable Stars and Stripes on a shiny pole with an eagle on top, was the white-haired, roly-poly figure of Senator Sam Ervin of North Carolina, whose dancing eyebrows and old-fashioned southern rhetoric gave him a powerful theatrical presence. People queued to get in, the famous and the unknown, and for a few weeks the crowded arena became, even to those of us watching on television from far away, a political crucible, bubbling with passion and fire.

'I'm a country lawyer,' Ervin liked to say, as he spun another folksy story, presenting a picture of a simple and decent man bewildered by the duplicity being revealed to him. But it was more complicated and fascinating than that. He was one of the last stalwarts of a vanishing and backward-facing breed, the long-serving southern Democrats who talked with ponderous reverence about democracy and the constitution in the manner of orotund preachers, but were simultaneously determined defenders of the segregationist past of the Old South. Ervin, like nearly all his Senate colleagues from the states of the Confederacy, had fought cunningly and stubbornly against every civil rights bill since Lyndon B. Johnson's time as a manipulative leader of the Senate in the 1950s, when the future president had started, step by tentative step and with serpentine guile, legislating to dismantle the apparatus of segregation that had been guarded in the South since defeat in the Civil War a century earlier.

It was Nixon himself in the late 1960s who developed a

'southern strategy' to persuade voters in the old confederate states that their conservative instincts would be better satisfied by voting Republican, something that had been anathema to white men and women in the South who were instructed in childhood to revile the party of Abraham Lincoln, and to cling to Democrats instead because they had been the states' rights party in the 1860s, and therefore the guardians of slavery against the northern Yankees who were trying to drive old Dixie down. The fact that, at least since Franklin D. Roosevelt and the New Deal in the 1930s, Democrats had become the liberal believers in the power of the federal government to solve problems didn't move the South at all. It was implacable, and wanted those Civil War labels to be indelible. What had happened to the Democratic Party elsewhere was not a matter for them: that was in another country.

So, well into the 1960s, in elections across the Deep South, Republicans were the outsiders, carrying the shame of the carpet-baggers who'd forced humiliating 'Reconstruction' on the South after its rout in what the losers still stubbornly called the War Between the States. The important contest mostly took place not on election day but in the earlier Democratic primary contest where the candidate was chosen who would certainly win. That also meant that in a regional system that amounted to a one-party state, once you were elected you were very unlikely to be removed, and because of the strict seniority rules of the Senate you would eventually be guaranteed control of one of the committees that are as important in determining policy as any Cabinet appointee put in place by a president. So the southern Democrats, long since separated from the drift of their party and forming a grumpy caucus of their own, tended to be older and more powerful than the rest of the Senate. By the start of the 1970s, however, they were on strictly borrowed time. The anomaly was bound to be corrected soon, and in Sam Ervin's starring role in those Watergate hearings we saw one of the last national performances by one of the old school who would soon be gone.

But there was a twist. Long-standing opposition to civil rights wasn't the kind of conservatism that would persuade a senator like Ervin to sympathise with Nixon. Any president who overreached himself seemed as dangerous to old Sam as a liberal who tried to railroad the South out of its traditional ways and, like his fellow segregationist in the Democratic majority on the committee, Herman Talmadge of Georgia, he showed a withering distaste for the machinations of the team that ran the White House under Bob Haldeman and John Ehrlichman, until their forced resignations as Nixon panicked. Day by day he made it clear that he thought they were ignorant interlopers in the proper exercise of government. Consequently, with a sharp Republican minority on the committee led by Senator Howard Baker of Tennessee (his refrain became a national catchphrase – 'What did the president know, and when did he know it?') the hearings heated up into a summer nightmare for the White House. The country watched a bipartisan assault come together, and it provided the bedrock of the case against Nixon.

This was a perfect overture to student life at Syracuse. Since I knew that I had a newspaper job to return to, I took most of my courses at the Newhouse School of Communications, despite a healthy scepticism about the likely usefulness of some of them. In some cases, I was wholly wrong in my doubts. For example, a class run by the veteran magazine journalist Leonard Robinson – who'd worked on the *New Yorker* with a galère of its finest writers – was an exploration into some of the best writing in America, much of which I still had to discover. Norman Mailer I'd been gobbling up for years, but Gay Talese and Tom Wolfe now became constant companions, one of their battered volumes always in my bag, and I discovered Gore Vidal properly for the first time. However, a bunch of us was also anxious to get to Washington, so we hatched our research project and began to phone journalists who were deep in Watergate.

In a number of expeditions over many months, we drank deep at the well, and managed to get time with some extraordinary and generous characters, like David Broder of the *Washington Post*, who years later became a friend and mentor, and it raised our spir-its, which were often tested in the dark cold of a Syracuse winter, with pitiless winds blowing from Canada across Lake Erie, only about 40 miles to the north. They also provided me with my first serious exposure to Washington and its ways.

The city still contrived to maintain a surprisingly sleepy character in those days, despite having government as its business and power its obsession. The streets were mostly quiet. Within a few streets of the White House you could wander past blocks of higgledy-piggledy wooden homes that were unpretentious and ramshackle, without a hint of grandeur. The streets stretching east from Capitol Hill were seriously ungentrified and raw indeed. Georgetown by contrast was smart, its undulating streets lined with elegant homes and many mansions, but even there you settled into a pace that carried an echo of the easy-going South and seemed on the surface to have little to do with glitzy city life. An illusion, of course, but a comforting one. We wandered along half-deserted streets where you barely looked to see if there was traffic before you stepped off the sidewalk. M Street running through Georgetown had in those days a jumble of individual shops and bars that gave it the feel of a country town rather than an upmarket quarter of the capital. At the weekends, the middle of the city emptied, because the powerful folk disappeared to other homes. On Sunday mornings it felt as if people were obeying an evacuation order.

The southern flavour was unmistakable, not only because Virginia lay just across the slow-moving Potomac River and in the summer the humid heat was often intolerable, but because of the obvious fact that the population of the city was overwhelmingly African American. People of government and business either lived in the suburbs or in well-defined enclaves, well away from downtown, which was not an area to explore at night. It was rough, but naturally that's where we tended to find places to stay (if the YMCA was full) because it was all we could afford. Less than a mile from the White House there was rampant poverty that was usually a shock to outsiders, if they discovered it. Also shocking to me was the realisation that so many Washington residents had learned to pretend that it didn't exist. I found out a little about street life in those days. The atmosphere, however, was a heady one for strictly political reasons. You didn't dare miss a news bulletin, or an Art Buchwald column inflicting another satirical wound on Nixon. The front pages shimmered with scoops. Week by week through the autumn of 1973, the revelations piled up. Then, on 10 October, Nixon lost his political bodyguard.

We'd been following for months the case of Spiro Agnew, the pugilistic vice president who had acted as Nixon's cheerleader against his multitude of opponents ('enemies'), and was now entangled in a string of corruption charges. He'd been under investigation for criminal conspiracy, bribery, extortion and tax fraud, and on that October Thursday he told the federal district court in Baltimore that he was offering no contest (the precise plea was 'nolo contendere') to the charge that he had taken regular kickbacks from contractors during his time as governor of Maryland. The payments continued after he became vice president, brown envelopes still being passed to him in the White House from the grateful recipients of his self-enriching political fixes. The shiny conservative hero, whose speciality was pouring scorn on the press ('those nattering nabobs of negativism'), was humiliated. Nixon might insist he wasn't a crook; his vice president certainly was.

Agnew escaped jail only because the authorities decided there was little point in prolonging the story and gave him a heavy fine and long probation. He borrowed a couple of hundred thousand dollars from Frank Sinatra to pay his bills, wrote a silly memoir and a worse novel, and was never heard from again.

This all interested me more than my class at Syracuse on the history of typographical design, for example, not least because that particular session was scheduled twice a week at 8 a.m., with a compulsory sign-in to make it even worse. These were two inconveniences that had never troubled me in my previous four years as a student. They meant, too, a long winter trek across a snowy park in the morning dark to get to school. In retrospect, it had been a fascinating class and perhaps I was unfair at the time. But on the weather front, I was often denied sympathy by my classmates, on the mistaken grounds that since I came from Scotland I must be used to the cold. In truth, I had never known anything like it. Onondaga Lake just outside town would sometimes freeze over from shore to shore, we had to run our shaky central heating system at full tilt in our rented wooden house at 428 Columbus Avenue because the wind had a way of getting in through the corners, and the streets away from the few main drags through the city would be coated in ice for days on end. Very happy though I was with my fellow students Danny Kaye and Phil Novak, the weather through that winter wasn't friendly.

They were great companions in our yellow-painted house, where we three had fled after a few weeks from a rather bare dormitory, Skytop, placed on a windy slope above the campus. Phil came from Chicago and was deep in religious studies, spending many hours meditating cross-legged, with a candle burning on the floor in front of him, and had a notably gentle spirit, which was just as well. He eventually became a professor of philosophy and religion at a Dominican Catholic university in California. Danny, who taught me the story of Brooklyn, was studying child psychology, and it was he who introduced me to many American enthusiasms that I continue to cherish, baseball among them. Being a Jewish New Yorker, he also revived my memories of days in the Catskills, never losing his amusement at the breakneck speed of my cultural immersion, and through our close friendship I also got my first real understanding of the steel-like bond that families like his felt with Israel. For most of that October he was monitoring news bulletins first thing in the morning to check the progress of 'our' forces in the Yom Kippur War. I had another friend whose brother was fighting in the Israeli army, and around me at Syracuse, which had a heavily Jewish student body and faculty, there was no doubt where most sympathies lay, in contrast to the attitude to Vietnam, where many Americans of their age were still bogged down, and about which a healthy majority of my fellow students was either angry to the core or, at least, profoundly uneasy and weary.

With my colleagues at Newhouse I'd spend long hours in the library, and there were many other friends with whom we watched baseball and American football. The university had long had a strong team in college football, known, rather awkwardly for a British student, as The Orangemen, under a famous coach called Ben Schwartzwalder who had just retired when I arrived, which meant that the team was about to slide down the rankings. But we knew that the university still chased after the best high-school players to persuade them to come to Syracuse. One of their tactics was to get two well-known alumni to phone the kids out of the blue to suggest that they should come – Alan Alda, the star of *M*A*S*H*, and Peter Falk, a.k.a. Columbo, the detective with the dirty rain-coat. I did try hard with gridiron, and have watched many games over the years, but have never quite got it. Rugby is so much more satisfying, and anyway I came to know that it's baseball that really tells the American sporting story, especially if it's Roger Angell who is writing it. Since he started to write in the 1940s, he has been to baseball what Neville Cardus was to cricket.

We did have fun around the campus. From a law student friend, Ken Fisher, I first got a glimpse into the machinations of New York Democratic politics, and also hung out a lot with a friend of Danny's in psychology, Rudy Duncan, from whom I learned one shameful lesson. He was African American, and after we'd known each other for a while, I asked him how he'd come by that name, since in my part of Scotland there were Duncans everywhere, and none of them was black.

He smiled. 'Guess.'

I couldn't.

'It's a slave name. Way back, somebody called Duncan owned my family. We had to carry the name.'

After that shivering moment, our friendship became closer, and such experiences made me realise that old truth about Americans, that those of us who share their language and part of their history are often tricked into believing we understand them much better than we do. So I was being educated in more than one way, and was lucky that in a wild political season, in a university where I was supposed to be spending time thinking about the practice and the ethics of journalism (and studying some history on the side), there was nothing sleepy or slow about my exposure to contemporary culture. It was helter-skelter from the start. Fortunately, there was a calm, domestic side to the story that gave my life a happy balance. By a chance throw of the dice, my first cousin Marcia had moved from Oregon to New York just before I arrived at Syracuse, and by the time I got there was living with her husband Mike and their two young girls, Joie and Aimee, about an hour down the road in Binghamton, where Mike was a librarian at the campus of the State University of New York. I had met them during my first visit in 1970 and we were a close gang. So I had a bolthole, and spent many blissful weekends with them, including my first Thanksgiving, and Christmas with my mother.

Mind you, she only reached New York after a chaotic series of flights that had been haphazardly reorganised, seemingly by the hour, thanks to the oil crisis and fuel shortages at home. Her original booking was cancelled, and a travel agent in Elgin, 15 miles from where she lived, didn't seem up to the task of keeping her in the loop, except in telling her that she could no longer go. She sent a simple telegram, which I knew must have been exceptionally painful, saying her great trip was off. Alerted by Mike – I happened to ring Binghamton by chance – I had to spend a long time on a street payphone in Washington to try to find out what was happening, and since this was long before electronic ticketing, let alone mobile phones, it turned into a nightmare. After a series of calls thither and hither, I eventually woke my mother in the middle of the night to give her the news that the airline had made alternative arrangements, of which she wasn't aware.

But at home the snow had piled up and the lights were out, and she had somehow to make it from the snowdrifts of rural Banffshire to Glasgow the next morning if she was to get across the Atlantic on her rebooked flights, which were taking her on a circuitous route. Of course, she had to write down my instructions in the dark. To put the tin hat on the whole affair, this was the first flight she'd ever taken, and she was heading into airports that would be brimming with angry passengers as confused as she would be. It was urgent, because the roads from home were nearly blocked, and as a result she got involved in a hair-raising race through a blizzard to Aberdeen, driven by our saintly village postmaster who was determined to get her onto the only train that would let her get south in time. When she arrived in New York a day and a half later, she proudly produced from her handbag the thick telephone directory that had been sitting on our front table at home when my call came from Washington and on which she'd scratched (perfectly accurately) my instructions in the dark, and then carried all the way with her in case she forgot any of the details. It was a particular relief to see her because we'd checked the passenger list on each incoming flight at Kennedy airport with increasing alarm, finding her name was notably absent. British Airways (still BOAC, just, in those days) had said, in a phrase I wouldn't forget for quite a long time, 'I'm afraid we seem to have lost her somewhere along the way.'

That long dark winter brought many memorable moments. One of the expected duties that came with my scholarship was attendance at the annual St Andrew's Night dinner in New York at the end of November. This turned out to be a mighty affair in the Waldorf Astoria, and I had taken with me from home my kilt and all the appropriate gear, booking a flight in good time from Syracuse for the great day. Unfortunately, some birthday party the night before meant that I overslept at Columbus Avenue, only waking up to hear the noise of a plane above our house and realising all too quickly that it was the one I was supposed to be on, already on its way to the city. A daft scramble ensued, but I did manage to make it eventually by late afternoon to the University Club on 5th Avenue and 54th Street where the society had kindly arranged for me to stay, a traditional and handsome gentlemen's club that was considerably more upmarket than my usual billets, but which set the scene for the evening. I was nervous at the prospect of walking down 5th Avenue in full Highland dress, but it taught me something I should have already known about New York. Nothing seems odd in that city. People do funny things: dress in unusual ways; go their own way. No one turned a hair, even though I had my *sgian dubh*, the black-handled dagger, sticking out of one of my socks.

When I got to the hotel, I was certainly glad I had made the effort. There was a vast horde in full swing, conforming to the old rule about Scottish cultural festivities: that when you are abroad, they always quiver with an over-the-top enthusiasm that would be embarrassing at home. Anything goes. We were in the giant ball-room of the Waldorf, big enough to allow a full pipe band to march up and down between the tables to entertain the banqueters. A lively time ensued (my only task was to stand and identify myself and get a boozy cheer, with a brief word of heartfelt thanks and no speech, thank goodness) with one awkward encounter, which occurred at the obligatory cocktail party in a comfortable room somewhere high in one of the Waldorf towers. Stories were swirling around that week about John B. Connally, the former Democratic governor of Texas, who'd been shot and wounded in the same car as John F. Kennedy in Dallas in 1963. Nixon had appointed him his Treasury secretary in 1971, because he was a conservative on the run from his party's liberals, and he subsequently ran 'Democrats for Nixon' in the 1972 presidential election. Now he was mired in accusations of bribery involving milk prices and the receipt of parcels of cash from people who stood to gain from a federal government ruling. At the party, I was talking to one of the tartan-clad guests, whom I should have realised immediately was unusually smooth and confident, and made the mistake of remarking that it was surely obvious to everyone that Connally (who was tried and acquitted the following year) was another wrong 'un like Agnew, or words to that effect. I got a slam-dunk put-down. 'Well, I had dinner with him last night. He's an old friend and a good man.'

I'd been talking unwittingly to a senior executive of Exxon, one of Connally's cronies in the oil-fuelled politics of Texas. I made what I could of it, and fled to the other side of the room as decently as I could manage. I remember the generosity at that moment of the main speaker, flown in from Scotland for the night, the industrialist Sir Iain Maxwell Stewart, who regaled me with happy stories of his golfing exploits with Sean Connery, naturally leaving me rather impressed. I never got the chance to thank him in later years, because there was a hidden sadness there: within a decade he had taken his own life.

I remain grateful to the St Andrew's Society for their generosity and the chance of a lifetime, and was glad to be able to express some of that warmth in speaking at their annual dinner in 2006, when they celebrated fifty years of the scholarship. The other main speaker that evening, however, is unlikely to be invited to return to one of their fine soirees. He was Fred Goodwin of the Royal Bank of Scotland, well into the approach to his fall from grace when he brought the bank close to collapse and became an arch villain of the 2008 financial crash.

Such excitements as the Waldorf dinner and others punctuated the academic year and gave colour to that grey winter. A few weeks later, in February, when we were beginning to think about our Watergate research project, I managed to get to Washington for the night of the British general election on the last day of the month. This was the election called in the chaos of the oil crisis, a miners' strike and the panicky imposition of a three-day week by Edward Heath's Conservative government, in which he decided to ask for a new mandate with the fatal slogan, 'Who governs Britain?', to which the electorate's answer was, roughly speaking, 'Not you, matey.'

I went to Washington on the usual Greyhound bus, which was becoming a bit of a long-distance shuttle (about a seven-hour journey). I had somehow inveigled my way into the British Embassy election results party up on Massachusetts Avenue, which was quite a hoot. I had reasoned that it would be difficult to follow the rolling results in any other way. That first visit to the building, and to the glorious Lutyens-designed residence next door, which I'd later come to know well, amounted to an exhilarating evening, with a blackboard set up at the party where some frenzied third secretary was chalking up the results as quickly as he could, and we listened to BBC World Service on transistor radios. I sensed a good deal of despair among the grander guests as it became evident that the government would probably lose its majority (although Ted Heath persevered through the weekend in a pretty hopeless effort to lure Jeremy Thorpe's Liberal Party into some kind of alliance before he had to give way, reluctantly, to his old combatant Harold Wilson). In the embassy I took trouble to avoid the ambassador himself, Sir Peter Ramsbotham, a diplomat of the old school, because although I am sure his manners would have held him back, I worried that he might ask an embarrassing question as to who I was and why I was there. I preferred youthful anonymity. I do remember, however, the kindness of Peregrine Worsthorne, who was deputy editor of the *Sunday Telegraph* at the time, and with whom I fell into an unlikely happy conversation and who generously offered me a lift home at the end of the party, with his wife Claudie driving. That was just as well, considering the quantity of embassy booze I had watched being put away with enthusiasm. We had a happy chatter about Nixon, about whom, from a determined but eccentric right-wing position, he had hardly a good word to say.

We journeyed contentedly down Connecticut Avenue. When it came to dropping me off, however, I was a little evasive, referring vaguely to a street junction somewhere close by. When they insisted, politely, on knowing precisely where I was lodging, I detected a distinct shock at the revelation that it was the YMCA. That was not a building either of them had ever approached before. But I was grateful, went to bed and locked the door from the inside, as usual. That was always the prudent course.

The months that followed were a time of high drama. Looking back at them from the perspective of the Trump era in the third year of his presidency, from the forty-fifth occupant of the White House back to the thirty-seventh, the contours of the story seem sharper than ever and perhaps more threatening. A special prosecutor who wouldn't be cowed, courts that stood firm and, above all, a significant cohort of senators and House members who realised eventually that if their grandiloquent speeches about the preciousness of American democracy were to be taken seriously into the future it meant a climactic confrontation with the president of the United States himself. As with the observation of Carl Leubsdorf about the Saturday Night Massacre, and his fears for democratic freedoms, the story of the spring and summer of 1974 penetrated the very idea of America that candidates of both parties self-consciously laid out in speech after speech. No Western democracy spends more time talking about its own constitutional history than the United States. Banishing self-doubt had become a public duty by the 1970s, which is why Watergate, with its toxic mixture of the profound and the trivial, proved so troubling to people in power. Doubt was everywhere.

By early March, the first guilty pleas had been entered by defendants on Watergate charges. The new special prosecutor Leon Jaworski was preparing to demand access to the White House tapes. In the office of Gerald Ford, the vice president filling Agnew's empty shoes, his staff were beginning to prepare for a transition that they knew might be on the way, because each time Nixon tried to cut off the investigation he failed, and his popularity sank further. Someone, someday, was going to hear the tapes. And almost no one believed that they would support Nixon against John Dean's accusations of cover-up. Otherwise, why would he argue so vehemently that they should never be released? Concern for constitutional propriety? Hardly. Everyone knew by that stage that such high-mindedness had no place in Nixon's White House, where John Mitchell, his former attorney general and campaign director in 1972, had said of Katharine Graham, proprietor of the hated *Washington Post*, that if the paper didn't desist from its investigations of him and others she was 'going to get her big fat tit caught in a wringer'. Mitchell was indicted in the first week of March, and a sealed briefcase from a Washington grand jury was delivered to the House Judiciary Committee on Capitol Hill in which they named the president of the United States as a co-conspirator.

The atmosphere through that spring was a curious mixture of sober high seriousness and music-hall entertainment as Nixon floundered. In terms of a Shakespearean tragedy, we were somewhere in Act 3 – the fatal mistakes made, the flaws revealed, the competing forces set implacably against each other and an emotional climax reached, from which everything else would flow. The inevitable descent to destruction was about to begin. Nixon's loneliness was obvious to outsiders – it was evident in the television addresses, the awkward public appearances where the more he smiled, the more you knew how much he was hating it all, the shrinking away of old friends – although no one could know how the deep darkness felt when he went late at night to his hideaway in the Old Executive Office Building next to the White House, watching the indictments pile up, hearing the first guilty pleas from his loyalists and knowing for a certainty that many others would follow.

The end game began on 30 April 1974, a year to the day after Haldeman and Ehrlichman resigned and John Dean was fired. Jaworski wanted to hear sixty-four tapes; Nixon offered to provide transcripts instead. So, like many others, I found myself queuing outside the government stationery office to see them for the first time. These tapes were going to tell the story at last. Nixon had got rid of Cox the previous October to try to keep them private, having offered the laughable compromise of handing them over for a behind-closed-doors review to the deeply conservative Democratic senator from Mississippi, John C. Stennis, a man who had only two claims to fame – his unswerving admiration of Nixon and the fact that he was notoriously hard of hearing. No sooner was the president's suggestion made public, than it became a national joke. Then there was the business of the eighteen-and-a-half-minute gap on the tape of a conversation between Nixon and Haldeman held three days after the Watergate burglary itself, which had been admitted to the courts before Christmas, and which was claimed to be the result of a mistake made by Nixon's secretary, Rose Mary Woods, when she was reviewing the tapes at the president's request. She said she'd taken a phone call and had mistakenly kept her foot on the erase pedal while talking. Unfortunately, the White House photograph produced for Judge Sirica to demonstrate this accidental manoeuvre, with Rose Mary Woods posing for the camera by way of explanation, showed her holding a posture more suited to an acrobat in the circus than a presidential secretary. She looked as if she had been caught in a yoga class that had gone wrong. Universal incredulity rained down.

The scene as the transcripts of sixty-four tapes were handed out to reporters from the government stationery office was extraordinary. The 1,250 pages were bound in 4-inch-thick volumes with light-blue paper covers, and reporters were running down the streets with multiple copies tucked under their arms. People were sitting on the ground checking particular dates in a frenzy, since by that time everyone knew the conversations that were of most interest to prosecutors and the congressional committees. Radio stations got actors to read the tapes aloud, hour after hour. Almost overnight, paperbacks were published carrying every word, and a million copies were sold in the first few days. Everyone was searching for the conversation that would tell all, but there was something else. You couldn't open the volume without coming across the words 'expletive deleted'. The transcripts had been filleted to try to preserve some of Nixon's fast-diminishing dignity. Within minutes those words became the label that might as well have been plastered on every tourist postcard of the White House as the emblem of the Nixon presidency.

Extraordinarily, despite the overwhelming evidence of shoddy politics and, after the first guilty pleas at the start of 1974, criminal wrongdoing, there was a big chunk of the population that was still minded to support Nixon as a wronged president, beaten down in

the way he'd always predicted he would be. Insecurity and resentment had been his companions all the way to the White House.

But he'd smashed his way to a second term in 1972, leaving
the liberal Democrat George McGovern with only one state
(Massachusetts) and the District of Columbia in his column, by far
the worst result for any candidate since the two-party system settled down more than a century before. He went to China, promised
peace in Vietnam (again). From that strength, he could argue that his
'enemies' had pursued him relentlessly and unfairly – just because
he was Dick Nixon! – and that journalists on the *Washington Post*
and the *New York Times* worked to an agenda the American people
didn't share. Like one of his Republican successors in the White
House forty-five years and eight presidents later, who fashioned
'fake news' into his rhetorical broadsword, so Nixon depended on
the idea that his concept of the truth had always been much finer
than the 'enemies' allowed, and that eventually he would prove it.
The tapes, unfortunately for him, proved the opposite.

'Expletive deleted' became a national catchphrase overnight,
and for some of Nixon's defenders even some of the non-deleted
language cut deep. I have a vivid memory of Senator Hugh Scott,
leader of the Republican minority in the Senate, emerging from one
of the office buildings on Capitol Hill to face the cameras. Scott was
a mainstream Country Club Republican lawyer from Pennsylvania,
opposed to hard-right ideology and committed through the 1960s
to civil rights. But he didn't talk about the courts or the possible
crimes when he gave his reaction. He was fighting back tears as he
spoke, saying he never thought he would live to see the day when a
president of the United States said 'Goddamn' in the Oval Office.
That caught it.

His reaction was telling, because it revealed how a national illusion was being challenged by the Watergate episode. Nobody with a
little toe in the real world could be remotely surprised by profanity
in private political discourse (LBJ had once said of Nixon's new vice
president, 'Jerry Ford can't fart and chew gum at the same time'),
but the presidency was wreathed in dignity and decorum and to see
it undermined in White House-authorised print was a shock to the
conservative, even puritanical, instincts of many Americans. Nixon

might sit in the Oval Office and say, 'I don't give a shit about the lira', as the tapes told us he did, but many Americans wanted to be spared that knowledge. It was possible that someday a president would come along who made a virtue of not caring, as one did indeed arrive in 2016, but in 1974 the lifting of the veil produced deep public discomfort.

The other reaction, very striking to an outsider of my age, was in the press. Talking to American journalists at that time was to realise how conscious they were of playing a public role, not least because at a time of constitutional consternation (could a president claim 'executive privilege' to keep private anything he liked?) they were themselves protected by the first amendment to that constitution, guaranteeing freedom of speech. The consequences of that guarantee ran deep, producing an atmosphere of high seriousness. Reporters were enjoying themselves, but writing soberly. Columnists were describing a constitutional crisis.

British newspaper readers have never been used to the strict separation of news and comment that was rigidly enforced in most American newspapers, because it's long been taken for granted that in the popular papers that were starting to become tabloids in the 1970s you got on the front pages exactly what you would find on the leader pages. American journalists were brought up quite differently, and on the major papers – *The Post*, *The Times*, the *Los Angeles Times*, the *Chicago Tribune* and more recent titles like *Newsday* – there was a heavily policed cordon sanitaire between the news pages and the editorial section where the columnists lived, and where all the editorial comments were made. By tradition, these pages had a separate editor who decided which columnists were invited to perform and what a leading article said. News reporters were kept well away. It was admirable.

When my colleagues and I spoke to journalists, perhaps at the National Press Building a couple of blocks from the White House at 14th Street and F, we were always reminded of the commitment they took so seriously, and for which they were 'enemies' to the White House. I've long had an affection for the independent traditions of American newspapers, still preserved in fine old titles – the Cleveland *Plain Dealer*, the *Seattle Post-Intelligencer*, the *Detroit*

Free Press, the *Toledo Blade* and the rest. A history that combined irreverence and boldness was on display every time we went into that building. It was a time when anyone working in a newspaper's Washington bureau – whether it was the *Times-Picayune*, the *Baltimore Sun*, the *Atlanta Constitution*, the *Boston Globe* – was in a state of perpetual excitement because they knew they were riding the wave of the story of a lifetime, but in the same way as American political language is always replete with a self-consciousness about the constitution, not to mention the supposedly enduring quality of the American Dream, journalists in the Watergate era found themselves reaching for the fundamental building blocks of their trade to answer the attacks being made on behalf of the president himself, and manning their barricades.

The argument between Nixon and the press about who was telling the truth was why there was such a day of celebration in newspapers and broadcast studios across the country when Ron Ziegler, Nixon's press secretary, took himself to the White House podium to recant. He announced, because of what was now undeniable, that all previous statements on Watergate – *all* of them – were 'inoperative', a wonderfully Nixonian construction. They were still there. They weren't being withdrawn. Nobody was admitting they were untrue. They just didn't work any longer, and therefore had ceased to operate. At least it had the advantage that, for once, it was true.

With the university year beginning to wind down and the House Judiciary Committee about to begin impeachment hearings, having been propelled into that course by a combination of the first guilty pleas, the indictments, the testimony to the Senate committee, and the tapes, Washington was clearly the only place to be. I had met Simon Winchester of *The Guardian*, who'd been given the prized correspondent's job in the United States as a consequence of his prize-winning work on the paper in Northern Ireland, and he was kind enough to respond to my tentative suggestion that it might help him in his small office if there was a dogsbody who could spend a little time organising the files (though such feats of organisation were not, and never would be, my strong point). He was happy to slip me a few dollars a week to help around the office and it meant I had enough pocket money to survive in town. I owe a lot to Simon. His colleague on the paper at that time was Hella Pick, State Department correspondent and a formidable operator. We hardly met at that time (Henry Kissinger being a more interesting interlocutor than me) but in later years we became colleagues on the paper in London and dear friends for ever afterwards.

One nice touch was that the *Guardian* office in those days was situated at 1750 Pennsylvania Avenue, a block west of the White House, in a building that had also been occupied by the operatives of the Committee to Re-elect the President in 1972. By this stage in proceedings everyone simply referred to it as CREEP, for brevity's sake, and because it felt right. So as the last act played out, that block took on a rather ghostly air. Soon, all the principal figures who had served in CREEP would be in jail, swept away as the waters rose.

The end game began when the House Judiciary Committee started impeachment hearings in May. I managed to squeeze into the room, having queued for most of the night, and I treasure the photographs I managed to take that day, catching the Democrat chairman of the committee, Peter Rodino of New Jersey, presenting the perfect picture of his character – an attack-dog prosecutor, but one determined to lift proceedings out of the morass of partisan political argument. His piercing eyes and gravelly voice became familiar to everyone, but he never let it suggest relish for the task, only determination. There was one individual sitting not far from me who interested me, because he seemed familiar, though he appeared to be dressed as a priest. It bugged me. Where had I seen him before? Afterwards, someone told me that it had been Robert Redford, incognito, who was already co-operating with Bob Woodward and Carl Bernstein for the film version of *All the President's Men*, their sparkling account of the saga that was published while the hearings were taking place. I have never been able to confirm the story, and I eventually gave up trying because, frankly, I like to preserve the notion that it's true.

The book revealed for the first time the existence of Woodward's source, whom the reporters nicknamed 'Deep Throat' (that film having been released in the Watergate summer of 1972) and who immediately took on a fabled character, a will-o'-the-wisp who seemed to be able to follow the most intimate discussions in Nixon's circle and simultaneously the progress of the FBI investigations. This was hardly surprising, because in 1992 he was unmasked as Mark Felt, deputy director of the FBI, then suffering from dementia and approaching the end of his life. Woodward's exploits in meeting him in underground garages around Washington, having devised a system of signals by which he could arrange a rendezvous, gave the whole story the flavour of a conspiracy thriller, and by the time the shades came down in the White House in the high summer of 1974 that is precisely what it had become – a tale of deception and desperation.

When the committee approved three articles of impeachment in July, there was not much doubt that the full House would eventually vote them through with its healthy Democrat majority and the rising number of defecting Republicans who could stomach Nixon no longer. But it didn't come to that. After the Supreme Court voted unanimously in July, in the case magnificently entitled United States v Nixon, to order him to hand over the tapes, the only question was how long it would take. Sure enough, the White House had to admit the existence of one devastating conversation – on 23 June 1972, just after the burglary – and the dam burst. Senior Republicans on the Hill, with Senator Barry Goldwater leading the charge, made it plain to Nixon that everything was over. If the House passed articles of impeachment and there were a Senate trial he would lose, with his support among the 100 senators perhaps dwindling to single figures. Goldwater, guardian of the conservative conscience, had written a memo to himself six months earlier questioning Nixon's mental state, and later described him as the most dishonest man he had ever met.

By this time, we later learned, Nixon's chief of staff, Alexander Haig, was already helping Gerald Ford's team to plan the succession he knew must come. The president's fall was nigh.

I was back home in early August when it came, watching the last act from a distance. For someone about to become a reporter, the experience had been much more than a political melodrama that I was lucky to have been able to observe; it was an introduction to the riddle of power. How can political ambition be contained? Are the deepest political friendships always destined to end in distrust and despair? What drives people on when they know they are heading for defeat?

On 8 August, Nixon announced in a televised address from the Oval Office that it was over. In a letter to Kissinger, secretary of state, he arranged to resign his office the next day, the first president to do so. He broke down as he addressed his staff in the morning, but as he boarded his helicopter to leave the White House lawn for the last time, he managed one final act of trembling bravado, thrusting both his arms high in the air in his familiar victory gesture, simultaneously making Churchillian V-signs with the fingers of each hand. From Andrews Air Force Base he flew to his home at San Clemente, California. Somewhere over the Midwest he ceased to be president.

I arranged for a friend to send me a copy of the *Washington Post* for that day, 9 August. It still hangs on my wall, a haggard image of Nixon staring out of it. A happy day. It was my twenty-third birthday.

CHAPTER 3

THE PURSUIT OF HAPPINESS

American political conventions choose presidents, and keep illusions alive. The vote counting for candidates – serious, and involving brutal deal-making in the raw – is turned into a circus, to let people who've made politics and parties their business revel in the idea that in the quest for power it's not only desirable to have fun, but necessary. The weariness of the candidates' trudge through the primaries and the mind-numbing months of speeches and interviews are meant to be transformed in the alchemy of a four-day party so that the nominating convention persuades everyone, inside the tent and across the country, that presidential campaigns are still happy crusades. Not compromises nor exercises in cynicism, but a search for something better.

They are therefore as American as baseball or pumpkin pie. Since my first immersion in a convention, in 1976, I have found them hypnotic events, despite all the nonsense that they attract. Despite their wild theatricality, you can experience moments of revelation: the loneliness of a candidate in defeat; the emergence of a figure of power who'd once seemed nothing; the creation of a political mood that comes in like a storm.

Even when most of the evidence points the other way, optimism is an obligation. If you're in politics, you have to believe it. The bigger, more raucous a presidential convention becomes, so the argument goes, the greater the campaign that will follow. They're exercises in pumped-up self-belief, all the hoopla of the speeches, the parties and the confected drama of the roll-call vote itself, a means by which 10,000 or 20,000 people can be lifted up for a day or two before they return home to a more prosaic world where the magic is a memory.

Sometimes it works, and sometimes it fails. When Jimmy Carter arrived in New York in July 1976 he was surfing a tide of optimism. After Watergate, and Gerald Ford's uncomfortable effort to steady the ship from the White House – greatly hampered by his unpopular pardon of Nixon – how could Democrats fail? But the shock had gone deep and Carter was a symptom of nervousness as well as confidence. The reason he won enough primaries through the spring and summer to make himself the nominee was that, like so many candidates before and since, he presented himself as someone who was almost outside politics, never mind that he was governor of Georgia. They needed, above all, a candidate who was different, and as disconnected from Washington as possible. A story almost as old as the republic.

When Carter began to scout out New Hampshire long months before the first primary of 1976, the most remarkable thing about him was that he was turning up in Nashua or Manchester or Tamworth carrying his own suitcase. This fact was reported with breathless wonder, as if he'd reinvented politics at a stroke. Where were the bag carriers and minders, the advance men and speech writers? Carrying his own suitcase! The man was either a naive southerner with straw sticking out of his ears, elected as a governor by accident, or someone with no real ambition. Probably both. Carter played this happily to his advantage, quite content to have people describing him as a peanut farmer (true) and not as a former senior naval officer on nuclear submarines (also true). After Nixon, it was a season for outsiders and he fitted the part perfectly. The more he sounded like a wide-eyed, slow-moving southerner, the better.

This meant that my first convention at Madison Square Garden in the summer of the American bicentenary came at a moment when the nation was preparing to make a break, because it needed one. It was tired of Washington shenanigans, wanted to forget a war that had ended in ugly humiliation in Vietnam, and Carter seemed to Democrats to be their best bet. He arrived in New York with a string of primary victories behind him and therefore more than enough committed delegates to ensure his nomination. There would be no trouble.

The Barnum & Bailey hype of a convention can sometimes catch the mood of the moment because of a happy combination of time and place, and that was Carter's good fortune. If you wanted to argue for a new direction, New York was certainly the place to do it. All the ills of the moment seemed to be illustrated in its streets. The city was failing. Street violence was obvious to everyone. Many Carter delegates from across the South, not party regulars, were coming to Manhattan for the first time, and there was much talk of their shock at taking a wrong turn into 42nd Street, and seeing hard drugs traded openly in doorways, porn parlours with a phalanx of prostitutes hanging outside the doors and shouting invitations to passers-by, drunks lying in the street, all in the view of cops who stood on the corner of Broadway or 8th Avenue, swinging their billy clubs and showing little interest in life around them. Many of them had probably been paid not to. It was a place that looked and felt on the slide, not least because its public finances were in chaos – many city employees sacked, and the salaries of the others frozen. The city was broke.

Like the whole country, it was feeling the consequences of the troubled 1960s, which further exposed the divisions between the races, between rich and poor, between the young and the old, in a way that shook Americans more deeply than anything since the trauma of the Great Depression in the early 1930s. In the canyons of New York you could see a microcosm of the country's pain.

Yet it was bicentennial year. Time for a party to celebrate 200 years of America on the Fourth of July. Broke or not, New York wouldn't be stopped. Independence Day fell at the beginning of the week before the Democratic National Convention opened and the city was going to celebrate, come what may, with the magnificent craft from the Tall Ships' Race sailing up the Hudson River and the biggest fireworks display the world had ever seen, so they said. What else would you expect? Even the arrival of the president was tolerated, despite his 'Drop Dead' moment, and he took a salute from the vast aircraft carrier USS *Forrestal* near the Statue of

Liberty, as the tall ships in full sail glided by on their way upriver like a pageant from the city's past.

I was there because I had been determined to get to a convention. What was Washington politics without some understanding of the flavour of a campaign? But there was a problem. Having finished my training course, I had begun two years' indentures – the fine old word was still being used – on the *Press and Journal* in Aberdeen at the start of the previous year. I knew, however, that the chance of the paper sending a reporter to an American convention was precisely nil. I'd had to make a heavy argument the previous year to get as far as the Scottish Conservative Party conference in Perth, less than 100 miles away.

I negotiated a compromise. I was going to the US on holiday anyway, because by that stage I couldn't keep away, so why didn't I file some stuff from the convention while I was there? It was agreed that there would be some (exceedingly) modest expenses if I did get some copy into the paper. The point was that I could therefore apply for accreditation from the Democratic National Committee in the name of the paper, which I did. I was in. I got the cheapest room I could find on their list of hotels and all was set. I will always maintain that I was the only reporter from the *P&J* until then to report from a convention.

So by the day of the bicentennial I was in New York, and by happy chance encountered an old friend from Aberdeen. Rhod Sharp and I had been students together – he was a couple of years younger – and he was that year's St Andrew's Society scholar, at Princeton in New Jersey. We didn't know it then, but we would later become BBC colleagues and witness many American political events together. On 4 July, we hooked up and decided we had to get a good view of the fireworks. There was one place that would certainly have the best vista on the harbour – the top of one of the towers in the World Trade Center. By means I can't recall – it seems extraordinary now – we got in, perhaps even by taking the name of the *Press and Journal* in vain.

That hardly mattered. Not only did we manage to get to the top floors of the North Tower, where the Windows on the World restaurant on the 107th floor was out of bounds to the likes of us because

Henry Kissinger and others were going to be partying there, but we discovered that it was possible to get up an escalator and out onto the roof, where people would be standing in the open air to watch the spectacle. This was extraordinary. A party was in progress outside, with nothing above us but the sky, behind the white railings that acted as a barrier and looked alarmingly flimsy. When it opened in 1973 the North Tower was the tallest building in the world, and we were at about 1,350ft, looking down on skyscrapers we'd always thought impossibly high. Vast sound speakers had been set up at the four corners of the tower to blast music across the harbour and the city as part of the co-ordinated sound-and-light fireworks show. We watched the whole performance, and were deafened by the sound, with a sense of disbelief. What were we doing there?

This memory has inevitably become a deeply poignant one in recent years. Having seen the towers on their way up in 1970, then got used to them in the refashioned cityscape when I got to know the place so well, it is a recurring shock to look down 7th Avenue from Midtown towards Battery Park through the gap where they once stood.

The bicentennial celebrations were an invitation – even an instruction – to Americans to enjoy themselves. Needing no encouragement, everyone began to speak about the promise that had been passed down the generations from the Declaration of Independence itself, that the rights to 'life, liberty and the pursuit of happiness' could never be taken away. Therefore the atmosphere of the first post-Watergate convention, nominating a man who confessed, in a deliberate act of humility, that he'd never met a Democratic president, had a feeling of starting again. Carter began his acceptance speech with the words that had become a catchphrase in his long and once-lonely campaign – 'My name is Jimmy Carter and I'm running for president' – and he later quoted Bob Dylan. America wasn't a country that was busy dyin', it was busy being born.

They were exhilarating days. This was a party that was trying to expunge its own memory of two disastrous presidential campaigns. In 1972, George McGovern, a man of palpable decency and beguiling innocence, had led a raggle-taggle army of young volunteers fired up by rage at Vietnam, and he flopped. A convention of comical incompetence in Miami had become so bogged down in procedural arguments and a prolonged vote on the vice-presidential nomination that he ended up starting his acceptance speech just before three o'clock in the morning, thereby guaranteeing that all but the hard core in the national TV audience had switched off and gone to bed. Even taking a great Woody Guthrie song as his theme – 'This land is my land, this land is your land, this land belongs to you and me' – and getting the whole convention to sing along, he couldn't rescue matters. It was the start of a doomed campaign. 'Come home, America!' was his rallying cry. The country stayed away.

And if anyone in New York was minded to look back further, to Chicago in 1968, there were even worse memories to dredge up. With the assassinations of Martin Luther King and Bobby Kennedy fresh in their minds, and the war dominating everything, it was bound to be a febrile convention, with poor Hubert Humphrey, once the brave bearer of the liberal standard, now a vice president humiliated by his association with the departed Lyndon Johnson and therefore lampooned as an architect of war. In practice it got even worse, when Mayor Richard Daley, *capo di tutti capi* among big-city bosses, let loose his cops and the Illinois National Guard on demonstrators in the streets, and politics gave way to running battles, tear gas, flag-burning festivals and brazen police brutality that was witnessed on television across America. It seemed to be a matter of pride for Chicago that the city could rough people up with more relish than anyone else. When Senator Abraham Ribicoff of Connecticut spoke from the podium about 'Gestapo tactics on the streets of Chicago', Daley leapt to his feet in the Illinois delegation, yelled at him for being 'a son-of-a-bitch' and told him to perform an impossible sex act on himself. Days of wrath.

Humphrey was nominated on the scorched earth of the Windy City; Nixon won in November.

It was impossible, even for a young outsider like me, to erase these memories. They were the folklore of the time and part of the reason that Democrats in 1976 wanted Carter, the Sunday school teacher from Plains, Georgia. But the past was never far away. Heading up a long escalator on the first day of the convention – towards the

Pennsylvania Railroad Lounge, which is where much of the foreign press was holed up – I encountered, coming the other way, Hubert Humphrey himself. He was in a bright seersucker suit, beaming with that apple-cheeked smile at all the passers-by, and behaving as if he were still the candidate, putting a hand out here and there, giving a wave as he went by. You knew that there was a speech waiting to come pouring out at the slightest invitation. Twinkling through it all, the indefatigable campaigner, despite everything. I have a photograph of him, snatched after he passed on the down escalator, which shows him from the back. But the shape of the head, the outstretched arm to answer some shouted greeting, make him unmistakable. I thought of it the next day, when I ran into another figure from '68, in odder circumstances.

I had been prowling around on the floor of the convention, because there was nothing like immersing myself among the delegates. They were grouped state by state, and in each of the delegations, even when an important speaker had got to the podium, there was usually a churning political argument – as well as displays of the kind of childlike exuberance that's part of the convention story. People wearing Lincoln-style stovepipe hats and an impossible number of badges, a man waving a state flag in some act of loyalty but making himself look as if he was sending a signal of distress; people snoozing, wearing straw hats saying 'Happy Days Are Here Again' and then singing along to the band that struck up between speakers. I found that I had to take a brief break for a call of nature. At that time security was so light as to be laughable to anyone of the post-2001 generation, and I slipped into a men's room just off the convention floor, near the stage. I was standing there minding my own business, so to speak, when I heard someone come in and stand not far away. Glancing up, I realised with a tremor that it was Mayor Daley himself. Mr Chicago. The Boss. To many Americans of my generation, the godfather of corrupt big-city machine politics. I caught sight of the unmistakable drooping jowls, and the dead eyes.

It was a tricky moment, for obvious reasons. I washed my hands. So did he, at the other end of the line of basins. There was no one else there. I was about to approach him on the way out, as politely as I could, but he slipped out through another door before I had the chance, nodding vaguely in my direction as he did so, presumably as an act of normal politeness. In retrospect, it was an embarrassing journalistic lapse on my part. I should have made sure that I was able to get a word. But the challenge of ambushing Mayor Daley in a bathroom was one that I was content to admit that I wasn't yet up to.

The convention was notable for a barnstorming speech from Representative Barbara Jordan of Texas – the first African American woman to be elected to Congress from a southern state – which had them dancing in the aisles for what seemed an hour, and another keynote from Senator John Glenn of Ohio, the former astronaut, who succeeded only in proving that just because you have been up in space it doesn't mean you have anything interesting to say. It was the end of his hopes of becoming the vice-presidential nominee, Carter opting instead for Hubert Humphrey's liberal protégé from Minnesota, Senator Walter Mondale.

That week was an introduction to the lexicon of American campaigns, the words and phrases that roll down the years and never go away. Carter's assertion that America's best days were ahead of it, the evocation of 'the people' as the vast multitude forgotten by government in Washington, the declaration of faith in the American Dream that would ensure that each generation would have new opportunities to grasp – a catechism memorised by every presidential candidate before and since. But this was a moment of genuine hope for Carter, who could believe that he was presenting Americans with the choice of a different kind of leadership as he headed into the campaign against Gerald Ford (who just managed to hold onto the Republican nomination the following month in Kansas City, against a Ronald Reagan insurgency that almost swept him away).

So Democrats left New York fired by the politics of optimism. The atmosphere was certainly exhilarating. For me, it was also a little strange, summed up in a midweek episode that was quite unexpected and left me with the bizarre feeling that I'd spent the whole time on a stage set.

One of the people who were helping to herd foreign journalists around Madison Square Garden was a character who seemed vaguely familiar. In conversation, I discovered why. He was George, the brother of Telly Savalas, then at the apex of his fame playing the TV detective Kojak, the wise-cracking, lollipop-sucking New York detective who was bald as a coot and gave quick-fire social commentaries on the state of the city and its violent underbelly as he chased down another villain. George had played a part in the first series a few years earlier and his face had struck a distant chord.

He told me that some scenes for the next series were being shot in Manhattan that week. The studio work was done in Los Angeles; the street scenes in New York. Would I like to go along? The arrangement was made and I was picked up by a car from the studio the next morning. Soon I was somewhere on the Lower East Side where they were shooting at a bar. I'd brought a camera, because I wanted to write a piece for the paper (likely to be more interested in *Kojak* than Walter Mondale, I reckoned) and thought I might get some shots. Unfortunately, the director got the wrong idea.

Seeing me wandering around with my Pentax, he concluded that I must be some kind of official photographer. I was scared to disabuse him, because he seemed grumpy and I thought he might tell me to vamoose, or something. So I played along. Each time a scene was set, on the street or in the bar, and the cameras were ready to roll, just before he cried 'Action!' he'd signal me forward to take a couple of shots. I was sweating with anxiety, trying to look as if I knew what I was doing. I survived for a couple of hours, and then there was a break. At that point things went awry.

I fell into conversation with Kevin Dobson, who was playing Bobby Crocker, Kojak's clean-cut detective sergeant (Savalas having disappeared into his caravan to learn his lines or have a lollipop). He was very friendly, and we strolled to a Mexican food stall at the next corner where I offered to buy him lunch. Unfortunately, my enthusiasm got the better of me and I squeezed a taco so hard that a glistening ball of chilli mixture shot out of my napkin and settled happily on his shirt and suit. Splat. Thinking back, I can still see the sticky rivulets of meat sauce running down his front. Panic ensued. The trouble was that when filming resumed he had to be wearing the same clothes, for obvious reasons of continuity. So he had to be removed to a caravan, his clothes taken off and whisked to a nearby laundry. Shooting was put on hold. Kevin was amused by it; the director wasn't. In the afternoon I decided it would be better not to hang around to take more pictures, and made an early departure uptown as fast as I could.

Months later, back home, I watched the episode containing those scenes. I fancy I caught a glimpse of my shadow with a camera on one of the mirrors in the bar. I like to think so, anyway. DS Crocker's suit looked fine.

Carter's victory over Ford five months later was meant to be the moment when the country passed out of the Watergate era. The trouble was that, having chosen a quite different kind of president, many Americans decided quite quickly that they didn't like the difference after all. Carter's southernness was one of the problems. Even in the 1970s, when Atlanta was transforming itself into a cosmopolitan city and shedding some of its past and Carter could claim to have been a progressive, reforming governor of Georgia, his style seemed to grate on people outside the South. The likeable candidate was less likeable in the White House, where too many people found the country Baptist style an irritant. His main problem, though, was the economy. However much he might deserve international acclaim for bringing Anwar Sadat and Menachem Begin together to sign the Camp David Accords and break down some of the barriers between Egypt and Israel, on the home front everything seemed stagnant.

There was an energy crisis. In Nixon's time the OPEC oil embargo on the United States as a consequence of its support for Israel in the Yom Kippur War had exacerbated a problem that had been building up for a decade. America couldn't pump enough oil to satisfy demand, and new environmental protections were putting extra limits on production. In 1974, a speed limit of 55mph was placed on all highways to cut gasoline consumption. But it was Carter who reaped the whirlwind. A few days after he entered the White House he delivered an address to the nation from his fireside, wearing a cardigan and talking like an off-duty teacher, in which he described a challenge that he said was the moral equivalent of war. 'By acting now, we can control our future instead of letting the future control us.' But it wasn't a message the people wanted to hear. They were infuriated by queues at the pumps and fast-rising gas prices, hardly having had to think about them before, and they didn't warm to lectures about energy-efficient homes and nuclear power, let alone talk of an oil tax. Americans' lifelong love affair with the car and the truck was precious, and Carter appeared to be the president who wanted to bring it to an end. His popularity plunged.

Three years later, I saw him unexpectedly at Union Station and the scene summed everything up. I was waiting for a train to New York, and noticed a few – not many – besuited men wearing earpieces. Secret service. Then, strolling onto the platform, there was the president of the United States, without fanfare. He was taking the train to Baltimore for an energy conference, making a point about cars and planes and energy. Ahead of his time, you might think, but out of tune with '70s America. I found it cheering to see a president behaving so straightforwardly; but many Americans did not.

The virtues of speaking softly, marshalling careful arguments, appealing to a sense of moral purpose, turned out to be more desirable in theory than in practice. He spoke frankly about a crisis of confidence that he identified in the country, whose roots went deep. Politically, he was stirring up trouble, because presidents who talk of decline usually find themselves heading for the door, but it was Carter's way and he wasn't going to change. Just because he was softly spoken didn't mean he wasn't stubborn. Together with a micromanagement style in the Oval Office which was widely mocked (he was reported to be insisting on seeing the bookings for the White House tennis court, and people believed it), the administration didn't present the intended picture of an outfit that was younger, fresher and quicker on its feet than Ford's White House. It looked instead like a team that wasn't a team, with little confidence in its own ability.

His staff – 'the Georgians' – became an emblem of it all. They were not familiar with the ways of Washington, it was said. Well, in 1976 that had been the point. But they found it difficult to escape the caricature of southern outsiders, as when Hamilton Jordan, Carter's chief of staff, was ridiculed for apparently overindulging at a banquet, peering down the dress of the Egyptian ambassador's wife and announcing to the table, 'I can see the pyramids!'

And then came the Iranian hostage crisis. In November 1979, at the height of the revolution that brought Ayatollah Khomeini to power, fifty-two American diplomats and citizens were taken prisoner and held for 444 days. It's hard to exaggerate the feelings that their ordeal engendered back home – a blend of blazing anger and humiliation. Americans didn't like the feeling that they were powerless. It produced a tide of patriotism but not one that was helpful to the president. When he addressed the nation in April 1980 to give details of a rescue attempt that had gone wrong – a combination of dust storms and mechanical failures hobbling the helicopters that were meant to get the hostages out, one of them crashing into a tanker aircraft and killing eight US servicemen – it was a humiliating admission of failure. Carter was being honest, but that wasn't enough. Had the operation succeeded he would have been a hero, and as a consequence would surely have had a good chance at a second term. Instead, he'd fumbled the ball while the world watched. And it was an election year.

So that summer I was back in New York for his second convention, which had none of the plain-sailing ease of his first. The reason was that, once again, there was a Kennedy on the ballot.

Senator Edward Kennedy's pursuit of the presidency was wild and melodramatic, combining excitement and dejection, and marking, more definitively than most people realised at the time, the end point of a political age. It rekindled memories of a lost romance in politics (at least for many Democrats) and seemed to some to promise all the fervour of another march to what his brother had called the New Frontier. The presidential cycle means that these moments of instant excitement are almost inevitable as the primary season approaches – the system makes them necessary – and a Kennedy candidacy was always going to have an especially rich flavour. In the end, that was all it had. The taste was attractive but the substance missing.

He would almost certainly have been a candidate sooner, of course, had his partying not led to grisly tragedy a decade earlier. A campaign worker for his late brother Bobby, Mary Jo

Kopechne, died in his car on 18 July 1969 (two days before the first moon landing) when he drove it off a wooden bridge in the dark on Chappaquiddick Island after a party during a regatta weekend on Martha's Vineyard, the adjoining island off Cape Cod in Massachusetts. His ten-hour delay in reporting the accident, the determined efforts to summon help from friends and lawyers at dead of night before telling the police, his vague account of what happened when he left the party (and the strange turning his car took, onto a road that led to nowhere but a remote beach), his nationally televised broadcast of explanation, which raised more questions than it answered, produced a surge of public hostility. When he said in that broadcast that in his confusion after the accident he'd wondered if a curse did indeed hang over the Kennedys, it was a crudely judged appeal for sympathy that didn't move most Americans and infuriated the rest. The 37-year-old senator was marked as the Kennedy who would never be able to emulate his slain brothers and run for the presidency. His suspended jail sentence for leaving the scene of an accident, and the settled public belief that he wasn't telling the truth, apparently put an end to it.

But Kennedys persevere. Ten years passed before he dared to take the chance. As a liberal irritated by the Carter administration, a senator with a formidable legislative reputation and one personally at odds with the president on domestic causes that were dear to him, by the summer of 1979 he was angry enough to try to snatch the Democratic nomination from Carter, buoyed up by the support of people who decided they wanted a change and were ready to turn to a Kennedy again. By August, one poll even suggested he might beat Carter in the primaries by a margin of more than two to one, a once-unthinkable prospect. It was fantasy, but the lure was irresistible. Then in one interview, the truth slipped out.

He sat down on Cape Cod with Roger Mudd of CBS for a TV film that was clearly intended to coincide with the campaign launch. The senator answered questions about Chappaquiddick with obvious discomfort. Then Mudd, a senior correspondent whom Kennedy had rightly trusted to do a straightforward interview, asked the simplest of questions. Why did he want to be president? Kennedy's answer was bumbling and unfocused, devoid of any clarity. Embarrassingly vague. He sounded as if he'd never thought about it seriously, and was running because it was a family tradition. His words trailed away, leaving the impression of a man without purpose. A veil had been lifted.

Chris Whipple was a young reporter for *Life* magazine who witnessed the encounter. Thirty years later, after Kennedy's death, he recalled what happened when the Mudd interview had been recorded. He drove a short distance with the senator for a *Life* photo session that was planned on the Cape Cod seashore near his home. But Kennedy refused. 'My brothers were associated with those images,' he said. Whipple saw a man looking out to sea with 'a thousand-yard stare', who realised that his rambling answer to a straightforward question would be a sharp revelation to everyone, and perhaps to himself. Whipple said, 'I will always suspect that – despite the battle he waged for the nomination in the months ahead – on that August morning Kennedy knew something. The campaign was over. His heart just wasn't in it. The game was up.'

His campaign pitched and yawed through the spring, Kennedy veering from the excitement of a stump speech to some huge crowd to the despair of yet another shouted question about Chappaquiddick in a shopping mall, which was almost a daily occurrence. Time hadn't healed the wound, nor dulled the public appetite for scandal. He won the New York and California primaries but never seemed on course to beat Carter's delegate count. There were some flashes of the natural campaigner, and the sharp tingle of a liberal crusade in the run-in, but by the time he arrived in New York for the convention in the second week of August 1980, the chance of a famous upset had disappeared. The president would be the candidate. However, conventions are dramas and there was one last act to come.

The week was dominated by the Carter–Kennedy choreography. Would they make peace? Clearly their animosity had intensified during the campaign. It was reported that Carter said he wanted to 'whip his ass' and Kennedy's feelings about him were well known – that the president's leadership at a time of trial was inadequate to the task. For party reasons, with Ronald Reagan having swept to the Republican nomination in Detroit the previous month, it was important that these differences should be patched up and that they shouldn't go their separate ways at the start of the fall campaign. But first, in old Boston style, Kennedy was ready for his last hurrah.

I happened to have a grandstand view. A friend in Edinburgh, Nancy Drucker, was the daughter of Edwin Newman, the veteran NBC newsman who was anchoring the network's radio coverage of the convention. He was friendly and generous, and after we had lunch on the first day of the convention he suggested that I might come into the NBC radio booth and join a panel to comment on proceedings on the floor – on the very night that the nomination would be decided. To my astonishment, the other participants were Theodore H. White, whose *Making of the President* books (starting with Kennedy in 1960) I'd been devouring for years, and Miz Lillian Carter, the president's mother. This was a cast list in which I felt myself having, at the very best, a minuscule walk-on part.

Having duly lost the nomination (Carter eventually got 64 per cent of the vote on the floor), Kennedy spoke to acknowledge defeat, on a day when his lieutenants engaged in such petty fiddling with the convention timetable with the Carter team that it almost produced fist fights backstage. The speech was largely written by Bob Shrum, whom I later came to know, and it allowed Kennedy to let himself go. Eloquent and passionate, now that everything was over, he seemed to cast off the hesitancy that had crippled his campaign. At the last, here was a candidate who had found his voice, released because all hope had gone, and spoke with style and guts. The peroration was memorable, and Madison Square Garden went wild. He quoted Tennyson – 'to strive, to seek, to find, and not to yield' – and said, 'For me, a few hours ago, this campaign came to an end. For those whose cares have been our concern, the work goes on, the cause endures, the hope still lives, and the dream shall never die.'

The demonstration of support on the floor lasted for the best part of half an hour.

Up in the NBC box, White spoke of a speech that had produced one of the great convention moments. I burbled for a bit. But it was when we came off the air that Miz Lillian, a twinkling lady with a gracious southern style and a warm wit who was three days away from her eighty-third birthday, produced a line that was rapier-sharp. 'Why,' she said, 'that sure was a wonderful speech. Truly wonderful. I sure hope nothing happens to that boy.'

To which there was really no adequate reply. We spoke for a little while, and she slipped away. 'What a lady,' said Teddy White.

The convention ended with the coolest of handshakes on the platform after Carter's acceptance speech, Kennedy having to be manoeuvred towards the president to do the deed. White later wrote that Kennedy's disdain and his refusal to accede to Carter's effort to get them to raise their arms together, boxer-style, made him look like someone who'd just had to attend his chauffeur's wedding. It was hardly a joyous occasion, the biggest laugh of the night coming for a Freudian stumble by Carter, when in paying tribute to Humphrey, 'HHH', who had died eighteen months before, he mistakenly referred to him as 'Hubert Horatio Hornblower', a fine label for the old speechifier. As Democrats drifted away from New York, pretending that a truce had been sealed, they were in truth walking into the path of a political tornado that was about to rip across the landscape. Kennedy's speech had tried to recapture the spirit of his brother's New Frontier, but the Reagan victory that was already in the making would radically recast that dream for a generation and more.

Convention week had been exhilarating, with one touching footnote for me. During the week I visited Eddie Condon's jazz club on 54th Street – now no more, because it burned down – a place I often enjoyed. By some accident of timing I missed another journalist whose regular haunt it was – Robin Day, the broadcasting giant, who was in town presenting *The World at One* for BBC Radio 4. He too visited the club in that week, with his producer, Eleanor Updale. Ellie and I didn't meet until a few years later back home, and eventually realised we'd both been at the convention, listening to the same speeches, and had sat in Eddie Condon's on different nights. It amused us. The next time we were in New York together was in the winter of 1986, on our honeymoon.

A second coda to the convention came at the end of the following summer. I was spending a weekend on Martha's Vineyard with two friends, Peter Pringle and Eleanor Randolph, who had rented a house there and who'd become close friends throughout that summer in Washington. The high heat of summer had passed, days were just beginning to shorten, the wind was brightening the barbecue fires and there was one last party. Eleanor had covered the Kennedy campaign for the *Los Angeles Times* the year before and as a consequence we were all invited to spend the day at the senator's annual party at 'the compound', where the Kennedy homes cluster on the Hyannisport shore, 25 miles or so away. The easiest way to get there was to fly, so we hired a tiny plane (for a surprisingly modest sum) and hopped across Nantucket Sound, fetching up at the gates of the compound to find a Boston Irish party in full swing. It went on all day. There were barrels of Guinness and vats of clam chowder, Irish whiskey and improbably energetic games of touch football on the lawns and the beach. Ethel Kennedy, Bobby's widow, was enticing people into a yacht that she was sailing oceanwards; people were singing Irish ballads down by the shore. You could see that a maudlin tone would infect everyone before proceedings were over.

The afternoon had a few bizarre twists. I found myself throwing a rugby-shaped ball around with a guy maybe a decade younger than me, whom I thought I recognised. Where from? Even as I asked the stupid question, I realised the answer. He was one of Bobby's eleven children, Christopher, who had the look of his father about him. The other slight embarrassment was the discovery that a well-known British journalist had hooked up with a famously frisky woman reporter from the *New York Times* and was disturbing the bushes at the edge of the lawn only a few feet from the crowd – with great vigour – as a consequence of what the papers might call, delicately, an amorous encounter. We moved away to let them get on with it with as much privacy as was possible, which wasn't much.

That aside, the afternoon left me with one sharp memory. I was standing together with Peter, a *Sunday Times* and *Observer* veteran, on the porch of the main house, where the Kennedy parents had raised their family. The senator came across and we had a conversation. In the midst of it, to my astonishment, he held out his arm in a gesture of welcome and uttered the unlikely words, 'Have you met my mother?' And there she was.

Rose Kennedy was ninety-one, a tiny birdlike figure wearing a wide, soup-plate straw hat. She was full of beans, and in her rasping Boston voice asked us if we'd seen 'the president's house'. No was the answer, obviously. So she strode off across the lawn and let us into JFK's home, where we entered rooms that seemed pretty much as they must have been left in November 1963, when it all came to an end. The children's pictures on the piano; the family mementoes. A ghostly simplicity clung to everything. We were glimpsing the relics of an era gone; a place where memories would never die but which had turned, in a few years, into a past that couldn't be recovered. She spoke a little about family evenings there, then led us away.

Eventually, the revellers began to trek back to Boston, and the day was over. We squeezed into our little plane and jerked merrily over the sound to Martha's Vineyard. As we did, I remember looking down just before we landed and seeing beneath us the outline of the island that juts out to the east of the Vineyard. Chappaquiddick.

There was nowhere better to quicken the senses about the profound political change that had taken place in the preceding months. The 1960s and '70s were behind us, and slipping away fast. We were in the Reagan era.

CHAPTER 4

THE GENIAL REVOLUTION

The shadows were lengthening on the White House lawn on the evening of 4 July 1981 when I first saw Ronald Reagan. It was his first Independence Day as president, and quite important for him to look relaxed, because Washington was still wondering how much damage had been done in the assassination attempt three months earlier, a couple of miles away outside the Washington Hilton. His performance that day was a perfect emblem of the presidency he wanted to create.

Surrounded by sober young men in blazers, white chinos and straw boaters with red, white and blue ribbons, he appeared on the lawn, where the crowd was waiting for the fireworks display on the Mall. He spoke briefly, warmly and disarmingly. We watched him pose with Nancy on a tartan groundsheet, then he disappeared to join Frank Sinatra on the balcony of the South Portico. The junior White House staff – many of the women in long dresses – partied sedately on the lawn. Over the fence, the huge throng that had gathered to hear the Beach Boys play at the Lincoln Memorial looked rather different, and through the railings suspiciously sweet smoke drifted from the crowd. Different Americas at play.

I was able to savour the first phase of the Reagan era thanks to the *Washington Post*. After the unexpected death in 1979 of one of its senior editors, Larry Stern, the British journalist Godfrey Hodgson, who'd known Washington for two decades and wrote about America with élan and rare insight, persuaded the *Post* to co-operate with some newspapers in London to establish a fellowship in Stern's name for a young journalist from home to spend time on the *Post*. Stern had had a particular penchant for British writers, a string of whom were regular campers in his house when they were passing through Washington. I was the second fellow in 1981, invited after an interview in London with Ben Bradlee, the executive editor, whose tussles with Nixon through Watergate were the stuff of journalistic legend. I got the news when a telegram arrived at my flat the next morning – he did everything in style – that said simply, 'Welcome to The Washington Post – Bradlee'. I have it still.

I got there just before Independence Day. There was talk of what I, a non-American, might do on the day. I said it might be fun to go into the Appalachians, wander about a bit in the backwoods and write something about the American heartland.

'Crap,' said Ben. 'Everybody does that.'

I asked nervously what he thought might be a better idea.

'Go to Reagan's party. I'll fix it.' And he did.

The young staffers who crowded around were all short-haired and well scrubbed, looking like missionaries about to make a house call. Reagan himself had that strange air of perpetual relaxation, a fixed calm that made him look as if he'd just been lifted from the porch in a Norman Rockwell painting. The wider atmosphere, however, had an unmistakable formality. Everyone was wearing a stars-and-stripes lapel pin and there was a rigid politeness in conversation. The famously easy-going atmosphere of the Carter years had been banished at a stroke. The trick with Reagan's unfailing geniality was to understand that it was a carapace. Around him there was high seriousness. Lou Cannon, the *Post*'s White House correspondent, who'd come from California to cover the 'Reaganauts', whom he knew so well, subtitled his biography of the man who'd grown up in Hollywood 'The Role of a Lifetime'.

I was struck by the Beach Boys crowd through the railings and the next day wrote a short, mild piece for the paper, suggesting that these were two different sides of America on display and that perhaps there was a gap in understanding between them. Hardly a revelation. But at the top of my copy an editor had added a line saying that I had just arrived in Washington as the Stern Fellow from abroad. The White House complained to the paper, insisting that it was disrespectful for a foreigner to write like this on Independence Day. I was surprised that such inoffensive comments, which would have passed without comment in any British newspaper, could produce such a reaction. Since I was hardly expecting a White House invitation, it didn't cause me to lose any sleep.

But soon afterwards there was another complaint, and a more serious one. I'd been sent to Cook County Jail in Chicago to interview Ziad Abu Ein, a Palestinian accused of bombings in Tiberias in Israeli-occupied territory, who was facing extradition. His case had been taken up by the Arab American community – led by a former South Dakota senator of Lebanese descent, James Abourezk – who argued that there was strong alibi evidence proving him innocent, and that the proper extradition procedures were being compromised because of Israeli pressure. The prisoner's claimed alibi and the retraction of two 'confessions' related to the case were not accepted as relevant evidence by the American courts, and he eventually became the first Palestinian to be extradited from the US to Israel, where his supporters claimed he would not get a fair trial. He was tried, found guilty and jailed, but released in a prisoner exchange in 1985. In 2014, when he was a minister in the Palestinian Authority, he was shot dead by Israeli forces in the West Bank. Back in 1981, my report on the case caused a former deputy attorney general of the United States to demand space on the *Post*'s editorial page to take issue with my understanding of the American legal system (although I remained confident I was right).

Having become a political reporter at Westminster for *The Scotsman* three years before, I was well used to the rough and tumble of the game. But this was heavy artillery. When a message arrived saying that Bradlee wanted to have breakfast with me at his regular table in the Madison Hotel across the street from the office, I thought my time was up, having hardly begun.

He insisted that we had Bloody Marys, and I concluded that I might well be heading for the door. Not at all.

'Let me tell you something. This is the table where I took Woodward and Bernstein when they screwed up one of their Watergate stories, about the money. You're annoying the right people. Enjoy yourself!' We had a happy breakfast. All his young reporters could tell the same kind of story about a lovable man who knew when support was needed and how to give it. We were in touch for the rest of his life and, like that of countless others, my admiration and gratitude remained.

Half Boston patrician and half Mississippi riverboat gambler, as someone once put it, Bradlee was hopelessly handsome and bold, a man towards whom heads turned sharply even when he'd reached ninety. His voice was frequently a bark, but always alluring – demanding attention, offering a deal, proposing a ruse or a bit of fun. Whether he was pouring a bone-dry martini – 'C'mon, another pop?' – or telling a hapless hack that his copy made his eyes glaze over, he was the embodiment of chameleon charm, able to morph in a moment from street-fighting editor to cultured boulevardier, a social pied piper with perfect French, an ear for any good story and an eye for a beautiful woman.

The *Post* at that time was adapting to a profound change in the culture of Washington. I learned that the paper's relationship with the Carter White House had been appalling – in common with most of the rest of the press – but the Reagan era was promising a shift that wasn't simply a changing of the guard in personnel, but also in ideology. When this president said that government wasn't the solution but the problem, he meant it. A culture change was beginning that warmed the cockles of Margaret Thatcher's heart as she pursued her own radical programme, however much she might have doubted the solidity of his intellectual core. Instinct was enough.

Reagan, however, had a bumpy start. The economy showed little sign of recovery. And there was widespread suspicion of the claim that deep tax cuts – favouring the wealthy – would produce the stimulus the economy needed. One reason for that suspicion was that one of my editors at the *Post*, William Greider, pulled off a journalistic coup by winning the trust of David Stockman, whom Reagan had appointed his budget director, and who was a fervent evangelist for supply-side economics based on a formula of tax cuts and huge reductions in government spending. But, as he acknowledged to Bill Greider in a series of long private conversations over many months, the policy was far less coherent than he (and Reagan) liked to make it appear. Supply-side policies were, he said, a Trojan horse for 'trickle-down economics' in which those at the bottom of the heap had to hope some benefits would eventually come their way, on a wing and a prayer. It was precisely what Bush, now vice president, had meant in the primaries with his jibe about 'voodoo economics'. When Bill's long article appeared in *The Atlantic* in late 1981 – running to nearly 20,000 words – it was called 'The Education of David Stockman', and the subtitle quoted him saying, 'None of us really understands what's going on with all these numbers.' There was a storm, and Stockman was holed beneath the waterline, saying afterwards in an interview that he was 'taken into the woodshed' by the president to be dealt with.

He survived through Reagan's first term but, revealed to be an ingenue conducting a hit-or-miss economic experiment that he was trying out for the first time, never recovered the air of certainty that he'd brought to his crusade to curtail the role of the federal government. He was increasingly beaten back by congressional leaders, Republican as well as Democrat, who found sound political reasons in their states back home for protecting parts of the budget.

It was a typical exercise in insight by Greider, a gifted writer and a warm companion, who later left the *Post* to write for *Rolling Stone*. He was one of a phalanx of writers on the paper who gave it such a rich character – serious observers like Peter Osnos, Dick Harwood, Haynes Johnson, Bob Kaiser, Jim Hoagland, Dan Balz, who combined high intellectual rigour with razor-sharp journalistic instincts. For a young journalist they were a generous inspiration, as well as having the gift of knowing how to pass on their knowledge and their skill. I sat at their feet. In that summer of 1981, they were all trying to work out what the Reagan era might mean, because no one could be sure. There would certainly be the usual run of crises – when he caused chaos by dismissing thousands of air-traffic controllers, because they'd gone on strike, his popularity dipped further – but how far would he succeed in turning the country in a socially conservative direction? At the beginning, it wasn't clear. He'd had a natural surge of affection after surviving the assassination attempt outside the Washington Hilton in March – 'Honey, I forgot to duck,' Nancy reported him as saying – but the public had not yet decided whether or not his administration was going to be competent.

That Washington summer gave me a glimpse of the changing of the guard. Reagan and his men rode into town as outsiders, just as Carter's southerners had, but with a quite different style. Although his administration was packed with the kind of Republican appointees (like their Democratic counterparts) who sail in and out of office according to the fortunes of their party, returning to sumptuous law offices between spells in government, the atmosphere had an ideological sharpness that was new. I was living happily in Georgetown in the basement apartment of a fun-loving socialite, Joan Bingham (who rejoiced in the sobriquet of the Merry Widow), and in its peaceful streets you couldn't miss the collective intake of breath at the arrival of the Californians. When Reagan's chief of staff, Ed Meese, came to lunch at the *Post* – with Katharine Graham presiding – it was obvious behind the polite banter back and forth that he wanted to deliver a sharp message: you people are going to have to prepare for a different kind of president. He meant what he said about government, and liberal ways were going to be challenged. That had one benefit in the town fuelled by politics, where they watch the comings and goings at the White House with the obsessive fascination of gamblers gathered round a poker table: there was an air of excitement, even among people who had no time for Reagan's attitudes, and liked to joke about a First Lady who'd consult her private astrologer before advising the president about the timing of one of his pronouncements.

It was less obvious then, but in the years that followed, Reagan became, outside the United States, the most misunderstood president of modern times. The caricature of the celluloid cowboy who held onto his cue cards when he got to the White House was fair as far as it went, but misleading. The depth of the change that he brought to Washington was consistently underestimated abroad by people who focused on his limited capacity and found it hard to acknowledge the powerful political spell that he cast on the generation that flourished in his shadow. Reagan changed his country; probably more profoundly than he ever knew.

Not surprisingly, Margaret Thatcher got the point. She visited him late in 1981 in his first year in office, fired up by the knowledge that Americans had elected a fiscal conservative with a penchant for Cold War rhetoric and a vision of ever-smaller government. Quite soon she learned the truth – that she would have to balance her enthusiasm for everything he stood for with her knowledge of his limitations. But she could be content that he was inspiring an emerging army of American conservatives who, only a decade earlier, had been a faction in the Republican Party and not its soul. She recognised there a reflection of her own rise to power.

On that first visit, she was accompanied by her foreign secretary, Lord Carrington. He recalled an incident after her first White House meeting with the president, reports of which percolated quickly through the upper reaches of Whitehall. In his memoirs, Carrington places it in the White House. The version I have heard from an official who was a witness sets the scene instead in Blair House, the government guest house across Lafayette Square. The words are the same. In this diplomat's account, the prime minister was having a large glass of Scotch, as she often did in the evenings, and was high with excitement after the encounter with Reagan, which had been as warm as she had hoped. She began to talk in detail about her impressions.

Carrington gestured at the ceiling, making a circle with his finger – suggesting that it would be wise for them to assume that the room might be bugged. But Thatcher was fired up, and carried on happily, though dropping her voice. Tapping the side of her head, she said of Reagan: 'Peter, there's nothing there.'

From the beginning, she realised she was dealing with a politician of instinct rather than calculation, let alone intellectual originality. Sir Nicholas 'Nico' Henderson, whom she had recalled from retirement from the Paris Embassy to go to Washington as ambassador, was open about it years later in conversation with his old Labour acquaintance, Tony Benn. In his diaries, Benn reports Henderson as saying that he couldn't tell him the truth about Thatcher's view of Reagan because of the damage it would do to British–American relations. There was no illusion on her part, but less than a year after that first visit she was able to use the personal bond with Reagan to secure valuable American help in the Falklands conflict – which a number of powerful administration officials wanted him to withhold – and in so doing almost certainly rescued her premiership after the Argentine invasion. She wrote in her memoirs that without the timely delivery of the latest version of American Sidewinder missiles from Washington, 'we could not have retaken the Falklands', the islands that Reagan called 'that little bunch of ice-cold land down there'. He saved her.

Caspar Weinberger, the defence secretary, was Thatcher's firmest ally, passing on any help that he could, in materiel and intelligence. By contrast, Alexander Haig, secretary of state, infuriated her by suggesting that the best way the United States could show its support for Britain would be with a display of strict neutrality; and Reagan's ambassador to the United Nations, Jeane Kirkpatrick, quickly became the bête noire of the British, their fire-breathing antagonist. She'd been dining at the Argentine Embassy on the night of the invasion, which seemed appropriate, because she wasn't shy of making it clear that Latin American hard men were much more to her taste than European types, especially if they were in London.

Those of us watching the Falklands conflict from Westminster became aware that Reagan tilted the balance. Al Haig's visits to London were awkward, the press conferences in Downing Street devoid of warmth. We were aware – although the detail would take time to emerge – that the enterprise was laden with risk and that without substantial American help Thatcher was, so to speak, sunk.

She needed to play Reagan like an old violin, and he responded. Her lifelong gratitude – summed up in the picture of her kneeling in obeisance at his coffin in the Capitol in 2004 – was well founded. The queen conferred an honorary knighthood on Weinberger when he left office in 1988. He knew why.

By the time of his death, Reagan had acquired a saintly reputation at home, even among some of those who wouldn't have thought of voting for him. The transformation was startling. There had been little hint of that lasting strength when he set off on his fight for the White House. In 1980, it wasn't clear until late in the campaign that, even with Carter's shaky public standing, he would prevail. There was still resistance because of his age (a paltry sixty-nine) and many mainstream Republicans remained suspicious of his ideology, which George H. W. Bush had said during the Republican primaries relied too much on 'voodoo economics'. But in the televised debates, when Reagan patronised the president with a smile – 'There you go again!' – and with one repeated question to voters – 'Are you better off than you were four years ago?' – he was able to paint the Carter years as a time of decline. And, as eloquent testimony, the hostages were still in the embassy in Tehran, with Washington apparently powerless.

In the last forty-eight hours before election day, Carter sped from coast to coast in what everyone could see was a desperate effort to shore up support that was sliding inexorably away. It was a rout, and on Reagan's coat-tails came a Republican majority in the Senate for the first time since 1955. But the most painful part of Carter's humiliation came on Inauguration Day in January. The new president gave the day an extra theatrical touch, delivering his address from the west front of the Capitol with the crowd spread down the Mall towards the Washington Monument, making a symbolic move from the other side of the building where all his predecessors in the modern era had spoken from the east steps. A former California governor was telling Americans that, like frontiersmen of old, they should once again look westwards for opportunity and fulfilment.

The climax to the drama, as if he had scripted it himself, came within an hour of his taking the oath of office when Iran announced the release of the hostages. No one has satisfactorily solved the mystery of the Iranian deal that got them out. Gary Sick, who had worked on the National Security Council, published an account a decade later in which he claimed that Reagan's campaign manager William Casey, who had a background in intelligence and was appointed as CIA director after the election, brokered a deal with Tehran in the course of the campaign that promised arms deliveries via Israel if the hostages were kept safe and only released after Reagan had been elected, thereby avoiding an 'October Surprise' that could have handed Carter the election in a moment of national celebration at a prisoners' homecoming. Barbara Honegger, who worked on Reagan's campaign, supported the thrust of Sick's theory. Two separate congressional investigations in the 1990s, however, failed to produce clinching evidence, leaving the case unproven. But around Washington there was no doubt. Casey was generally assumed to have managed a nifty and eventually spectacular undercover manoeuvre. If that was true, it certainly wasn't the last shadowy arms deal in Reagan's time. Fourteen administration officials were indicted in his second term in the unravelling of the Iran–Contra affair in which arms had been sold illegally to Iran, the proceeds being channelled secretly to anti-government guerrilla forces in Nicaragua, despite a congressional ban on such support.

Iran may have remained the great target of American conservatives for decades afterwards but, oddly enough, their hero Reagan owed a great deal to Tehran, seat of the revolution that would torment the United States for decades to come.

Quickly, more quickly than political Washington had expected, the Republican orthodoxy shifted rightwards. Visits towards the end of Reagan's first term felt as if they were to a different city, where the conservative tide was flowing strong and heavily suited men of the American corporate establishment had quietly taken control.

One of my generous guides through that political thicket in Reagan's first year was David Broder, the *Post*'s pre-eminent political writer and a nationally syndicated columnist of renown. Dave had been caricatured in Tim Crouse's cult book on the press in the 1972 presidential campaign, *The Boys on the Bus*, as an ultra-cautious, high-minded scribe, dealing with the rest of the rat pack as if he were a Methodist minister trying to control an unruly congregation. It wasn't entirely unfair. A conversation would often morph into a civics class, and he wrote with ascetic precision rather than bravado. But he was a man of powerful insight about people, who valued friendship and who knew how he thought his country should work. A journalist, too, of iron integrity. Politicians who tried to ingratiate themselves with him – he would take their calls in his private glass box in the middle of the newsroom, surrounded by teetering piles of books and newspapers – found that he never succumbed to flattery, and would coolly make up his own mind. The harder they tried, the more headmasterly Broder's demeanour would become.

He drove me to Atlantic City in August of that summer to the National Governors Association conference, and when we arrived at our hotel there was a sheaf of messages waiting at the front desk, all asking for some time with him. 'Who would you like to have dinner with?' he said. When travelling with Broder, it seemed that you could take your pick. We agreed that if we wanted to have a fun evening, Jerry Brown of California was our man.

Brown was first elected governor at the age of only thirty-six in 1974, and by 1981 he'd already had two modest but frisky tilts at the Democratic presidential nomination. He clearly had staying power, but I didn't realise how much (almost certainly, neither did he). In 2010, he decided to try to be governor again, and served two more terms. When I sat down with him in San Francisco in 2018, he was approaching eighty but talking about the 'resistance' to Donald Trump with all the freewheeling enthusiasm that had been the most obvious characteristic when I encountered him in Atlantic City for the first time. He was unconventional, clever and throwing ideas around like toys. We had an argumentative dinner of the best, friendly kind, with Broder quietly puncturing some of his more fanciful pronouncements. Dave – whom I was able to count a friend for the rest of his life – was kind enough to fend off the governor's henchmen when they expressed hostility after I wrote a piece about our conversation, in the course of which I alluded to him as 'Governor Moonbeam', the stinging nickname pinned on him by Garry Trudeau in his satirical *Doonesbury* newspaper comic strip. It wasn't a label he liked.

That encounter revealed what was preoccupying political liberals. A deep anxiety that the thrust of the social reforms that sprang from the 1960s – steady progress, as they saw it – might be reversed. Brown himself was looking for new inspiration – he went to Japan the following year to immerse himself in Buddhism to try to discover something new about himself – and it was impossible not to feel that, for all Reagan's problems, the alternative hadn't yet found a voice. There was a challenge coming that would have to be met.

This was impressed on me even more by a visit to a Democratic beanfeast in Detroit. I wanted to write something about Walter Mondale, who was using his experience as Carter's vice president to make himself the unquestioned front-runner for the Democratic nomination in 1984. He agreed to talk on a trip he was making to address a dinner of the United Automobile Workers union in

Mo'town itself. It was in honour of a retiring bigwig in the union, one Irving Bluestone, who'd been chief negotiator throughout the 1970s for half a million employees at General Motors when they were among the best-rewarded industrial workers in the country. Mondale, who'd always enjoyed the support of organised labour, was on home ground.

We spoke on the plane from Washington, and he said he'd enjoy a late-night gossip. First, the dinner. It was a huge affair, displaying the American love of dressing up. A nation that rightly prides itself on homely informality still finds it impossible to resist the urge to put on fancy dress. When Americans decide to be formal, they go for broke: everyone at this union dinner appeared to be wearing patent leather shoes, and their tuxedos were sharp. Here was a gathering of political heavyweights on the Democratic side, but taking place in Michigan, a state that Reagan had won by a huge margin. The extent of Reagan's blue-collar support in 1980 had shocked them, and they suspected, rightly, that there was much more of that to come. That explained the downbeat quality of the evening. Mondale's speech was routine and flat. It lacked fire, surprisingly from someone who was purporting to be ready to take on Reagan, but it was obvious that in the UAW the Carter years were not seen as good ones for the men who built America's cars, however much they might pay homage to Mondale's support for organised labour throughout his time in public life. He was feted, but this didn't feel like a crusade in the making, more a melancholy remembrance of things past.

Later, we repaired to his suite in the Detroit Hilton and spent an hour or two alone. He produced a bottle of whisky and spoke about what Democrats needed to do if they were going to challenge Reaganism. He well understood that the president had succeeded in recasting the language of politics, appealing directly to the profoundly individualistic feelings of most Americans and, in his beguilingly simple way, suggesting that the ills that had perplexed them for a generation could all be traced back to the relentless growth of government, its costs and its conviction that Washington always knew best. Mondale's answer was, of course, the old one that he had learned in Minnesota at Hubert Humphrey's knee – a combination of collective strength in the workplace, fair taxation, civil rights protected by the courts and government that counterbalanced the power of corporate interests to protect individuals. But it was a song that too many people hadn't wanted to hear the previous year. They looked for something new. What would make them change their minds? He didn't have an easy answer.

There was news from home that he was anxious to discuss. The Labour Party had elected Michael Foot as leader about nine months earlier, and the schism had opened that led to the 'Gang of Four' breakaway to form the SDP and the debilitating left–right struggles that would not only keep Labour from power until the late 1990s but threaten to destroy it. Mondale had known leading figures in Labour for years – Denis Healey, in particular – and he was perplexed by the reports he was getting from London. Thatcher was proving as difficult a target as Reagan.

'What's happening to my friends? Why?'

He was plaintive, suspecting that electoral retreat would take a long time to reverse. The same, he acknowledged tentatively, was true for Democrats. They couldn't assume that people would abandon Reagan, any more than a divided Labour Party could confront Thatcherism and win. What message would they have for car workers in Detroit who might be fired up by Reagan's appeal to individualism, which he described as their birthright? Recalling that conversation much later, it was clear that he had a sharp sense that despite Democratic rhetoric about the economic prospects of many Americans under Reagan – which he could encapsulate clearly and with passion – the landscape had changed. The America to which he and Carter had appealed successfully in 1976 had moved on.

I have a lingering memory of the man who would be president wandering across the room in his boxer shorts, preparing for bed, with a glass in his hand and a gloomy look on his face. We'd had a bit of a laugh, but on his part there had been a dark undercurrent. I knew then that the road ahead didn't look as inviting to him as he'd expected.

The next time I heard him speak was at the Democratic convention in San Francisco in the summer of 1984, after a roller-coaster primary season in which Senator Gary Hart had shaken him with accusations of out-of-date thinking and the Rev. Jesse Jackson had picked up an average of about 20 per cent of the vote with his 'rainbow coalition' of liberal interests, including, for the first time in a presidential contest, a gay and lesbian movement. Mondale was fairly easily nominated in the end, but he was an uncomfortable candidate, lacking the fire that the convention saw in Jackson and particularly in Governor Mario Cuomo of New York, who talked of forgotten people who had no place in Reagan's 'shining city on the hill' that was meant to be America.

That week in California was the prelude to a campaign that marked the transition of Reagan from the divisive and at first rather unpopular interloper to fatherly commander-in-chief. He asserted that the country was confident for the first time in two generations, and was recapturing something of the certainty that middle-aged Americans had been left by their parents, and then somehow lost, like a religious faith gone sour. Cuomo's divided country and its social problems were subjugated in an argument about spirit.

Reagan's image was caught in a famously effective political commercial, filmed in the California sunshine, that portrayed a country beginning to find itself again. 'It's morning again in America ... and under the leadership of President Reagan, our country is prouder and stronger and better. Why would we ever want to return to where we were less than four short years ago?' It set the tone, and Mondale could do nothing about it. In November, he won his home state of Minnesota, but the forty-nine others all voted for Reagan, many by huge margins. The industrial states were his, and so was the whole of the South. The Democratic coalition that Mondale had known all his life was gone.

Reagan's political triumph was to keep 'morning again' bright in American minds, even when his administration was shaken by scandal. The Iran–Contra revelations in the second term pulled his senior team apart and produced a host of indictments. But although the administration had to admit illegality – and contempt of Congress – Reagan himself suffered surprisingly little damage. It was a spectacular illustration of the way in which he managed to place himself almost outside his own administration – as if he were some kind of latter-day monarchical figure, always at one remove from the grubby machinations of the Oval Office. There was truth in it, of course. He preferred the homilies in his weekly radio address to arm-twisting on Capitol Hill; a speech of pieties came naturally to him when a closely argued economic text did not. When Americans saw a president who wanted power to be a simple and genial affair, many of them believed they were recovering, at last, what they thought they had lost. If it was an illusion, so be it. Much of America felt good.

The picture was completed by the decline and fall of the Soviet Union. By the mid-1980s, there was much less of the Cold War rhetoric that Reagan had deployed enthusiastically in his first term, talking of a 'Star Wars' defence system to confront an 'evil empire' and pursuing new weapons deployments in Europe against a strong tide of popular opposition there. Mikhail Gorbachev's ascent produced the most unlikely but significant coming together of American and Soviet leaders since Franklin Roosevelt sat down with Joseph Stalin.

Reagan had a stroke of luck that came at the right moment, from an old friend. The Thatcher government was able to pass on much of the intelligence flowing from Oleg Gordievsky, the spy of spies. He had been recruited by MI6 in the 1970s and found himself a few years later in a position in Moscow (and for a period, remarkably, in the Soviet Embassy in London) to provide the kind of information, in quality and volume, that surpassed anything his handlers had seen before or perhaps had ever expected to see. The best of it reached Thatcher directly – although even she didn't know his name until he was safely out of the Soviet Union – and Washington was in the loop. The Reagan administration was getting a clearer picture of Kremlin politics – and, in particular, the depth of the Soviets' exaggerated fears of a nuclear first strike by the West – than it was able to get from its own sources. When Thatcher described Gorbachev as a man with whom she could do business, and Reagan joined the chorus, they were operating with the assistance of Gordievsky's intimate observations. It was therefore ironic for him (as well as life-threatening) that when he had to flee Moscow in 1985 it was not because of a security lapse on his part, but a blunder by some of his most grateful customers and admirers.

It happened in Washington. The quality of Gordievsky's intelligence was impressing the CIA so much that, without telling London, they determined to find the source. MI6, naturally, guarded the identity of their precious spy with great care. As Ben Macintyre of *The Times* describes in his account of Gordievsky's secret life – based on conversations with him over several years – Washington pieced together fragments of the story and, alighting on a clue that the source might have served in the Soviet Embassy in Copenhagen in the 1970s, narrowed the search to Gordievsky. Unfortunately for them, they were ignorant of a spy in their own backyard. Aldrich Ames of the CIA had recently sold himself to the Soviets – a cash transaction rather than an ideological conversion – and it's assumed that it was he who passed the news to Moscow that Gordievsky was a double agent, thereby throwing him to the lions. He realised the KGB was on his trail in May 1985 and had to set in train an emergency 'exfiltration' involving a wild car chase across the border into Finland, which had been part of an MI6 rescue plan for years, but was so risky that those involved could have no confidence that it would succeed. Gordievsky survived by a whisker, plucked in a split-second manoeuvre from a hiding place among bushes in a lay-by near the border to be wrapped in an aluminium-foil blanket and stuck in the boot of the car, and only made aware that they had crossed into safe territory when an MI6 officer in the front seat stuck into the cassette player a tape of the famous theme from the Sibelius tone poem, *Finlandia*.

The 'special relationship' is a phrase that causes amusement in Washington because it's thought to be an uncharacteristic piece of British overstatement, though harmless enough. If it means anything, it's a reflection of the intelligence and defence co-operation that remained close throughout the Cold War. They are the ties that bind. American taxpayers might be surprised, for example, if they knew how much they put into the British code-breaking and interception centre, GCHQ. The Gordievsky story is an episode that makes the point eloquently. Without the sharing of his intelligence it's unlikely, in the view of many of those who served Reagan and Thatcher in those years, that the relationship with Gorbachev would have developed as it did. The history of the Cold War would have been quite different.

It's a helpful prism through which to see the transition of Reagan. When he spent ten days in Europe in the summer of 1984, just before his second winning campaign, he was still the president who stirred up angry demonstrations because of his hawkish defence posture, and the fact he hadn't moved on from the rhetoric of the 'evil empire' speech the year before. His image remained that of an inadequate president. Tip O'Neill, Democratic speaker of the House, gave him credit for nothing when he spoke to James Reston of the *New York Times* in late 1983. 'He only works three to three and a half hours a day. He doesn't do his homework. He doesn't read his briefing papers. It's sinful that this man is president of the United States.'

But watching him on his trip to Ireland in 1984 was to see a president apparently untroubled by any suggestion of sinfulness. His visit to the village of Ballyporeen in the south-west corner of Tipperary had the flavour of an amateur production of *Brigadoon*. He dropped in from the sky to visit the home of his great-grandfather, who emigrated to the US, and despite the comical sight of military helicopters and hundreds of security men looking uncomfortably out of place around the tiny village and its surrounding green fields and potato patches, sodden from the rain, he managed to amble around as if he were just another dewy-eyed elderly American paying homage to the old country. After he left, the village pub was renamed the Ronald Reagan. When it closed, twenty years later, they took the sign over the door and transferred it with the fittings from the bar to become an exhibit in the Reagan Library in Simi Valley, California, which seems an appropriate resting place for one of the old boy's stage sets.

Those of us who snoozed on a seemingly interminable bus journey that day from Galway to Ballyporeen, made palatable only by supplies of Guinness and oysters, were aware that everywhere he went (with the notable exception of Tipperary) there were demonstrators. Faculty members in Galway had stayed away when he was given an honorary degree; there were crowds of protestors in Dublin shouting about cruise missiles and policies in Central

America. He smiled all the way. Reagan's capacity to sail through such stormy waters with apparently unfailing calm was a gift that few politicians are given.

That was how he survived Iran–Contra and left office in 1988 with a higher approval rating than any other departing president since the Second World War – 63 per cent, according to Gallup. When the Berlin Wall was breached a year later, Reagan basked in the glory. I watched Gorbachev in Washington on his second visit (the first was in 1987), when he repeated several of his walkabouts, his car stopping on the short drive from the Soviet Embassy on 16th Street to the White House to meet George H. W. Bush, letting him plunge into crowds like any Western politician. That extraordinary sight, of a Soviet leader being mobbed in the street by enthusiastic Americans, cemented the profile of Reagan as the peacemaker, precisely the label that no one would have dreamed of pinning on him in the first term.

A decade after the wall came down, I was in Berlin, to mark the occasion for *Today* on Radio 4. There was an air of polite excitement in the city. Mstislav Rostropovich played the Bach cello suites at the Checkpoint Charlie museum, as he had done ten years before in front of the wall, after racing to the airport in London with his cello so that he could play an accompaniment to the raising of the Iron Curtain. We crouched at his feet with a microphone, as he whispered loudly that he would let us record for no more than two minutes. I'm afraid we ignored him. I spoke to Daniel Barenboim about what it had been like to play a Beethoven piano concerto in the Philharmonie in West Berlin to an audience that had flocked from the East for an experience that had been impossible for more than three decades. He was tearful at the memory of it. But the most intriguing event of these days was a colloquy about the end of the Cold War, which my producer Roger Hermiston and I found out about just in time, with three of its most important participants talking together – Helmut Kohl, Mikhail Gorbachev and George H. W. Bush. They sat together and reminisced.

Bush was asked, of course, why he hadn't come to Berlin in 1989 to give a presidential victory dance on the wall, as Reagan would almost certainly have done.

I recall that his reply was directed at Gorbachev. 'Well, I didn't know whether or not you'd be there next week.'

And Gorbachev replied (in Russian), 'Neither did I.' They laughed.

It was altogether a remarkable conversation as they recalled the atmosphere of the time, with Kohl – sitting in the middle – interrupting at one point to say, 'And then of course there was our friend in London …' His shoulders heaved and they all had another laugh, no doubt recalling some of their difficult conversations with Thatcher, whose determination to have victory in the Cold War was matched only by her anxiety to prevent the reunification of Germany. An awkward posture. There was nothing she could do to slow down the process, which culminated in German Unity Day in October 1990, the month before she resigned, for quite different reasons.

Long afterwards – in 2018 – I spoke to one of the American diplomats most involved in the Cold War and the united Germany, John Kornblum, who'd also attended that Bush–Kohl–Gorbachev discussion. He'd seen it all in the second half of the Cold War – exchanges of spies on the Glienicke Bridge, escapes across the wall, the to-and-fro exchanges between the occupying powers in West Berlin and the Soviets in the East. He was at the Brandenburg Gate in 1987 when Reagan delivered his famous line, 'Mr Gorbachev, tear down this wall.' It pleased Kornblum, not least because he had written it. Looking back, he remembers it as a message not so much to Moscow, but to the West German government in Bonn.

I thought up the Reagan speech and I organised it. We did it for one very specific reason, because at that time there was again a change of eras. It was the end of the Soviet Union, the one country that would profit the most from the end of the Soviet Union was trying to prop it up, and that was Germany. Why were they doing that? Because they felt that if the Soviet Union was to disappear, or if East Germany was to disappear, there would be war. So their major goal in life was peace. Given their recent history one can understand that. But we in the United States, joined with the British and the French too, were of the view that this was completely the wrong thing to do.

I was involved in all this. George H. W. Bush was probably one of the wisest presidents we've had. And he had a very very learned and wise security adviser [Brent Scowcroft]. And they knew exactly what you were saying, that the real goal had to be about putting Europe back together and not to be that we've beaten somebody. And it's been said many times – but I actually saw this myself, Gorbachev told me this personally – that this phase went so smoothly because of the close personal relationships between Gorbachev, Helmut Kohl and George H. W. Bush. They were in touch all the time and they knew what was going to happen. Kohl and Bush in particular were very successful in convincing Gorbachev that they weren't going to dance on his grave – that this was going to be done in a co-operative way. And I think that was why it worked, to tell you the truth.

Domestically, Bush was unable to appear in command, which was why he lost to Bill Clinton in 1992. But, before the first Gulf War in 1991, it was he who would set the tone for the end of the Cold War in a way that Reagan would surely have found difficult. But in doing so, Bush helped to add lustre to the Reagan era, which could be associated in perpetuity with the end of the conflict that had divided Europe and dominated American foreign policy for nearly half a century.

Reagan's political work at home, however, had an influence that was just as profound. A politician who had little interest in intellectual debate, beyond routine restatements of his small-government individual-liberty principles, transformed the American conservative movement. When he arrived in office conservatives still saw themselves trapped in a struggle with mainstream Republicans who wanted to keep them in their place; by the end of his second term they had confidence, as well as money and organisation, that would change America.

Outsiders often find 'conservative' a confusing label in America, because there it indicates that someone is outside the centre-right mainstream, whereas in Europe it is the other way round. When Barry Goldwater stormed the Republican convention in 1964 – before losing to Lyndon Johnson under a mighty landslide – his credo was laid out in his book *The Conscience of a Conservative*, which rejected the kind of mild conservatism espoused by the Republican establishment and argued for fiercely limited government, unswerving faith in free markets and a war on any attempt to offer a collectivist solution to any problem. He was a lousy candidate, but hugely influential. With the likes of the astringent William F. Buckley and his *National Review* magazine providing intellectual ballast, conservatives began to coalesce into a movement that became much more powerful (and respectable) than the old repositories of far-right activism and prejudice, like the John Birch Society, whose version of anti-communism was so virulent that they ended up accusing President Eisenhower, the best-known soldier of his generation, of treason. The movement for which Goldwater was the beacon began to grow, and by the time the Heritage Foundation was founded in 1973 as part of a think-tank network that was growing fast and attracting serious money, the groundwork was being laid for the Reagan era. The outsiders were coming in.

By 1981, when he took office, Heritage, for example, was spending more than $5 million a year and had become an intellectual powerhouse for conservatism. With the American Enterprise Institute, it became a sounding board for the ideas that Reagan distilled into simple language. The consequence was that judicial appointments took the country in a socially conservative direction, deregulation became seen as one of the prime purposes of government, and a generation of conservative politicians and thinkers gained confidence, and got a scent of power.

By the time Reagan left office, the nostrums of the 1960s seemed an age away. American political language had changed, and its institutions were reshaped. As well as its successes, the Reagan administration made many mistakes, failed in some of its prime economic objectives and mired itself in scandal. But by the end of the 1980s, America had changed. Conservatives who took Reagan as their model and inspiration were ready for an advance that they could never have expected a decade earlier.

No president has enjoyed mocking himself so much. He once said, 'I have left orders to be awakened at any time in case of national emergency, even if I'm in a Cabinet meeting.' But it was another ruse. Behind the bumbling facade that was always there when he wasn't on a platform with his cue cards, Reagan was the intuitive leader of a movement that wanted a creed they could cherish. In a way, it was masterly. His simplicity was the perfect answer to their prayer.

But the grandfather of the modern conservative movement, Barry Goldwater, loathed the import of religious fervour into the thinking that sprang solely from a particular reading of the constitution. He told the Senate in 1981: 'We have succeeded for 205 years in keeping the affairs of state separate from the uncompromising idealism of religious groups and we mustn't stop now. To retreat from that separation would violate the principles of conservatism and the values upon which the framers built this democratic republic.'

When people asked him what he thought of the evangelicals who, through the 1980s, became the vanguard of a new social conservatism, his usual reply was 'Nuts', frequently with a pithy adjective attached. As he put it in relation to one of the most prominent television evangelists, 'I think every good Christian should kick Jerry Falwell right in the ass.' Goldwater disapproved of the way constitutional conservatism was being fused with an evangelical moral crusade. But that alliance produced a burgeoning conservative movement that had more ideological confidence, and much more money, than ever before.

One administrative act at the end of the Reagan years catches the flavour, a ruling that harked back to an age long gone and changed the country more profoundly than most people predicted at the time. In 1987, the Federal Communications Commission abolished the 'fairness doctrine' that had applied since the 1940s to the licensing of broadcasting organisations, putting an obligation on them to air different points of view on matters of public importance and to give them an equally fair hearing. It did not lay down rigid rules about how balance should be achieved – giving equal time to opposing arguments, for example – but simply put a duty on broadcasters to serve the public interest by striving for fairness in their output. By the end of Reagan's time, such concepts were deeply out of fashion. 'Freedom of speech' was everything, which meant that the more money you had, the more you could spread the version of events that you preferred. It was a free-for-all.

The FCC's decision changed what Americans were going to hear.

Within a few years the shock-jock culture had hijacked hundreds of radio stations and turned the airwaves into an ideological battleground. Especially on the right, conservative talk-show hosts fought to outdo each other like fire-and-brimstone preachers of old vying for the biggest crowd by whatever means they could find. And with the advent of cable news, television was going to go the same way. The most significant consequence came in 1996 with the birth of a cable channel that had a piquant connection to Reagan's Hollywood past.

Just before he was elected governor of California in 1966, he did a land deal that guaranteed that he would be rich for the rest of his life. He sold most of the rugged terrain on his Yearling Row Ranch in the Santa Monica Mountains north-west of Los Angeles to one of the big six film studios in Hollywood, which wanted more land where it could shoot westerns on the trails and canyons. Three decades later, the co-owner of that company turned it into one of the most powerful and unruly offspring of the Reagan era, changing the culture of television and the American public discourse.

The studio was Twentieth Century Fox, the boss was Rupert Murdoch, and the product of their union was Fox News.

CHAPTER 5

THE ROARING NINETIES

The loneliness of a long-distance presidential candidate has a hypnotic quality. You see it revealed on a windy plaza where the crowd is unaccountably thin, in a glimpse backstage where the figure at the centre of it all looks stricken at the moment of defeat and artifice falls away, in panic-stricken eyes when an interview goes wrong. Lying beneath layers of brash speech and sound and confected excitement, and moments of inspiration if you are lucky, you sense a persistent feeling of solitude. It is the natural product of two powerful impulses in any presidential quest – single-minded obsession and emotional excess. The candidate's challenge is to disguise one with the other.

Bill Clinton, who came to dominate the American 1990s, found politics such a natural trade that he understood that truth without instruction. In the closing days of the New Hampshire primary of 1992, feeling the precious jewel of his ambition slipping from his fingers as the campaign floundered, he spoke to a crowd jammed into the Elks Club in Dover, near the state's eastern seaboard, dead-tired but determined on one last push. If they gave him a second chance, he said, 'I'll be with you till the last dog dies.'

He knew he had to beg, and the natural language of a southern campaigner came bubbling up. His Louisianan soulmate James Carville, who always talks slowly as if he is soaking up the heat and lingering with a po-boy sandwich in New Orleans, reminded him almost hourly that he had to 'shake every hand' until polling day, and the candidate pressed hard on the gas pedal, which is what he loved to do when that last dog was threatening to expire. Indeed, if it weren't, he would have been strangely disappointed.

His panic, however, was real. In his ear, and touching all the voters in New Hampshire, was the siren voice of a nightclub singer who said they'd had a twelve-year affair – Gennifer Flowers was armed with taped phone conversations which she brandished as proof – and the accusation from opponents that he had dodged the Vietnam draft. His hopes were evaporating. Aware that if he were knocked out he would never get another chance, and knowing that his private pollsters predicted collapse, he braced himself for a last stand. 'The press only talks about a woman I didn't sleep with, and a draft I didn't dodge,' he told *Nightline* on ABC, taking the whole business head-on. The fight to be 'the comeback kid' had started three weeks earlier, when the Clintons, man and wife, decided to go on prime-time national television – on the evening of the Super Bowl, no less, just after the game – to fight back against Flowers, who was placing herself before the electorate as the lover who could stop a would-be president stone-dead, not the first or the last of her breed.

On that Sunday night in January, sitting with her husband on a sofa in a hotel suite in Boston, wearing a demure black hairband and holding his hand, Hillary Clinton established her character to watching Americans with a few sentences, and imprinted an image on the public mind that would trouble her in later years but which, on that edition of *60 Minutes* on CBS after the Super Bowl, sprinkled some magic dust into the mix. 'You know, I'm not sitting here, some little woman standing by my man like Tammy Wynette, I'm sitting here because I love him, and I respect him, and I honour what he's been through and what we've been through together. And you know, if that's not enough for people, then heck – don't vote for him.'

It's thought that perhaps 50 million Americans watched that display of defiance – an infinitesimal fraction of them with a vote in New Hampshire – which the campaign knew had to be powerful enough to offer him support, but not dominating enough to make him appear a man with no backbone of his own, and therefore a soft touch. Or, in the word all candidates are taught to dread, 'unpresidential'. Nixon, characteristically, could not resist an acid intervention from his retirement seclusion, saying in an interview soon afterwards, 'If the wife comes through as being too strong and too intelligent, it makes the husband look like a wimp.' Strength! Intelligence in a woman! What was America coming to?

Tammy Wynette herself, a soulful southern belle, said Hillary Clinton had insulted every American, man or woman, who loved 'Stand By Your Man', and her fifth husband revealed to anyone who wanted to hear that the interview had made the self-anointed queen of country (in a disgraceful slur on Emmylou Harris, in my view) 'madder than hell'. But she hardly mattered – the prize was too important. George Stephanopoulos, who was in the thick of that fight, and on his way to the White House, said afterwards, 'We bet a whole campaign on a single interview.'

At that moment, storing up TV footage that would later play back as a hostile soundtrack to her own attempts at the presidency, the Bill–Hillary White House story began. Like the opening scene of a TV saga meant to span a decade or more, it glistened with melodramatic promise. Ironically, the appearance wasn't even intended to secure victory in New Hampshire – among Democrats, the popular senator from next-door Massachusetts, Paul Tsongas, had the top spot wrapped up from the start – but was simply a fight for second place, to allow Clinton to stay alive, like that last dog, until the primary votes across the south where, as governor of Arkansas, he might establish himself as the likely Democratic nominee. They threw the dice because they had to, and their audacity paid off. The Clintons were the story of the year, and their undisguised ambition, shot through with some calculated bravado, brought them to power. They were the believers in a more liberal America who were open about their failings, like most children of the 1960s, but able to paint a post-Reagan America in appealing colours. On the economic prospects for ordinary voters, healthcare and race, Bill Clinton – brought up in the poor South by a single mother after his father was killed in a car crash before he was born – cut through the untroubled conservatism of the Bush years with eloquent verve. The torch was being passed on, taken from a generation that was fading away. And look what was coming along. A disadvantaged kid who'd become a Rhodes scholar at Oxford and later a reforming governor aged only thirty-one, but who nonetheless retained that most precious commodity in American politics, the role of the outsider.

In winning, however, he was the agent for a tide of opposition of such toxic intensity that before the end of the decade the country was more troubled than it had been when he came into power, despite undeniable evidence of the economic expansion he'd promised. He left office after two terms with Gallup ratings that were higher than any president's since before he was born, and all but delivered the White House to his own vice president, Al Gore, who would have led the first three-term Democratic administration since FDR. But from scandals real and imagined there was a legacy that Bill Clinton never wanted – a culture war that, even two decades later, would divide the country much more painfully than any of his own campaigns and which would define the start of the new American century.

At the end of the '92 campaign I watched him on a balmy fall day in a college football stadium just outside Atlanta, on the Sunday before polling day. Behind the platform, the leaves on the trees had turned to brown and gold, a low sun was throwing shadows on the field and the crowd was in picnic mood. By happenstance, Reagan was speaking on the other side of the city. The former president was paddling happily in nostalgia, evoking the idea of an old America that, by implication, had been in place before George H. W. Bush took office and had slipped away during his presidency, leaving it to the mercy of tax-and-spend Democrats to bend to their will. The Clinton rally was clearly the one to witness – the future usually being more intriguing than the past – but the Reagan event delivered some gems that shone with the gleam of the future.

Daniel Becker, running for election to the House in the ninth congressional district of Georgia, reminded everyone, before Reagan arrived, how the politics of the South encourages you to go for broke. The *New York Times* reported the next day that he contrasted the morals of the 'mainstream media', a term then only beginning to catch on, with the Bible – 'my journal' as he described it in patronising style – safe in the knowledge of which source the crowd would choose to believe, all of them brought up to shiver at the instructions of every Old Testament prophet, and to feel the flicker of hellfire at their feet.

On Clinton, Becker let go with gusto. 'What my journal calls him is a rebellious, philandering, fornicating, adulterating liar.' Getting into his stride, he delivered the thrust the crowd had expected and they duly cheered. 'My publication doesn't say he's going to the White House, it says he's going to hell.' Nowhere else would do for the likes of him.

Reagan himself always avoided such language – descriptions of eternal damnation never appealed to him, having spent so much of his life in Hollywood – but the movement to which he had bequeathed an absolutist political message was taking it forward.

Clinton, in contrast to the old charmer who was already beginning to seem grandfatherly and frail, was young, and looking ahead. At his rally on that Sunday, he paraded a phalanx of great Georgians, including the Atlanta Braves' baseball hero Hank Aaron, who'd beaten Babe Ruth's record of 714 home runs – in a game I'd watched on television in Syracuse back in 1974 – and in so doing had expunged the memory of a time, decades earlier, when Major League Baseball had been an all-white affair. At the time when he was born, as a black American, no one would think that he had a chance of becoming a Major League ball player. It didn't have to be explained to anyone watching: Aaron was a representative of a different South.

But a notable absentee on that platform was Jimmy Carter, the only Georgian to become president. For the Clinton campaign, his presence would have been too backward-looking, so the former governor of the state, never mind a former president, wasn't welcome at the party. This had to look like a new generation. Years later, at a dinner in Atlanta, Clinton recalled that rally, claiming that there were 25,000 people in the football ground – a reasonable estimate – which was greater than the majority by which he won the state two days later, with the thirteen votes it had at that time in the electoral college. Clinton appeared fresh on that afternoon, before heading north to Iowa and Wisconsin for rallies until late in the evening, but the truth about the cost of a presidential campaign in the last days had been revealed more clearly on the day before, in an encounter with his running mate, which was a telling vignette of the climactic days.

It produced little of value for the BBC, I'm afraid, and that is often the way of things on the road. You labour away, sweeping up all you can, realising that sometimes there is a little gem in the dust. But you can't predict where and when you will find it. So it was with Al Gore. My producer, Colin Hancock, and I thought we were on to something, having managed to get onto his plane on the last weekend before polling day. Here is what followed.

We flew south from upstate New York, having been promised an interview on the journey to Chattanooga, near his family home in Tennessee. We had guaranteed *The World at One* an interview for Monday, the eve of polling day. The trouble was that the vice-presidential candidate was so exhausted that he couldn't stay awake. Colin and I lurked as enticingly as we could at the front of the section of the plane where he lay while his travelling press corps flopped out further back, rendered as comatose as the candidate by having listened to the same stump speech, with only one new sound bite attached each day, for the previous two months. They had waited, day after day, for something to happen. It hardly ever did, because running mates never produce news unless they find a way of making a fool of themselves, and the reporters amused themselves instead by adding on every flight some new graffiti to the inside of the plane, which already looked like a kids' playground, with multicoloured walls and pieces of souvenir tat – 'Welcome to Dubuque, Iowa!' – hanging on strings from the overhead racks, to remind them where they'd been on their madcap wanderings. When they spoke, it wasn't about Clinton–Gore economic policy, but about getting home. Throwing away the suitcase before it finally fell apart. Sleeping without the prospect of yet another flight to Michigan – and on to Nevada, if they were especially unlucky – the next day.

Up front, we fancied we could hear the candidate snoring. It was late – we'd get to Chattanooga after midnight – and the chances of Gore giving us time after the plane landed were, approximately, zero. Somehow, he had to be woken up.

We threw ourselves on his staff, pointing out – we thought it was the clincher – that we had forked out a substantial sum to get on the plane (they charged commercial rates, plus) and that our programme (a flagship BBC outlet, blah, blah, blah ...) would be rather unhappy if its investment produced a blank tape. This cut no ice. Did we know how much the *New York Times* had paid to follow him at close quarters for months? Unfortunately, we did. I already knew that we were getting tangled up with one of the settled rules of American politics – that foreign press and broadcasters are always at the back of a long queue, unless the reporter in question is fortunate enough to have established a happy relationship with a member of staff – in some cases, even an affair – that allows a special request to zip through. We were not in that position, and had to fall back on the faithful backstop – a miserable appeal to human pity.

Unfortunately, such feelings are in short supply at the end of a campaign, when most staff members look as if they have just experienced a nervous seizure or are dependent for survival on a desperate concoction of drugs – perhaps both – and, even if the individuals concerned are decent, who've spent so much time on the road swatting away reporters that causing a little offence to someone from far away who'll soon be going home is not at all troubling. Indeed, it often seems to give them pleasure. In truth, I have often thought, who can blame them?

To our consternation, however, after no sign of life from the front section of the plane where the candidate was asleep – we could see a long leg and a foot sticking into the aisle, hinting at impenetrable inactivity – we realised that we appeared to be starting our descent, with time running out. We made a last, anxious push, not quite tearful, but getting on that way. There was, at last, a shaft of pity. The candidate would be jolted into life and asked – again! – if we might join him. And he said yes, because he respected the BBC, or so we were told. By now the plane was dipping, and we knew we didn't have long.

We crouched down, thrust a microphone in his face, and began. Al Gore is not a sparkling interviewee at the best of times. As I was reminded years later, he will happily engage in a thoughtful discussion that takes a little time, and deliver the goods, but even in campaign mode he is no master of the quick-fire exchange. Especially when his head is nodding with exhaustion and he is finding it difficult to keep his eyes open. We limped through a few routine questions – it was hardly the moment for cheery badinage – in the course of which his voice drifted off, and his mind along with it. He was obviously looking forward to getting home to Carthage, Tennessee, and some more welcome sleep. I found myself hallucinating. Perhaps he might suggest that we join him on the drive home for a longer conversation. Calm down. He buckled his belt for landing, closed his eyes, and we were done.

In the absurd excitements of such moments, when the tiniest breakthrough can seem like a triumph, we were content. We had an interview with the next vice president (possibly). Not for the first or the last time, I wondered how surprised listeners might be if they knew the contortions that are required to snatch a little time with your target. When it is effortless, or when someone shows unexpected kindness, or has a particular affection for BBC Radio (increasingly common in the United States, I should say), or is a friend or returning customer who genuinely wants to talk, it feels like the first day of spring. Too often it's a long winter's night.

We landed in Chattanooga in the dark. Gore was driven away, fast. At least there was an exciting message to pass to the office the next morning. We set off to search for the cheapest motel we could find, singing the 'Chattanooga Choo Choo' in our delight – 'When you hear the whistle blowin' eight to the bar, then you know that Tennessee is not very far ... '

Election day – in the United States as almost everywhere else – is often spookily calm. After all the noise, there is a tingling silence, because it is done. You wait with frustration for the dam to break, while people amble to polling places keeping their intentions to themselves – feeding on rumour ('Georgia's slipping away!', 'Michigan's back in play!', 'George has told Barbara they've lost!'), most of which turns out to be bunkum, spread by enthusiasts who need to keep themselves excited, even when there is nothing to say. In the early 1990s, the torrent of speculation, fact and rumour on social media outlets wasn't even a trickle. We had no mobile phones, let alone algorithms on laptops spewing out running precinct tallies of turnout and a tide of airborne gossip to excite us, only rumours in fragments (most of them rubbish) and the simple arithmetic of electoral college votes, which by that stage we knew as well as the old times tables from long ago.

On this one, we conceived what we thought to be a clever idea. The economist John Kenneth Galbraith was still going strong, at a lively eighty-four. By now it was old hat that at Clinton head-quarters they had a sign on the wall put up by Carville saying, 'The economy, stupid!' to get to the core of things and remind everyone what the campaign was about, so why not travel to the mountain top (Galbraith's home in Cambridge, Massachusetts, near Harvard Square) to talk to the guru himself, whose rumi-nations on everything since the Wall Street Crash had influenced three generations? There would be plenty of time to be back in Washington before the polls closed. Galbraith told us on the phone that we would be welcome guests. I should note that Roger Mosey of *The World at One*, one of the BBC's most brilliant editors and a close friend since our first happy days on that programme, didn't jump for joy when we left a message saying we were on our way to Boston. To tell the truth, he was furious. But I still think we were right, and he was wrong. Usually, it was the other way round.

That election was the first I experienced from start to finish, in regular visits, and also the one that clearly, in retrospect, marked the opening of a new era in politics. Clinton, the first president born after the Second World War, was a break after twelve years of Republican control from the White House and we would learn only two years later that he'd be the catalyst for the fulfilment of the revolution on the right that Reagan had announced. Those whom he had inspired were ready to take to the streets. They transformed politics, and our trade too. The accompanying changes in broad-casting, with the growth of cable news and a fashionable disdain for the once-prevalent obligations of balance and fairness in news, were recasting the American national debate.

Broadcasting was changing fast at home, too. Technology was allowing all of us to operate far more speedily and flexibly on the road, and the BBC was waking up to a new era in the transmission of live news. I was one of the many presenters and correspondents who had been part of an exciting experiment during the first Gulf War in early 1991, when the controller of radio news and current affairs, Jenny Abramsky, was far-sighted (and brave) enough to turn over Radio 4 output on FM to rolling coverage of events in the Middle East after Saddam Hussein's invasion of Kuwait and the launch by George Bush, with enthusiastic British support, of Operation Desert Storm. The six-week ground campaign was covered in a way that had never been attempted before. We weren't going to pop up when something happened; we were going to be there throughout, day and night.

It would be absurd to say that there weren't longueurs in the coverage. Indeed, quite a few. Waiting for an uninformative briefing from an unknown American soldier, delivered in army-speak in an airfield far away, is not a recipe for excitement. Hearing about a battle two days after it has taken place is frustrating, particularly when you can be certain that the account is only part of the truth. So all of us had to learn to keep things going as best we could, without the helpful disciplines of time-limited programmes and pre-recorded material to call upon. Everyone had to learn to busk it, and we did. Correspondents from an earlier age – notably Christopher Lee, a former BBC defence correspondent and a silver-tongued radio man – were able to talk for as long as they liked, with the occasional interruption by a general or a historian of the Middle East eager to talk about the schism in the seventh century that produced the Sunni and Shia branches of Islam, or the history of the Persian Empire. We welcomed to the studio anyone who had anything to say about desert warfare, the mechanics of a Scud missile, the twentieth-century reordering of the Middle East. Sykes and Picot, the two mandarins from the Foreign Office and the Quai d'Orsay who redrew the map to suit Britain and France after the Great War, were introduced to a generation that had never heard of them, because it was the borders they drew that were still causing most of the trouble, nearly a century on. Listeners got a flavour of life in Baghdad, and the sound of the Arab street. And who cared if it was in the middle of the night?

Naturally, there were strange episodes during the long hours we spent in the studio. One night, my wife, Ellie, gently pointed out to me (in St Thomas' Hospital in London) that I had an ugly stain on my shirt, which I must have brandished throughout a three-hour stint in the studio that afternoon. It was a large black patch of meconium, evidence of the birth of our third child, Flora, earlier that day. Whether my colleagues knew what it was and felt it would be embarrassing to point it out, or just didn't know, I can't say. But I wasn't at all bothered when I found out, partly because of the family excitement that we all felt on that day – and because there were no cameras present on 'Gulf FM' – but also because that studio had become a kind of domestic annexe in all our lives, albeit as a consequence of war.

However much was concealed, as ever, in the fog of conflict – the 'truth' about the scale of the Battle of Medina Ridge and other fierce engagements, for example, would take many months to emerge – a different kind of war reporting was being encouraged. There was no going back. And if listeners wanted to discuss the ethics of 'embedding' reporters with the troops, thereby accepting some military censorship, more time was available to talk about why it was right or wrong. There was a context to the campaign that had never been available in such detail and at such length, and an opening for listeners to participate.

Within a few years you could be forgiven for thinking that it had always been like this.

The experience of 'Gulf FM', as we knew it, was profound for the BBC. Radio 5 Live was born two years later as a direct consequence of those two months. Just as television in the United States was starting to invent rolling news (Sky at home had begun to develop it in 1989) – with profound implications for the public discourse, and therefore for politics itself – we were starting to explore a different way of doing our jobs. Listeners were learning to expect more out-and-about reporting, and to have a grandstand seat at events with a better view than they had ever known. Simultaneously, the tools of our trade were getting sharper.

When I spent weeks in the US towards the end of 1991 recording a Radio 4 series called *America's Crisis of Leadership*, it was with heavy old Swiss Nagra reel-to-reel machines, which, along with the trusty Uher recorders, were correspondents' friends on the road for a generation. That series was produced by Anne Sloman, who for decades inspired some of Radio 4's most imaginative broadcasting, and I have sharp recollections of her in both a white-hot Texas sun and in a New York snowstorm, protecting the machine and our precious tapes from the elements. This was a physical challenge, as I learned with Anne and others on many occasions, notably on a journey with her in Cambodia in 1992. We were returning from an eye-opening expedition for a series on UN peacekeeping operations, which involved some scary rides in helicopters rented by the UN that had served in the 1980s Afghan war, complete with bullet holes and their vodka-soaked Russian pilots, and an exhilarating ride down the Mekong in a rubber dinghy driven by the Royal Navy at speeds I had not thought possible, when we had an encounter with a dour security official at Phnom Penh airport. He insisted that every reel of our tapes be unwound to inspect them for anything suspicious (an utterly pointless exercise – how did he intend to play them?). The trouble was that they amounted to thirteen hours of recording, and unwinding them could be catastrophic. Our entire project was threatened. Anne dealt with him in a fashion that he clearly wasn't used to, and when he suggested that at least our tapes should be subjected to magnetic screening – which might have wiped them clean – he discovered that he had gone too far. As people who got into a fight with Anne often discovered, even if they were wearing a military uniform, it was more sensible to fold.

Soon, with digitalisation, the old machines ended up on the shelf. There was no longer any tape, nor recorders that sometimes threatened to dislocate a shoulder. By the mid-1990s, we were using satellite dishes that got ever smaller over the years, and were able to get a signal through the kind of rainstorm that earlier versions couldn't handle. We could park up at a roadside or on the roof of a multi-storey car park, a favourite spot from which to try to make contact with the satellite that we knew was hovering somewhere over Brazil. Checking into a motel or hotel, we would try to get a room with a window opening in the right direction, so a compass was always part of the kit. It was an exhilarating time because we could bring listeners closer to events and broadcast clearly, without having to wait to edit tape in a friendly radio station and then hang around until a line to London became available, probably at a cost that entailed some haggling. We could be fleet of foot.

Editing no longer involved cutting tape with a razor blade, a gloriously subtle business in its day, and could be done on the move. I have fond memories of driving through the Carolinas during a later campaign with Alexis Condon of the *Today* programme in the back seat editing our report on his laptop with his usual dexterity, but having to do it with a blanket over his head because of the strong sun. When he emerged from his tent after several hours, having had only an occasional break for a smoke, there was a perfectly crafted piece of reportage, with my script, interviews with candidates and voters, all interwoven with street sounds and birdsong along with campaign songs and speeches. I can't remember the sequence of events on that particular night, because they all tend to collapse into one endless journey, but we probably found a motel car park, then erected the little satellite dish in the car headlights in a few minutes, wiggled it around to find the orb in the sky above Brazil, and beamed it home, as clear as a bell, ready for morning broadcast.

Thinking back to the time before these changes brings to mind Bill Clinton's remark about the arrival of the internet. When he took office in 1992, he likes to say, you could count the number of proto-websites going up online on the fingers of one hand, but by the time he left office, in 2000, his cat Sox had his own web page.

The *Crisis of Leadership* series produced by Anne as Clinton came over the horizon was well timed. A period of expansion and dominance had covered the lives of almost every American alive, and now the Cold War was over, the wall gone. Although Bush, cannily and wisely, refused to crow about victory, because he was well aware of the schisms and battles that were likely to follow the collapse of Soviet Communism, for many Americans it was proof of their power, and of the country's 'exceptionalism', which guaranteed power and glory. Why, then, was their country beset by such troubles at home? Cities that couldn't eradicate the poverty in their midst, schools that were slipping behind others in international comparisons, racial divisions that wouldn't heal, too much violence in the streets, and a Congress that seemed happier when it was caught in gridlock with the White House (or between its two

Houses) than when it turned to clean decision-making with compromise and common sense. American government seemed clunky, and Bush lost the White House for one overriding reason – he couldn't produce at home the economic and social success to match the power the country seemed to project abroad.

It wasn't the maverick intervention of a third-party candidate that did for him. Ross Perot was a pesky Texan billionaire with iron self-confidence and an unfortunate resemblance to the cartoon character Mr Magoo, but exit polls after the election suggested strongly that his votes came almost equally from those who would have voted Democrat and those who would have voted Republican. Bush lost because the president abroad and the president at home seemed to be two different men. A tendency to be accident prone in public didn't help, as in 1992 when he had the misfortune to vomit into the lap of the prime minister of Japan at a banquet in Tokyo (in an American election year!). Served him right for playing tennis beforehand with the emperor, said a host of one of the late shows that were starting to become bolder and much less deferential on American television.

I had a long conversation in the course of the *Leadership* series with Larry Eagleburger, a Bush intimate who was deputy secretary of state. He summed up Washington succinctly, aware that world power and overbearing influence weren't enough. 'We muddle through. We're not efficient as a government. We never will be.'

The 'shining city on the hill' promised by Reagan was a mirage, and that truth became the American torment through the 1990s.

Clinton, however, began in confident style. Inflation and unemployment were low, and although he abandoned plans for deep tax cuts for middle-income earners in favour of deficit reduction, he could point to an economy that was growing. And in foreign affairs – at a point where all the later difficulties of his administration had barely shown themselves – he achieved one remarkable coup. In September 1993, he choreographed a famous handshake at the White House, cementing the agreement that had been negotiated secretly in Oslo over many months under which Israel would allow a measure of autonomy in Palestinian territories which it had occupied since the Six-Day War of 1967 in return for a declaration by the Palestine Liberation Organisation that it recognised the State of Israel, renounced violent opposition to it and recognised that nearly 80 per cent of historical Palestine was Israeli.

Yasser Arafat, a bogeyman to most Americans, turned up in Washington to sign the accords with the Labour prime minister of Israel, Yitzhak Rabin. I was there with the BBC's diplomatic correspondent, Paul Reynolds, who'd been stationed in Jerusalem in the 1980s, to broadcast the outcome live. By chance, I was staying in the same hotel as Arafat, and in the course of a couple of days the place had started to sound and feel like Beirut – music, food and Arabic chatter gave it a Middle Eastern flavour, including the enticing smells – much to the bemusement of those American tourists who had arrived in Washington from Missouri and points south and west to explore the historical sights of the city and found themselves swept up in a crowd of excited Palestinians who every now and then would line the lobby to let Arafat pass, dressed in combat gear and waving all the way from the elevator to his car as they cheered him on. For Clinton, who liked nothing more than arm-wrestling negotiations behind closed doors, it was exactly the kind of event he'd come into politics to supervise.

Afterwards, however, he confessed that there had been a potentially ruinous hitch when both leaders (and old enemies) were inside the White House, waiting to be led outside for the announcement from the Rose Garden to the world. Arafat was beaming, putting a hand on every shoulder, preparing for the moment that so many had thought would never come. Rabin was not looking so happy. He told Clinton that they could go ahead, just, but without the handshake.

Clinton told him that if that was the case, everything was off. He would not preside over an announcement that didn't end with a handshake, and he was prepared, sadly, to send everyone home. It still rankled with Rabin, who was facing fierce political opposition at home, and knew Arafat's penchant for showmanship.

Eventually, he retreated.

'Okay,' he told Clinton. 'But no kissing.'

Journeying to Washington during Clinton's first term was exhilarating, because the place was changing so much. With healthy majorities in both Houses, a Democratic president could afford to be bold. Clinton asked Hillary to pursue healthcare reform – keeping-it-in-the-family being more acceptable in the United States than in most democratic countries – with the aim of building a universal system of insurance. The failure of that effort was one of the signals that Reagan's conservatism had permeated more deeply than liberal Democrats liked to admit. And the hard evidence came, with a whirlwind, in the midterm election of 1994.

The results were dramatic, but I also remember it as the night the lights went out.

During the early evening of that November Tuesday, the pattern of the returns was becoming clear. It was a Republican rout, with Democrats almost certainly losing control of the House of Representatives, which meant trouble for Clinton. Not only would healthcare reform, already bogged down, be doomed, but he'd have to fight hard to get the funding for the kind of federal budget he wanted. The House holds the purse strings in Washington. As usual, we were watching results in the BBC office on M Street, about six blocks from the White House, a place that over the years has become a home from home for me and where I have had many friends. The pattern of results firmed up. We knew there was a Republican victory party in a downtown hotel not far away, so it made sense to get over there and speak to whoever we could, and perhaps even broadcast live into *Today*, which went on air in London at 1 a.m. Washington time. We had no doubt that the party would still be going on, because it was the Republicans' night.

On that visit we had with us Graham McHutchon, a BBC studio manager who was a wizard of on-the-road broadcasting. Graham was one of the most experienced of SMs – the talented and dedicated group whose professionalism keeps the nervous system of BBC Radio going. He could rig an outside studio in an hour or two, find clever solutions to the most challenging technical problems, and always had about his person a spare microphone or the very piece of cable or plug that was needed, urgently, to connect two machines that otherwise wouldn't speak to each other. I watched in wonder at the end of the negotiations on the Maastricht Treaty in the Netherlands on a freezing morning in 1991 as he somehow managed to find an ideally positioned hotel room from which he could drop a microphone out of the window, with a cable perhaps 35 feet long, which could be grabbed at street level far below by my colleague John Sergeant and poked in the face of the prime minister, John Major, as he came out of the hotel to go to the last round of negotiations, and was therefore hooked up live to London. On any trip away from the studio, Graham was a man you always wanted to have by your side, and a good friend.

That evening in Washington he wanted to see how we could set up a live broadcasting point outside the hotel from which we could speak live to *Today*. We had one of the early satellite dishes – much clunkier than the later models that could fit into a briefcase – and we had to find a reliable power source to broadcast from the street. While we pondered this problem, I went into the hotel ballroom, which was packed with revelling Republicans watching the results with ecstasy (the mental kind, I think), and a good deal of beer. I spoke to Haley Barbour, chairman of the Republican National Committee and later governor of Mississippi, and Senator Phil Gramm of Texas – both, to use Thatcherite terminology for their ideological positions, as dry as desert sand. They said it was a night when not only the tone and colour but the very nature of American government was going through a fundamental change that would not easily be reversed. They were right. The argument was no longer about taxes or health, nor even war and peace, but about how government itself should be conducted. When they spoke about a second American revolution, they meant it. They were challenging many of the assumptions underpinning the growth of the federal government over decades, and the influence of a broadly liberal Supreme Court.

Meanwhile, outside, Graham was surrounded by partying Republicans who thought it was a hoot that the BBC was at work in the middle of their celebrations. But he had solved the technical problem. When I came out, he showed me a line of trees that was decorated with early Christmas fairy lights, twinkling away. Clearly there was electricity coming from somewhere. Digging around, he had found the power source. So we got everything ready and he unplugged a spindly tree. Unfortunately, because of some complicated wiring system of which we were unaware, it brought darkness down on the whole street. The high-spirited Republicans found the scene hilarious, and continued to party up and down the street as we tried to broadcast in the blackness, interrupted every now and then by a bibulous party worker whizzing out of the hotel's revolving door and bawling a southern hog-call to the audience across the Atlantic.

It was one of the occasions – I remember so many, at grassy roadsides, in airports, on the seashore and up a mountain, once in a disused palace in Rome where I had to conduct a live interview with the foreign secretary, who was sitting at home in Oxfordshire while I was lying under a table to try to keep the traffic noise at bay – when it is tempting to explain your predicament to the listening audience. But except in the most extreme circumstances – pointing out that there is a pipe band practising in the next field, for example – it's wise to remember the reason for the broadcast, not the passing discomforts the reporter or presenter may have to face. Why should they care?

However, the Night the Lights Went Out was important. It brought onto the national scene the Republican whip in the House, Newt Gingrich of Georgia, the quirky politics professor who had effectively mounted a coup and would be the new Speaker, a role that confuses the British because it demands none of the non-partisanship expected of the Speaker of the House of Commons. The Speaker of the House on Capitol Hill is the political kingpin, the boss of the majority party, and Gingrich was already promising on that night to shake the whole place up with his 'Contract with America', a piece of radical populism that thrilled the most conservative elements in his party and laid out a path that would still seem familiar twenty-five years later.

Conservatives – an increasing number identifying themselves as born-again Christians, for whom their God trumped any mere president – were building a well-funded popular movement dedicated to the memory of the Reagan years, propelled by fiscal conservatives, a number of gifted ideologues and an evangelical movement that had once been suspicious of political activity but was now fully engaged on the Republican side. Such questions as prayer in schools, abortion and the freedom to own and carry guns became the focus of heavily funded campaigns all asking the brutal question: which side are you on? There was no middle ground, and the era of Country Club Republicanism with George H. W. Bush, who had never appealed to right-wing ideologues, nor they to him, was already a world away.

Gingrich himself had a relatively short career at the top, but he changed America. Tax cuts and welfare changes were a direct challenge to Clinton's view of the world, and he encouraged more than one government shutdown – paralysing parts of the federal administration – in pursuit of his goals. But much more significantly, he altered the tone of Washington politics. The Republicans who chanted 'Newt! Newt!' at his rallies wanted a battle, and so did he. Language got rougher, ideological positions hardened, and all politics was polarised. You chose your side and fought for it, knowing that the others were the enemy. Gingrich exhibited the rumpled ease of a wacky teacher who liked to chew the fat because it was fun, but in truth he was in for the kill.

Clinton's presidency therefore became the battleground for a culture war, with the melodrama of his private life a flickering backdrop that excited and encouraged his opponents. The rhetoric across the conservative–liberal divide took on a poisonous tone. The sexual harassment claims against Clinton made by Paula Jones, dating from Arkansas days, were a threat to the White House that wouldn't go away, and when Monica Lewinsky turned up – in the form of taped recollections with a friend, Linda Tripp – she quickly became a public femme fatale, and the balloon went up. The story of her liaisons with Clinton, and his awkward and duplicitous denials, became not only ludicrous but a running national joke. Soon after he had despatched the ageing Bob Dole in the 1996 election with some ease, the White House was forced into a defensive mode that lasted until the Senate voted down impeachment three years later. By that time, Gingrich himself had gone from the Republican leadership and the House itself, mainly because of an extra-marital affair with a woman more than two decades younger than he was, and his Contract with America was in tatters. He was a shrivelled figure in disgrace, swathed in irony as Clinton faced impeachment, but his work was done. Few American figures in modern times have combined such inadequacy in power with such lasting influence.

I had sharp glimpses of that crisis from a long-standing friend, Sidney Blumenthal, who became special assistant to Clinton in 1997. We had met in London more than a decade earlier, thanks to David Broder, and had a rolling conversation over the years, in his time on the *New Yorker*, then through his roller-coaster years in the West Wing of the White House, up to the time he was subpoenaed in the Lewinsky affair, through his later campaign work for Hillary, and into his research on a majestic three-volume biography of Lincoln. For me, Sid's ups and downs were a kind of temperature gauge of American politics, but our friendship has never wavered.

By the early 1990s, Sid, though still a journalist, was part of the Clinton circle – it was in his home that Hillary first met Tony Blair and Gordon Brown – and it seemed inevitable that he would end up in the White House. So when the Lewinsky affair began to unravel, he was inevitably in the thick of it, and one of the characters Republicans loved to hate. The House Judiciary Committee appointed an independent special counsel, Ken Starr, whose investigation became the engine of opposition to Clinton, churning through every allegation, from the serious to the absurd, and turning the political atmosphere in the process into a miasma of mistrust and conspiracy. Starr was assisted by Brett Kavanaugh, who would end up as a Supreme Court justice, appointed by Donald Trump in 2018, but in truth it was less of a legal investigation than a rolling political assault.

Among the president's opponents, Clinton became the physical embodiment of everything they loathed about liberal America, and the temperature rose fast. The wilder conspiracy nuts had never had it so good. And across the great divide, for their part, Clinton's defenders saw the growth of 'a vast right-wing conspiracy', as Sid Blumenthal and others were apt to put it. I can vividly picture Sid drawing for me on a sheet of White House notepaper a Venn diagram showing in its interlocking circles the connections of Republican leaders to right-wing billionaires (the Koch brothers of Kansas being the favourite demons) and to such publications as the *American Spectator*, dedicated not so much to the regular pursuit of political aims, as to the destruction of the Clinton presidency by whatever means possible. It was a frenzied time.

Clinton's resilience, however, was remarkable to behold, under personal pressure that would have broken many characters. There was a good illustration when Tony Blair made his first visit to Washington as prime minister in early 1998. Clinton, whose relationship with Blair's predecessor, John Major, had not been warm, laid on a spectacular welcome. At dinner in the White House they ate from plates gifted by Eisenhower and Reagan, and drank from Kennedy's crystal glasses. The papers were full of Lewinsky stories, but the president was determined to put on a dazzling show. Blair couldn't conceal his excitement at being placed on a table with Barbra Streisand, and Hollywood was on show as well as every serious figure from Capitol Hill. In the White House on the afternoon of the dinner we could hear from the East Room rehearsals going on for the late-night cabaret and were requested not to reveal before the dinner what we'd overheard – because we could hardly have failed to identify the hands on two pianos out on the west terrace: Elton John and Stevie Wonder.

In the spirit of that time, a colleague suggested, good-naturedly, that he hoped Elton wasn't going to sing 'Don't Let the Sun Go Down on Me'. That was not broadcast.

Clinton's cool was revealed at the joint press conference in that same East Room that traditionally brings to an end any visit from a head of government.

The White House press corps, having been deprived of a presidential press conference for some time, were determined to get stuck into Lewinsky matters, after the obligatory opening exchanges about the US–British relationship. Having watched a good deal of Blair close at hand at home, I could see that he was unusually nervous, I assumed on Clinton's behalf. The best moment came when Wolf Blitzer, then White House correspondent for CNN, preceded his question with an acknowledgement that the revelations of Clinton's liaisons with the young intern had made life difficult for all concerned.

Then, quite mildly, he said, 'At this minute, what is your message for Monica Lewinsky?'

Clinton hesitated, and looked down. Blair gripped the lectern in front of him more tightly.

Then the president shook his head, and smiled. 'That's good!' The place filled with laughter. Clinton joined in. 'At this minute, I'm going to stick to my position.' That was to say nothing. And he was off on another subject, with a classy sidestep.

I interviewed Blair later, before he took a helicopter to Camp David for a weekend with Clinton. We were in the official government guest house on Lafayette Square, coincidentally called Blair House and which therefore seemed to underline the prime minister's favoured status in Clinton's Washington. But I learned in the course of our conversation that the atmosphere inside the White House was icy. Domestic bliss was notably absent. It was clear, however, that even as a political leader of little experience at that time Blair was impressed – astonished might be a more accurate word – at how Clinton had been able to put on a public appearance of calm and control against such a lurid backdrop.

They were troubled times for Clinton. In the midterm elections later that year, with apparently little chance of restoring a Democratic majority in the House, he campaigned in the dark shadow of the Lewinsky affair and the threat of impeachment. Forty-eight hours before election day, I watched him in Baltimore, going to church.

New Psalmist Baptist is a huge African American church (Martin Luther King used to say that America is at its most segregated on Sunday mornings) where services go on throughout the day. The choir was swaying, the pastor warming up in style, hours before Clinton arrived. I was with Gordon Corera, then a producer on *Today* (later appointed BBC security correspondent), a friend who was a companion on many election forays and a walking encyclopaedia of American politics. We spent most of the morning sitting in the congregation – everyone dressed to the nines – listening to the strains of 'This Little Light of Mine' and the congregation's gospel favourites, and discussing how Clinton would appear. Strained? Angry? Desperate?

Warned that he was close, we went outside to see the presidential limousine approach through the crowd. Clinton was alone in the back seat (his wife away from Washington – it was a bad time), unsmiling it seemed, and with a pallor. He didn't look to be in a glad-handing mood. What could he say to the congregation, which was about 2,000 strong? For months he'd been engaged in an excruciating effort to extricate himself from accusations that he had committed perjury in testimony in the Paula Jones case, first denying a sexual relationship with Lewinsky then admitting in a televised address from the White House that he had indeed behaved improperly. No garment worn in the White House had ever become such an object of public scrutiny and voyeuristic fascination as the blue dress that Lewinsky claimed to have held back from her dry-cleaners because it still carried the stains of presidential semen.

And here he was in church, asking for votes. But he was brilliant, as we should have expected. Starting quietly, in the old southern style where you fashion a long crescendo that saves the explosion for the end, he threw himself on the congregation. Indeed, he might as well have cried aloud, hands raised to the heavens, 'I have sinned!' After all, what's the point of a Baptist service without a confession of sinfulness? And the congregation, aware that we are all fallen, loved it. What better on a Sunday than to welcome a sinner come to repentance?

There was some subsequent controversy about his visit, because after the service he attended a reception in an adjoining build-ing, which was in effect a fund-raiser for Representative Elijah Cummings, the local Democratic congressman – who, after his death in 2019, became the first African American to lie in state in the Capitol – and it was claimed that he had breached the divide between church and state. This was an amusing complaint, because anyone who has travelled through the South or the Midwest during an election season knows that from the pulpits of many evangelical churches you don't just get a whiff of fire and brimstone directed at politicians (usually liberals, of course) but a torrent of rage.

Clinton certainly had no qualms on that Sunday about whipping up the vote. The governor's race in Maryland was close, and impor-tant. He was determined to win it (and did).

At that nadir of his personal and public life, Clinton was still capable of delivering a lesson in campaigning. And, despite the sound of his opponents battering on the White House walls, he understood that he retained the affection of many Americans, perhaps more than many Republicans were inclined to admit.

At the height of the affair, when it was clear to everyone that the president had tried to cover up his sexual appetite, I drove out from Washington one day, to get well away from the political hothouse. Deep in rural Virginia, in a conservative part of the state, I spoke to a group of late-middle-aged and elderly ladies, having lunch together in a diner. I expected them to be unanimously hostile to Clinton. They certainly didn't like the idea of sexual acrobatics in the environs of the Oval Office, which they thought gave the whole business a near-sacrilegious quality, but they were surprisingly forgiving.

Two of them reminded me that they had raised families during the 1960s and '70s. Did I think they didn't understand what changing times meant? They hardly knew a family that hadn't been touched by separation or divorce, or a drug problem, or an episode of mental ill-health. Trouble-free personal lives were rare. Clinton, for them, wasn't an unusual man. They certainly didn't like bad behaviour in a president and couldn't approve of it. But, to a degree that struck me forcefully, it didn't surprise them, not because they were cynical but because they were realistic.

The following year, Clinton was impeached by the House but cleared in the Senate trial that followed. That his vice president, Gore, was nearly elected to succeed him is a reminder that the hysteria on Capitol Hill generated by the Lewinsky affair had not become an epidemic. His popularity when he left office at the start of 2001 was higher than almost anyone (except perhaps Sid Blumenthal and Clinton himself) would have predicted during the summer of the blue dress.

Gore himself believed he would win. The events that turned the election the other way were the most extraordinary in a presidential race since John F. Kennedy squeaked home in 1960 by a margin so narrow that Nixon, the loser, came under great pressure afterwards to challenge the result on the grounds that evidence of fraud could be uncovered in Illinois (especially in Mayor Daley's Chicago) that would reverse the result. Nixon refused, some say because political machinations in that election were not confined to Illinois, nor to one party, and he knew it. This issue returned, like a clap of thunder, forty years later almost to the day.

George W. Bush fought a Republican campaign that was based on the 'compassionate conservatism' (his phrase) that had served him well as governor of Texas, rather than the vitriolic style that had taken hold in Washington through the battles with Clinton. Both he and Gore had been reared in the political establishment – one the son of a president, the other born of a long-serving senator – and they fought quite a conventional battle. Everything changed, however, on election night itself.

I was in Washington trying to make sense of the results and recall the confusion that reigned in all the American networks. Relying on a mixture of exit polls and 'real' votes, they began to predict around eight o'clock in the evening that Gore had won Florida, which made him a strong favourite to become the forty-third president. There was much more to come, with some close races across the country, but he appeared to have leapt forward. Within an hour, however, the networks were in embarrassing retreat, no doubt cursing the software that analysed the precinct and county tallies to the point where it was deemed safe to call a state for one side or the other. They had jumped too early. Bush was now expected to win Florida, and the presidency was back in the balance.

The next few hours were tantalising, until the nationwide totals turned the spotlight back to the Sunshine State. It would be decided there, because we reached a point where, in search of the 270 electoral votes required to win, Gore had 255 and Bush 246. New Mexico and Oregon were so close that the results wouldn't be confirmed for days (Gore won them both by a whisker), but they weren't big enough to make the difference. Everything depended on Florida. Its twenty-five electoral votes would decide the presidency.

Sometime after midnight, Gore was told that Bush was ahead by 50,000, which seemed to put an end to it, and he rang him to concede the election at 2.30 a.m. in Washington, although we didn't know that at the time. Just before the 8 a.m. news bulletin on Radio 4, we decided that it was safe to tell listeners to *Today* – not without the slight tremor of fear that always grabs you at these moments – that we were going to have another Bush in the White House. Even as we did that, Gore was being told that the tide had turned once again, and the margin was shrinking. In Palm Beach and Broward counties he was piling up votes. He abandoned the public announcement he was about to make in Washington, and rang Bush back at 3.30 a.m. to inform him that he was withdrawing his concession.

Nothing like this had happened in living memory. Truman–Dewey in 1948 was a famous turnaround, but people weren't watching it on live television. The handful of votes between the candidates meant that the Democrats couldn't accept the result in the state that would decide the election. The inevitable happened. Like two divisions of the 7th Cavalry, lawyers swarmed over the horizon to take the election out of the hands of the candidates and the voters, whose job was done, to settle it in court.

Planeloads of them headed south to Tallahassee, the Florida state capital, where George W.'s brother Jeb was governor. Democrats believed they could prove that the result was unreliable and force a recount, not least because of previous scandals in Florida. The Miami mayoral election two years earlier had been overturned when it was discovered that a large number of votes had been cast by people who were either in prison (and therefore couldn't vote) or in the city's cemeteries, and therefore in the same position for a different reason. In the course of the next month, a battle of wills took place across the state, where some counties began manual recounts of votes and others did not. By late November, the Florida secretary of state, Katherine Harris, decided to certify the results – Bush over Gore by 537 votes, or 0.009 per cent of roughly 6 million cast. But that could not be the end of it. The court arguments rolled on, with Democrats trying to force Harris to open the ballot boxes.

Americans waited for more than a month after polling day to find out who was going to become president. The Bush team in Florida was led by James Baker, the Texas lawyer who had been secretary of state to the candidate's father (with the most unforgiving smile in politics), and Gore assembled the cream of the Democratic legal fraternity to try to get a state-wide count ordered. Over the weeks of argument, Americans learned much about a counting regime that, had it been reported from a developing country after a disputed election, would have produced scepticism, laughter and perhaps outrage. They heard painstaking explanations of the comic phenomenon of the 'hanging chads', little bits of paper sticking to ballot papers that had not been fully punched through by some outdated polling machines and were therefore not counted in many precincts, despite the intention of the voter being quite plain. They also got a glimpse of the ways in which the parties have ingenious ways of trying to disqualify voters whom they expect not to be helpful to their cause.

No one can know what a state-wide recount would have shown. Republicans have argued that Bush's margin would have been greater, and Democrats the opposite. But in the end, the Supreme court in Washington decided that it was not its place to dictate to the Florida authorities, and in making that decision – which outraged Democrats – it ensured a Bush presidency. Republicans were in command of the State House in Tallahassee and were going to do everything they could to seal a victory for the governor's brother.

I was in Washington on the night the Supreme Court, which had already overruled a decision by the Florida Supreme Court to order a manual recount across the state, announced its decision. Gore's fight was over. There was a remarkable statement that evening from Justice Antonin Scalia, a conservative hero who was still on the court when he died in 2016. 'The counting of votes that are of questionable legality does in my view threaten irreparable harm to petitioner Bush, and to the country, by casting a cloud upon what he claims to be the legitimacy of his election. Count first, and rule upon legality afterwards, is not a recipe for producing election results that have the public acceptance [that] democratic stability requires.'

Democrats cried foul, but the decision in Bush v Gore, SC 531, by a vote of five justices to four, was the final judgment. Gore conceded. Once again it drew the court into the heart of the political battle, where it would remain. Three presidents later, when Donald Trump got the chance to make three appointments that swung the court decisively rightwards, I was reminded in Washington, while making a documentary on the way that nine justices had shaped the political scene, that you could hardly overstate its importance in the ideological battle. A senator said, in an echo of the old Clinton motto, 'It's the court, stupid.'

The turbulent decade ended in the confusion and anger of those weeks, with an election that seemed to settle nothing. In particular, it left questions that would roll down the years and trouble many Americans on both sides of the divide about the operation of the democracy of which they are so proud. Gerrymandering by both parties, efforts to disqualify voters and the old worry about money and politics were exacerbated by the new threat – only vaguely understood at first – of interference by the invisible power that technology had put in the hands of the ruthless and the unscrupulous.

The 1990s, crowned by the most contentious presidential election of them all, were the prelude to an age of bitter politics.

CHAPTER 6

WARTIME

Probably the most surprising words I heard in the tumult after 9/11 were calm, but puzzling. They came from Tony Blair, who had been turned by the cataclysm into an iron-clad ally in war of the United States and the most intimate friend of the Bush White House. Sitting in the garden of 10 Downing Street, more than a year after British troops had gone into Iraq and the strains in his own party getting more obvious by the day, the prime minister spoke about the Americans with whom he'd made common cause and said simply, 'I never quite understand what people mean by this neocon thing.'

Innocence or bravado – who can say? We were having an on-the-record conversation about the story of the war, thirteen months after the invasion in March 2003 and at a moment when the political tide that had run his way for so long was beginning to turn. Yet the evidence that he remained unflinching in his commitment lay in the fact that he had little interest in the ideological forces that had shaped the administration in Washington since 9/11, nor their roots. He was convinced in his own mind, and that was all that mattered. With a little hesitation – because I suspected I knew the answer – I asked him if he had read the founding document for the Project for the New American Century, the think-tank for neoconservatism in the 1990s, which provided the playbook for the warriors in the administration, most notably Dick Cheney, the vice president.

'I can't say I have,' Blair said with a smile. 'What's in it?'

The phrase that sprang to my mind was 'benign global hegemony'. It didn't bother him. Blair unbuttoned, but determined. His answer was all the more surprising because in the days before 9/11, with Bill Clinton still in the White House, he'd made a speech in Chicago on 24 April 1999, that seemed for the neoconservatives who were setting the tone for foreign policy among Republicans to be an encapsulation of their world view – that there were circumstances in which Western intervention was not only justified but a matter of duty, even if there was no direct threat (as in Kosovo in the Balkans, then under siege from Slobodan Milosevic's Serbian forces, where Blair was determined to play a role).

His admirers believed that their idea of a more activist America, evangelical in trying to spread its influence and values wherever it could and unembarrassed by military might, had found a champion in Europe. Summing it up in his Chicago speech with a biblical reference, Blair said, 'Just as with the parable of the individuals and the talents, so those nations which have the power have the responsibility.'

Those of us who listened to him that day – more than two years before 9/11 put his thoughts to the test – realised that he was using the invitation to address the Economic Club of Chicago to pursue his dispute with Clinton about sending troops into Kosovo, which he wanted to do and Clinton didn't. It was at times a furious argument, and Blair's success at convincing the president to commit ground troops was a serious factor in his later dealings with Bush. British prime ministers don't often change a president's mind on military questions; and when they've done it once, they like the idea and try again.

On that one-day Chicago trip from Washington he enjoyed another of his American welcomes, which he was getting used to. Mayor Daley, son of The Boss and inheritor of his father's political machine, gave him a hero's reception – he was the first sitting British prime minister to visit the city – and closed the freeway from O'Hare airport so that the Blair motorcade could arrive downtown in style. In retrospect, the speech was the foundation for his policy in Iraq, arguing that liberal democracy demanded more than passive defence; sometimes it was right to fight for its values, even far away. Yet five years later, in 2004, with the complications and chaos (as well as the casualties) in Iraq becoming more obvious after the deceptive ease of the invasion itself, we sat in the Downing Street garden and he professed ignorance – even perhaps a lack of interest – in the ideology that drove many of those in Washington with whom he'd thrown in his lot.

The story of the year-long discussions and arguments leading to the invasion was complicated – more so than some of his most severe critics are willing to admit – but that conversation reminded me sharply of the posture that he struck from the beginning, which, for him, needed no ideological underpinning from American neo-conservatives or anyone else. He was convinced. It took me back to his transatlantic trip, nine days after the 9/11 attacks. We all clustered in St Thomas' Episcopal Church on 5th Avenue, where he felt at home surrounded by High Anglican statuary, sitting with Bill Clinton and Kofi Annan, the UN secretary general, with the families of many of the sixty-seven British dead in the congregation behind. He spoke of a 'surging of the human spirit' at a moment of grief and agony and, making a deliberate reference to the Blitz in the Second World War, he pledged that Britain would stand with its old ally the United States, now under attack.

These were days in which America changed Tony Blair. Instinctively aware of the scale of the implications from the moment he heard the news of the attacks (while he was preparing to address the Trades Union Congress in Brighton) he was plunged into the whirl of diplomacy that he knew from the start would lead to some kind of military response from the United States. The only question was how far it would go. He was in Paris and Berlin before crossing the Atlantic, and from the plane had a conversation with President Mohammad Khatami of Iran, which would have been nigh-unthinkable a few years earlier. To make the point that he felt no animus towards Islam, his people made it known that he was carrying a copy of the Koran with him on the trip. However, this wasn't a one-off gesture. In truth, as he told me at the time, it had become a habit as a consequence of a conversation with Chelsea Clinton, of all people, who'd told him that she found it inspiring and kept a copy with her. Blair, although he is much less 'churchy' than some suspicious critics like to paint him, does have an interest in spiritual thinking (although the kind he finds much the least appealing, ironically, is that practised by many American conservatives). From then on, the Koran became a standard component of the prime ministerial baggage.

That visit was the start of eighteen months of turmoil that split his government, brought huge demonstrations into the streets against him, but cemented a place for him in modern American folklore. After that visit to St Thomas' Church, he went straight to the White House, where his ambassador, Christopher Meyer, noted that after a private meeting with George W. Bush in the Blue Room – the two men spent twenty minutes alone – he emerged with the appearance of someone who had changed. He had assured Bush that he would support an attack on al-Qaeda and the Taliban in Afghanistan, and was given an assurance – the American decision had been taken at Camp David four days earlier – that Iraq was a question for another day. But afterwards, some of those closest to him recognised it as a turning point. In his own mind, Blair would find it hard to turn back.

That evening, he listened to Bush addressing both Houses of Congress, and got a standing ovation just for being there. 'Thank you, friend,' said Bush from the rostrum in the House of Representatives.

Everyone knew that preparations for war would be beginning, because most Americans expected nothing less than military retaliation, somewhere, sometime. Those with long memories spoke of Pearl Harbor, six decades earlier, and the day that Franklin D. Roosevelt said would live in infamy. Targets, costs, military objectives and the huge risks were all subsumed into a public cry for revenge. Yet bubbling up through the defiant language, promising that the perpetrators would be found and punished, there were plenty of signs of anxiety at the prospect of another military adventure. Too many had not ended well.

A couple of months after Blair met Bush in the White House, before the agonies of the run-up to the Iraq invasion took a grip, it made sense to make an American trip that didn't begin and end in Washington. There would be plenty of time for that, and for the inevitable festival of diplomacy at the UN in New York, where Bush would surely try to get backing for whatever he chose to do in the coming months, or years, and where Blair would have to decide how far his commitment should stretch, perhaps how much his government could take. That autumn, with the images from ground zero still vivid in everyone's minds, the smoke and dust and rubble having changed the face of New York for ever, I wanted to shake up the mood, and experience a few days with people at home, away from the politics of terror and war. There was a good place to go, and an obvious time, when I hoped there would be very little political talk, and not too many arguments about war. I wanted to leave that behind for a few days.

The experience was an interlude that remains for me a passage of brightness in the dark after 9/11.

In November, I spent Thanksgiving in New England. The six states in the north-east corner capture for me much of the best of America. Their sense of history and civic tradition – the proud small-town democracy that means more there than in any other part of the country – gives New Hampshire or Vermont or Massachusetts a rich flavour. Drive north out of New York and within a couple of hours you start to pass through towns and villages that were established before independence, and the white churches on village greens, the Pilgrim history that's everywhere in graveyards, on street signs and in place names, give these parts a beguiling personality, with certainties that – even in late 2001 – were surely still secure. The townships in the hills still resonate with the physical echoes of their history; they've resisted more urban desolation than most; Yankee families still speak of little patches of land grabbed happily from George III; many people still carry a route map of the Revolutionary War in their heads. It has never lost its lure for me, whether on a windy Cape Cod shore or in the gentle folds of the Berkshires, in summer or winter, in the hills or by the sea. I had never spent Thanksgiving there, however, and I knew that for many families, less than three months after the cataclysm, this American homecoming would have greater significance for most people than they'd known before. This is the moment in the year when people with no family find they're offered a hearth for the celebration dinner, when old friendships are renewed, travelling children come home and the generations sit down together.

The national celebration of the first settlers' harvests, with its roots in seventeenth-century New England, was turned into a national holiday by Abraham Lincoln in 1863, in a decree that called on people to step outside themselves on the last Thursday of each November and give thanks for the prosperity that had come their way, with family and with strangers too. Though the Civil War was at its height, with characteristic grace he added 'peace' as a blessing they should celebrate. Every year, it's the moment to find America looking at itself.

So to Tamworth, New Hampshire. My New York friends Ted Smyth and Mary Breasted have a summer home there, and they suggested that if I wanted to taste a real Thanksgiving, Tamworth would deliver. It lies in wooded country in a granite bowl just south of the White Mountains, which rise to more than 6,000ft, and the hamlets that surround the township have looked for generations much as they do now. The celebrations were sure to follow the usual pattern; life had to go on.

I drove west from Portland, Maine, and within two hours drew up at the Tamworth Inn. I rang Peggy Johnson, whom I'd been told would sort me out, and then, thanks to an embarrassing mishap, I got to know the town quite well in less than an hour. There was no danger of sinking into a mournful post-9/11 mood, because the weekend began comically. My rental car had a locking system that was far enough ahead of its time to cause me some confusion. How precisely it happened I can't remember, but I found myself marooned on Main Street with the keys to the car locked securely in the boot. I had arranged a few local visits – a turkey farm was the first stop, for Thanksgiving reasons – but it seemed now as if nothing was going to happen. The car was impenetrable, and the turkey farm more than a mile away. I would also be late for the rehearsals for the town play in the little theatre round the corner. To put the tin lid on proceedings, my phone was inside the car (although, unbeknown to me, it had already been rendered useless by the granite mass of the hills around). Tamworth then revealed itself.

My friend of twenty minutes, Peggy, hoisted the storm cones. From one of the two stores – not the other one, which is called The Other Store – came a key for a similar-looking car. The key, of course, was sitting in an unlocked car – a standing rebuke to the suspicious visitor from London. It didn't work. But Dan, the police officer, was on his way. Meanwhile, we went into the town hall, outside which the stricken car sat, and inside which we passed through a door bearing the legend 'Town Clerk and Tax Collector'. This was where the town government resided, under three – only three – 'selectmen', chosen each year at a town meeting in which Tamworth turns itself for a day, like many places across New England, into a Greco-Yankee city state, sorting everything out in a cheering moment of direct democracy. A new selectman joins the town government, to replace the one whose three-year term is over. It goes round and round, as it has since sometime in the middle of the eighteenth century.

Fascinating, but not the answer to the armoured car, which had now turned into a safe-cracker's nightmare. Dan Poirier, the police officer, had brought a bendy piece of plastic, possibly confiscated from a housebreaker, with which he was attacking the windows. A minor crowd was gathering at the street corners, eddying round the scene while managing to be unobtrusive. Scott, the local forester, came along. He had various bars and gadgets in his truck, but nothing that wouldn't leave Dollar Rent-A-Car wanting a large refund, or possibly a replacement car.

The pace was quickening. The play rehearsal was about to start. A teacher arrived. He was Richard Posner, from Essex back home. He and his wife ran an alternative school, in Peggy's house. The children coming to the play rehearsal milled around him.

'Why here?' I asked him.

'Look around you. Why not?' he said.

The kids wondered how to get into the car. They poked and prodded along with Dan. The shop door jangled as people came out to look. Cars slowed down even more than usual as they tootled along Main Street. The librarian was wheeling a cartload of books packed in old whiskey boxes back from the store to her renovated building (the Cook Library, 1895) and she paused to sympathise.

The bell on the Congregational Church, which makes all its white boards shake once every hour, began to boom. There wouldn't be time to get the turkeys before the curtain went up at the rehearsal.

Then came Jerry, summoned from a garage not far away. He opened a burglar's dream box of tools. Lying before us were coat hangers, plastic rods, wires of all sorts, wooden plungers and sticks, and many bits of string, together with implements that looked as if they were a job lot from the last dentist to leave Tamworth. He began to fiddle and jiggle, and Dan the policeman went off on his rounds, tactfully avoiding the skilful denouement. Word had spread. When Jerry sprang the door and the alarm hooted for several minutes to inform all of Tamworth that the deed was done, it was as if the whole thing had been a rehearsal for the rehearsal.

We went to the turkey farm, on Turkey Street (where else?), where 640 corpses were lined up in neat, respectful rows ready for the town's fridges, and then set off for the theatre, pausing only to hear the story of a wild mink that in the course of the previous evening had savaged two innocent ducks (before their appointed time at Christmas) and to be told all about the town doctor who died without issue, having led a quiet life like his doctor father before him, but was found to have left $16 million in his will, a good portion of which came back to the town in new building, community enterprises and lots of white paint, one of which outcomes was the refurbishment of the theatre (1931), where even now the children of Tamworth were being transformed into cockney urchins for the annual production of *A Christmas Carol*.

They were sorting out the door to the office of Scrooge and Marley, making sure it would open properly in the first scene. There was a moment to think. Tamworth had shown itself already to be a warm and confident community, a close and easy place where after an hour or so at the soda fountain in The Other Store or on the creaky boards of the lounge in the Tamworth Inn you could sense a genuine tranquillity. The woodsmoke rose straight into the sky, the last of the fall leaves crackled underfoot, birds skittered along the riverbank, and from Turkey Street a procession of carcasses made its dignified progress to the kitchens of the townsfolk, ready for Thanksgiving Day itself, which had turned the roads coming north from Boston and west from Maine into a crawling homeward pilgrimage.

Then, a surprise. I had talked to Peggy of 11 September, of course. Katie at The Other Store had a cousin who'd been in the World Trade Center, and had got away from the second tower just in time. Everyone knew someone who knew someone. They spoke of people who'd got news of a death with all the downbeat horror of a telegram delivered in another era about battles far away. People here had been part of the national trauma. She said, 'You know, I wonder if we've moved on too quickly.'

It was a piercing shaft. Her tone was poignant, wondering if human beings were getting too good at managing the recovery from horror.

There had been much talk over the ten weeks of a country that wouldn't be cowed by terrorism. The ubiquitous wayside pulpits urged resolution in the face of attack (though one just outside Tamworth did say, boldly, 'Pray For Our Enemies') and the natural urge was to celebrate community and democracy – the business of not being done down by terrorism. But moving on 'too quickly'? Under the confidence of places such as Tamworth, which especially at Thanksgiving time can cling to the old ways and values that endure down the generations, there was a fear that the deep shocks of New York and Washington would be absorbed almost too efficiently, at least by adults. For children it was different. One 10-year-old put it like this: 'It's scary. I don't really understand why. I'm scared every morning.' Her friend, eleven, said she still wondered how it was that people in other countries who were probably just like her parents could do what they did to the people who died. They spoke openly about the apprehension that they thought was maybe too often concealed by their parents and grandparents.

Peg Custer was the rector of the little Episcopal church, St Andrew's-in-the-Valley, and she had glimpses of that fear. Getting her turkeys ready for the drop-in Thanksgiving dinner in the church hall, for people who didn't want to be alone, she spoke of churning anxiety. 'People say to me, as a priest, that they have a strong sense of the unknown, and it scares them. I've had to counsel many people with real fears. It goes deep.' You couldn't have a conversation for more than a few minutes without evidence of that insistent uncertainty breaking the surface. Christine at the Tamworth Inn: 'It's been a bad, bad time for every one of us.' Irene at the Whittier Store: 'I just hope it turns people back to community and family. We need it. There's been awful sadness here. Awful.' Everyone said they had never expected to be under attack; but they knew that now they were.

Under the bubbling bonhomie of Thanksgiving lay a lake of anxiety. Peggy's fear about dealing with it too easily, too quickly, was really a concern that its presence could not be acknowledged openly enough. Its existence couldn't be denied, but the pressure to return to a triumphant normality as evidence of victory over evil might cause it to be pushed out of mind as a deliberate act of defiance. That would not be right.

On the edge of town was a higgledy-piggledy electric sign, the letters spelling out a birthday greeting to Robin (twenty-six) and also announcing to passers-by, 'We Will Prevail'. It caught the ambiguity of the moment. Hold to your course; but this could be war. As the families of Tamworth lit their candles and drew together at the festive table the next day, there was no escaping the truth. Take the Watkins clan, clustering together at their ancestral cabin on Lake Chocorua, under the witch's hat of the pointy mountain where the Indian chief of that name is said to have flung himself from the peak to deny the advancing white men his scalp, cursing the valley below, where they say nothing grew for a generation afterwards.

Their table represented Thanksgiving at its best. Grandparents, children, aunts, uncles, cousins, friends, a student from Beijing studying nearby and busy falling in love with New England, two Nepalese friends, a German student, an in-law from Bradford, England, having fun – but talking about the war, too. Where would it end? Was it possible, John Watkins said from the head of the table, to hope that good might come out of it all? Could a greater understanding of the outside world come to Americans? They agonised, even as the festive bird and the squashes and relishes and special family recipes for green tomatoes and onions did their rounds, and everyone dug into bowls of black beans and gleaming peppers and attacked a mountain of potatoes, with pumpkin pie to come. This was a celebration with a melancholy undercurrent breaking a surface that, everyone knew, wouldn't settle.

Down on the lake, where e. e. cummings and Henry James both came for escape, a loon hooted across the water. The night drew in. Lights sparkled in the trees. At the Beechers' house the family celebrated, but a grandfather, who remembered arriving as a GI at Berchtesgaden to clear up after Hitler, wondered if the grand-children playing at his feet were doomed to experience another century of war.

And not far away, at another blazing log fire in another cabin in the woods, Admiral Ralph Weymouth spoke of peace. He first sailed in a US Navy cruiser in 1938, from which he watched bombs falling on Barcelona. More than thirty years later, after Vietnam and a couple of decades of gnawing disillusion, he became a star of Veterans For Peace and still, in his eighties, was speaking with the glittering eye of a believer. He described the Middle East tragedy with a weary familiarity, spoke of hope that people would emerge from the horrors of 11 September and its aftermath with a newly fashioned commitment to say 'never again'. He doubted it, but he was doing his best.

Everywhere there were pinprick reminders that behind the cele-bration was the unknown. At St Andrew's-in-the-Valley the diners were asked before raising a fork to name one thing for which they could be thankful that day – the kind of exercise that is so nat-ural to most Americans and so embarrassing to non-Americans. More than one said, with real feeling: 'Still being here. Just being here.' This wasn't melodrama, but the still, small voice of reason. Everyone believed there was still much to fear. Anthrax? There was a scare on about parcels of white powder being sent in the mail. War? Another attack? People shivered.

Tamworth was itself and not an emblem of the whole country – although it had more poverty than the casual glance suggested, and a drug problem that lay just under the surface, it had little of the churning despair that afflicted urban America – but it exhibited the electricity of the moment in its own way. In the the-atre – 'Dickens is better than Neil Simon, for me,' said the man

playing Scrooge, proudly – they romped. By its lakes, they treasured the placid life. In its community, they played. The women,
taking their cue from the Women's Institute 'Full Monty' calendar
back home, had made an arty version of their own, with tasteful
shots of twelve Tamworth nudes (spanning at least five decades, I
guessed, although I didn't ask) made decent by strewn branches
and flowers, carefully placed babies, an artist's easel and, in one
special case, a flute. 'I'm June,' said Amy Berrier – for that was her
month in the calendar – when I went to see her. I almost said that
I didn't recognise her with her clothes on, but in Tamworth that
was already an old joke.

I decided that Peggy's nagging worry that too much from that
year might be put behind them too quickly – which arose from a
determined effort to face the truth squarely – wouldn't come to pass.
No one had forgotten; no one would let it go. Children were asking
questions; grandparents were finding ways of avoiding answers and
running out of time. People who worked in New York, or whose
children did, had moments that weekend when they looked out
towards the trees, and away from other eyes. No one knew what
these months promised, at home or on a battlefield. They knew,
however, that they were on a journey, and led by others.

You can never be in New England without thinking of Robert
Frost, its poet. On that trip I drove to the place where he lived for
a while in New Hampshire, near the woods – 'lovely, dark and
deep' – where, on a snowy evening, he said that he had many miles
to go before he slept. He described the things in that landscape and
among these people that lasted. In his poem 'The Bonfire', he wrote:

> Haven't you heard what we have lived to learn?
> Nothing so new – something we had forgotten:
> War is for everyone, for children too.
> I wasn't going to tell you and I mustn't.
> The best way is to come up hill with me
> And have our fire and laugh and be afraid.

Laughter and fear summed up that Thanksgiving weekend pretty
well. Family, companionship, warmth in a place where everyone

could remember the gift of security. But running through it, in every family and among each group of friends, the certain knowledge that the new century promised danger.

In the year that followed, a course was set in a series of meetings between Bush and Blair and a prolonged transatlantic argument about the value of such intelligence as was available from Iraq, which turned out to be rather less than the most rigorous proponents of war wanted, and much thinner than they expected. The political fever at home was high; in the United States the atmosphere in the months before the invasion was, on the surface, less troubling to the administration. For me, paying several visits in that period, the march to war was marked by a few memorable encounters, especially in Washington and New York.

At the end of a snowy day in Washington, out at Andrews Air Force Base about half an hour's drive from the city, Tony Blair was drinking tea and talking about George W. Bush. It was the last day of January 2003 and he'd spent much of it in the White House. I asked him what he'd say to people at home who were accusing him of being led too easily into war against Saddam Hussein by an American president to whom he was in thrall. He said that people who thought like that should realise that the truth was worse than they thought. 'If George Bush wasn't raising these questions, I'd be raising them myself.'

He spoke with determination, knowing that there was a timetable for war and that the effort at the United Nations to get a second Security Council resolution on Iraq was starting to look hopeless. The resolution that had been passed unanimously by the Security Council in November, UN 1441, said that Iraq was in material breach of obligations it had given to the UN but, with the Russians and the French determined to ensure that a failure by Saddam to comply was not an inevitable trigger for war, Britain, as a co-sponsor of the resolution, had to say before the vote that no 'automaticity' – authority for an invasion – was built into 1441. The Security Council would have to be consulted again about what measures to take. Sir Jeremy Greenstock, the British ambassador, added, 'We would expect the Security Council then to meet its responsibilities.'

Now, in January, Blair was in Washington to try to get Bush's support for a second resolution that would go further, and give him the authority at home to argue that war would only come with explicit approval from the UN. But at the White House, he failed to get that support.

The scene, described to me later, was intriguing. Bush and Blair had spent time together and the president, taking longhand notes in pencil, knew what Blair wanted. But as they came downstairs from the private quarters on the first floor to face a news conference in the East Room, Bush's press secretary, Ari Fleischer, took fright. Hearing what the president intended to say he suggested that it would be better not to talk about a second resolution. After all, wasn't it implicit in everything administration officials had been saying anyway? There was no need to go further. The British officials present concluded that he simply didn't want to hear evening news programmes telling a story of Bush succumbing to UN pressure, because that was not how it was meant to be. Condoleezza Rice, the national security adviser, was on Blair's side, but Karl Rove, Bush's political pollster and enforcer, was not. He nodded in agreement with Fleischer: say nothing about another resolution.

If Blair had argued at that moment, would Bush have changed his mind? Probably. He owed Blair a great deal because he allowed the president to say to critics that there was an international coalition determined to be tough with Saddam. America was not planning to go to war alone, and the prime minister who had found just the right words in the aftermath of 9/11 was the most admired of allies.

As someone who was there described it afterwards, 'All he had to say was – George, I need this.' He didn't.

Out at Andrews, Alastair Campbell, Blair's director of communications, was hurrying him along. He said there was fog rolling in, and if Blair didn't get out to the plane quickly he might be marooned in Washington, with the House of Commons waiting for a statement the next day that he wouldn't be there to give. This all sounded unlikely – the fog didn't seem as dense as that to me – and I realised later that, because of what he had witnessed in the White

House, Campbell was anxious to avoid too much second-resolution talk, and wanted to get Blair away from a microphone. Sometimes, that was his job. The fog helped.

The problem may have been that Bush was simply unaware of the parliamentary atmosphere in London. Blair seemed to him not only resolute, but secure. At home, it felt different. Two weeks after that visit an anti-war demonstration in London attracted a vast crowd. The organisers claimed 2 million people took part, the police thought it was 750,000, but whatever the truth about the numbers it was huge. For most of them, the Bush administration seemed a warmongering lot. The truth was more complicated.

Behind the facade of unity in the face of terrorism, a struggle unfolded about the scale and the timing of an Iraq invasion. General Colin Powell, secretary of state, was one of the leading voices in Washington for caution. He understood the likely cost of war, and for him it was important to use Blair's unstinting credentials as an ally not to press the case for an early invasion but to help him confront the hawkish voices around him, especially those of Cheney, Paul Wolfowitz (number two to Donald Rumsfeld at the Pentagon in the Bush first term) and one of his own under-secretaries, John Bolton, who would enjoy a brief comeback years later, long after the Iraq withdrawal, as Donald Trump's national security adviser. Powell had a running conversation with his opposite number in London, the foreign secretary Jack Straw, which at important moments meant they spoke almost daily, on one day alone eight times. When I provided one morsel from these conversations in a book in 2004 (*The Accidental American: Tony Blair and the Presidency*) there was an instant and predictable denial from the State Department. I had expected it.

They could hardly admit that the secretary of state had described a group that included the vice president, Dick Cheney, as 'fucking crazies'.

However, from information that I had good reason not to doubt, I knew it to be true. No one with the slightest contact with the White House circle could doubt it, either. They knew that Powell, who had served as chairman of the Joint Chiefs of Staff under the president's father during the first Gulf War in 1991, was infuriated, as an instinctive military man, by the ideological certainties that others wanted to apply to day-to-day negotiations and military planning. It was clear in London that he didn't want to embark on a full-scale invasion of Iraq without unambiguous authorisation from the UN, and that his position was close to the British prime minister's. Blair had understood from the start that, however much he was convinced about the rectitude of a confrontation with Saddam Hussein, he wanted to work through the UN, not least because his own government might fall apart if he didn't. For the neocons (although Bolton preferred the simple description 'pro-American'), driven by the belief that America's destiny must lie in its own hands, the UN represented an impediment, an obstruction in the exercise of foreign policy.

When Bolton served briefly as American ambassador to the UN from 2005, he said – tastelessly, you may think, in the city of 9/11 – that if the top ten floors of the UN building were removed (they housed the senior officials in the secretariat and the peacekeeping department) it wouldn't make the slightest difference to anything. That was a harbinger of the contempt of the Trump era that he would help to stoke up before and after his brief tenure as national security adviser. His ideological ferocity and Trump's wayward decision-making were never going to blend, and when he left in a rancorous parting in 2019, he and the president were not even able to agree whether he had resigned or been fired. The drooping curtain of Bolton's moustache, tended ever more carefully through the years like the favourite corner of a maturing garden, has always reminded people of Ned Flanders, the evangelical neighbour of Bart Simpson in the cartoon world of Springfield, who always wants to do the right thing for the town. But that is misleading. Bolton's career has been dedicated to the proposition that there is no more miserable creature on earth than the 'do-gooder'. No Ned Flanders he.

Visiting a number of leading neoconservatives over those years, I became aware of the fervour with which they despised any form of politics that didn't spring from unbending ideological conviction. In more than one cheerful and hospitable encounter with Richard Perle, the hawk of hawks, I recall his gentle soft-spokenness as he

poured coffee in the shadow of the trees in his garden, simultaneously expressing relish for some approaching conflict, which he
thought would come along sooner rather than later. His deep-set
dark eyes would watch you with something like pity if he suspected
you weren't responding with appropriate enthusiasm.

He was one of the intellectual creators of the neocon movement, having been a member of the group around the conservative
Democratic senator Henry 'Scoop' Jackson in the late 1960s and
early '70s who found themselves ideologically marooned, because
they combined a belief in some liberal social values – drawn from
Roosevelt's New Deal era – with a rigorous anti-Soviet posture that
dominated their thinking to such an extent that it could never fit a
'progressive' profile. Electrified by the Reagan years, they became
the vanguard of a movement that tried to forge a new foreign
policy doctrine for conservatives, with which to confront liberal
internationalism.

One of Perle's deputies when he served in the Pentagon in the
Reagan years was Frank Gaffney, who became a neocon firebrand, specialising in assaults on Islam, on which subject he was
almost impossible to outflank. Despite Perle's protection, he lasted
at the Pentagon for less than nine months, because his opposition
to the flow of policies in the Middle East under successive administrations made him, even as a member of a Reagan cast of proud
outsiders, just too much of a troublemaker. As an illustration
of the spirit of the neocons, it's worth remembering his dispute
with Grover Norquist, whose exotic name is little known outside America.

Norquist is a jovial, rumpled man, who believes that America
would be a better place if tax rates, and the place of government in
people's lives, reverted to the way things were in, roughly speaking,
the 1890s. I remember a car journey with him – he'd kindly offered
to drop me off at my hotel on his way out of town – in the course
of which he said that it would be a good thing if tax rates were
about what they had been before Teddy Roosevelt was elected in
1900, with the federal government funding a bit of defence and not
much else. In other words, twentieth-century forms of government
should be dismantled. It is unwise to get into a discussion with him

about healthcare, for example, unless you believe that only a free market in doctors and drugs will do, and that anything else takes you on a socialist roller-coaster to the netherworld. You'll never find a middle way with Grover. To his supporters, he's Mr Valiant-for-Truth; to his critics, he's nuts. Eventually, his proposals on tax would capture Republicans on Capitol Hill to an extent that he probably never expected, and he basked in the adoration of the Tea Party movement. Looking back to the early years of the century, in the ideological battles in the conservative movement that flowed just under the surface of the Bush administration, you can detect a clear signal of the feelings that would allow Donald Trump to succeed more than a decade later. In the conservative movement, people spoke about ideological purity but the real test was in never giving way. Serious argument was less important than victory, and the whole business had the flavour of a seventeenth-century religious war. Belief was everything.

Frank Gaffney, for example, didn't think that Grover Norquist's position on tax was radical enough, though it went much further than anything Barry Goldwater had said four decades before. And why didn't Norquist subscribe to the complete neocon vision of America in the world? There was a reason for Gaffney's ire, which eventually showed itself. He accused Norquist, whose wife is a Palestinian Muslim, of being in league with the radical Muslim Brotherhood, and therefore part of 'an influence operation [that] is contributing materially to the defeat of our country', which came quite close to an accusation of treason. The American Conservative Union, with which they were both involved, got itself into a terrible tangle. Gaffney was eventually banned from its events, until he was reinstated by the intervention of Bolton. Years later, in the year Trump was elected, a Gaffney ally challenged Norquist's place on the board of the National Rifle Association, to which every conservative pays dutiful homage, on the grounds that it had been infiltrated by anti-American Islamic extremists. To any outsider this would have the flavour of a comic opera, perhaps a Marx Brothers romp, if it didn't involve some people who have the ear of presidents. It's hard to go through the story of such family fist fights without bringing to mind the kind of determined factionalism that defines many far-left groups and sends them into regular tailspins.

When Blair and his officials had to deal with the Iraq question, therefore, they knew that they were dealing with some members of the administration, and a wider circle of neocons, who saw the cause – irrespective of the status of intelligence about alleged weapons of mass destruction – as the opportunity they'd long cherished. The figure who best represented them – albeit in a style that was soft-spoken and often cheery – was Dick Cheney.

I was given a reliable account of an evening at Cheney's house, where the vice president was having a drink in the evening sunshine with friends in the autumn of 2002, when the Security Council was deep in its argument about where the UN should stand on an invasion if Saddam, as everyone expected, wouldn't budge. The official residence of the vice president is in the grounds of the Naval Observatory next door to the British Embassy on Massachusetts Avenue, but on this occasion Cheney was not expressing fraternal feelings towards his neighbours. He mused over his drink, and expressed frustration at having to try to find a consensus on the Security Council in New York.

'We're only there for Blair. There's no other reason; no justification. We're told we have to do it.'

He and Rumsfeld at the Pentagon wanted to attack Iraq in February. Blair persuaded Bush to stretch the timetable – though the president wouldn't go beyond March because of the difficulties of going to war in the summer heat – in the hope of getting his second resolution. But the British knew that Cheney was not on their side. Throughout the long months of planning he had been the conservative watchman who wanted to make sure that Bush didn't give too much ground.

Just before an important meeting at Camp David in September 2002, where Blair was anxious to get Bush's commitment to a UN process, Cheney made a speech in which he cast doubt on the usefulness of any weapons inspection programme by the UN, which Blair was insisting must be carried through, because he was aware that if there wasn't one, he would face some resignations in his government that might even bring him down. In the days before that meeting one British official who was going to be involved at Camp David got a phone call from a former ambassador from the Clinton era who had access to a private intelligence network. His message was simple. 'Watch out. Cheney's going to be there.'

Sure enough, when Bush and Blair were preparing to talk alone, Cheney settled into a corner chair, immobile, with – as one British official put it to me afterwards – 'that funny little crooked smile on his face'.

Blair got his commitment to American support for UN authorisation, but in turn the American side was now convinced that Blair wouldn't turn back. He wanted the UN involved, but he was also committed to supporting an invasion. The question that interested the Americans (almost as much as it interested his own Cabinet at home) was this: when had he decided?

In April 2002, he'd gone to the Bush family ranch in Crawford, Texas, a place that many people find a touch bleak – it's about 25 miles west of Waco, of massacre fame – but the president loved it. There is still some mystification among those who accompanied Blair there about what passed between the two leaders. Their closest advisers – including Condoleezza Rice – had to leave Bush and Blair alone at the ranch and were taken for a Tex-Mex supper in a raucous restaurant on a strip mall in Crawford, where their evening was interrupted by the arrival of a consignment of embroidered leather cowboy boots, each pair tailored for a particular guest. The British contingent at the table was wondering what Blair was saying back at the ranch, as they tried on their boots.

The condition that Blair believed he succeeded in extracting from Bush at that meeting in return for his support was for a resumption of efforts to bring the Israelis and Palestinians together, which had become moribund. But as one of his officials put it afterwards, 'It was a condition that never became a condition.' The White House didn't deliver, but Blair was already too far down the track to change course. By the time he went back in the summer, the Americans were convinced he'd stay the course.

Blair himself argues that it's wrong to imagine that Bush was set on war at that point, though the preparations were being made. In our conversation in the Downing Street garden in 2004, he said, 'It is absolutely right that throughout the whole of 2002 the Americans were looking at – and we were looking at – what happens if there is no way of dealing with this issue other than military action. What is not true is that the Americans had decided to take military action come what may. That is not true. I happen to know that, from my conversation with President Bush all the way through.' Even some of those close to the two men will never agree about whether that was true or not.

When war came – after all the rows over intelligence, the controversial British dossier about weapons of mass destruction, the ups and downs of the UN weapons inspections, the political upheavals in Blair's government and his party – the question still puzzled some of those who had been with him through these meetings. They were observing a formidably close personal relationship between president and prime minister, but was there still a lack of understanding across the Atlantic? Did Bush underestimate Blair's political problems at home, and did Blair fail to grasp fully the depth of the neoconservative desire to attack (which was certainly greater than Bush's own)?

The episode reveals how much was still hazy, even in an alliance that could hardly have been closer. Bush and Blair spoke often, and they liked to talk alone. For many months, Alastair Campbell conducted a daily video conference call with his White House opposite numbers – nothing so intimate nor sustained had happened before – and Jack Straw and Colin Powell were probably talking more often than any secretary of state and foreign secretary ever had. Yet it was not until about ten days before the invasion that Bush made the surprising offer to Blair – perhaps realising fully for the first time the depth of his political troubles – that he could keep British troops out of the coalition if he felt it necessary. When the phone call came, Blair said, 'No thanks.' He'd committed himself, and wasn't changing his mind.

This convinces some of those around him that throughout the eighteen months following 9/11, although he certainly wanted UN authorisation and worked for it, and did harbour some vain hope that Saddam would crumble and let the weapons inspectors do their work, he was determined not to step back. In the view of one senior figure who was there throughout, there were times when Blair's commitment seemed even more obvious, perhaps more visceral, than Bush's own.

The phone call came around the time that President Chirac of France made it clear – as had been obvious for months – that France would not back any explicit UN support for invasion. The UN effort was over.

The French role in the Iraq affair revealed how strange its relationship remained with the United States. The suspicions about transatlantic power, embedded in Paris since Gaullist days, were no surprise, but it was remarkable how quickly many Americans identified France immediately after 9/11 as an unreliable ally, summed up in the mockery of the conservative *National Review* magazine, which coined a phrase that promptly entered the public discourse, picturing the French as 'cheese-eating surrender monkeys'. The feelings were reciprocal.

I recall one of Chirac's senior diplomats entertaining a dinner table after an outburst of anti-French feeling in Washington. A congressman was demanding in a piece of theatrics that French fries be taken off the menu on Capitol Hill and replaced by 'freedom fries'. The diplomat said that this was disturbing. He had even heard that some New York restaurants were removing French wines from their lists. People were drinking wine from Oregon! Even, *quelle horreur*, from Pennsylvania. Then the punchline. 'Things are so bad that I have heard a terrible rumour going round the Quai d'Orsay that the president himself may even stop reading Proust!'

In the long weeks at the UN, those of us who were trying to chart the course of the negotiations became familiar with three particular poker faces among the permanent representatives who sat on the Security Council. For the British, Sir Jeremy Greenstock, as austere in public as he was jovial in private, who looked like the schoolmaster he'd once been (at Eton); for the Russians, Sergey Lavrov, later Vladimir Putin's foreign minister, wearing the heavy grey features of a reincarnated Andrei Gromyko from Cold War crises long ago; for the French, the graciously subtle and perfectly dressed Jean-Marc de la Sablière, former diplomatic adviser to Chirac at the Élysée Palace who had been sent to the UN after 9/11 to make sure that France did not acquiesce in war unless the threat from Saddam could be shown to be overwhelming (which they never believed it would be). With the Americans represented by John Negroponte – whom the others believed was given so little freedom of manoeuvre by Washington that he was embarrassingly hobbled in negotiations from the start – they were the figures who, with Kofi Annan, the secretary general, would effectively decide the grounds for war or peace.

Throughout the autumn of 2002, as they came and went from the Security Council Chamber, the British, French and Russian ambassadors seemed to become ever more like caricatures of their own countries, whatever their private thoughts.

Greenstock was the drafter, par excellence, who was meant to find words that could satisfy everyone. Resolution 1441 was the result, passed unanimously, but as 2002 became 2003 it became obvious that the chances of a second resolution – with more cover for Blair – were fading fast. In the hall outside the Security Council Chamber, at the British delegation's HQ, in the watering holes up 3rd Avenue, scepticism was rife. There was great suspicion about the weight that could be given to such intelligence as there was – caution that was later shown to be wise – and the French and the Russians were never going to accept that enough time was being given for UN-sponsored weapons inspections. Dominique de Villepin, the French foreign minister, assailed Colin Powell at a meeting of the Security Council in January, arguing that there was no justification for war. Powell was irritated by Villepin, anyway, because he considered him aloof and arrogant (a view that had many supporters, even in Paris), but thought his behaviour at that meeting was insufferable. In turn, the French thought the Americans were bullies. *Plus ça change* ...

When war did come, on the night of 19 March 2003, most Americans supported it, although the depth of feeling among those who did not was profound. Bush's approval rating, according to Gallup, jumped above 70 per cent, but then began a long decline, interrupted only by a burst of excitement at the capture of Saddam Hussein in December that year.

America had appeared to be united by 9/11, but in truth the

consequential war divided it. Indeed, by the time we all became embroiled in another presidential campaign, Bush's position looked vulnerable. On the Democratic side, the populist governor of Vermont Howard Dean – a social liberal and fiscal conservative – electrified anti-Bush voters with his anti-war rhetoric. But Dean was the latest in a long line of presidential candidates who soared high before the primaries began, only to discover that his waxen wings melted when he met real voters in the polling booth, and to fall back to earth. It didn't take long for Dean to dive.

One day, in an old theatre in Manchester, New Hampshire, I watched him being introduced to a big crowd by Martin Sheen, who was then playing President Bartlet in *The West Wing*, and the trouble was that Sheen appeared to be a more palatable choice than the candidate, having more bottom. Dean seemed to be driven by an ego that was just too obvious. So it proved. He lost New Hampshire – though he had expected, since he'd served as governor in a neighbouring state, that he might be favoured. Localism in New England, however, sometimes works the other way.

In any case, he'd already shown that he had feet of clay. In the Iowa caucuses in January, the former front-runner slithered to third. That would not have mattered much in itself, but he demonstrated on the night of the results that if he'd ever had good political judgement, it had deserted him just when he needed it most. In his concession speech, promising in traditional fashion to fight on and prevail, he whooped and squeaked so much that it became known on the spot as the 'I Have a Scream' speech, which was cruel but funny. The result was that by the time he got to New Hampshire, where the veteran Massachusetts senator John Kerry crushed him easily, his bright star had faded to a modest twinkle. The Dean phenomenon was over.

Kerry's campaign leading to November was notable for one ugly development, one of the most effective smears in modern American politics (although there are admittedly many competitors for that title). Clearly, at a time of war, Kerry was fortunate in having a distinguished service record in Vietnam to present to voters: it meant that in engaging in constructive criticism of the Iraq War for which public support was on the wane – and he refused to take a simple anti-war stance – he could not be accused of a lack of concern for servicemen and women, nor of 'anti-Americanism'. However, a group calling themselves Swift Boat Veterans for Truth tried to change that.

Raising a vast amount of money – at least $8 million, from well-known Republican donors – they challenged Kerry's account of his military service, during which he'd served in a Swift Boat unit in Vietnam, claiming that he misrepresented his own role and that his criticism of aspects of that war were unfair, even treacherous. Kerry fought back as hard as he could – enlisting many former comrades who said he was the victim of a smear – but some of the mud stuck. It was a classic attack of the 'no smoke without fire' variety that evidently convinced some voters that Kerry was not all he seemed. Such independent evidence as there was left little doubt in any neutral's mind that he was unfairly demonised. It was, however, a harbinger of campaigns to come, an indication of how the relentless repetition of a charge, however baseless, can prove impossible to dispel.

Kerry did come close in the end, Bush prevailing in the electoral college with thirty-one states to Kerry's nineteen, but only winning the popular vote by a narrow margin. Indeed, on the morning of polling day in Washington, rumours were circulating among Democratic Party operatives that the ground was shifting their way. At a lunch with Democrat friends, where their phones were buzzing with rumours of happy early exit polls, there was discussion of who would be getting which job in the new administration. One person present was hoping to be appointed as an ambassador in an interesting embassy. It was one of the better lessons I have had in the dangers of listening to scuttlebutt on election day (or indeed in the days just beforehand): it's always wise to wait. By the time I prepared to go on the air in the evening on BBC Radio 4 to present the overnight results programme, those companions were already aware that their expectations had evaporated, and that their belief that Bush had returned to Texas in gloom, there to contemplate the end of his presidency, was hopelessly premature.

There was a typical jumble of campaign memories in that year – chasing General Wesley Clark to Las Vegas, when he still thought he had a chance of becoming a Democratic general-president;

catching up with Kerry outside a fire station in New Hampshire, where the night was so cold I had to get someone else to hold my microphone; finally managing to gatecrash a Karl Rove briefing for Young Republicans in a New York restaurant and blocking the door so that he was compelled to give an (uninformative) interview in order to escape; visiting the Florida county where stories of the 'hanging chads' of 2000 were still sending a tremor through politics; discovering again that for all his reputation abroad as a president without fluency, Bush on the stump – in an aircraft hangar in Georgia or a field in rural Pennsylvania at midnight – was still an amiable, formidable force.

But a pair of linked memories stands out. At the Democratic convention in Boston in the summer, I joined my old friend Rhod Sharp for one of his *Up All Night* programmes on BBC Radio 5 Live. We were high up in the auditorium, near the roof, where we could see that everybody down below was having a good time. Carole King had played the night before; Ted Kennedy had given a barnstorming welcome to Boston – 'my hometown' – and there was a sense of optimism among Democrats. Then, on the air with Rhod, we watched together the keynote speech delivered on the Tuesday night by a young Senate candidate from Illinois – propelled unexpectedly into a winnable race because a sex scandal had forced the Republicans to change candidates – of whom many Democrats had never heard. The major TV networks didn't bother to broadcast the speech live. Later, they wished they had, because it was remarkable. For some of us it was the first time we'd heard the name. Barack Obama.

He coined a phrase that would be the title of his second book, the audacity of hope. And if Democrats – divided by the war, aware of Bush's stubborn and genial appeal – left Boston with lively tread, it was because of that speech.

'It's the hope of slaves sitting around a fire singing freedom songs. The hope of immigrants setting out for distant shores. The hope of a young naval lieutenant bravely patrolling the Mekong Delta. The hope of a mill worker's son who dares to defy the odds. The hope of a skinny kid with a funny name who believes that America has a place for him, too.'

The linked memory was of meeting that skinny kid in Chicago a couple of months later. I remember the date very well because earlier I was in Cleveland, Ohio, and took the chance to spend an hour in the Rock & Roll Hall of Fame where my producer, Gavin Allen, and I were given a piece of sad news by a man at the front desk, who realised we were from London. John Peel, our BBC colleague and one of the most original broadcasters of our time, had died. It was a strangely appropriate place to hear that melancholy news, surrounded by Elvis's sparkly jumpsuits, Lead Belly's guitars and drum kits that you could imagine having a life of their own. But we had to head on to Chicago, where we had a date at Jesse Jackson's church on the South Side.

We found it, with a little difficulty, and discovered inside that a large group of campaign workers were about to go out leafleting, a pleasingly old-fashioned bit of campaigning. They were getting their briefing from the candidate, who introduced his wife and family, and said he'd be heading into the streets too, with his bag of Vote Obama stickers, just like any old canvasser. He had time for an interview, but he requested politely that it should be done outside. Fine, but I wondered why. Soon it became obvious. In those days he couldn't get through a ten-minute conversation without a cigarette. So we stood in the street as he puffed away, and he spoke about the prospect of Washington, how much he had to learn, but about how he believed that the theme of his speech at the convention was the message that people wanted. They needed hope of escape, a little glimpse of fulfilment.

We said goodbye. Afterwards, I sat with Jesse Jackson, and when we had recorded something and I had switched off the microphone, I asked him more about Obama. He was a brilliant speaker, certainly, and a person of obvious intelligence and charm. But why did Jackson think he was something so out of the ordinary? He spoke for a while about his own cohort from the 1960s, the people who marched with Martin Luther King – Ralph Abernathy, Andy Young and the rest – and were now getting on in years. 'It can't be one of us,' he said. 'That generation can't produce an African American president now. There's too much history, heavy history, and anyway time has passed.'

I was listening with a natural scepticism. 'The skinny kid with a

funny name' was almost certainly going to become an Illinois senator. But a president? Steady on.

Jackson was in a benign, happy mood. He shook his head.

'Watch him,' he said. 'This is the one.'

CHAPTER 7

TWO RACES OF A LIFETIME

In many places across America, in cities and small towns and hamlets, on planes and trains, in bars and diners, I can hardly count the conversations in which I was told that neither Barack Obama nor Donald Trump could be elected president of the United States. Eight years apart, the message was the same. Their campaigns, so it was said, were phantoms that would dissolve into nothing, because nature wouldn't permit anything else. Each man was carrying a burden that was too heavy. I remember a locker room in a Minor League Baseball stadium in upstate New York, where the coach warned me politely and quietly in 2008 that I should not take seriously what his players told me about how they would vote. They might talk respectfully about Obama into a microphone, but at the polling place they would not vote for a black man, full stop. 'Not yet,' he said, shaking his head. 'Not yet. Believe me.' Eight years later, just after a raucous Republican convention where Trump broke most of the rules of politics in a few wild days, one of the canniest political reporters in America looked me in the eye and said that I needed to understand one fact about the coming election. 'Hillary Clinton could win this one from jail.'

Each of these two candidates, therefore, was entitled to regard election night as a revolutionary event, and they did. Although in the closing weeks of his campaign, Obama's victory, unlike Trump's, had begun to seem to most Americans the likeliest outcome, he was still able to portray it as a moment when people could 'bend the arc of history', as he put it in his victory speech just after midnight in Grant Park in Chicago. 'If there is anyone out there who still doubts that America is a place where all things are possible, who still wonders if the dream of our founders is alive in our time, who still questions the power of our democracy, tonight is your answer.' When Trump claimed his own victory in New York in 2016 he argued that his brash, unorthodox scramble to power, in which the shrewdness of his pollsters and tacticians had been disguised by his blustering style, lifted him above politics to a higher zone than his predecessor had ever occupied.

'As I've said from the beginning, ours was not a campaign, but rather an incredible and great movement made up of millions of hard-working men and women who love their country.'

When he addressed 'those who have chosen not to support me in the past, of which there were a few people ...' the crowd laughed and hooted on cue. He had seen them all off – his detractors, the Republican rivals who had called him coarse and crude, the people who questioned his business acumen and his wealth, and, stretching beyond them into the distance, the dismal crowd who loved Washington and its ways. Bringing these speeches to listeners at home in the early hours of the morning was to wake them up with startling news: the once-impossible had come to pass.

These two campaigns painted vivid colours on the America of the new century. It had come to think itself drained, shaken cold by 9/11 and then frozen by a financial crash seven years later. An age of excess was over, and an era of decline had begun.

Theirs were the arguments that shaped the country for the new century. But Obama was hobbled from the start. He lived his whole time in office under the shadow of the global panic that followed the collapse of Lehman Brothers in mid-September 2008, seven weeks before his election, and all its miserable consequences. The crisis helped him get elected, because Republicans had to shoulder much of the blame, but it weakened his presidency. As voters made up their minds, all Americans were facing up to the truth that in the preceding nine months under George W. Bush, while the Federal Reserve had been trying desperately to pump some life into a jittery economy and to prop up financial institutions that had once seemed secure – guaranteeing to underwrite Bear Stearns, which had teetered on the brink of disaster with $10 trillion in securities promising to go up in smoke if it collapsed – the banks had been playing a life-and-death game of pass the parcel.

Middle-income Americans learned that their mortgages had been contrived and then sold on through financial instruments so complicated that no one fully understood them, invented by algorithmic wizards who didn't seem to care, and certainly hadn't grasped the truth that the very intricacy and cleverness of their inventions concealed from sight an ocean of bad debt that left Wall Street's 'masters of the universe' running around like penniless punters who'd been fleeced in a shell game on a street corner. The certainties of progress were challenged, the pillars of the financial system wobbled, and the new century was bringing in fresh humiliation on every tide.

Americans saw their country back at war in the Middle East, where the news from Afghanistan and especially Iraq wasn't of 'victory' but of spreading chaos, and learned that the financial certainties they'd taken for granted – which moulded their lives through assumptions about housing, healthcare, security at work, college fees for the kids – were no longer reassuring, but had been turned into promises that didn't stand up. At that time, travels across the country revealed a gulf, filled with anger, between those who had always thought they knew what to expect and those on high who were trying to explain why such beliefs were no longer appropriate for a world in which money moved in mysterious ways, but couldn't always deliver the wonders it had promised to perform.

This was the dark background for the two most unexpected and dramatic presidential elections in the lifetime of most Americans, a dizzying swing of the pendulum, perhaps because it was a time from which to look back in anger.

The loss of faith was as profound in its own way as the one experienced by an earlier generation after the Wall Street Crash, who remembered with a sigh in the wreckage of the Depression the post-war optimism and cultural gaiety of the 1920s. F. Scott Fitzgerald chronicled that time in his novels and stories and said that the world just vanished could be conjured up for him in an instant by 'a ghostly rumble among the drums, an asthmatic whisper in the trombones' that swung him back to a hedonistic time of short skirts and jazz and wood alcohol when, through a haze of youthful exuberance, everything seemed destined to get better and better, with no end.

But, he wrote in 1931 in *Echoes of the Jazz Age*:

Somebody had blundered, and the most expensive orgy in history was over. It ended two years ago, because the utter confidence which was its essential prop received an enormous jolt, and it didn't take long for the flimsy structure to settle earthward. And after two years the jazz age seems as far away as the days before the war. It was borrowed time anyhow, the whole upper tenth of a nation living with the insouciance of grand dukes and the casualness of chorus girls. But moralizing is easy now and it was pleasant to be in one's twenties in such a certain and unworried time. Even when you were broke you didn't worry about money, because it was in such profusion around you.

Such reflections came strangely back into focus in the new century, when Obama and Trump appeared as the faces on two sides of the same coin, minted over a decade in a bleak atmosphere of financial troubles. Obama argued that he was the latter-day agent for the old confidence that had surged among black Americans and liberal whites in the 1960s, embedded in the youth culture of those days, and which he swore could be recovered and fulfilled. Didn't you remember that time, and how the prospect of change appeared to be real and close? But he wanted the torch to be picked up by a new generation. The '70s liberals had had their chance. After him, Trump turned it round, flipping the argument. The liberal dream was an illusion and a cruel deception, promising a world that could never be created, and the effort would deliver only betrayal. Better to forget it, he said, and accept that reality was a game of risk. You won or you lost, and that was all. Why not follow him, the man who knew how to play that dirty game?

He said this at his nominating convention: 'I have joined the political arena so that the powerful can no longer beat up on people that cannot defend themselves. Nobody knows the system better than me, which is why I alone can fix it.'

'I alone'? Entering politics to make himself a hero to those who wanted to challenge power? Even to some of his intimates that seemed bold. But he was deliberately raising the stakes from the start. Anyone who challenged him could expect an onslaught. And he was appealing directly to a beloved American stereotype, the man on the white horse who rides into town with guns at the ready, drawn to the fight because people in need are longing for him. And his challenger?

He portrayed Hillary Clinton as the epitome of established power, after eight years by her husband's side in the White House as First Lady and later four years as Obama's secretary of state. He created a dark and devious figure, subservient to mysterious forces, and guilty of 'terrible crimes', which boiled down in Clinton's case to the unwise use of a personal email account, which, when subjected to prolonged investigation by the FBI, revealed no significant breach of national security and little more than run-of-the-mill political tittle-tattle, which couldn't compete with the torrent that issued from Trump's Twitter feed. It was a 'dumb mistake', she told me, and that was all. But candidate Trump told his convention that it was evidence of a dark web of deceit, stretching further than anyone could know. 'Big business, elite media and major donors are lining up behind the campaign of my opponent because they know she will keep our rigged system in place. They are throwing money at her, because they have total control over everything she does. She is their puppet, and they pull the strings.' For Americans with a penchant for conspiracy, this was irresistible.

Voters who experienced these two elections, eight years apart, had never seen the like. The drama of the rise of the first black president gave 2008 an aura that no other contest in living memory could match; and Trump's campaign was the victory of the biggest outsider – the first president in the country's history with no experience of politics or the military at any level – that played out on social media platforms where powerful new forces were at work that were little understood, for example by millions of Facebook users who didn't know that a cheery post urging support for Trump didn't come from some friendly campaigner in Peoria, Illinois, but from a team in St Petersburg, Russia.

All that lay far in the future when Obama began his own quest for office. At the start of his year, 2008, I had a conversation during the first primary in New Hampshire with Joe Klein, who'd been writing about politics for more than thirty years and had a special fascination with the presidential primaries. His attempt to remain anonymous as the author of *Primary Colors*, his 1996 satirical thriller based on Bill Clinton's 1992 campaign, only lasted about six months, because a Shakespeare scholar at Vassar College, Don Foster, produced a devastatingly accurate stylistic analysis of his writing in *Newsweek* that sourced the novel to him, and forced Klein to acknowledge authorship, having previously denied it publicly. The book told an insightful story, exuding an atmosphere of alarm about the modern form of professionalisation in politics, the scene dominated by pollsters and consultants acting as hired guns for candidates – anyone will do if they've got the money – and building campaigns. A prescient piece of fiction. On this occasion, in the New Hampshire snow as we travelled together from an Obama meeting to watch Hillary Clinton speak in a school gymnasium, he said he hoped I realised that this was probably going to be the most absorbing struggle for a presidential nomination that we might ever see.

Two senators vying for the Democratic nomination for president. Hillary Clinton of New York, a former First Lady, steeped in politics from her youth and for much of her party the heir presumptive who had the fire and steel to become the first woman president. But then Obama, elected only in 2004 and with little legislative experience, with a thin national profile. But each of them brimming with political guile.

Klein said that it was clear even at that opening stage that this was going to be a rare contest, probably more intense than any he had witnessed before. I believed him, not least because we already knew that nerves on both sides had been rubbed raw, even before the real campaign had started. The intensity wouldn't spring from the fact that the rival candidates had a close relationship, but from the truth that they didn't.

In Iowa the previous Thursday night, with New Hampshire only five days away, Obama had stormed the Clinton citadel. The result was effectively a draw, but since she had been leading in the national polls throughout the winter and was established as a firm favourite for the nomination, his was a spectacular performance, subtle and cheeky and threatening all at once. The atmosphere on the Clinton plane that left Des Moines late that night bound for Manchester, New Hampshire, was described to me afterwards as 'grimmer than you can imagine'. There was a fight on. Obama would have to be dealt with.

For four days the pair raced from town hall to church, school to shopping mall, in a frenzy of hand-shaking and speaking. Watching Obama early on a Sunday morning in the homely old Palace Theatre, which had been welcoming candidates since the First World War, it was easy to feel the surge that he was beginning to command. His ease and eloquence were bringing out voters, and rousing passion in his campaigners. A middle-aged teacher was sitting beside me. She had travelled to hear him from the north of the state, just by the Canadian border, and I thought there was a danger that even before he had finished, she might have some kind of ecstatic seizure. Such devotion would morph in the course of the primary campaign into a feeling of moral superiority whose power was obvious but which (understandably) infuriated the other side. Obama's team had to cool it as the months went by, although they sometimes succumbed to the temptation not to try.

Yet an hour or two later, listening to Clinton with a crowd of more than 1,000, then watching her take questions for almost as long as she had spoken, happily getting into policy discussions about prescription drugs, healthcare exemptions and immigration, you realised that this was going to be a titanic struggle between two candidates who each had a grip on their supporters and an ability to lift the atmosphere, with words or with argument. They wanted to talk seriously, and to avoid nothing. For those of us tired of routine campaigns (not only in the United States), where listening to limp scripts from weak candidates becomes tedious very quickly, this was exhilarating. They were taking each other on with verve and gusto, and with plenty of sharp jabs. In another year, John Edwards, the persuasive North Carolina senator who'd been John Kerry's vice-presidential running mate in 2004 and who tried to edge through between them, might have seemed a serious contender. But in this company he was easily brushed aside, which was just as well for the Democrats, since not long afterwards his messy private life became a tacky story that ended in court and finished the political career of a previously saintly-sounding senator.

In the run-up to Iowa, when the Clinton team began to panic – late in the day – about being outmanoeuvred, and then through to New Hampshire, the two camps stoked up a good deal of mutual loathing. Even when the candidates were apparently being polite to each other, it was through gritted teeth. On the night after Iowa, they both turned up for a New Hampshire debate at St Anselm College, just outside Manchester. She attacked him for changing his position on healthcare, questioning his credentials as the Man of Change. The gloves were off. When one of the chairs of the debate asked how she felt when voters said Obama was the more likeable of the two, she admitted that it hurt her, and said, 'He's very likeable. I agree with that.' Pause. 'I don't think I'm *that* bad.'

He looked up, and his response seemed intended to be deadly. 'You're likeable enough, Hillary.'

Nobody had any doubt that this was going to be rough. Bill Clinton was still convinced that the Obama people had pulled some underhand tricks in Iowa, although he failed to persuade the candidate to make the charge publicly, and all of us heard enough from both sides to realise that, like a pair of pugilists preparing for fifteen rounds by eating pounds of raw meat, they were ready to hurt and be hurt. There would be blood, because nothing else would do.

The intimacy of the New Hampshire primary means that tiny communities can expect visits from half a dozen candidates of both parties, and every president in the modern era has had to go to tiny gatherings in town halls and restaurants there to meet voters – the old joke in the state is that you don't vote until you've met the candidates at least three times, in order to make a measured judgement. Fortunately, you get plenty of opportunity, because long before the presidential year opens, potential candidates trudge up north to start putting together an organisation ... just in case it's needed. The residents are caught in a near-permanent campaign. At one 2008 meeting, an elderly lady regaled me with stories of Nixon,

Reagan, Clinton and Bush. She'd rubbed shoulders with them all, like visiting preachers at her local church. New Hampshire treasures its face-to-face quadrennial political season, so much so that it long since established in state law that it must hold the first presidential primary in an election year (caucuses being regarded as an inferior way of choosing convention delegates).

The Obama–Clinton fight was a classic, in which you could hear them beginning to find the voices that would dominate the rest of the year, Obama, a pied piper in the snow drawing huge crowds in his wake and summoning up graceful speeches apparently from nowhere, Clinton (with Bill in tow) bringing to bear all her experience, grit and high intelligence in the argument about what Washington required. She had to stop Obama getting a surge, and she did, by a whisker. They each came away on the Tuesday night with nine pledged delegates to the convention. Effectively they'd go into the spring primaries neck and neck.

In Iowa, my producer Jat Gill and I had gone to Clinton headquarters as the results dribbled in from the caucuses held in halls and libraries and individual homes (when you are required to make your preference known by standing in a particular corner of a room, or standing under a sign bearing your candidate's name). We hadn't expected Obama to be the one making the victory speech that night. So at the start of the following week in New Hampshire, we were determined not to repeat the mistake. But, as it turned out, Obama had to concede there that his momentum had slowed just a touch, and that there would be a fight for every delegate going to the convention in Denver in August. He looked tired, perhaps surprised that he hadn't prevailed, and standing close to him as he spoke it was obvious how great the wear and tear of the primary campaign had already been, and how much more there was to come. Yet this was the moment when he began to repeat the words that became his powerful slogan on the long run home, 'Yes we can!'

It was going to be punishing stuff, and the winner would only emerge after a back-and-forth trek across the country, and no one had to remind Obama about the power of a Clinton campaign. 'We have been told we cannot do this by a chorus of cynics,' he said. 'And they will only grow louder and more dissonant in the weeks and months to come.' Yet surviving her retaliation after Iowa – in the state from which Bill Clinton had to become 'the comeback kid' to win – was the clue. This wasn't a campaign that was going to be stifled.

They rolled on for months, through which arguments about race exacerbated the hostility between the two camps. Like others, I was told of a tape – allegedly in the hands of the Republicans, who were supposed to be planning to use it as an explosive charge in the fall campaign – in which Michelle Obama was said to have used the racially derogatory term 'whitey' in a college speech. The Obamas said it had never happened, and let their rage be known. They never forgave those around Clinton who claimed that it was true. The bitterness on both sides kept spilling out.

When particular Obama remarks to a fund-raiser in San Francisco were revealed during the Pennsylvania primary campaign – at the point where she was beginning to threaten a comeback of her own – the Clinton campaign saw an opening and accused him of being 'elitist' and 'out of touch'. The candidate herself was more circumspect than some of her team, for whom the target was irresistible. Obama had been talking of disaffected voters in industrialised states, and said, 'They get bitter, they cling to guns or religion or antipathy to people who aren't like them, or anti-immigrant sentiment or anti-trade sentiment as a way to explain their frustrations.' It was a gift to Republicans who were naturally eager to create an unlikely bogeyman, the black candidate who was an elitist. To have him identified by Hillary was a bonus. Indeed, the episode was one they were still using eight years later to explain the appeal of Trump.

She would have cause to remember that episode, perhaps poignantly, in 2016, because her criticism of Obama for those words had exactly the same flavour as Trump's assault on her after she talked of 'the basket of deplorables' who supported him. So it goes, round and round.

Clinton did win the Pennsylvania primary, but lost North Carolina on the same night. Nearly everyone was concluding that by the early summer Obama would be the nominee, picking up many more convention delegates in the remaining primaries than

Clinton. The problem for Democrats was clearly to repair some of the damage and stage a unifying convention in Denver that would prepare the ground for the campaign against Senator John McCain who, in contrast to the Democratic fight, was having a relatively straightforward progress to the Republican nomination.

In an amusing footnote for students of Icarus-style presidential candidates, Rudy Giuliani, former mayor of New York and a future Trump lawyer-confidant, was the (brief) early favourite for the Republican nomination, but flopped when he had to face voters in primaries, a process he evidently found much more difficult than financing his campaign. He raised tens of millions of dollars in contributions, much of it from Wall Street, but withdrew in humiliation before the end of the primary season, owing more than $2.4 million to his donors and going to the convention in St Paul, Minnesota, with one solitary delegate committed to him – without question the most expensive delegate in American political history. I hoped Giuliani had at least bought him lunch.

But before St Paul, there was Denver.

All of us who arrived in Colorado for the convention recognised that we'd witnessed the first acts of a memorable drama. Obama's campaign had an electric force, but Clinton supporters were all over town, and promising emotional demonstrations of support for her (and Bill, who would speak). After a primary campaign that had lasted a full six months and pushed the candidates to their limits, there would be no easy return to calm.

In trying to heal the Obama–Clinton wounds, there was help from a shaky old hand. On the first night, the delegates watched a tribute film to Senator Ted Kennedy – then in the advanced stages of brain cancer – introduced by his niece Caroline, President Kennedy's daughter. The place went wild, and even wilder when the film ended because, to the surprise of most delegates, Ted himself lumbered on, having been transported to the backstage area by paramedics in a golf cart, an ambulance parked nearby to take him back to the hospital where he'd gone on arrival in Denver in excruciating pain from kidney stones. Having heard on the grapevine that he'd been flown to the city and was determined to speak, I squirmed into the Massachusetts delegation on the convention floor – where else? – to catch the moment. It was a genuine last hurrah from Boston, after all, and he duly boomed in old style, bringing them to their feet with his pledge that whatever happened he knew he'd be back on Capitol Hill in January to see the start of the Obama presidency. (He did survive to see the inauguration, standing close to Obama as he was sworn in, but died seven months later, at home on Cape Cod.)

By chance the next morning, I spied checking into the Brown Palace Hotel Theodore Sorensen, then in his eightieth year, John F. Kennedy's special counsel and speechwriter. We talked for a while, quite unnoticed, in the lobby. He said: 'This is an extraordinary moment for me. I'm going to have a few words to say to the convention and among them is the remarkable fact that twice in my lifetime I've had an opportunity to know and help extraordinary candidates for president – John F. Kennedy in 1960, forty-eight years ago, and Barack Obama this year.'

Without any difficulty, he identified Obama's sharpest weapon. 'Looking at him through the primaries, he seems to have a quality of being able to stand apart, inhabit his own space, be quite cool with himself on a platform, and that's an obvious comparison with John F. Kennedy. It's very true. He was cool. He was calm. It was one of his important qualities as president, particularly during times of great pressure and crisis. But he was also relaxed. He was at ease on the public platform.'

And so it proved in Denver. Despite the excitement it was difficult to create an optimistic convention, because of the alarms underneath. During Clinton's concession speech she was heckled by a group of middle-aged women delegates who wanted her to withhold support for Obama. Bill, who spoke late at night at a length no one else would have dared to risk, tried to apply some healing balm, despite his own anger, presenting the nomination of Joe Biden as running mate, for example, as a unifying act. But everyone wondered how Obama would handle his acceptance speech, for which they'd decided to leave the convention hall and fill the open-air Denver Broncos' Invesco stadium with about 80,000 people.

It was a hot, starlit night in the mile-high city as we watched a mile-long queue curling towards the stadium hours before the speech. But in the arena, the stage looked awful, dominated by a

New York harbour 1970, with the Twin Towers going up.

The war that wouldn't end: Vietnam protestors against Nixon, 1970.

All over: Carl Bernstein and Bob Woodward watch Nixon's resignation, August 1974.

A lack of convention chic at Madison Square Garden, 1976.

Old technology delivering the news from the convention.

© Diana Walker / The LIFE Images Collection via Getty Images

Ted Kennedy lays down the sword at the Democratic Convention, New York, 1980.

The face of defeat. Jimmy Carter at the farm, Plains, Georgia, 1980.

At home in front of the camera, Reagan in Ballyporeen, Ireland, 1984.

The ever-present flag. In the Governor's mansion, Austin, Texas, 1991.

Days of Innocence. The Clintons in Georgia, 1992.

Bush and Blair in step in the White House, 2003.

A national debut for 'the skinny guy'. Obama at the Democratic Convention, Boston, 2004

Hurricane Katrina. A city engulfed and national shame.

Over the top. Obama accepts the presidential nomination, Invesco Stadium, Denver, 2008.

At home. John McCain in his Senate office, 2012.

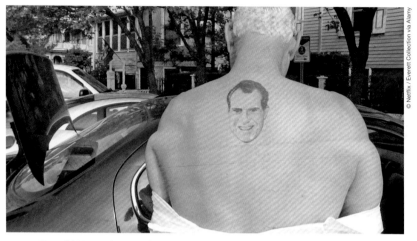

Donald Trump's street fighter. Roger Stone shows off his Nixon tattoo.

The truth about broadbasting. Finding the satellite atop a car park in Las Vegas . . .

. . . and on the boardwalk in Atlantic City. Campaign 2016.

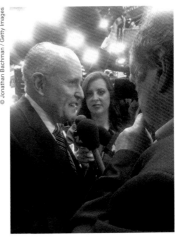

The Disrupters. Trump and Nigel Farage in 2016.

A word in edgeways, just, with Rudolf Giuliani on the Trump campaign.

Home from home. The Washington studio.

'What happened.' Hillary Clinton talks about her defeat, London, 2017.

Intimations of defeat in high summer. A deflated Trump returns to the White House in June 2020 after the Oklahoma rally that went wrong.

Almost alone. The day after the election, the President arrives in the White House briefing room to tell Americans, 'It's a corrupt system'. Refusing to accept defeat, he promised 'lots of litigation' and confirmed what everyone knew – that he would not leave office quietly, but instead with all the noise that had characterised his presidency.

Watching Joe Biden in the New Hampshire primary at the low point of his campaign, on the day he promised a fightback that would carry him to the presidency at the third attempt.

set that had a mocked-up Greek temple and was hopelessly over the top, making Stevie Wonder look weirdly out of place when he came on to sing (though Al Gore appeared happier among the fake marble columns). But Obama himself, demonstrating Sorensen's point, knew the danger of trying to look too confident or grand – he'd been burned before – and deliberately lowered the temperature. In front of an adoring crowd, he turned down the heat and opted for slow-burn oratory with no early flourishes, keeping lift-off for the end. 'Let us keep that promise, that American promise, and in the words of Scripture hold firmly, without wavering, to the hope that we confess.' It was a subtle piece of timing and rhythm, delivered forty-five years to the day after Martin Luther King's speech to the Washington march from the Lincoln Memorial. From high up in the stadium, with the crowd swigging beer and eating hotdogs as if the Broncos were playing at home, it sounded as if he'd been taking lessons from Bill Clinton. Unlikely, I thought.

Driving to Minnesota, because the Republicans were gathering in St Paul only four days later, I stopped at Mount Rushmore to see for the first time the presidential monument, where four of the greatest are carved into the granite, their faces each about 60ft high. In the car park, I saw two trucks with John McCain stickers on their back windows. It was easy to envisage him as another president – an American hero, an amalgam of feistiness and palpable decency, and a popular figure across the country. Obama was in a genuine fight. I'd talked to McCain, deep in a happy crowd, on the night he won the New Hampshire primary. I knew – we'd spoken a few times before, since he had a fondness for the BBC – of the natural appeal that he would have for many Americans who might consider voting for a candidate from either party, but who would be wary of a one-term senator like Obama with no administrative experience, and would perhaps remain instinctively reluctant to cross the racial divide.

But the Republican convention had an uncomfortable start, although the convention organisers did manage to extract some advantage. By a stroke of bad luck, Hurricane Gustav was threatening the Gulf coast, and McCain, like President Bush, who chose not to come north and addressed the convention by video link from

Texas, spent the beginning of the week in the South, just in case. In truth, the fact that the president only spoke for five minutes, without appearing in the hall, was a relief. He was an unpopular figure. The memories of Katrina, and the Bush administration's chaotic response, were too sharp for anyone to take a chance on a repetition. So the convention got off to an uneven start. Then there was Sarah Palin, a hurricane of her own.

McCain chose the governor of Alaska as his running mate not because he knew much about her, but because he didn't. McCain himself was regarded with suspicion by ideologues, and could easily be caricatured as a natural Washington insider, so he was persuaded to abandon his bold plan to recruit the Democrat senator Joe Lieberman, on the grounds that it might look like a Washington fix (which is exactly what it was). Instead it would be Palin, who'd become a star on the conservative talk-show circuit and could be said, unlike Obama, to have run a state. She was just the ticket, and in the convention hall, you might have believed it. I was sitting in the Kansas delegation when she gave her acceptance speech, feeling the waves of acclaim, and when she described herself as an 'average hockey mom' they let rip. 'I love those hockey moms,' she told them. 'You know what they say is the difference between a hockey mom and a pit bull? Lipstick.'

Her speech, horrifyingly crude to old-style Republicans, was electric. She told them she didn't want to use a luxury jet as Alaska governor, so she sold it on eBay, just like that, and the cheer threatened to take the roof off. Her later performances in the campaign convinced outsiders that the choice had been a mistake – by any rational calculation, it was a corker – but everyone in that convention hall who watched her lift the crowd knew that she understood intuitively just how to hit the spot. Years later, watching Trump bulldozing his way through the primaries, we all recognised the style. Palin, inadequate though she turned out to be when she faced even a mildly testing interview or tried to delve into policy at any level, was a trailblazer for the Tea Party movement that sprang into being during the Obama presidency, and the true forerunner of Trump.

But the fall campaign was too much for her. McCain was

sabotaged by her stumbles, family troubles and her fatal ignorance about world affairs. There were painful stories about tutorials organised for the putative vice president to teach her the basic outlines of twentieth-century history, after which her invariable response was said to be, 'Awesome!' When someone spread a presumably apocryphal story – but who can say? – that she thought Africa was one country, many people found it credible. All of it allowed the Obama campaign to turn her into a liability, a scary figure to the neutral voter. But in a harbinger of the Trump era, she was the one the party hard core wanted to hear. Each night fellow journalists would gather in the St Paul Grill across the street to eat before our late-night broadcasting stints, and it was remarkable to notice the change in atmosphere that Palin brought. Until she spoke, the place was quiet in the evenings, despite the crowd. Afterwards the whole convention rocked. McCain, indeed, had to try to calm things down in his own acceptance speech. No organised raucousness for him.

I watched one of the few rallies at which she and McCain appeared together, in Virginia not long before election day, and it was something of an embarrassment for the Republican campaign. Clearly, the crowd was there to cheer the 'hockey mom' and not the distinguished senator. After she spoke, a large chunk of the crowd broke away, not bothering to listen to the man introduced to them as the next president of the United States and heading for their 4x4 trucks parked in the fields outside. Her style might have irritated McCain, but he knew that she was a formidable presence on stage. By that point, he was looking his age, which was not surprising.

By contrast, Obama was gathering steam as November approached. Travelling north from Florida to Washington in the last few days we saw remarkable scenes at polling places in the South, where huge numbers of African Americans were taking advantage of the early-voting rules to get in line in the autumn sun and, in some cases, to queue for hours to cast their votes. Many of them were happy to say that they hadn't voted for a long time, in some cases almost never, and a number of those I spoke to in Florida, scene of the 'theft' of the 2000 presidential election, as many of them saw it, said they still could scarcely believe that, as one elderly man put it, waving his walking stick in the air as if trying to defy the gods, 'they will ever allow this to happen'.

There was, however, the big unknown. Would white voters (not only in the South) who told pollsters that they were Democratic voters do something different when they pulled the curtain behind them in the polling booth? No one could know, despite the vast crowds that Obama attracted in a progress north from the Deep South in these last days. His was the optimistic campaign, however, and those days crackled with energy, on a drive through the South with my producer Alexis Condon. It gave us a memorable picture of a country that knew the scale of the step it might take. In North Carolina, Obama voters could scarcely believe that they could win that state with a black candidate. They did.

On the night before polling day in Washington, where we were preparing for the next day's radio results programme, I tried to get across the Potomac River to Manassas in Virginia. Obama was due to stop there on his way home to Chicago. We had to turn back because the bridges were blocked by traffic, and because I had some broadcasting to do later we headed reluctantly back to the office, assuming some unlucky pile-up on the beltway had caused the jam. No. The reason was that about 100,000 people had turned up to hear Obama, just before midnight, at his last campaign stop, which happened to be near the site of the two battles of Bull Run in the Civil War, both of them won by Robert E. Lee's Confederate States Army, and therefore hallowed ground to the Old South. An extraordinary landfall for the last stop of the campaign by a black candidate. It was over.

The rivals for the presidency could hardly have been more different, in background, age, experience, culture, style. During the campaign, while reporting from Las Vegas – Nevada being a state that could go either way – I had an intriguing conversation about gambling, because it was reported that each candidate had a favourite game. This was obviously a matter of psychological interest.

I have made sure that craps has remained a mystery to me, apart from following Nathan Detroit's exploits under the Biltmore garage in *Guys and Dolls*, and listening to Sinatra. The baize-lined hollow tables that look like bathtubs, where players throw pairs of dice into the void, watched by the boxman sitting behind piles of chips at the rim, have always seemed to me an obvious invitation to disaster. But in Vegas or Atlantic City they're in every hotel lobby and people sit around them day and night, fingering their chips and chucking in their dice – most of them, I have observed, looking gloomy. Yet this was McCain's favourite game. Obama, on the other hand, prefers poker, which is comprehensible and harmless enough, unless you take it seriously.

I needed some help, so I went to see Howard Lederer, who's one of the most renowned players in the world and is known respectfully in Nevada as 'The Professor', for what I suppose are obvious reasons. He was sitting at a poker table.

'I wouldn't disparage either, but you know that craps is a game of pure gambling. Pure, pure entertainment. Whereas poker can also be a game of self-betterment.'

Self-betterment?

'When you're at the table, you're thinking about your opponent, and you're thinking about yourself. It's a very social game. And I think you grow at the table, if you allow it to happen. I don't think there's any personal growth happening at a craps table. But it's a lot of fun. And you know, I've played some craps in my day and I do think that it does speak a little bit to the personality and the type of people that the two candidates are.'

He explained how a craps game worked, or didn't, and afterwards I felt even more relief that I had stayed away from the tables. A festival of pure chance, the gambler's last resort. Howard's final words were, 'What you have to have as a poker player is an objective sense about yourself and your skills, and the skills of your opponent.'

A nice line for election night, and tucked away with gratitude.

I walked across the Bellagio Hotel, because someone told me that in one of the backrooms I would find Doyle Brunson, a poker player of legend who's said to have been the first man to make a million dollars from the game (legally, at least) when he started as a professional more than half a century ago. I asked a hopeful question, not expecting an interesting answer.

'Have you ever played poker with a politician?'

And Doyle Brunson said, 'Yeah. I played with Lyndon Johnson.'

Fortunately, there was a waiter standing near the table proffering drinks. I thought I might need one. It was like hearing someone say they had played pétanque with General de Gaulle.

'What was that like?'

'Well, Lyndon was just a good ol' Texas boy that liked to play poker. Oh yeah. And a very nice man.'

I asked if he was a good poker player, because when it came to games of skill and bluff surely he'd been a master. Nobody could read him better than himself.

Doyle, who had exactly the kind of leathery face you might expect and looked as if in his spare time he presided over a cowboy saloon in the desert with rattlesnake skins hanging above the bar, thought for a moment.

'I wouldn't say he was real good, but he was decent. Yeah, I'd say decent.'

Being a poker player, Doyle didn't display much emotion. None at all, to be honest. I tried to get him going on LBJ. What was the table talk like? How did he react when he lost? Nothing. It all stayed behind his eyes, which didn't blink very often. He was meticulously polite, but was disappointingly not in the business of gossip, even of the 40-year-old variety.

His final judgement was that Johnson had been better at politics than poker. He'd just met him here and there, after all, not across his desk in the Oval Office. Here and there? There were no details. Sadly, on that night, Doyle Brunson, the possessor of a temperament that was kept perfectly under control, would say nothing more.

Too long ago, he said. And McCain–Obama?

'Well, I've never seen Mr McCain play craps round here. Does play, though. And of course I've never seen Mr Obama play poker, but I hear he plays. It's quite interesting, isn't it? McCain's got a lot of bravery. He's an American hero. Obama is a velvet-tongued orator, I'll say that for him. I'm not sure who I would prefer. I wish they were on the same ticket.'

Then, a decision. 'I think that a poker player has good judgement. I think a poker player would be a good president.'

The poker player won.

Looking back to that campaign season from the standpoint of the Trump era, Sarah Palin's convention speech keeps recurring, like an earworm. Her populist tone became the war cry of a conservative movement for the new century: the Tea Party, dedicated to the proposition that, just as in Boston in the 1770s, taxation from far away – Washington, these days – was the source of most of society's ills. It was ramshackle and disorganised, and most of those who were propelled to Capitol Hill by its efforts proved lamentable figures when confronted with serious policy choices, but it was evidence of a powerful current that, years later, would give Trump his energy.

One particular visit to Kentucky, during the 2010 midterm election campaign, has stayed with me. I visited a couple who lived just south of the Ohio River, with Cincinnati just over the state line. Bobby Alexander, in his early sixties, had recently retired from the army, and was helping to organise the Northern Kentucky Tea Party, appalled by Obama and all his works, especially the Affordable Care Act – Obamacare! – which had been passed six months earlier, a significant extension of healthcare benefits to millions of Americans who had no insurance, though a long way from the universal cover many reformers wanted. To Bobby it was socialism, pure and simple. We had a friendly conversation in which I asked him in passing why he thought Margaret Thatcher – a hero, of course – had made a point in her three winning election campaigns of pledging faith in the National Health Service. This proved to be a conundrum that he couldn't fathom. It troubled him, but certainly didn't change his view of Obamacare, which, alongside infringements of gun rights, any liberalisation of abortion, gay marriage and increased federal spending on anything, was for him an assault on the freedoms in defence of which he'd worn his uniform.

He and his wife Gloria made my colleague Jasper Corbett and me most welcome in their home. They were good people, taking in rescue dogs, doing their bit in the local community, baking cookies for a church event on Sunday. We sat on the porch drinking Earl Grey tea. They were passionate, without angry words, although there was a bumper sticker on their car outside saying Obama's inauguration was 'A day that will live in infamy!', FDR's description of Pearl Harbor. They only watched Fox News, because it confirmed their view of the world, and they would not read the *New York Times* because it didn't. Their favourite broadcaster was Glenn Beck, then a Fox commentator, who had organised a few weeks earlier a Washington march that he compared rather ludicrously with Martin Luther King's 1963 march ('I Have a Dream'), except that it was a demonstration for a different kind of 'freedom' – against big government, healthcare reform, abortion and gay marriage. Bobby and Gloria went along, in a fleet of Tea Party buses that helped to produce a crowd thought to have been about 100,000 strong. Beck spoke, and so did Sarah Palin. Bobby told us it was one of the most moving days of his life. I asked what was most striking about the event.

'It wasn't at all political,' he said.

Bobby and Gloria Alexander considered their outlook and beliefs to be separate from politics (which was the game that liberals played) and more of an attitude to life. The conservative movement had by then become a belief system rather than a political platform, the culture wars of the 1990s made flesh. Although the Tea Party spluttered as a movement, its influence was enormous. The reason that its congressional caucus folded a couple of years later was not that its views had passed out of fashion, but that after Mitt Romney's failed campaign against Obama in 2012 – which he fought on a centrist platform – the Republican mainstream absorbed the restive, impatient conservatives who wanted a more radical party and was transformed by it.

No wonder Donald Trump saw an opportunity. For a man who had apparently taken no serious interest in party politics – though I learned from one of his wiliest associates that he had made reconnaissance trips to New Hampshire as early as 1988 – the decision was always going to depend on a public mood rather than on a party operation of the kind that most candidates organise to try to win the nomination. His name had been touted around for years (in relation to both parties, naturally), unsurprisingly for a character who was an oversized public figure for three decades before he became president – a business mogul, followed obsessively by supermarket tabloids through a torrent of marriages and business deals, and a pouting presence in many American living rooms since 2004 on *The Apprentice* on NBC. Believing himself to be the embodiment of American achievement, it may have been inevitable that he would try his luck. Just at the right moment, the upheavals on the right of American politics presented an enticing landscape to him. With sure instinct, he recognised it for what it was – his natural habitat.

At first, his campaign for the nomination was widely mocked. Although he attracted about the same respectable level of support in the early days as Jeb Bush, governor of Florida and brother of George W., Republican pollsters and strategists were as dismissive of his chances as Democrats.

Not long before the start of the primary season, in autumn 2015, I had a first encounter with Anthony Scaramucci, a figure who would play a colourful minor role in the Trump story as fundraiser, cheerleader and, for a few wild days, one of the succession of unfortunates who agreed to become the president's head of communications in the White House, and regretted it. We talked in his office building on the East Side of Manhattan, where he ran his own investment firm, SkyBridge Capital. An ex-Goldman Sachs banker, Scaramucci, aka The Mooch, appears more of a pint-sized bow-legged street fighter in a sharp suit than a Wall Street banker, and we had a happy time talking about baseball (he owned a chunk of the New York Mets) and looking at the pictures on his wall, which showed him with sportsmen and politicians of all colours, including Bill Clinton, although he had co-chaired Romney's presidential campaign. At that time, he was backing Scott Walker, governor of Wisconsin, who turned out to be a hopeless candidate and fell away quickly.

And Trump?

'He's trying to find a way out,' Scaramucci said. 'Believe me. He wants out of this.'

Trump, he was sure, was in the race only for publicity to add to his fame and fortune, and not for serious political reasons. He predicted that the man he had once called 'a hack politician', who was divisive and even anti-American, would be out of the race by the spring, and had never expected anything else.

The next time I saw The Mooch, Walker was long gone, and he had quickly abandoned his alternative choice for president, Jeb Bush. Instead, he was raising money for Trump and helping him sew up the nomination.

The Trump bulldozer reached full power in New Hampshire in February, which it hadn't quite managed in Iowa. He was uncomfortable in prairie country, where his attempt to ingratiate himself with voters was patronising and therefore unsuccessful, telling them he had taken to their state to such a degree, having never visited it before, that he was thinking of buying a farm there. Senator Ted Cruz of Texas, on the other hand, was at home with the strong evangelical faction among Republicans, understanding the tracts of long straight roads, rural chapels and churches, and early teatimes, which to Trump were a distant world. I watched Cruz at one breakfast meeting in the town of Hubbard out in the flatlands, where we had to keep reminding ourselves that we weren't in church.

He spoke of the election as 'an awakening', quoted Scripture from memory and at length, and warned the crowd of about 300, crammed into a middle school, that one of the most important reasons for voting Republican was to avoid the appointment of a liberal Supreme Court justice who might bring about a majority on the court and in turn order all religious symbols to be removed from every gravestone in every burial ground in America. Every cross, every Jewish Star of David. Muslims weren't mentioned, naturally. He didn't provide any evidence, but was believed. 'We're only one justice away,' he told them. 'One justice away!' Apocalyptic stuff. Coming back to earth, one questioner who told a story, tentatively, of a family member facing critical illness who had been able to have medical treatment that he couldn't have afforded without Obamacare, was firmly put down. It was a revivalist meeting, and that was all.

A few days afterwards, at Cruz headquarters as the votes came in, they celebrated victory over Trump ('To God be the glory!' were the first words of the candidate when he appeared for the crowd). But the euphoria didn't last. In New Hampshire, where economic concerns were more important to most Republican voters than moral renewal, Trump crushed his opponents with a promise to breathe fire into the economy. Leaving the intimate handshaking to others – it has never been his preference, allegedly because of germophobia – he campaigned on rally platforms, flying home to New York every night because he said he liked to sleep on 5th Avenue and nowhere else. As we would all discover, he liked breaking the candidates' rules.

He barged his way to victory, dominating the debate in which all the candidates appeared, taking special care to mock Senator Marco Rubio of Florida ('Little Marco') who had shown threatening signs of life in the campaign but never recovered after his weak showing in New Hampshire.

Governor Chris Christie of New Jersey, a rough-and-tumble politician of the kind favoured by that state, helped Trump by giving Rubio a verbal kicking in the debate, accusing him of repeating pre-rehearsed answers like a robot. When the senator responded by repeating an answer he had already given, Trump led the chorus of laughter. Having belittled Rubio, he then turned on Christie in the days afterwards, with brutal success.

Cruz did continue to cause some trouble for Trump, and because he might be a threat in the later southern primaries, he had to be derailed quickly. A month after New Hampshire, Trump produced an extraordinary story, with the help of the *National Enquirer*, the supermarket tabloid specialising in conspiracy whose publisher was a friend. Trump noted, in an appearance on *Fox & Friends*, that it had published a picture said to be of Rafael Cruz, the senator's late father. He appeared to be having breakfast with John F. Kennedy's assassin three weeks before the president was shot in Dallas in 1963.

'What was he doing with Lee Harvey Oswald shortly before the death? Before the shooting? It's horrible,' said Trump. 'Ted Cruz, I don't think, denied it.'

As smears go, it was a corker. Cruz was incandescent with rage. Trump didn't offer any evidence, and wasn't challenged on Fox to explain the story. Job done. From then on he was 'Lyin' Ted Cruz'. In return, Cruz, infuriated by Trump's attacks on his wife, described him as a coarse man whose speeches were so crude that he wouldn't allow his children to listen to them.

Watching Trump at work during the first primary campaign in

the Music Hall, an old theatre in Portsmouth, New Hampshire, it was instructive to talk to his audience. Many of them were young and had evidently come to the meeting out of curiosity rather than zealotry. A number cheerily confessed to a simple desire to see this character in the flesh, because the chance didn't come along very often. He was an American phenomenon, and one that had to be witnessed. Trump, walking on to his theme tune, Puccini's 'Nessun Dorma' ('*Vincerò!*' – 'I will win' – the tenor sings), introduced his children in fashion-parade style, and gave his routine stump speech, short and staccato, consisting of little more than an assertion that he would Make America Great Again, because he possessed powers that were denied to anyone else.

These were the first glimpses of Trump's momentum. But he certainly didn't impress everyone. When I sat down with the newspaperman Joe McQuaid, publisher of the *Manchester Union-Leader*, he described Trump as an inadequate bully. He'd been amused that one of the writers of *Back to the Future*, Bob Gale, had confessed the previous year that he'd drawn on the character of Trump in the 1980s to create the character of Biff, the school bully in the film, who threatens his classmates and cheats at everything, calling anyone he doesn't like (namely, most people) 'butthead'.

The *Manchester Union-Leader* has a long and colourful conservative history, described by George McGovern during his 1972 campaign as the worst newspaper in America. Its long-time publisher, the late William Loeb, was notorious for his vicious crusades against any candidate he didn't like (destroying the Democrat favourite Ed Muskie in 1972, for example, by publishing such poisonous stories about him and his wife that the candidate broke down in tears in public, and folded). Post-Loeb, the paper was still deeply conservative, but without most of the bile. McQuaid, an engaging publisher-editor, said he'd been visited three times by Trump in search of an endorsement.

'He thought he could come here and demand it,' he told me in his office. 'He didn't understand that he couldn't.'

On one of his visits he presented McQuaid with a signed photograph of himself.

'You know where I keep it?' McQuaid asked us.

He showed me into a little lavatory off his office. There was Trump on the wall, just where McQuaid thought he belonged. He laughed.

But it was a brutally successful campaign. The destruction of Jeb Bush, for example, was complete. He had flopped in Iowa, and Trump was ready to finish him off, describing him as 'a low-energy light bulb', a label that hurt because it spoke the truth – a display of Trump's instinctive gift for the killer thrust. Bush was unimpressive on his feet, and prone to rambling speeches and malapropisms. At one New Hampshire stop, after he made what he considered a rallying cry for a strong commander-in-chief (himself), and there was silence from the audience, he said, without appearing to smile, 'Please clap.' Not surprisingly, that became a favourite clip online.

I sat at one Bush meeting, of modest size, in a township in the north of the state, where he was accompanied by his mother Barbara, the former First Lady, then aged ninety. She was welcomed warmly by the crowd of mostly elderly Republicans and spoke with spirit in support of her 63-year-old son. Not a meeting for the young at heart. He couldn't, however, rise even to that occasion. It was a snapshot of the old Republican Party, which was about to be flattened by Trump.

After New Hampshire, there was no stopping him. Chris Christie fell away, and a bold attempt to carve out a moderate path to the nomination by John Kasich, governor of Ohio, attracted much of the anti-Trump vote but could never match his power. At one of his meetings in the Virginia primary, I ran across Newt Gingrich, who was in no doubt that Trump would win, and not a candidate like the mild Kasich, thoughtful though he was. Why? 'Trump is like Andrew Jackson,' said Gingrich simply, Jackson being the swashbuckling seventh president of the United States who claimed to have fashioned the young country's democracy for 'the common man'.

By the time Trump arrived in Cleveland for the Republican convention, his command of the party's troops was obvious. His rhetorical style was their battle cry, with memories of McCain and Romney wiped away. The event was turned into a festival of Clinton-baiting, with the retired general Mike Flynn leading chants of 'Lock her up!' (Unfortunately for him, he was later convicted of lying to the FBI.)

There were Republicans there who were horrified, but none of them spoke up. Chris Christie materialised once more on the platform to say that as a former prosecutor he knew all about making charges stick. He read out a list of 'crimes' committed by Clinton, urging the crowd to join him in a cry of 'Guilty!' after each one, which they did. If someone had suggested the return of public executions, we sensed they that would have cheered even more loudly.

There were conservative commentators who were appalled. Charles Krauthammer, the neoconservative *Washington Post* columnist who yielded to no one in his disdain for the Clintons, wrote that Trump was an affront to American democracy, which he didn't understand and was betraying. Later in the campaign, Krauthammer wrote this: 'This election is not just about placing the nuclear codes in Trump's hands. It's also about handing him the instruments of civilian coercion, such as the IRS, the FBI, the FCC, the SEC. Think of what he could do to enforce the "fairness" he demands. Imagine giving over the vast power of the modern state to a man who says in advance that he will punish his critics and jail his opponent.'

Trump simply ignored such criticism. The investigation into Clinton's use of a personal email server when she was secretary of state from 2008 to 2011 was enough. It was perfect conspiracy material, because the less that was known about what the emails contained, the more sinister Trump could make them sound. At every stop he urged WikiLeaks, which said it had a huge cache of hacked Democratic emails, to publish them. 'I love WikiLeaks!' he would say. And if the Russians were holding emails too? 'Bring it on! Publish!' The campaign was to be as much an attack on his opponent as a set of promises, with assistance welcome from anyone who would join the fun, for whatever reason.

At rally after rally, he responded to the crowd's chant with remarks like this one, in Pennsylvania – 'Lock her up is right! She should be in jail!' The posters and slogans on hats at Trump rallies often said more about Clinton than they did about him.

No one had seen a candidate like this, and he knew it. I talked about him in Cleveland to one of his oldest associates, the epitome of the political trickster, Roger Stone. He was wearing a white suit and the producers of a Netflix film – *Get Me Roger Stone* – filmed our conversation. He told me and my producer Terry O'Neill that the movie would be seized by the CIA if Trump became president because it would be too hot to be allowed on the air. I wasn't sure whether or not he was joking. He also predicted that if he was interviewed on the BBC he was afraid that his London tailor in Savile Row might hear him and pursue him for some unpaid bills he hoped had been forgotten. I knew that was no joke.

He had first dabbled in politics as a teenager, shouting down the liberal Nelson Rockefeller at the 1964 Republican convention in support of Barry Goldwater, and had gone on to work for Nixon, since he enjoyed the capers of the characters who perpetrated all the dirty work we came to know as Watergate. Stone is the only man I have spoken to, as far as I know, who has an image of Nixon tattooed on his back.

Stone's business associate in the 1980s was Paul Manafort, another Trump intimate who was one of his campaign chairmen, and was jailed on multiple counts of fraud in 2019, after courts heard about an intricate web of financial deceptions around the world, and his work for Russian interests in Ukraine, which he had avoided declaring, illegally, to the American authorities. Stone, who has since said he was being persecuted by the Justice Department and the Internal Revenue Service, has known Trump for more than forty years and, sitting not far from the convention hall while a plane circled overhead trailing a sign saying 'Hillary – Prison 2016!', he spoke about his friend.

His triumph, said Stone, was to have wound up the party of the Bushes, whom he considers no better than the Clintons, whose charitable foundation he describes breezily as 'organised crime'. At last there was a candidate he could warm to, the one for whom he'd been waiting for so long.

'Trump is the outsider who has changed everything. This is like nothing we have seen before. The times have changed completely.'

Was he fit to be president?

'He's smart – don't forget that – and he listens, probably more than you think.' In other words, he knows exactly what he is doing.

But, I said, how would he deal with the big questions and, for example, with Vladimir Putin?

That produced Stone's most interesting answer. 'Putin will respect him more than he respects Obama, I'll tell you that. They have a lot in common.' A similar view of power, he meant, and the way you handle it.

And how could he counter Clinton in the debates, given her command of detail and political experience, not least as secretary of state?

'She has a glass jaw,' he said simply. The battle was going to be like a prize fight, nothing less. If I had been innocent enough to think that the debates would be measured and deliberative affairs, which I was not, that would have removed the last doubt.

Stone, who was later convicted of witness tampering, obstruction of justice and making false statements, was one of Trump's links to Russians during the campaign, the network that became a focus of Robert Mueller's investigation when he was appointed special counsel the following year, and subsequent congressional investigations. When we spoke in Cleveland, Stone said he had no doubt that this was going to be 'the dirtiest, most bruising' campaign of them all. He was certainly in a position to know.

Weren't people entitled to be concerned that the wall-to-wall political ads on television during state and national campaigns were now overwhelmingly negative, a non-stop rolling attack ad from one side or the other? There was nothing new about that, said Stone. Did I not recall that in Lincoln's election in 1860 a leaflet had been circulated in Illinois accusing him of fathering a mixed-race child?

I realised that Stone saw himself as the inheritor of a proud American tradition.

As if to underline the melodramatic tone of the convention, the following morning I witnessed an unusual sight in the area that was set aside for radio, which was dominated by conservative talkshow stations and their over-the-top hosts, sitting in a long row and addressing the folks back home in various stages of excitement. I was working with my producer, Terry O'Neill, when we were interrupted by a commotion, and round the corner tumbled two men, apparently one in pursuit of the other, pushing everyone aside as they raced through, like schoolboys having a prank. One was Roger Stone and the other Alex Jones, prince of the conspiracy theorists,

who believes, among other things, that 9/11 was a put-up job, the
federal government planted the Oklahoma City bomb that killed
168 people in 1995, the Sandy Hook massacre of schoolchildren in
2012 was an elaborate hoax, and that elements of the moon landing
were faked for some dark bureaucratic purpose.

That scene summed up the weirdest of conventions.

Hillary Clinton's, by contrast, was a traditional affair. Her
nomination, however, had involved another street fight, this time
with the Vermont senator Bernie Sanders, determined to push the
Democrats leftwards. He stirred up a movement that had spirit,
beating Clinton in New Hampshire and announcing that he'd
see it through to the end, which he did, although it became clear
early on that he would not be nominated. He played a similar role
to Clinton's own in 2008, when she refused to concede the nomination to Obama until the end. In his left-leaning populism he
demonstrated a different version of the Trump movement, which
understood exactly where to pitch its appeal to those who felt themselves to be outsiders in contemporary America. The difference with
Sanders was that his strongest appeal was to students and young
professionals who felt that their promise wasn't being fulfilled.
They, rather than older, disgruntled blue-collar workers, were his
vanguard. At the party after his New Hampshire victory it was
striking to realise that a majority of his campaign team guzzling
their celebratory beers hadn't been born when Bill Clinton became
president. Despite Sanders' own age – we called him the Rip Van
Winkle of Vermont – you could see why they found it easy to think
of Hillary Clinton as a figure from the past.

It was frustrating for her, because she believed that she was
the natural voice for the dispossessed. Indeed, it was in trying to
explain that, after the conventions, that she unwittingly played into
Trump's hands with words that proved unwise and even reckless,
especially when edited and compressed by her opponents, which
they were always bound to be. They should be quoted in full.

At a fund-raiser in New York on 9 September, she said:

You know, to just be grossly generalistic, you could put
half of Trump's supporters into what I call the basket of

deplorables. Right? They're racist, sexist, homophobic, xenopho-
bic, Islamophobic, you name it. And, unfortunately, there are
people like that. And he has lifted them up. He has given voice
to their websites that used to only have 11,000 people and now
have 11 million. He tweets and retweets their offensive, hateful,
mean-spirited rhetoric. Now, some of those folks – they are irredeemable, but thankfully they are not America.

But the 'other' basket – the other basket – and I know because
I look at this crowd I see friends from all over America here. I
see friends from Florida and Georgia and South Carolina and
Texas and – as well as, you know, New York and California – but
that 'other' basket of people are people who feel the government
has let them down, the economy has let them down, nobody
cares about them, nobody worries about what happens to their
lives and their futures; and they're just desperate for change. It
doesn't really even matter where it comes from. They don't buy
everything he says, but he seems to hold out some hope that their
lives will be different. They won't wake up and see their jobs disappear, lose a kid to heroin, feel like they're in a dead end. Those
are people we have to understand and empathise with as well.

In making the very point that Trump's appeal to the forgotten
was one that had to be understood and turned, in her view, into a
more positive answer to the sense of desperation, she handed him
a priceless piece of ammunition with those words 'deplorables' and
'irredeemable'. The qualifications and context were forgotten, and
they dogged her for the rest of the campaign.

Trump supporters wore them with pride on their baseball caps.
That's what she thinks of you, he would tell his crowds. In por-
traying Clinton as a monstrous elitist, the words became code for
everything that was wrong with the Democrats and their candidate.

Their three debates were the stage for this argument, in which
Trump showed that he had no interest in playing by any rules. In
the first two, in New York and St Louis, he demonstrated that he
was not going to adopt a different persona for the confrontation,
all the while mocking Clinton for taking a day or two away from
campaigning to prepare. Why should he? He'd be himself – saying

he thought Clinton should be in jail, that her husband was guilty of serious sexual crimes (this from a candidate who'd been heard on tape boasting about his sexual conquests of women who couldn't help being attracted to powerful men) and calling himself smart for avoiding taxes.

At the end of the first debate on Long Island, Trump himself came into the so-called 'spin room' where normally the candidates' staff and chosen spokespeople come to put a gloss on proceedings. On that night no neutral could doubt that Clinton had 'won', appearing by far the stronger candidate of the two.

I managed a brief word with Trump over the rope that kept him just apart from the throng. He said it was a fact that the instant polls being done as the debate ended were all showing him winning with the public. When he disappeared through the curtain again, I checked and found – not surprisingly – that what he had said was untrue. The polls were showing the opposite. He had made it up, and was rambling in a way that was unusual for any candidate. It was an early glimpse of the wild stream-of-consciousness style, if that is the appropriate word, that we would come to know so well. It was appropriate in that campaign, I suppose, to start with a lie.

When they met for the final debate in Las Vegas in October, it looked as if Trump's efforts were going to fail. He was behind in the polls and any chance of victory seemed to be slipping away from him. Yet he didn't change tack in an effort to revive the campaign. In Vegas, where everything is a gamble, he doubled down.

Taking a step that no one had seen a candidate take before, he refused to confirm to the moderator, Chris Wallace of Fox News, that he would even accept the result of the election (unless he won, in which case it would obviously be fair). He had made accusations about irregularities in electoral registration, all unspecified, as if they were part of the web of deceit with which his opponents were trying to ensnare him. 'I will look at it at the time,' he said. 'I will keep you in suspense. What I have seen is so bad . . .'

Even for a candidate who had broken new ground in conspiratorial theory and name-calling, this was remarkable. It caused a number of commentators who had already written him off, noting that polls in the states that would probably decide the election (with the notable exception of Ohio) were steadily favouring Clinton, to conclude that he was now flailing around in desperation. His crowds might be enjoying his promise to seal the Mexican border ('Build that wall!' they chanted at every stop), revelling in the anti-Clinton rhetoric, and convinced that he would be the biggest job creator in American history, but there weren't enough of them to put him in the White House.

Clinton certainly left Las Vegas convinced that she had won all three debates, and so did all but the Trumpist commentators. But the last days produced the 'October surprise' that all candidates have come to fear, the game-changer that comes from nowhere.

Exactly a week after that debate, with the pattern of polls looking settled, James Comey, director of the FBI, announced that he was reopening the bureau's investigation into the emails on Clinton's personal server. A laptop had turned up belonging to Anthony Weiner, the estranged husband of a senior Clinton aide, Huma Abedin. The FBI said that messages were found on the laptop that may have originated from Clinton's server, presumably sent to Abedin. He did not say that there was any reason to suspect wrongdoing, just that the emails would be examined. After the tumult died – after election day, in other words – it became clear that there was no sign of classified material on Weiner's laptop. It had no bearing on the matter, and the episode had been an unnecessary distraction. It is hard to dispute Clinton's claim that Comey's surprise statement on the Saturday ten days before the election was deeply unfair. It hit her campaign like a wayward meteor. Clinton's people were thrown into a desperately defensive mode, and Trump was able to suggest that all his suspicions had been proved right. Something was stirring in the undergrowth and it wasn't quite right. Didn't I tell you?

At that moment, Comey was a hero. Later, with Trump in office, that view would change and the FBI director would be fired for taking too much interest in Mueller's Russia investigation. But ten days out from the election, Trump could hardly have wished for better news. The rest of the campaign was dominated by questions directed at Clinton, not at him, and he knew exactly how to play it with the crowds. The truth would soon be out, he'd tell them. The revived FBI investigation produced nothing of significance in the end, but by then it was too late for Clinton.

Talking to her more than two years later about those days, she gave me her verdict on Comey:

Well, he cost me the election. There's no doubt that he cost me it. You could see my numbers drop precipitously. And I know that, because I have polling data and not just what we have, but other polling data too. You know, it would have been different. I would have won. I fought back from his really ill-advised inappropriate comments in the summer. Fought back. We had a good convention by everybody's account. I won the debates.

We were on a very solid footing until the Russian co-operation with WikiLeaks and the weaponising of those emails that were stolen, and not only that, as Mueller points out in his second indictment, the Russians hacked into the cloud where very valuable information that the Democratic Party – and my campaign – had stored, and they stole it. We always were wondering how did they know who to target on Facebook. Who were these people that they were clearly going after?

And however he knew it, Trump knew it. He mentioned WikiLeaks 161 times between the day that they dropped the emails and the day of the election. So there was just a lot going on at the same time. But Comey? Absolutely called the election.

'It still hurts?' I asked her, although the question was unnecessary.

'Well, it's infuriating.'

In the last days of the election, I spoke to The Mooch once more. We were five days away from the vote, and his judgement was that the balance had tilted slightly towards Trump. 'We have a 50 to 55 per cent chance that he wins,' he told me in his office. I was fairly sure that he didn't believe it, but it was obvious that Comey had ridden to their rescue.

The most memorable exchange, however, came after we'd talked for a while and were walking towards the elevator. I mentioned the indiscipline in Trump's Twitter account, which had already become an unruly scattergun, firing off in every direction.

Scaramucci took me by the arm. 'I can tell you one thing. Donald has agreed that if he's elected, the Twitter account is controlled by the communications staff. It's fixed.

'No more tweets.'

I have fond memories of that comment, several times a day.

The next morning I called on the Clinton campaign headquarters, across the East River in Brooklyn. I had spoken before to Joel Benenson, her strategist, and we talked just off the big room where the campaign staff were working on their get-out-the-vote plans for Tuesday. He is a man who wears a naturally downbeat, even gloomy, expression, and although he insisted that the news was reassuring for Democrats from the key northern states that could deliver victory, even without Ohio – the 'blue wall' of Wisconsin, Michigan and Pennsylvania couldn't be breached – I detected a feeling of unease that hadn't been there in the campaign two or three weeks previously. The Comey intervention had been a nightmare, though he didn't put it that way, and had blown them off course.

Bill Clinton, regarded by some in the campaign as an irritant, was pressing – shouting, some have said – for more attention to be paid to Michigan and Wisconsin, where he could smell the sour prospect of defeat. His advice was not taken. In those closing days, post-Comey, they realised that not enough work had been done to insure them against a final swing towards Trump. It wasn't huge, but it was enough to turn into reality what had once seemed to Democratic partisans, and many others, a mathematical impossibility. A campaign that had often been too controlled, too centralised, with a candidate who had spent too much time in a bubble (with such strict limits on press access that many fair-minded journalists were angered), could not recover momentum.

It was time to go on the road for the last time in the campaign. North Carolina – won by Obama in 2008 and 2012 – was being targeted heavily by both sides, and the president was due to speak there on the last Friday night, just outside Charlotte. We turned up to see a shirt-sleeved Obama, on a mild autumn night, speaking to a crowd of perhaps 8,000 in an open-air arena where he told them of the momentous choice that lay ahead, between progress and retreat. It was one of his last campaign appearances as president and marked by the relaxation that had become so familiar. The event had an unusual intimacy, despite the size of the crowd. I recall the person standing beside me noticing that the military aide with the nuclear 'briefcase' chained to his wrist, which contains the military codes available to the president in an emergency and is never more than a few feet from him, was unusually obvious, walking directly across the platform behind the president and unfortunately being picked out by a stray spotlight.

'Trump. Imagine!' the man said to me.

Coming out, we spoke to three African American women of around thirty, one of whom had served in the air force. They were strong Obama supporters, but, as politely as they could, they indicated that although they would vote for Clinton on Tuesday, and certainly not for Trump, they would have preferred another candidate – a telling reminder of the dip in the Clinton campaign at the end.

Early next morning we drove east, because Trump had scheduled a short stop for an airport rally. There had been little notice, but a large crowd turned up, probably 10,000 strong, who waited in the sunshine for the first sight of his plane – with TRUMP emblazoned on the fuselage, of course. They were a cross-section of the local community, ordinary people with kids perched on their shoulders eating ice creams. There were a few hairy bikers who seemed to be from the Steve Bannon part of Trumpland – some white nationalist stickers were on their machines – but in the main this was middle America at play, not even particularly concerned about chanting 'Lock her up!' too often. They were normality on display.

My *Today* colleague Jonathan Harvey said, as the plane appeared, 'He's going to win, you know.'

Trump spoke briefly, got back in the plane and took off for the Midwest. His travels seemed haphazard in those last few days, but they weren't. They were meticulously targeted. He was touching the tender spots, and on Tuesday we knew why. North Carolina, Wisconsin, Michigan and Pennsylvania all fell to him – by quite narrow margins, fewer than 80,000 votes when everything was tallied – but they gave him his victory.

We were on air all night from the BBC Washington bureau on M

Street, and the tide was turning by midnight. Liz Chadderdon, who had worked on many Democratic campaigns, was speaking for that side in our results programme and began the evening convinced that Clinton would sail home safely, just as her Republican counterpart, John Reid, was preparing to explain the reasons for a Trump defeat. But she began to look more anxiously at her phone as she got information from Pennsylvania and Michigan that was not yet public. It was going wrong. John Reid, meanwhile, was finding it hard to believe the messages he was getting from Republican sources. In New York, Clinton stopped work on her acceptance speech and went to lie down for a short time.

By midnight, eastern time, the Democrats knew it was over. The 'blue wall' across the Midwest had cracked. The popular vote was won across the country, but states were lost that should have been held, which was enough to give Trump victory in the electoral college, taking him past the 270 electoral votes he needed and probably once believed, like all but his most devoted acolytes, were beyond him.

We got a call through to Trump Tower just before midnight – 5 a.m. in London – and tracked down The Mooch. He was happy to talk, but just before we put him on the air, he took another call. He told me that he'd just been informed by the Republican National Committee that he was allowed to say that they could be sure Trump would now be the forty-fifth president of the United States.

It was always going to be The Mooch, wasn't it?

CHAPTER 8

A CULTURE OF CONTEMPT

Inauguration day was cold, damp and gusty. Walking back from a viewing stand where I'd had to take binoculars to get a proper sight of Donald Trump on the west front of the Capitol – the hair, the jaw, the scowl, the joy – we were reflecting on his address as the rain moved in. A voice said, 'Not a speech. An extended tweet.'

We were gazing into the inhospitable drizzle, unsure what 'America First' portended for everyone. As we packed away our gear, the helicopter carrying away the Obamas dipped over the crowd, seeming with a tilt of its blades to make a farewell salutation before it took them to Andrews Air Force Base and thence to Chicago. Putting politics away for a moment, I mentioned to a friend on the *Washington Post* that on the way home I was hoping somehow to secure a ticket in New York for *Hamilton*, the musical that had opened on Broadway a few months earlier and which had turned one of the framers of the constitution into a hip-hop star. He said, 'You do realise that the script for the first Trump administration won't be written by Alexander Hamilton. It'll be by Mario Puzo.'

Setting a Founding Father against the author of *The Godfather* seemed appropriate for the moment, on a day of extremes. Trump's slogan on that morning was the one that had been on the banners of the American isolationists who marched against Europe as it drifted towards war in the 1930s, although it's fair to say that his knowledge of history is so vague that he had no idea that 'America First' was once chanted by Americans who were waving swastika flags and cheering Hitler. He was in no doubt, however, that 'making America great again' was going to be divisive. That was built into his first address as president, because politics for him was a fight-back against destructive forces, and he was intending to lead as he had campaigned, by setting winners and losers apart, and reminding everyone that forgiveness was for wimps. This wasn't going to be an administration like one of Lincoln's – 'with malice toward none, with charity toward all' – but much more like Puzo's picture of street life in 1950s New York, where the fight for control was just as rough as it needed to be, the family and its business at the heart of everything.

We walked past the Romanesque greystone Old Post Office building with its majestic clock tower, a few steps across Pennsylvania Avenue from the headquarters of the FBI, which had been converted in the previous couple of years into a hotel and was welcoming its first guests for the inaugural celebrations that weekend, with familiar letters shining above the door – spelling out TRUMP.

Another property, another financial outlet for the presidential brand, and one that he would almost be able to see from the family quarters in the White House five short blocks away. No such commercial operation had ever been tied so closely to the presidency. Yet it was the dispossessed for whom Trump claimed he had been elected. He was the conduit for their anger, and there was a striking link, even in those first days, between the feelings that he turned into a political movement, and his own sense of self. Behind all the bravado, the bullying manner and the torrent of insults, there was persistent evidence of the feeling of humiliation that he shared with many of those who felt, rightly, that they had been left behind.

The builder to whom quite a few bankers in New York wouldn't lend a cent; the socialite who lived high above 5th Avenue but still had the air of an outsider among the super-rich; the developer whose buildings had to be taller and shine brighter than any built by his rivals; the Johnny-come-lately Republican who grabbed the nomination in a street fight with the remnants of a once-dominant party establishment that looked down on him, angry at the way he had elbowed them aside. He enjoyed that victory, but never tried to conceal his own anger. He was the guy determined to beat those who demeaned him, knowing inside that they would never desist. Like the publisher of the *Manchester Union-Leader*, they'd consign photographs of him to the darkest corner of the smallest room.

No president has ever opened the workings of his mind to the people as Trump has done, and evidence of this kind of thinking emerges almost hourly. It was true on the day he walked into the White House as president, and true more than two years later, when you might have expected the fever to have passed. Not at all. The temperature never dropped; instead, it rose.

There was no cooling off. A particularly telling moment came in his speech to the Conservative Political Action Conference in March 2019, an event that has become the most important conservative festival of the year, when everyone gathers round the flame. His performance stands as a template for many others that were to come, in which a president is turned into a variety act – ready to go jump through hoops, stand on his head, and generally cause amusement. Trump was a particularly well-timed guest, having just returned from Vietnam and his summit with Kim Jong-un of North Korea. Perhaps the fact that the summit had failed prompted the introspective remarks that followed, because he launched into a long, mostly impromptu speech, which included some extraordinary riffs on favourite themes. He claimed that the special counsel Robert Mueller had deliberately hired hard-core Democrats to serve on his investigation, including someone, unnamed, who had 'the worst reputation of any human being I've ever seen'. They were, he said, 'all killers'. No one at the gathering asked him precisely what he meant. To any other audience these remarks would have suggested that something had gone wrong with the speaker, but he was cheered to the echo through a speech that one presidential historian, David Rothkopf, thought might have been, at around two hours, the longest by a president in history, just beating the oration in 1841 by William Henry Harrison, which was delivered in such cold and wet weather that he developed pneumonia and died soon afterwards.

Trump finished in apparently robust form, however, but revealed that despite the cares of office he had not forgotten the dispute about the size of his inaugural crowd. It gnawed at him and just wouldn't let him go. For those of us who attended both Obama's first inaugural address and Trump's eight years later, there was nothing to argue about. Trump spoke on a miserable day, but for whatever reason his crowd was thin compared to Obama's. A fact. But so what? Nobody spent much time thinking about it, because in the wider scheme of things it hardly mattered. Yet somewhere in the White House it still rankled and, true to form, he translated it into a hoax, another attempt by his enemies to belittle him by underhand means. Was there nothing they wouldn't do to try to humiliate him? The president revealed that he'd been looking at a picture of a scattered crowd taken on the day – two years on! – and had found that he was looking at a photograph taken quite a time before he rose to speak. Without any evidence, he was suggesting that it had been circulated deliberately in order to do him down. Wasn't that just the kind of thing that they spent their time cooking up against him? Each attack on Trump himself was interpreted, naturally, as more evidence of the American decline – 'carnage' he'd called it in his inaugural address, to the bewilderment of the former presidents who were there – that had to be reversed. The two were indistinguishable in his mind.

Presenting the crowd confection as proof of a hoax, he told his audience how he had looked down on the throng from the Capitol on the day he took the oath. 'And it was wide! Wide! We had a crowd – I've never seen a thing like it. And I have to live – I have to live with "crowd size"! It is all a phony deal, folks. But I saw a picture just the other night of practically no people. It was taken hours before our great day.'

Leave aside the fact that after more than two years in office, sitting in the White House, he was still poring over pictures of his inauguration in search of proof that the claims about crowd size were wrong, perpetrated by political opponents who, as he said in his speech, were people who hated their country. The telling line was, 'I have to live with "crowd size"!' Forget the threat of war in the Middle East, North Korean nuclear tests, economic uncertainty, gun violence, racial unrest, climate change; he was complaining that he still had to endure the accusation that his crowd was smaller than Obama's. An unforgivable assault on his pride by the people Ted Cruz called at the same conference 'bat-crazy Democrats'.

Finding a rational explanation for this speech – in the course of which he said that the Democrats' 'green deal' would mean the *disappearance* of the American car, full stop, and *all* air travel – is not easy. The *Washington Post* columnist Eugene Robinson called it unhinged. Trump was certainly tired. He'd been to the Far East, but the speech was also delivered in the week that his former lawyer, Michael Cohen, had testified to a congressional committee that the president was a 'liar', a 'conman' and 'a cheat'. So perhaps it was natural that he would return, in anger, to reassuring themes, all the old favourites. 'Crooked Hillary', his recent discovery of the weakness of his former friend, the sacked attorney general Jeff Sessions, whom he accused of a betrayal (yet another one) by recusing himself from the Russia investigation, the madness of wind power, his own powers of diplomacy, which had been hard to discern at his Vietnam summit, and – of course – the size of the crowd for his inaugural speech, which had been particularly admirable he said, because women had chosen to walk to the Mall in bad weather, 'in high heels in many cases', just to see him.

No one who heard it – including Nigel Farage, who had been invited from London to receive a Brexit hero's welcome – could have imagined this was a prepared oration. Not only was it unpolished, to put it politely, but after the opening sentences it hardly had any structure, and no coherence. Nonetheless, it was authentic, oozing the spirit of the man. One listener (admittedly not associated with the organisers, the American Conservative Union) called it a stream of unconsciousness. Trump himself attempted an explanation, when he got into his stride about ten minutes after he stood up.

'You know, I don't know, maybe you know. You know, I'm totally off script, right ... you know, I'm totally off script right now. And this is how I got elected, by being off script. True. And if we don't go off script, our country is in big trouble, folks. 'Cause we have to get it back.'

This was the essence of Trumpspeak, the conflation of his own style with a vanished 'great America', because the two are inseparable in his own mind. And the more instinctive, unpredictable and impulsive his thoughts, the greater is the America that swims into focus, as if inspired to reveal itself by his words.

It is the kind of speech that his supporters have come to know and love. But the CPAC event stands out as a fine example of the atmosphere he had created in Washington, only two years after his seismic victory. In a way, it is evidence of the depth of that achievement. He had no doubt that he could accuse senior public officials of corruption and criminality, most newspapers and broadcasters of venal impropriety, smear any member of Congress who didn't support him as anti-American, and face no consequences. 'The base' would stay strong, and indeed would want more. Happily, he would make sure they got it.

Forty-five years earlier, Nixon couldn't match any of this, even in the throes of his decline and fall. Members of Congress are accused by Trump of crimes, his own government agencies are trashed, old friends are consigned to deep darkness for acts of betrayal, former business partners and lawyers are branded lifelong liars for turning on him (with the invariable caveat that the lying only became obvious to him at the moment of betrayal, when the hidden truth was revealed at last), and almost all journalists and broadcasters are lumped together as determined purveyors of 'fake news', out to hoodwink 'the people', the exceptions being Fox News and the *National Enquirer*, the supermarket tabloid of the Cruz–JFK assassination story, which bought up the story of Trump's pay-off to the porn star Stormy Daniels specifically in order to suppress it, in a deal done at his lawyer's request. The publisher happily admitted afterwards that it was what the tabloids call a 'catch and kill' deal, a favour to stop the story influencing the election. Trump once wondered aloud, in public, why the paper had never been awarded a Pulitzer Prize.

Two years in, it would be natural to suppose that a performance like the CPAC speech suggested that the pressures of office were beginning to take their toll. In truth, there was nothing extraordinary about his statements, except that no other president in modern times (or possibly since the foundation of the republic) would have delivered such a litany of complaint against former friends, as well as political opponents, and laced it with quite so much self-pity. On the attack, Trump is always talking as much about himself as about those whom he's trying to bring down. The speech wasn't at all out of character, but emblematic of his presidency. Disorganised and fevered, impulsive and angry.

The consequence of this language coming from the seat of power has been a change in the common culture. He has normalised a public discourse framed by insult, to the extent that contempt has become one of the defining characteristics of his era. Great Americans on one side; cowards, liars and cheats on the other. Trump supporters in one camp; America-haters and losers in the other. In between? Forget it. It's just natural to attack the other side, as natural as if you're haggling over the price of a vacant building lot in New York City, where anything goes.

And what is the point of winning if you can't pour contempt on the loser?

When Representative Justin Amash announced on 4 July 2019 that he was leaving the Republican Party to sit as an independent in Congress, the president of the United States took time, on Independence Day, when most of his predecessors have tried to find uplifting words, to say this in a tweet: 'Great news for the Republican Party as one of the dumbest & most disloyal men in Congress is "quitting" the Party. No Collusion, No Obstruction! Knew he couldn't get the nomination to run again in the Great State of Michigan. Already being challenged for his seat. A total loser!'

Obviously, there is nothing new in overblown, melodramatic rhetoric in American politics – southern demagogues, in particular, would breathe hellfire at each other day and night, because insults were a currency as homely to them as grits for breakfast – but even weak or bullying presidents of both parties have been constrained by a sense that the White House is not the place for it. However much they might have cursed and raged in private (or broken the odd commandment here or there), no president in the modern era has wanted or has felt able to turn the office into an engine of contempt. Yet, quite deliberately, Trump did it from the start.

Warming up with his crude descriptions of Obama from his Twitter bully-pulpit before the 2016 campaign – 'inelegant and unpresidential', 'a pathetic excuse of a president', 'a racist', 'can you be that thick?' – he has hardly passed a day in the White House without letting loose a stream of invective towards someone who has displeased or challenged him. Intriguingly, the fiercer the attack, the more likely it is to be followed by a reminder of the qualities that he believes set him apart from the political throng, and the assertion that it is only his enemies who harbour self-doubt.

As he put it, before he became a candidate, in a tweet that serves as a model of his style, 'Sorry losers and haters, but my I.Q. is one of the highest – and you all know it! Please don't feel so stupid or insecure, it's not your fault.' What would Roosevelt, Kennedy, LBJ or even Nixon have made of such messages?

The unbroken tide of insult was so insistent that it came to shape the days. The majority of Americans who, according to all reputable polling evidence, believe it to be unpleasant, ill-judged or something far worse, have had to adjust to the knowledge that he will not stop, come what may. The Twitter feed is as immutable as the weather. Each time, when a moment has come at which people have asked, 'Surely he can't say that?', he has said it again, and turned up the volume.

At the death of John McCain, whose long imprisonment in North Vietnam had turned him into a hero for most Americans, the president made no effort to go back on his criticisms of a man who had offended him grievously – most probably, by being a Republican who tried to work across the aisle in the Senate (notably with Ted Kennedy) in an effort to find a consensus on immigration reform. McCain wanted to devise a 'pathway to citizenship' for the millions of undocumented migrants living in the United States, many of them settled for a generation and more, with working children and grandchildren educated in the US who probably spent less time wondering about how to pare down their tax bills from the Internal Revenue Service than Trump himself, or his lawyers. And, with an intimate knowledge of the Mexican border from his own state of Arizona, McCain didn't think that the wall was a solution to anything. To Trump, heresy.

McCain, Trump complained, shouldn't be considered a war hero, because he was taken prisoner after he was shot down near Hanoi in 1967. That was a sign of failure; this president preferred people who weren't captured. McCain's vote against the wholesale repeal of 'Obamacare', when his brain cancer was at an advanced stage, was the last straw for Trump, who ignored his frailty. 'He was horrible,' he said after his death, and during McCain's funeral service at the National Cathedral in Washington in September 2018, Trump took himself off to play golf on one of his own courses.

There could hardly be a more public expression of contempt from the White House. By that time, most Republican senators, though deeply embarrassed by the McCain episode, had evidently decided that there was nothing they could do to moderate Trump's language or change his style and they went along with it, with varying degrees of comfort, in the hope that they'd be spared an assault from the White House that might bring an end to their careers in some future Republican primary through a confrontation with a Trumpist insurgent.

Take the case of Lindsey Graham, the ponderous and lugubrious South Carolina senator who at first opposed Trump's nomination in 2016 on the grounds that he wasn't a true conservative, then complained loudly that he didn't understand defence or foreign affairs, and later accused him of slandering his dead friend McCain as he went to his grave. Go back to election year. 'You know how to make America great?' he had tweeted in 2016. 'Tell Donald Trump to go to hell.' When the Republicans nominated him nonetheless, Graham's judgement was that his party had gone 'bat-shit crazy'.

Then spool forward. For the likes of Senator Graham there is nothing so persuasive as flattery from the top. By mid-2019 the senator had folded up in a heap, and was happy to be flown meekly to Florida for the launch of Trump's 2020 campaign, mouthing superlatives about his presidency as if he had never doubted the inevitability of the eventual triumph. He admired the president's golf style – he now claims to have discovered the 'real' Trump while playing a round with him, on one of his own courses – and any worries about Trump's 'schizophrenic' relationship with Putin, as he once called it, had apparently evaporated. For the president, another victory to enjoy and another trophy to be stuck on the wall, like the head of a stuffed moose that he could pat on the nose as he passed. His rhetorical blunderbuss had downed them all.

But Trump's challenge to orthodoxy was not, clearly, in language alone. The cultural upheaval wasn't simply a challenge to the way presidents were expected to behave and speak, but to institutions. Speaking just before the inauguration to James Fallows of *The Atlantic* – a veteran journalist who had also spent time in the Carter White House – I got a vivid account of a liberal's attitude to Trump's election, one that he believed, even before the new president took the oath, was going to shake the foundations that many Americans believed solid and immovable. This was no blip on a screen, he said, but a challenge that took the country back to its darkest days, in the Civil War.

Fallows said:

I am old enough to have been around for the assassinations of John F. Kennedy and of Martin Luther King, and the Vietnam War, and then the Iraq War. There are a number of disasters and crimes and tragedies that have afflicted this country. But they were crimes inflicted upon it, or mistakes it made for reasons that seemed good at the time, as with the Vietnam War with that long build-up to it. This was the democratic system for a variety of odd reasons but now we are elevating a person who expresses complete disregard, indeed contempt, for the institutions of democratic governance in the long run – those of compromise and openness and accessibility to the press, and adherence to the norms on which any democratic society depends, from being transparent about your tax information to not having conflicts of interest, to not talking cavalierly about locking your enemies up.

So the American democratic system has set up for itself, in my view, the toughest test it has faced for at least a century. Now, the Civil War in the 1860s was the sternest test America has faced through its history. But this is, I think, the second sternest test – worse than Watergate forty-plus years ago.

There was more adherence even by Nixon to the norms of government than there is by Donald Trump. So we will see whether those norms actually are resilient or whether there is a challenge too great for them to absorb. I believe they will show their resilience, but that is not an obvious or automatic proposition right now. So this has been a very difficult year for American democracy.

Fallows was speaking before the inauguration, and the curiosity is that although Trump would surely not agree that his was an attack on 'democracy', because he had his own idea of what the word meant, he would certainly accept that he was trying to dismantle the norms of the system, whether institutions or ingrained habits. Everyone had learned during the campaign that they meant nothing to him. In particular, he had no respect for wisdom or accumulated experience in government, a concept that appeared to offend his conviction that he could see around the next corner before anyone else. Hadn't he said in the campaign that he knew more about ISIS than his generals, and didn't need the help of CIA intelligence to navigate the world? After the inauguration, some of his officials had to begin to accept that he meant it.

I spoke in early 2017 to a State Department lifer who had reason to understand. Tom Countryman became a diplomat in the early 1980s and, between foreign postings, worked in counter-terrorism, in the US delegation at the UN, on the staff of the National Security Council and, from 2011, was assistant secretary of the Bureau of International Security and Nonproliferation, dealing with Russia and arms reduction. He worked at the heart of the foreign policy and security machine for three Republican and two Democratic administrations, serving as a non-partisan official for presidents and secretaries of state of different colours, from Reagan to Obama. In the week after the inauguration in January 2017 he was told, in a phone call that came without warning, that his services were no longer required. He was out.

His description of the incoming administration, which he'd observed taking shape during the transition from election day ten weeks before, was dark. When I asked him to describe it, he said his mind went back to his first foreign posting as a young diplomat, fresh from university, when he was sent to the American Embassy in Belgrade, where Slobodan Milosevic was putting together an oppressive regime.

'What I saw in Serbia when Mr Milosevic achieved the presidency in some of the first free elections ever held in Serbia, and watched how he used his victory to consolidate complete power over the press, over the judiciary, and over business through his support for a widespread net of corruption – well, the parallels I see between Mr Milosevic and Mr Trump are frankly frightening, and growing stronger every day.'

We were talking after the Trump administration had been in power for only a few weeks. I was recording his words for broadcast, so this was no late-night ramble from a disappointed man, but words from the heart. He was making a remarkable charge – that the president was following a path that the United States had been trying to close off around the world for generations, and which represented the way of its adversaries. To Countryman, a twenty-five-year veteran of his country's foreign service, through which he dealt with many different forms of autocracy, the warning was as clear as crystal.

'I don't take for granted that our institutions will actually resist an authoritarian move like this.'

Observations like Countryman's, from a public official who had never engaged in partisan politics, lead you to the heart of the Trump conundrum.

Freedom or authority?

Trump campaigned on a programme of personal liberty, with the traditional promises from the right of smaller government and freedom for business, all presented as the change that would bring prosperity to those who had been left behind, and who resented the interfering hand of government from far away. It spoke to the mainstream of the conservative movement, despite the disdain of many of its intellectual leaders for Trump. Before his decision to run for president, he had shown no sign of having any discernible ideology, save for a general view that people like him should pay less in tax and be allowed to get on with their businesses with minimum interference from anyone. About the social issues that moved many of the voters who eventually supported him – conservative evangelicals, in particular – he had said little. No one knows, for example, what he really thinks about abortion, which he never opposed in the past but which 'the base' abhors. His success in the campaign was to throw together all the issues that could be seen as matters of individual freedom – trashing any 'collectivist' idea like Obamacare along the way – and simply appeal to all those who felt that most of the bad things in their lives were brought on by big government. He would sort it out by appointing the right kind of judges, the promise they'd been waiting for.

Except, as the campaign demonstrated in his strange waltz with Putin, his admiration for authoritarian leadership was obvious from the start. Some voters, who had been waiting for some kind of political messiah, thought he represented the nearest thing to a libertarian agenda they had known; but in Trump's hands it was fused with a desire to exert authority without the intervention of congressional committees, or bureaucratic encumbrances that claimed the right to check a president's power, not to mention those pesky courts, which needed to be sorted out with an injection of right-minded judges. Freedom in Trump's America was to be achieved without too much awkward freedom of thought.

Before the midterm elections in 2018, as his foreign policy veered hither and thither, he threatened a jet-propelled trade war with China, and revealed the depth of his worries about where the Mueller investigation would lead with a torrent of invective. I spoke to some of his opponents outside Washington about how they would challenge the drift of policy, and indeed the power of the Twitter-fashioned rhetoric coming from the White House. They understood it could not be wished away, because although his approval ratings were historically low for a president at that point in his first term, the bullishness of his hard-core support would always give him hope that he could power into a second term. 'The base' was firm, and ready to fight.

But if you want to find the antithesis of Trump's America, head west to California.

I visited Governor Jerry Brown, nearly eighty years old at that point but still carrying something of the liberal swagger that he'd brought to the political scene in the 1970s when he was first elected. Now in his second flowering – he was elected governor in 2010, fully twenty-eight years after finishing his first incarnation, when term limits obliged him to step down after eight years and two

terms – he sat in an office looking across San Francisco and spoke
of the Trump administration with the kind of angry wonderment
that the president himself usually directs the other way – towards
California.

'Trump is highly unusual in the positions he's taking – the sharp
break with his predecessors, the instability of his behaviour and the
pronouncements that change so rapidly, the identification with a
relatively small subset of the American people – maybe 20 per cent
of them. These are all unusual. Most political leaders try to build
their constituency, not contract it.'

So how do you challenge such unorthodox leadership?

I think the position of California is doing its work in going
against the policies of President Trump. On immigration, public
provision, you name it. Here is one thing, but the policies that the
Republicans and President Trump are pursuing are also highly
dangerous to the world. They're undermining American solidar-
ity and unity – the fundamental unity that is enshrined in the
motto *e pluribus unum* and our constitution. So I think we have
the Washington problem, and then we have the California activity. I would say more people throughout the country are called
upon to take action.

That action, in California, has centred on immigration.

America has many people who are undocumented who've come
here, for the most part – overwhelmingly – to seek a better life,
mostly in the southern part of this state and across the border
from Mexico. California has millions of these people. Now,
Trump has not said he's going to round them up like some authoritarian regime but he *is* harassing them. Everything is reduced to
pandering to the nationalist minority that are Trump's base. I
would say for the most part in Washington it's more of a political
game that's being played to use xenophobia, use the crimes of
some to be ascribed to the many. So we're in a real pickle here in
the United States. We have someone at the helm who is tearing up
much of the fabric of what made America in the last twenty-five

to fifty years. So, yeah – California needs to protect itself. We also need to change America.

His argument was that the state was happy to obey the law in properly sanctioned deportation when the evidence was clear under the law, but would use the courts to block mass deportations. San Francisco would be a 'sanctuary city' – refusing to co-operate with immigration authorities if, for example, they tried to deport an individual who had entered the country illegally but had not committed any crime since. Cities across the country have co-operated in that effort, to the fury of the White House. There was a historical precedent, from a dark time.

What we're saying is we're not going to co-operate with his round-up. We used to have something called the underground railroad in the time of the Civil War, when the American Negroes – slaves – went to the north for refuge. People broke the law because they felt the natural right of liberty was being offended.

Well, now we have something different, but we have families, we have workers. The California economy depends on the work of many of these people who Trump is scaring the hell out of, and at least purporting to deport.

We spoke about a speech delivered a few days earlier by George W. Bush, who said he wanted a return to civility in politics, because he worried that it had gone. Brown said, 'We need some intelligent leaders who are both rhetorically effective and mentally alert, and clear in mobilising an electorate that sees what's going on. I want clarity, but also caring. We have neither right now.'

High above the city, with his dog Calusa sniffing at my trousers (no doubt scenting our little Bess, although she was 6,000 miles away) – the cross-bred Border collie–corgi had recently acceded to the title of First Dog of California – we looked down towards Market Street, one of the main city thoroughfares, and there, unmistakable because of the bright-blue bird on the top corner of the otherwise anonymous brown building, was the headquarters of Twitter. At that time, the president's tweets numbered around

65,000, and counting. For a moment it seemed as if that building, just another city office block, was housing them all in a contemporary Tower of Babel, from which one unmistakable and insistent voice was barking louder than all the others.

California has always been surfing dreams, and that moment did seem to take us into a different sphere.

Brown, leading a state where Clinton got more than 61 per cent of the vote in 2016, was speaking of a cultural antipathy to Trump's nationalism that goes deep in his California, where the Latino, Asian and African American communities put together outnumber the non-Latino white population, and which has always seen itself as a melting pot, as diverse and ever-changing on the west coast as New York City is on the east. It is easy, in the company of Jerry Brown, or indeed Congressman Adam Schiff – whose district covers Hollywood – to feel the tide of liberal anger at Trump. Schiff told me, before the midterm elections that brought Democrats to power in the House and therefore allowed him to become chairman of the powerful House Intelligence Committee, that he believed that the country faced an assault greater than many of its citizens yet realised:

> You can go back to World War Two, and then say that somehow what we're facing now is a greater challenge to the country than that. It's a different kind of challenge, obviously, but I would imagine that the level of division in the country is not unlike what we saw during Vietnam. The level of dysfunction is frankly unprecedented, and that's what makes this such a historic challenge.
>
> This is the time to stand up and be counted. The next generation is going to ask us what we did at the time that country really needed us.

But it's impossible, of course, to understand Trump by talking to his critics. They may tear apart his policy platform, accuse him of dangerous warmongering in the South China Sea or the Persian Gulf, assail him on his 'hoax' rhetoric on climate change – Brown says California is 'burning up' and it's bound to get so much worse that no president can avoid a confrontation with reality – but they know well that the 2016 result was no fluke. Whatever their criticisms of the Clinton campaign, their anger at the Comey intervention, they're aware of the depth of the feeling that Trump was able to tap and which still runs strong. You need to go elsewhere to find it.

I felt its pull in West Virginia, just before the midterm elections, at a time when in the league table of states it had the fourth-lowest per capita income in the country, and the third-highest unemployment rate. The state is tucked into the Appalachians, and a journey into the folds of its hills and valleys, driving westwards from the Washington suburbs in northern Virginia, takes you in a few hours from prosperous and high-tech booming America to land that seems forgotten. Its pockets of poverty are obvious everywhere, and the scars and the husks of its old industries litter the landscape. Its small towns are struggling to rescue their charm and their very personalities. In 2017, the state had the third-highest rate of opioid overdose deaths across the country. Caroline Foreback of the TV station WVNS, in the old mining town of Beckley, told me that visiting south-east West Virginia now was 'like landing on a moonscape … everything seems to have gone'.

You can take a little underground train into some old mine workings that have been turned into a museum for tourists, where just under the surface you can see the once-rich seams of coal that used to fuel the factories and the steelworks that dominated the part of America that now has to bear the insult of being called the 'rust belt'. A couple of generations ago it was the pride of the country. You don't have to search far for the source of the anger.

Hinton, a small town of 2,500 people about half an hour's drive away, near the confluence of the Greenbrier and New rivers, is trying hard to revive itself, but there is too much evidence of what it once was for that to be an easy task. It used to be an important stop on the Chesapeake and Ohio railroad, and called itself a railway town. The *Cardinal*, which rolls from New York south to Washington and then turns west to Chicago, still stops there three times a week, a reminder of old times, but for most of the time the station is quiet and the track deserted. When the train does stop, few passengers get on and off. Chris Meadows, the city manager, who's working to revive Hinton with new developments in the old brick warehouses associated with the railroad, talks with nostalgia about the way things were. Now, the young folk of Hinton mostly leave.

This is beautiful country, streaked with wooded gorges and high hills, but – like northern Kentucky, the western fringe of Pennsylvania and southern Ohio – it has found itself looking back and not forward. That is why Trump got a higher percentage of the vote in West Virginia in 2016 than in any other state – nearly 70 per cent.

I watched him at a rally in the midterm campaign in an airport hangar in Huntington, where the south-west corner of the state juts into Kentucky and Ohio, and there was one campaign sign that almost everyone in the crowd was holding up – TRUMP DIGS COAL. How right they were. The crowd gathered long before Air Force One arrived, to see the man who shared their view that coal was not a fuel of the past, but the route to prosperity. It was not an accident that his campaign had received unstinting financial support from the fossil fuel industry. He spoke that afternoon of new mines opening up; you could have heard the cheers from underground. In truth, although his administration had already reversed Obama-era regulations that were meant to accelerate the closure of coal-fired power stations, no industry analyst thought the historic decline in employment was going to be reversed. Yet on that day, his hair flying dangerously into the wind despite the attention it had no doubt received, he presented this as the opening of a new era of mining for coal, as they once did across Appalachia.

'You know what I say? Don't worry about it, I'll just figure it out. Does that make sense? I'll just figure it out. The Democrats want to raise your taxes, restore job-killing regulations, shut down your coal mines – and, by the way, they *will* shut down your coal mines. You know that! That's one thing I can guarantee.'

Did they believe that he would 'just figure it out' and all would be well? They certainly crowded round him. During the rally, a few people got up for a chorus of 'Lock her up!', a chant that by that stage had acquired an antique flavour as a battle cry from an old field of victory, letting him know that they'd been on the road with him and were never going to doubt him. He represented their culture, not 'the other', and that was enough. It was just as well that they thought of him as a representative of their anger, and not someone who had come from nowhere to inherit the promise of the American Dream. Because, as he never says in these speeches, he was left a fortune by his father.

In the first debate with Clinton, he said, 'My father gave me a very small loan in 1975, and I built it into a company that's worth many, many billions of dollars.' Not quite. A *New York Times* investigation in 2018 calculated that in various ways from the mid-1970s onwards, his father, Fred, passed on to him $60 million (worth perhaps $140 million today) to pursue his property ambitions and to rescue him from some of the dips and dives that have punctuated his career. In making a virtue of his wealth, Trump usually points to himself as someone who has taken the road open to every American, allowing them to turn a pittance into a fortune by hard work and guile. The truth is more complicated, to put it gently.

The Huntington rally was telling. Trump spent much of his speech expressing mystification at the misrepresentation of his record – the rising job numbers (true, though less spectacular in scale than he claimed), the fact that some coal mines were open for business again (again, a claim with a sliver of truth but greatly exaggerated), and the progress he was making on building his Mexican wall, which produced cheers and a happy old shout from the campaign, 'Build that wall!' But the whole performance had a defensive air, acknowledging that he wasn't believed, as though that was incomprehensible. The recurring line was, 'Can you believe it?' Beyond the slogan – MAGA ('Make America Great Again'), which was emblazoned on many of the baseball caps in the crowd – it was a simple litany of complaint.

And his opponents revelled in the chaotic management in the White House – successive chiefs of staff who found it hard to defend the president in public and who had a precarious short-term existence, one press secretary who was reduced at a bad moment to hiding in bushes in the White House grounds to avoid reporters, nominees for Cabinet posts who turned out to be incapable of answering simple questions about their responsibilities at confirmation hearings. It was easy for Democrats to laugh, and for the late-night TV shows to have a festival of fun. But Trump demonstrated that, whatever feelings of resentment and even humiliation might be bubbling up inside him, in public he was unembarrassable. As he had shown in the campaign, he just didn't seem to care. The private angst that became the talk of Washington from his earliest days in the White House was accompanied by public boasts that spiralled to the sky. I heard him say in West Virginia that he had created, personally, the greatest movement in the history of the United States. He says it everywhere, and no one in the crowd seems to mind.

He had succeeded, in a way Americans hadn't seen before, in bringing to power a counter-culture.

His attitude to authority, to traditional mechanisms of government, to the balance of power that dreamy politicians celebrate as the constitutional holy grail of America, was one of impatient antagonism. People growing up in the Vietnam era remember the tide of alternative thinking that swelled up on campuses and in the streets in which America was imagined as a different kind of place. The movement was wild, often contradictory, and fuelled by passions that were allowed to run free. But eventually it subsided. America became a more conservative country again.

Trump, bizarrely, succeeded in installing a counter-culture in the White House, just as iconoclastic and with all the gut passion that the liberal-left had displayed in the late 1960s. Where McGovern had lost – badly – in 1972, Trump had won. The world turned upside down.

At a gun and knife show in Pennsylvania in 2018, surrounded by modern weaponry, civil war relics, advertisements for fearsome tasers to use against burglars, and posters reassuring everyone that God loved guns, I spoke to some converts. This was telling, from a man in late middle age who was no more than a regular hunter in the neighbouring hills and not a gun-obsessive. A Republican of moderate views who had not warmed to Trump at the start.

'I am a respectable man, I wanted somebody who was intelligent, who had a good knowledge and command of the issues, and I was stuck with the concept that being polite, being appropriate and being professional was the way to go. Then you have somebody like a Trump who is so difficult to deal with, crude or lewd or whatever.

But look, he can definitely make his point. So I am pleased with the way the administration is turning out.'

He represented Trump's victory, having been persuaded. Another said: 'The change America needed was that you don't need professional political people, where they are in office and one hand washes the other. He wants to clean up the country, whereas the politicians – they want to clean up on the country and take the money.' For him 'the politicians' were a group from which Trump stood apart.

This was Pike County, Pennsylvania, on a bright winter's day, with ice on the Delaware River, where Trump got 60 per cent of the vote. At this juncture people weren't deserting him – for all the embarrassments coming out of Washington. They were feeling more than ever that they were right in what they'd done. A risky ride, but why not? For outsiders, a sobering reminder of the feelings that had propelled him to office.

On the face of it, he seems an unlikely figure to be the 'clean-up kid'. He has lived his life on a financial roller-coaster and his complicated financial affairs will remain the subject of myriad investigations as long as he remains in office, and perhaps will prove his Achilles heel. When I talked to people in Atlantic City, including the Republican mayor, just before his inauguration, about his venture into the casino business there – 'the eighth wonder of the world', he called it – the word they would not use to describe the chaotic financial collapse of his enterprise and his subsequent hasty departure was 'clean'. But the promise to 'drain the swamp' had done the trick: someone had to say it. Even those who were suspicious of him, and perhaps wouldn't lend him a dollar, were willing to give it a shot.

At this stage, he was already reshaping the United States. Appointments to the courts at every level that pleased small-government conservatives, the most radical environmental policy for decades in which the balance was deliberately shifted towards oil and mining interests, a notably austere and often harsh immigration regime (in a country built proudly on the promise brought by newcomers), a bonfire of government regulations, many of them the product of patient bipartisan agreement over decades. And maybe most startling of all, a presidency that addressed itself to the

American people in a way no one had known before. The benefits that would come by the end of his time in office might not be obvious to everyone – in the view of liberals, the consequence would be disaster and a backward-looking country – but enough of them were willing to give him a chance. Convinced that America had been in decline, they wanted to give it a jolt.

He was slaughtering herds of sacred cows. Sitting down with a prominent conservative, Diane Katz at the Heritage Foundation, the think-tank that sees itself as the guardian of the Reagan inheritance, you will find mystification at any alternative view of the world. On climate change, for example. I asked her why there was a president who seemed to be at war with science.

'No, on the contrary, the war with science goes way, way back – decades – and it has to do with the politicisation of science. For me, policy prior to the Trump administration on climate change and global warming was entirely politicised and it has led to this myth about climate change.'

A myth?

'Of course! Why do so many scientists swallow the myth? I'd love to know!'

Such conversations have a way of not getting very far.

At the gun and knife show, among the blades and handguns, rifles and pepper sprays guaranteed to give an assailant 'a very bad day', anyone would realise how Trump had given them a voice and legitimised their hurt, so that they felt emboldened to say publicly what they might have muttered privately before. Carrying a microphone, and therefore identifying myself as a near-certain manufacturer of 'fake news', there were quite a few people who made it clear with a surly shake of the head that they had nothing to say. I did meet one character, prowling along trestle tables heavy with fearsome hardware, who was happy to let me into his world.

'This is a country that has been under a political system that keeps a lot of truths from the American people. Donald is making them realise that. The worst thing we could have done is to vote for Hillary Clinton. The Clinton family – if people don't believe me, they can look it up – things are starting to come out now. People who are against the Clintons all of a sudden end up dead.'

Again, not a conversation likely to reach any kind of happy conclusion.

This is the true flavour of Trump's America. A genuine feeling that people who have been forgotten are getting some attention again, but one that's infected with a lust for antagonism, partisanship and, frequently, the kind of conspiratorial thinking that's encouraged daily from the Oval Office itself. A toxic mix, in which legitimate grievance is electrified by bitterness and contempt. From the other side, it looks like a breeding ground for trouble.

Soon after leaving the gun show, I sat down in New York with Philip Bobbitt, professor of jurisprudence at Columbia Law School, and a noted historian. He also has a significant political pedigree, being a nephew of Lyndon B. Johnson, which means he knew the White House during Vietnam, having spent some summers there in his student days. He later served there under Carter, George H. W. Bush and Bill Clinton. Being a scholar who is careful with words, his criticism of a sitting president is couched as moderately as he can manage.

It isn't just Trump's temperament, or policies – it's that he has never spent one hour in public service. He doesn't have that knowledge and experience to draw on and he hasn't had to cultivate talents of persuasion, respect, patience, tolerance.

He said during the campaign that 'I will never lie to you', which I found odd as he was lying all the time about so many things, but what I think he meant was: 'I will always let you know how I feel.' And when you have a public that is disillusioned with the elite and conventional methods of information, it's not surprising they fall back on something they do know – which is how to read another person's genuineness and whether they are really telling you what they think. So I think that's exactly what he meant – there's no political correctness, he will tell you exactly what's on his mind. The problem is that is grossly insufficient for solving public problems.

I wondered how damaging that might be.

It depends on whether or not we will be shocked, as I think we will be, by what's happened, and then pull back and say we have to listen to the voices that put Donald Trump in office. We have to, for their good and for our own good. We don't want to have one of these wretched experiences again. If that's the consequence, if we can find a way to reach out to those disaffected parts of the population who are rightly, quite rightly, outraged by being ignored and patronised, condescended to, then I think the damage will be temporary maybe, even salutary.

If, on the other hand, this just leads to further alienation from a large part of our body politic – the feeling that, well, now what do we do, the idea that it must be hopeless because the president has been driven from office by some conspiracy – then I think we'll be worse off than we were at the beginning.

For Bobbitt, proper invigilation of Trump and proper congressional and judicial investigation where it's warranted have to be accompanied by an understanding of the legitimate anger that was the bedrock of his campaign. The problem, however, is that such an appeal to tolerance runs counter to the very spirit of the administration that pushes the public mood in another direction. Given a chance to rise above the fray, to apply some healing balm, Trump always resists. Present him with a sensitive problem, deserving a delicate touch from the White House, and he will fumble it.

When the Ku Klux Klan and other white segregationist and nationalist groups held a 'Unite the Right' rally in Charlottesville, Virginia, in August 2017 – in a row over a statue of the military leader of the Confederacy, Robert E. Lee – they fought a bloody pitched battle with liberal protestors, one of whom was killed. Hawk Newsome, who leads the New York chapter of the campaign group Black Lives Matter, was there. He described the scene to me.

'When we went to protest, we saw men in camouflage gear with huge guns, and neo-Nazis with signs saying "Kill Jews", "Kill Niggers". The Ku Klux Klan and skinheads had shields, sticks, guns, knives, pepper spray, goggles – they were prepared. I looked down at my phone and – boom! – I was hit with a rock. There were fights, people hit with hammers, it was terrible.'

Afterwards, the president said he thought there were 'very fine people' on both sides in Charlottesville that day. Criticism rained down from the elders of the Republican Party, as well as from his political opponents. 'Fine people' in the midst of a crowd of neo-Nazis, carrying guns and threatening to kill Jews and 'Niggers'? Mitt Romney spoke in the days afterwards of 'an unravelling of the national fabric'.

Not for the first time, when the president qualified his comments, presumably as part apology, and then retreated again, he made things worse. The episode reminded everyone how much the old racial wound still hurts. Sitting in New York, recollecting the day, Newsome said, 'The hate is in your face, it's outright. We have people who worship Trump as if he's a god. He can do no wrong. You have Bible-belt Republicans who draw all their ideals from the Good Book. Donald Trump is violating God's code, the commandments, and they choose Donald Trump over Jesus. Well, that's amazing to me.'

These were the early signs of a presidency that by the beginning of the last year of his first term was the most chaotic America had known in the modern era. The tweets of Trump's early days, which many people had taken as evidence of a fragile, tormented personality, and not much more, had turned into a conveyor belt of abuse, layered with fantasy and untruths that were so blatant that reporters spent their time not so much checking his messages for veracity – because the inventions were usually so obvious – as arguing among themselves whether he knew what he was saying, and just didn't care, or whether he had passed into a state in which he had lost the ability to distinguish between fiction and truth, and had created a world so consumed by his boiling rage that it had none of the characteristics most people would associate with normality.

He pursued a foreign policy that scared allies (and delivered some of them in northern Syria to a Turkish war machine), and seemed never to deviate far – in Ukraine, the Middle East, the Far East and Europe – from a path that would suit Vladimir Putin. At home, by the end of 2019, he had doubled the deficit that had been one of his bitter complaints about Obama. And through it all, his financial affairs – despite the work of lawyers trying to prevent disclosure of his tax returns, or the conviction of yet another business associate – were threatening not only to sabotage his chances of re-election, but to raise the spectre of the ultimate punishment, impeachment in office.

It had once seemed as if the willingness of the Republican majority in the Senate to defend Trump's stumbles, mistakes and challenges to the constitution and the courts knew no bounds. By his third year no one could be sure, and Romney's sceptical voice was no longer alone.

It had been clear in the 2016 campaign that this was a candidate who wanted to create a presidency of 'self'. Every success would be the produce of personal vision and guile, the combination that he often called genius. And failures would be the consequence of enemy forces so jealous of his talents that they visited their anger on all Americans. It was not a long journey from those campaign rallies to football stadiums filled with jeering crowds at the start of the 2020 campaign ready to defend anything he had done and to march under his banner till Doomsday.

One greatly respected presidential historian and election analyst told me privately that his lurking fear was one he hadn't known before. 'Having watched this guy in office – unable to lead an administration, sending out illiterate messages, stuck in front of daytime TV for his only intellectual stimulation – I think to myself that if he thought in late 2020 that he was going to lose the election, he might do anything. Anything.'

He went on to canvass a thought that he knew was circulating in Washington, propelled by the erratic performance of a president who evidently saw no value in continuity among his advisers, particularly in national security and defence. He reminded me that in Nixon's last days, which were so dark that some of his staff feared for him, General Al Haig, chief of staff, took steps to review the protocols required to authorise a nuclear strike. As he put it to me, 'Haig probably didn't have the power, but he didn't want some kid sitting in a bunker somewhere getting an order that he had to carry out.' As a result, Haig tightened the system that kicks in if a president reaches for the codes in the nuclear briefcase that is never more than a few feet from him. The idea that a president can launch a strike alone is a myth, because in practice there are checks and balances that come quickly into play, but Haig took the trouble to bolt down the chain of command through which the order had to pass. The question was: had the generals put in place a similar insurance policy for Trump?

We were sitting on a beautiful university campus, sweet oleander on the air over the lawns, in an office with posters of decades of presidential campaigns on the walls – FDR and Willkie, Stevenson and Eisenhower, then all the rest, including posters and bumper stickers for a host of long-forgotten characters who had a moment in the sun, such as Dick Gephardt, Jack Kemp, Gary Hart, all of whom thought they would be president one day, and were swept out by the tide. A political tradition was displayed on the walls (and the ceiling, and the table top) but the conversation was about how difficult it would be to restore after Trump, however he went.

I know, from first-hand knowledge of one conversation, how George W. Bush suspects it might end. He tells friends he knows the pressures in the Oval Office, even on a president who waves away briefing papers and advice – 'I don't need to read the same thing in the same words every day,' Trump said in 2018 of the morning intelligence report to the Oval Office. Bush's view is that the weight of office will eventually hit Trump harder than he knows.

He adds two more problems to the mix. First, Trump almost certainly – by his own boast – has the unhealthiest diet of any president in living memory. All those burgers and dogs in the sessions in front of football games and *Fox & Friends* on TV. Second, he is seventy-one and clearly, from his own speeches, filled with anger and hurt. A troubled man. Put all those together, and Bush has expressed the view that if you were making a good guess, you might well surmise that one morning he might be found dead in bed.

An unkind but accurate observation would be that the conspiracy theorists, to whom Trump has given such succour, would be launched on the journey of their lives. Forget Oswald, the Texas School Book Depository and the Grassy Knoll, it would be a festival of madness.

Such was the atmosphere across America, particularly among people who'd touched power, as Trump began his campaign for re-election. No one could watch him at the rallies where he railed against the Congress, joked about the UN, climate change, immigrants from Mexico or Puerto Rico, and conclude anything other than that he had succeeded in a task that he had relished from the moment he came down to the lobby of Trump Tower on 5th Avenue in New York in 2015 and declared himself a candidate for president – making America an angrier place.

His currency is contempt. Speeches are brimful of it; his tweets shimmer with disgust for anyone who opposes him. Former administration officials – never mind if they were secretaries of state or chiefs of staff or national security advisers – become 'dumb as a brick' or 'weak' when they're finally pushed onto the down escalator to the street. The culture of his country has been infected in his time, and by his efforts, with a contemptuous air, and the public discourse soured, not just in the White House or on Capitol Hill but across America.

Early in 2019, I wanted to take a trip during which I wouldn't set foot in Washington, nor sniff any gossip, however delicious it might be.

So, with an old song in my head and a train ticket in my pocket, I went to Chicago to start a long journey.

CHAPTER 9

'DON'T YOU KNOW ME, I'M YOUR NATIVE SON'

SOUTH

Landing in Chicago two years on from the inauguration, at the juddering midpoint of his first term, it felt odd not to be regretting Washington. After all, the Mueller report on the Russians was said to be nearly complete (although it wasn't); the first confrontation between Trump and the new Democrat-controlled House had shut down chunks of the federal government; and with the New Hampshire primary a year away – only one riotous year! – the Democrats were beginning to agonise about presidential candidates. Yet I was staying away deliberately, to make a journey I wanted to take slowly. It had been in my mind for a long time. Maybe some fellow passengers might want to talk politics, or maybe not. I didn't mind. I would start in one favourite city, then travel to another that is more than ever America's most idiosyncratic and disturbing, and also visit a shrine. I would travel, too, with a haunting song in my head.

> Good morning, America, how are you?
> Don't you know me, I'm your native son,
> I'm the train they call the City of New Orleans,
> I'll be gone five hundred miles when the day is done

No interviews with politicians; no day-by-day schedule; just a journey with its serendipitous encounters, between two cities a country apart. The here-and-now would be freshened by memory, and maybe history.

One of the cities has a pedestal in American folklore sculpted from gangsterism and political corruption, the other is a place of a different kind, with an odour and aura quite its own – oozing out of a steamy, jazz-driven life that attracts outsiders and then often leaves them bewildered when they go, even more so if they've taken the trouble to delve deep and tried to understand it. Between them they project the power of urban America, and reveal its fragility. If you travel from Chicago to New Orleans, it's worth taking the time to abandon airports and take the train, because a proper journey between such places should involve enough time for proper acclimatisation, and because the rhythm of your translation from the Windy City to the Big Easy is set by the Mississippi itself, which moves gently alongside you for much of the way.

It's also true that one of the best ways to feel America's contemporary sense of loss is to get onto the railroads. They built the country, gave it iron sinews. Prairies and deserts could be crossed, the Rockies were no longer a barrier and the oceans could be joined. Railways also breathed prosperity. The cattle were driven from deep in Texas north to Kansas City, then shipped by train – dead or alive – to the stockyards of Chicago, where the trains also carried the grain from the prairies to the rest of America and, through the Great Lakes, to the world. That network allowed people to move and prosper, bringing east and west together, and the trains spoke of the commodity Americans had been reared to treasure, allowing the spirit of the early settlers to drive them on to another frontier. The giant locomotives of the Union Pacific, Illinois Central, the Chesapeake and Ohio, the Kansas City Southern and all the others, represented energy and discovery. They could roll through storm and tempest, carry coal out of the Appalachians and then steel from Pittsburgh, conquering the vast landscape once and for all.

The romance of the railroads slipped quickly from everyday consciousness into distant memory after air travel became possible for middle-income families in the late 1950s. Quite quickly, they started to forget those bulging, hooting locomotives with their cowcatchers and cabooses and clouds of steam, the drivers and engineers, and the gentle itinerant army of hobos who knew only that they had to be on the move to somewhere. The towns in the midst of nothingness that only sprang up because the railroad passed through them began to shrink and die. The folklore faded – those stories of gamblers on the train from New York to Florida (the *Silver Meteor*) who were said to win and lose fortunes as the train rolled through the Carolinas in the night, or of jazzmen travelling north to Chicago who played all the way from the South so loudly that you could hear them from the fields as the train rolled by. These images came to represent a fondness for the past. Even in the commuter-packed north-east corridor from Boston through New York to Washington, where the trains have revelled in a spirited renaissance in the last four decades, two great stations – Grand Central in New York, which was only saved from the wrecking ball by a public campaign in the 1970s, and Union Station in Washington, which was rescued from decrepitude for the bicentenary in 1976 – are a reminder of a past that remains more solid than the overcrowded big-city airports that, since they were turned in an instant into anxious security zones after 9/11, have become places that many people would like to avoid, but think they can't.

Climbing aboard a long-distance train is therefore taking a happy step backwards. Many Americans, even in middle age and beyond, have never ridden the railroad. Eighty per cent of farms in the Midwest were once within 5 miles of one of the great lines. Now, unless you live in one of the handful of urban areas where proper commuter networks survive, you don't think of taking the train. Yet that decline – of the 90,000 passengers now travelling daily on 300 trains, the overwhelming majority are on short journeys around urban centres – has its own attraction. The lure of a journey that's a break with the ordinary. Who chooses to spend a night on a train, rattling around on tracks that bear the scars of years of carrying heavy freight in mile-long trains, and why?

I left Chicago, heading south, on a shivery January evening. There was a storm on the way, and Chicagoans were hunkering down for a familiar few days of bitter blasts and snow blowing in from Lake Michigan on a north wind. Near Union Station, a pillared 1920s Beaux Arts monument to the golden age of steam, the wind was zipping through the curving tunnel of the Chicago River, between buildings that tell the story of twentieth-century architecture in stone and concrete probably better than anywhere else, and are one of the city's great boasts. I was warned that when I got back from the South, in six days or so, the place would look and feel different. Sidewalks would be packed with snow and there would be ice floes on the lake. With the wind-chill, it was going to feel like 25 below, probably more. In between, however, I'd be in balmy climes. If there was rain in New Orleans, which there usually is, it would be warm and soft, because snow is unknown on the Gulf coast, half a continent away. There would be a sultry haze on Lake Pontchartrain, which has never seen an ice floe in its life, and whose shoreline residents would consider such a thing an alien intrusion, probably sent deliberately from the north. The train I was catching was set on a fabled route, almost due south, eventually picking up the course of the Mississippi after passing through Illinois, Kentucky and Tennessee, before rattling down into Mississippi and Louisiana, then settling into a long slow curve round the shore of Pontchartrain to reach the city. Steve Goodman's song, recorded by Arlo Guthrie in 1972, distils all the nostalgia for such journeys into this one, and describes a particular longing.

> Night-time on the City of New Orleans,
> Changing cars in Memphis, Tennessee,
> ... the steel rails still ain't heard the news ...
> This train's got the disappearin' railroad blues.

There is nowhere better to think about it all than on a train, because it takes you away from the noise and confusion and makes a soundtrack of its own. It's especially exhilarating when the route follows the Mississippi, America's bloodstream, through the playgrounds of Tom Sawyer and Huckleberry Finn. Where better to wonder what kind of country America is now?

This route south links two cities that are distant in culture and style, representing different sides of the American personality.

Chicago is the Big City personified, with a famous history of political corruption and gangsterism, but, paradoxically, with a commitment to public art and culture that is as notable as that in any city of comparable size anywhere in the world. New Orleans, although on the crime front able to give Chicago a wild run for its money, has a quite different heritage. Where Chicago has an appetite for trade and political power, getting things done, and still cherishes Irish and Italian cops (uniformed equivalents of the hard-nosed political operatives from the same roots), New Orleans has Creole and Cajun food, a self-conscious desire to slow down rather than to speed up, and a propensity for delicious self-indulgence of which jazz is the natural outpouring and a sparkling decoration. This train connects two opposing worlds. One is the industrial hub of the Midwest, where St Patrick's Day is the great annual festival – I've watched them turning the Chicago River green with special powder, the early-morning signal on 17 March that the day has come at last – and, by contrast, the other seems a piece of the United States that is moored offshore, where everything is done differently. Customs, street life, the very climate. By law, they bury their dead in vaults above ground, because otherwise graves get flooded and coffins have a scary way of popping up from the depths; they eat alligator meat and po-boy sandwiches, and throw themselves wantonly into the feasting at Mardi Gras, when the streets are filled with jazz and carnival costumes in wild parties that get their energy from an intoxicating amalgam of Catholic ritual and persistent pagan customs that trace their ancestry to a galaxy of voodoo gods.

At Union Station in Chicago, just west of the river, they still call out the names of the trains. The *Empire Builder* to Seattle, the *Cardinal* to New York, the *California Zephyr* to the west coast, and the *City of New Orleans* heading south. Conductors whoop and holler to get their last passengers aboard, blowing their whistles with gusto. A clanging bell tells you that you're about to roll. Travellers familiar with the ritual pull down the blinds in their bedrooms, strap on their eye masks and prepare to sleep, but when my train began to move there were many bright, excited faces at the windows, to the sound of a drawn-out, mournful horn. They had little thought of sleep. The train was long, and took a while to get up to speed, pulling itself gradually into the night, through the first snowflakes of the coming storm.

Leaving Chicago, the train was smooth at first, because these are lines that are part of the commuter network. In other words, the bits of the railroad that make money. Passengers are told that it will get less comfortable later on. This is a polite way of saying that since the years of sharp decline in the 1950s and '60s, when the tracks were allowed to deteriorate, full-scale modernisation was postponed, year after year. Amtrak, the semi-public corporation that has run the system for nearly fifty years, gets a federal subsidy that runs at between $1 and $2 billion a year and therefore has an annual crisis that is a regular fixture of the congressional calendar. Washington has always tried to get Amtrak to lurch towards life without subsidy, and has so far failed. But the pressure to cut back has meant that investment outside urban areas has been patchy.

Before long, the city slipped away in the darkness that had already come down. We settled in for a bumpy night.

Having known the secrets of sleeper trains since my youth in northern Scotland, and still regarding them as one of the most exhilarating forms of travel (leaving a dark and rainy London late in the evening and waking up in the Highlands is a thrill that never fails), I was perfectly at home in my tight compartment when the seats were turned ingeniously into a bed by the gutsy flick of an attendant's arm. I wondered what it was like elsewhere along the train. Arlo Guthrie came into my head again.

> Dealin' card games with the old men in the club car,
> Penny a point, ain't no one keepin' score,
> Pass the paper bag that holds the bottle,
> Feel the wheels a-rumblin' 'neath the floor . . .

There were indeed people playing cards in the club car, but they weren't hobos with bottles of rye in paper bags, they were a group of retirees on their way to join a cruise to Mexico on a towering liner with a dozen decks (they carried pictures of it, presumably for inspiration, which didn't work for me) and they weren't playing poker, but patience. There wasn't a single pile of coins on the table. They'd never taken the train for this trip before, and it was for the purposes of adventure, one as big as the coming cruise itself. Forget convenience, they thought, this will be a blast. I suggested that we might talk a little bit about Donald Trump, and they said they'd rather leave that to the morning, if I didn't mind. They were, I think, Republicans but I concluded that they were trying to forget, and I wondered how many people on this train had climbed on board because they were trying to get away from something.

I'd already met a youngish international lawyer, Dutch by birth but New York-based, who was on the second leg of a circular New York–Chicago–New Orleans–Atlanta–New York marathon simply because he was trying to write a law textbook – for which he won my pity from the start – and found that it was easier if he headed into the unknown. For him, the train was a travelling writing room where he was in his own sphere and only needed to answer the phone if he wanted to. He was in an invisible place, unconnected to the world outside, and on the move through the night. I told him I liked the feeling, too. But I noticed that he wanted to talk to people, when he wasn't worrying about explaining torts. I could see why. We were both enjoying the sensation of being in a gang and yet at the same time apart, in our own protected space. That's the thing about the train. You can plunge into the mix or withdraw at your whim. Stare out of the window for an hour, then split a beer in the club car and hear a story. Meet someone, avoid another. Retire to your room with a fat book, pull up the blinds and watch the darkened fields slip by, catch the lights in the little townships along the way. Feel them passing in the night as you roll south, retreating back into themselves. Then, if you want, you can venture out and join the others.

There were quite a few families, the kids excitedly unused to the peculiarities and etiquette of trains, but I noticed that the five or six Amish families I'd seen in the halls of the station at Chicago, dressed in rigorous plain style, the men's hats and women's head-scarves straight out of the seventeenth century and the young men sporting square Dutch beards, surrounded by children in impressively arranged bands, didn't seem to be with us on the train.

This was hardly surprising, I realised quickly, since the hedonistic delights of New Orleans are certainly not their preferred poison. But you do see Amish in noticeable numbers at stations all across the eastern side of the country, because Amtrak does well with that community, as a consequence of their view that flying is one of the more objectionable elements of the modern world, a feeling that many people with distinctly non-Amish approaches to life have come to share.

It was a cheery train, mostly. So far, there was no sign of any of the people who end up on board because they've been banned by an airline for some unspeakable behaviour, and who might be a trial. There were a number of characters with wide eyes and penetrating stares whom I marked down as potential ancient mariners to be avoided, unless I might feel inclined to hear an endless bedtime story. Others I categorised as train travellers who were there because they suffered from a serious fear of flying, a condition more common than most of us remember. They were presumably enjoying the feeling that there was nowhere for the train to fall. Not quite true, but you can see why they like to believe it, and I decided without any evidence that they had that look about them, whatever it is. Perhaps we would all have a conversation in the morning. And, being America, there were some people who, I suspected, were only on the train because they were simply too large for any kind of plane that wasn't a military transport. As usual in such company, there were also those who were obviously determined to strike up a conversation whenever they could, as an irritating act of public duty, and those of the opposite persuasion who lifted a book to their faces (a Bible, possibly) when they felt that someone was about to try to break the ice. I was pleased to find, however, that the train manager had been reared in the talkative school of conductors, and I suspected he was ready to blether through the night if he got half a chance. He was going as far as Greenwood, Mississippi, where we'd pull up in mid-morning, and where he'd pass the baton to a colleague who never ventured further north. We had a preliminary foray into the story of the train, which Amtrak tried to withdraw in the 1970s, only to change their minds when people came to know Arlo Guthrie's song and saw the *City of New Orleans* as an emblem of an America gone, one that they treasured and wanted to rekindle in their minds. Why did he like the train?

'It's my family. I love my wife – don't get me wrong – but I get to know them on this one journey, in a few hours, and I see everything.'

'Everything?'

'If I wrote a book, I tell ya, I'd be worth a million dollars. Remember, some of them are here for a day and a night.'

With the end of laid-out dinner service and tablecloths – long gone – the patchy elegance of the old days has faded away, but everyone seemed to spend a comfortable night. Even after an hour or two, the faces began to seem familiar. There was no singing, and the club car closed suitably late but before anyone in party mood got the idea of getting wired in for the whole journey. Breakfast would happen when we left Memphis, just after dawn.

'People are better when they're on the train,' the conductor said. 'They change. That's what I think, anyway. Opposite on an airplane.' He sounded quizzical but in reality had no doubt that life is more troubled and less appealing from the minute you climbed down the steps to the platform.

'They get away.' Wise man.

I kept the blind up, because every now and again there was a little starburst of light from a hamlet or a town. We made a couple of unscheduled stops, for no obvious reason, and the whole train settled quietly for a while, surrounded by spreading dark fields where nothing was moving. Eerie moments of quiet, broken only by a few bursts of laughter coming from a compartment a little way down the corridor, where people were apparently determined not to sleep, I hoped because they didn't want to miss something.

The conductor did his late rounds. He told me the timetable was only a rough guide. Things happened on the railroad. We should arrive in mid-afternoon, but who could tell? We certainly wouldn't be early. For once, reassuring words. So sleep was easy, comfortable and deep.

In the early morning, while the outside of the train glittered in strong winter sun at Memphis, a group of African American young women got on and settled down in the observation car. Why were they going to New Orleans?

'Fun.' They laughed, as if only a fool might imagine that anyone would go to New Orleans for anything else. I asked one of them how the fun was going to be made.

'I'm going to show off my titties.'

Okay, fine. Instead of continuing further down that road, I mentioned Donald Trump and the government shutdown. This certainly marked me out as a probable bore – or at least someone who didn't realise that the train should let you forget the world for a while – and they were a little surprised, before entering into the spirit. With very little prompting, out it came. They were deeply unhappy. They all held down decent jobs in Memphis, with friends who were federal employees who'd had their pay cheques stopped because Trump and Congress couldn't agree on a budget.

'We all know people that are suffering. Really suffering. Not just because of this shutdown but other ways.'

'Other ways?' I said.

'You know. Everything. We're hurting, and you know it.'

Another said, 'Food stamps, opioids. You hear what I'm saying? It's plague time.'

None of them was a Trump voter, and they were getting what they expected. Under all their infectious jollity there was polite but vigorous anger. We talked for a while about what should happen, and as with so many conversations on this subject, it became obvious that they didn't see any easy way of fixing what they called 'the problem', a catch-all word for a dozen and more anxieties and complaints. One of them turned out to work for the Memphis police department (not, I should say, the one who was planning to show off her titties). She was not happy.

There's an irony here. They were hostile to Trump – to his personality and style, his approach to life, his way with women – but had sympathy with the idea that Washington had to be shaken up, to be cleaned out by somebody, Trump's 'draining the swamp'. They just didn't want him to be the drainer-in-chief, because they suspected that he would like to repopulate the swamp with alligators of his own choosing, probably of a nastier kind than the ones who'd be flushed out of the swamp in the first place. They were caught in a familiar bind. They'd got a shaker-upper, but of the wrong sort. What to do? I detected severely limited enthusiasm for the campaign that Hillary Clinton ran, but her tormentor troubled them even more.

We talked for a while, and it was obvious that they considered themselves lucky to have jobs, all the luckier because they knew many people who hadn't. The more we spoke, the more it became clear that they felt a great distance from the world of politics, not because they had particularly radical ideas, nor because they were obsessed by the state of the country, but simply because, as African Americans, they felt that even after eight years of Obama in the White House there was still a gaping cultural gulf that many Americans in power, with Trump as their emblem, simply wouldn't or couldn't cross, maybe because they didn't know it existed, let alone how wide it was. And after Obama, with so much still the same for them and their friends, they wondered aloud if the pain had got even worse because they had hoped briefly for so much more.

'I don't blame him, of course,' one of them said. 'A graceful man.' She looked out of the window for a while. 'You know, good.'

We were rattling hard as we passed from Tennessee into Mississippi, the train jerking on the rails as if we were careering downhill. In a way we were, because for the next 300 miles or so, running parallel to the great river itself, which forms most of the western border of the state, we were heading into one of the poorest parts of America. Before the Civil War, Mississippi was cotton rich, a state that plantation owners thought was the definition of prosperity, but its economy has never escaped its nineteenth-century destruction. The poisonous legacy of slavery has proved a formidable obstacle to the state shedding the memories of that time. Its most recent effort to become more prosperous has consisted mainly of legislation, conceived in desperation, to allow gambling on boats moored on the river, which has been moderately successful in financial terms, but the truth is that for most Americans outside the South, Mississippi remains a backward place, bound by an umbilical cord to a past that the rest of the country wants to forget.

Looking out from the train, there was little to see that wasn't bleak and, in the wet mist of the morning, dispiriting. Long trails of trash littered the scrubland along the track, and broken old cars lay higgledy-piggledy along the route, as if they'd been dragged there to make some kind of point. The potholed roads we saw were more or less empty, with only the odd rusty truck to be seen. Life from this angle looked thin and grey, random and rough. Intriguingly, a fellow passenger from the cruise party offered the thought that one of the reasons it was a good idea to take the train was that after the interstate network was connected in the 1950s, towns tended to swivel outwards to the roads, and away from the railroads, turning themselves inside out. The result was that when you travelled by train, she said, you got a vista that you couldn't get from the roads and you saw places properly.

True, but it didn't mean that the vista was uplifting. On the flat-lands of this part of the South, there was a weary sameness to the communities and down-at-heel strip malls, with no lift on the over-grown landscape, hardly a hill to be seen and no happy contours, only a view that convinced you that you were in run-down America. Lazy creeks, trailer parks, boarded-up stores. It's why so many of the young who are brought up there, even in the state capital, Jackson, which is the biggest town in the state but still has a popula-tion of less than 200,000, try to escape if they can. In state-by-state tables of household median income in recent years, Mississippi has usually come bottom. In most of the other league tables it's also in the basement or nearby.

As we approached the Louisiana border, I sat for a while with a woman from Memphis. She was African American, about to turn forty, and wasn't being paid because of the government shutdown. She worked for the Food and Drug Administration and her job involved food inspections. She wasn't interested in talking about the politics of Trump or Washington – nor indeed about her own financial position, although with elderly parents she said she was struggling to manage in the way she'd like – but about how strongly she felt about public servants who were involved in protecting public health and maintaining standards, in her case checking on food in schools and other public facilities.

She wished that more people would speak about the importance of these services, in which she was exceptionally proud to work.

As we conversed, I realised how often in many parts of America today – away from New York and California and the other liberal-leaning states – you never heard such an impassioned case being made for public provision. The change in the climate has been so stark, the political rhetoric so tuned to self-help, and much public dialogue so contemptuous of 'weakness', that such talk even seemed to be startling. It was once normal.

This turned out to be a good preparation for New Orleans, where the question of what individuals can expect from the community has been stretched to snapping point.

The train crossed the border into Louisiana and started its circuitous approach towards the city, almost as if it wanted to prolong the arrival by stringing it out as long as possible. The landscape changed. There were some flashes of tropical colour, a lushness in the undergrowth that spoke of heat and damp, straw hats on the people waiting at level-crossing gates. A slowing-down. The sun was bright, and we could tell that outside it was getting warm. We started to see the creeks and pools of the bayou glistening in the light, across a maze of unruly canals. But they had an unlikely stillness. Nothing seemed to move, except the birds – a few blue herons, black crows on the high branches, and dozens of white egrets, which are like skinny pelicans with very long legs who like to stand on one of them for a while before taking off in a slow sweep over the thick foliage that covers everything down to the water. You could hardly tell where the land ended and the creeks began. Vast green fronds and their tentacles covered everything on a green and brown landscape, where all living things seemed to have become entangled over time with something else.

That easy-going confusion was the right introduction to the city. Everything warm and sluggish, thrown together in a lazy embrace. The trees twisted and gnarled in a grotesque tableau. Now and then the water broke and you realised some creature was swimming just underneath, probably one of the destructive nutria – elsewhere they're known as coypu – who've long colonised these waterways, burrowing into the banks in the mud below the surface and chomping away at the foliage and the trees. They're giant swamp rats that grow up to 2ft long and look like beavers, inhabiting a dark amphibious underworld. I suspect they are not pleasant company. The train made one of its unexpected stops, and there was a telltale ripple on the water. I thought I saw a touch of slicked-back brown fur, then it was calm again. The scene was immobile for minutes on end, but you knew that the stillness was illusory because this is a stormy place and often, despite its effort to promote a sultry charm, quite ugly underneath.

In a few minutes here, the sky changes dramatically when the clouds sweep in without warning and warm rain begins to drive across the landscape. In the evening, a boiling sky can promise you storms and havoc. The levels in the bayou might rise quickly, and on the wide surface of Lake Pontchartrain, which the train was now circumnavigating and which stretches to the horizon with nothing to break the flat line of the sky, waves seem to rise from nowhere. All around, there were signs of the last storms – tree trunks, splintered branches, high piles of vegetation – reminding everyone that soon, for a certainty, there will be another one. This landscape has that expectation built into it. You are always between one storm and the next, so people talk of them as if they're fixed points on a calendar, measuring out the days. As a consequence, everything on the landscape reflects that truth.

Even I-10, the interstate highway that runs from Jacksonville in Florida due west all the way to California over more than 1,000 miles, is supported here on high concrete stilts round the edge of the lake, because no one can be sure of how high the next surge might be. The train conductor who took over at Greenwood – he had no interest in getting to Chicago and the snow – was a New Orleans man, and he was preparing to give us a talk on our entry into his city, regarding it as a duty. He identified the birds from the observation car, talked us through the world of the bayou and the levees, which were built like the dykes of the Netherlands as a guarantee that the sea would never take over. But he pointed at the level of the water. People in these parts do it by reflex, as they might tap a barometer.

'That's high, but it can go higher. Nearly to the roadway. Gotta watch it.'

To those of us listening to him it looked a fragile and precarious highway, another part of the edgy atmosphere that this part of the South generates for itself, and jealously guards. Nothing is permanent; everything you see is on the move. The vegetation has a tropical lushness, the colours are bright and deep, the roll of the water has a languid rhythm of its own and the bare trunks of the cypress trees that poke out of the water look like abandoned mooring posts for boats that have gone and will never come back.

Where a cloudy sky meets the water in a haze, there were a few flares from the oil refineries that were the only breaks on the straightish line of the horizon. Down here, you're never far from one.

We were getting towards the city now, and the conductor was pointing to the new levees built to protect it from the waves when the storms came, because most of New Orleans sits precariously below sea level, with the Gulf of Mexico just above it. He was at the wide window in the observation car, and as the fringes of the city came into view, he started to talk about the event that made the city familiar to many people who previously hardly knew it, and brought to Americans a crisis so unexpected, and for most of them so shocking, that it stirred up thoughts about the state of their union. You can't come to the city without realising again the lasting significance of the events that unfolded on the morning of Monday 29 August 2005, when Hurricane Katrina, which had been heading west from Florida for a week, spun out of the Gulf and hit the coast.

The conductor, a big burly man in his fifties, said to us: 'I didn't believe this could happen, but when I saw what was happening to my home, I feared for my life. That's no lie. I did. Imagine that.'

One of the other passengers expressed surprise. The big man in charge of the train said simply and emphatically, 'Madam, I was very scared.'

The nightmare wasn't the wind, but the water. As the hurricane moved across the sea from Florida, gathering speed from the warmth of the Gulf and at one point stretching across its whole span from east to west, people were warned that it might be the big storm they'd been taught to fear, and were advised to get out. The governors of Mississippi and Louisiana declared a state of emergency, and eventually, early on the Sunday morning after long days of observation when Katrina became a hurricane and then a tropical storm and then a hurricane again, the mayor of New Orleans, a city of about half a million people, ordered a mandatory evacuation. Nothing less would do. 'This is going to be an unprecedented event,' said Ray Nagin, and in that at least he was right.

Many left immediately – the highways were clogged and chaotic within an hour or two – but many didn't go, either because they refused to take notice of the authorities, had no hurricane history (like the out-of-state gamblers carrying on with abandon in Biloxi, not knowing the casinos would be flattened), or because they simply didn't have the means to get away, nor anywhere to go. For a large number of those people, it was a fatal predicament. And, anyway, the evacuation order was too late. The levees couldn't hold back the water. Overnight, dozens of them folded under the pressure, and let the waves in. By midday on the Monday, streets were inundated, with tidal water filling the arteries of the city. By the time the disaster reached its height, 80 per cent of New Orleans was underwater. Tempests and floods are part of American life – tornadoes in the Midwest, hurricanes in Florida and the Carolinas, ice storms in the northern states – but no one had seen anything like this.

The mayor then made an appeal to the federal government that surely ranks as one of the most humiliating ever to be issued from an American city hall. As he spoke, thousands of people were crammed into the Louisiana Superdome, the football stadium, because they'd had to flee their homes. They were in a terrible state, but Mayor Nagin said the city couldn't feed them. He asked if Washington could help, because he couldn't.

Most Americans could hardly believe the catastrophe of the next few days. How could so many people die in a flood that had been predicted year upon year? (The figures are uncertain, but the National Hurricane Center puts the number of deaths in the city itself at more than 1,000, many from chronic illness and weakness, which meant they couldn't withstand the shock of the storm.) The rest of the country asked the obvious questions. Why couldn't fleets of assembled buses reach the city to rescue people who were crying for help? Why, despite more than $10 billion pledged in the early days from a panicky White House and Congress to try to save the city, did the mayor have to appeal to charities across the country to get food to the people in the stadium (where some of them died on the floor from heat exhaustion), or to those perched on the roofs of their houses, surrounded by foetid and poisonous water, with nothing to eat or drink? They were as lost and battered as any refugees from a war zone, but they were Americans, and at home.

Of those who died, the overwhelming number were old, poor and black. The waters that rose across the city, and stayed long after the hurricane blew itself out further north, left an indelible mark on the country, and exposed the truth about the kinds of lives many Americans were leading, especially if they were black.

Afterwards, the Pew Research Center published survey data that revealed a telling and ugly aspect of the truth. Of those questioned by Pew soon after Katrina, two-thirds of African Americans said they thought that the response by state and federal authorities would have been faster and more efficient if the victims had been white. But the view among white respondents was the reverse. Among them, 77 per cent said race had made no difference. Two perspectives revealing the divide in outlook, and in understanding.

Soon after Katrina, the novelist Richard Ford, who was born and raised in the city, wrote about the catastrophe for *The Guardian*.

In America, even with our incommensurable memories of 9/11, we still do not have an exact human vocabulary for the loss of a city – our great, iconic city, so graceful, livable, insular, self-delighted, eccentric, the one Tennessee Williams believed care forgot and that sometimes – it might seem – forgot to care. Other peoples have experienced their cities' losses. Some bombed away (by us). Others gone in the flood. Here now is one more tragedy we thought, by some divinity's grace that didn't arrive, we'd missed. But not. Our inept attempts at words only run to lists, costs, to assessing blame. It's like Hiroshima, a public official said. But, no. It's not like anything. It's what it is. That's the hard part. He, with all of us, lacked the words.

Parts of the graceful and eccentric city were rebuilt, and if you wander around the French Quarter – which wasn't destroyed because it sits just a little above sea level and was largely spared

the deathly threats of 19ft surges – you might be persuaded that
the heart of the place, which people travel from other continents
to see, was unaffected. You have to remember that the quarter's
streets became an island in a city most of whose streets were sub-
merged, and which had become a bigger island itself, marooned
from the rest of the country. People talk about it all the time. I
supped a bowl of gumbo with a barman in his thirties who'd come
home from Atlanta after Katrina to help, and who said that as a
consequence of what he saw he would never leave again. There was
so much still to do that he thought he couldn't bear to leave his
city. Everyone has a story – of an old man who used to sit on the
street corner of Basin and Iberville rattling his tin cup and singing
quietly but after Katrina was never seen again, of houses in outer
districts that disappeared as quickly and completely as if they'd
been taken out by precision bombing, of families dispersed far
away from the city who couldn't or wouldn't return, of funerals
that went on for weeks. Of the revelation that there was greater
poverty than most people had cared to admit. Of a horrifying
incapacity to survive.

Even coming to the city many years after Katrina – and I hadn't
visited it since the old century – you encountered a story that's
embedded in these streets and can't be removed. While I was there,
I recalled an American trip soon after the storm – far away from
New Orleans – when I was shaken by some of the hostility from
elsewhere in the country, laced heavily with contempt, towards
the victims of Katrina, almost as if they'd conjured up a hurricane
as a ruse to get $10 billion for their city and therefore deserved
no sympathy. It was a minority tide of complaint, but surprisingly
potent in conversation and in social media exchanges. What gave
them the right to federal funds? How dare these parasites parade
their helplessness in front of the world! Although huge numbers of
Americans gave generously to charities who did their best in New
Orleans, some others turned the shame of what they saw on television into anger directed at those who bore the brunt. Evidently the
truth hurt, and cut deep. Those whose lives were changed for ever
by the storm might find many ways of describing their lives, marked
by poverty and stubborn injustice, but they would be unlikely to

reach for the favourite all-American word of those who criticised them – 'freedom'.

A day and night in the city therefore had a melancholy touch. New Orleans is so determinedly different – though despite its lingering wonders the French Quarter has always had an off-putting tourist-driven side – that it defies comparison with anywhere else. But somewhere in those streets is a clear, unmistakable spirit – smoky, hedonistic, rich, with a wildness that often seems to hint at violence of some kind. Richard Ford tried to catch it when he wrote about Katrina, looking back.

I have a memory of my father and mother drunk as loons on New Year's Eve, in front of Antoine's. It is nearly midnight, 1951. There was no place to leave me, so they had their fight (only an argument really) in front of me. My father held my mother against a wall on St Louis Street and shouted at her. About what I don't know. Later, when we were in bed in the Monteleone, with me between them and the ceiling fan turning, they both cried. So. What of Antoine's now? What of the waiters who a week ago stood out on the street in white aprons and smoked? What of St Louis Street?

I have a memory of a hot and breathless summer. It is many summers joined into one. My mother took me on to the Algiers Ferry, an open boat with cars driven on to the deck. Out on the great sliding brown river, there was the only hint of breeze you could find anywhere. Back and across to the foot of Canal Street. Back and across we went. She bought me pralines. I held her hand during it all, until the sun finally fell and the hot night rose. So, now, what of that river? And the Algiers Ferry? And Algiers? All memory resolves itself in gaze.

And a last one, more up to date. My wife and I are walking home from a friend's house down tree-shrouded Coliseum Street. It is 2003 and eleven on a warm January night. We are only steps away from our door, just in a cone of street light, when a boy hops out of a car that stops and says he will definitely kill us if we don't hand it over right away. He has a little silver pistol to persuade us. Let's say he's 16. And he is serious. But he laughs when we tell him we don't have a penny. And it's true. I pull my pockets

out like a bum. 'You people,' he says, almost happily, his gun
become an afterthought. 'You shouldn't be out here this way.'
He shakes his head, looks at the pavement, then drives away. He,
that boy – he'd be 19 now – I hope he's safe somewhere.

The questioning. 'What of Antoine's now?' Well, as Richard knows,
it survived the storm, the elegant restaurant that opened in 1840,
only thirty years or so after the Louisiana Purchase, when Thomas
Jefferson doubled the size of the United States for $15 million by
buying New Orleans and its surrounding territory from France. But
the writer also knew that although you can still sit there in front of a
vast platter of oysters, as people always have, and hear jazz hanging
on the sultry air when you go out onto St Louis Street, something
has disappeared. It's estimated that at least 300,000 people were
permanently displaced by Katrina, and that the cost of the damage
amounted all told to more than $100 billion, if such a thing can be
calculated.

Spending a day and a night in the city gave me time to revive
old memories – the fish from the Gulf, the sidewalk cafes beside
the water, jazz in one of the crowded little clubs well away from
Bourbon Street, even a cemetery, because I remember the startling
sight of one of them on my first visit decades before. The city must
have some of the most melodramatic burial grounds in the world –
filled with ornate and fairy-tale tombs that are there to make a
show, many of them convincing you that someone was determined
to make a joke of death, and turn it into a party. But as well as
feeling the warmth of these old experiences, I was conscious of a
city that had been hollowed out. Physically recast – after Katrina
there were some serious suggestions that it should be abandoned
altogether – but showing the scars of human misery. In a city of
atmospheres – special flavours that you can't taste elsewhere – there
was a new layer of sadness that would remain.

NORTH

New Orleans had darkened my mood, even as I waited in the sun
to board the train north. The city had seen the abyss open up, and

looked over the edge. I wondered how many of the people in the streets for the weekend, or the football fans in town for the LA Rams–New Orleans Saints NFL play-off (the Saints lost) had taken a Katrina tour. I found I hadn't wanted to. Again on the train, as the sun went down in an hour or two and the water blackened across the lake, I heard passengers talking about the storm: they'd heard things in the city that had made them pause. They spoke quietly, respectfully.

Back in the observation car – it was already feeling like home – I met three women who were, I guessed, in their early sixties. They'd got away from their husbands in Memphis for the weekend, and we spoke for a while about what they'd done in the city. Jazz, a boat ride, shrimps and crab cakes. Cocktails at the Hotel Monteleone, where people like to imagine they can see the ghost of Hemingway at the bar. They quizzed me in turn, and were happy to declare themselves watchers of BBC America, and one a listener to BBC World Service on a local radio station that, like many others across the country, carries it through the night hours. It was then inevitable that Trump would force himself into the conversation, and he did.

Two of them had voted for him, with reluctance, and the other had supported the Libertarian candidate (Gary Johnson, who got about 1 per cent of the vote). She knew it was a protest vote, almost a spoiled ballot and a shout of anger, but in different ways Trump and Clinton had appalled her. She had never thought of voting for the Democratic candidate (although she had in the past) and she found herself unable to face the alternative. Almost any other Republican, yes. Trump, no. She expressed her feelings in an interesting way.

'It's not taxes. Not Obamacare particularly. It's the way we talk to each other. There aren't friendly discussions that we used to have. Some of my friends get so angry because I didn't vote for him. It didn't used to be like that. We're becoming less civilised, and I worry about young people. What are they going to think about America?'

Her companions joined in. They spoke about a public discourse that was being poisoned. About being screamed at from TV screens. Being told what to think. The America that they believed in – and still tried to bring to bear on their own lives at home – was civil and friendly. Neighbourly. A world of cookies, backyard barbecues and church boot sales. They were saddened that friends, on one side or the other, wouldn't speak to each other because of Trump.

'Everything's too wild. Angry. That's what's happened.'

'I regret it so much,' another said. 'And don't know where this is going to end up. I just can't see.'

Such conversations have become common. For every person you meet who will praise Trump as the bold change-maker who was necessary, you'll find another (or perhaps two or three) who'll express a feeling of something lost. Often it's laced with anger, because naturally he stirs up as much outright hostility as loyalty, divisiveness being his stock-in-trade, but underneath the back-and-forth argument about whether he's right or wrong there lies a more subtle and profound concern about the country. If politics becomes even more tribal, more money pours into one-issue campaigns, media outlets become pulpits for zealots, where do you find thoughtful deliberation? Goodwill? Even for some of those who voted for him, he represents the opposite.

We spoke for quite a while. As we broke up, one of them asked about Brexit. I kept it very short.

Heading north through the Mississippi flatlands, the heady warmth of New Orleans seemed far away, its colours and louche ways part of another country. The curtain had come down, and Memphis would be different.

By just after ten we were there, pulling up at a platform that seemed more suited to a rural halt than a city station, and because I needed cheering up I walked from my shabby motel to Beale Street, where you can still hear soulful music at every turn. Two singers with back-to-back battered and hollowed-out grand pianos, with good electronic keyboards installed in their carcasses, were still having a riotous time at 2 a.m. playing rockabilly and blues to an enthusiastic barful of people, and the night seemed young again. They were duelling at their keyboards with all kinds of songs – sometimes playing together, sometimes taking turns – when I thought that dawn couldn't be far off, so I slipped away. I had business in the morning.

I don't know why, but I had never seen Graceland.

Sunday morning. There was music coming through the open doors of a church or two along the way, some kids with guitars and a drum kit on a street corner – why? It was just after nine o'clock – and then an early caravan of tour buses all following the same road, Elvis Presley Boulevard. The house is cocooned in parkland that has been retouched by Las Vegas and Disneyland, with shiny pink pavilions and spangles everywhere. The first thing you see as you walk towards the ticket office is Elvis's private jet (for a hefty fee you can join a VIP tour that lets you stick your head inside) and then fast-food joints that pay tasteless homage to the King's diet, which encompassed many monstrosities, like bacon, peanut butter and grape jelly sandwiches on fried bread. You take a buggy across to the house, passing through clumps of southern magnolias, pecans and red maple trees before you're driven up the slope of a curving drive to the white-pillared portico. Then respectful guides, who look as if they're in a church porch about to hand you a hymn sheet, shepherd you inside, where everyone speaks in a whisper.

The first thing I noticed was the age of the visitors. I should have known. There was lots of white hair, walking sticks galore and quite a few motorised chairs. Why should I have been surprised? When Elvis died in 1977, at forty-two, the generation that had been first to know him was well into middle age. There were kids around on this Sunday morning, and even before the real crowds started, curious visitors of all ages from around the world. But the elderly Americans were the most interesting. Their jiving days were far behind, but I liked to think of them in their bobby socks jumping up and down in front of black-and-white TV screens at a sight they'd never seen before, with their parents shouting disapproval from the next room. The singer raised on gospel was doing what nobody had done in the same way before: bringing black and white music together. The reason so many people in the South hated rock 'n' roll wasn't really because of sexually provocative gyrations, it was because the music was doing what was prohibited at lunch counters, on buses, at the swimming pool. Crossing the racial divide.

It's something Memphis always understood better than most places in the South, because anyone was welcome to dive into its musical melting pot. When Elvis started with Sun Records in 1954, two years before 'Heartbreak Hotel' made him an overnight star, he was a singer who did things white men weren't supposed to be able to do. This crooner had soul, and the world changed. Many of these elderly people visiting Graceland on Sunday morning could remember it all. They looked at his white piano at the far end of the parlour, the wild decor and the stained glass, the kitchen with all his televisions that still managed to seem modest and homely, the dining table laid for guests with his favourite china, listened on their headphones to the recorded commentary telling his story, and took themselves back.

I asked a visitor, elderly and slow, what he was thinking at Graceland. It was his first time.

'An American boy. That's it. All through. An American.'

His wife said, 'How could you not love that boy?' She spoke as if he was a child who had just wandered off one day.

Hearing my accent, she asked if I knew that The Beatles had come here. I had a memory that they'd had their only encounter with Elvis somewhere else, not in Memphis (I checked later, and found that it was Beverly Hills), but Graceland is the palace to which everyone was meant to trek on a pilgrimage, so why have a dispute that might spoil things? We were all enjoying ourselves, and there was music everywhere.

There isn't much wandering to be done in the house, which is not as large as most people expect, and no one is allowed upstairs. But it's hard not to step through the front door without remembering that, four decades on, his death has a sharp resonance in contemporary America. The notorious George 'Dr Nick' Nichopoulos filled him with prescription drugs of the kind that are now causing a deadly addiction epidemic. Its existence used to be denied by Trump, but it is now so visible in communities across the country that it cannot be ignored. Trump has had to approve federal funding, though he wraps it up in talk about his Mexican wall, as if most of the opioids are being brought to America by criminal migrants rather than dispensed by neighbourhood doctors and pharmacists. In one of the worst states for overprescription, West Virginia – poor, with high unemployment – state figures show that in 2017 healthcare providers prescribed 81.3 doses of various kinds of strong painkillers for every 100 people. As an illustration of the culture of American medicine, with drug companies bent on marketing and many doctors allowing themselves to be driven by financial incentives, it's a telling commentary on the way public health has been ignored.

Dr Nick was suspended and put on probation for overprescribing. The district attorney in Memphis concluded that in the first eight months of 1977, leading up to Elvis's death, he'd prescribed 10,000 doses of drugs for him – amphetamines, barbiturates, narcotics, tranquillisers, sleeping pills and hormones. At the autopsy, Elvis was found to have recently ingested codeine, morphine, Quaaludes, Valium, Valmid, Placidyl, Nembutal, phenobarbital and butabarbital.

His death was a harbinger of the crisis that now touches many Americans. Of the 72,000 deaths that were categorised in 2017 as having been caused by a drug overdose, 49,000 were from medically prescribed drugs (or the many powerful ones bought over the counter). Drug-related fatalities account for a majority of deaths of those under fifty; every day, more than 130 people in the United States die after overdosing on opioids; the Centers for Disease Control and Prevention estimate that the total 'economic burden' of prescription opioid misuse is $78.5 billion a year. Extraordinarily, male life expectancy is falling for the first time in living memory thanks to opioids. Surveys conducted on behalf of the American Psychiatric Association in 2018 suggested that one in three Americans knew someone who was addicted to painkilling drugs, and that nearly half thought it was a crisis that affected people like them. The penny had dropped.

It is deeply ironic that the knowledge of this crisis certainly helped to propel the anger that fuelled the Trump campaign (and certainly didn't threaten the pharmaceutical giants). It was simply an element in the popular feeling that something had gone wrong in America. Yet the crisis identified by multiple federal agencies – excoriated by Trump as a matter of course – is difficult to manage when you have a public health emergency in a country where the concept of 'public health' is, in some quarters, an ideological no-go zone, with a president determined in principle to tear up federal regulations and to slash funding to Medicaid and Medicare, two programmes that provide a significant amount of anti-addiction help.

Feeling the pain is not the same as curing it.

So as I drove back to Memphis, with a taxi driver who insisted on taking me to Elvis's childhood home, where the boy would sit on the front step on a summer evening to sing to the neighbours, and to the church where he responded to the rhythms of gospel music almost as soon as he could walk, the nostalgia for the first great era of rock 'n' roll was pricked by the feeling that his decline and death were just as all-American as the culture he absorbed and turned magically into something of his own.

For relief, I spent the afternoon listening to more music, from a group of elderly blues musicians who plucked a few people from their brunch-munching audience, who, remarkably, were able to give a great account of themselves onstage. Memphis is different. It cheered me up.

A quiet night followed. Heading north in the dark I spent time with three retired men of the breed that I'd come to know well in that week, people who just liked long train journeys. One of them was visiting a son in Michigan and then taking another train to San Francisco. A hard-core traveller. As always with Americans, family history came pouring out. A Czech mother, a Midwest upbringing, the navy, kids in all four corners of the country. A grandmother who was from somewhere in Scotland. An island, maybe? Not sure. Behind his reminiscences was the conviction that there was less promise for the young generation in the twenty-first century than there had been for his own, half a century earlier.

'I was a submariner. Always said I left the navy 'cause my boat kept sinking.'

Another passenger worked on oil rigs in the Gulf. 'Two weeks on, one week off. Sometimes go north to Memphis to chill. Clubs. Anywhere.'

The submariner's friends joined in. 'Yeah, we know about living with the water.'

'Eighty-four days underwater. Think about that. Sturgeon-class subs.'

The other said: 'Real fast. So fast the Russians couldn't follow.'

'Tried to chase us. Couldn't keep up.' They all laughed.

'Meant we could chase them hard, though,' said his friend.

They spoke for a while about whether the Russian crews had enjoyed it as much as they did.

'Never met them. But kinda knew them, if you follow. Never far away.'

In the Trump era, were the Russians now friends?

'Hard to tell, wouldn't you say?'

I asked them to imagine a conversation between Donald Trump and Vladimir Putin. They laughed, and offered to buy me a drink.

Sleep. In the early morning, we could see that it was cold outside. The heating on the train had been turned right up. People knew what was waiting in Chicago. Ice. Warnings that temperatures were dropping so far below zero at night that it was dangerous to go out without some serious wrapping around your face.

When we arrived, however, the sun was shining. The city was cold but bright. Crossing the river and walking downtown, you felt its exhilarating power. I once asked Jim Dickinson at the *Washington Post*, a proud Midwesterner, what the city's secret was. 'Chicago has balls,' he said simply. When Mailer arrived for that chaotic convention in '68, he wrote, 'Chicago is the great American city. New York is one of the capitals of the world, and Los Angeles is a constellation of plastic. San Francisco is a lady.' Chicago ain't no lady.

It's hard to describe its personality without revisiting two cataclysms – the fire that destroyed most of it in 1871, and the most famous scandal in American sport nearly half a century later. They're both etched on the city's face. The Great Fire destroyed nearly 20,000 buildings and left about a third of the city homeless, a Katrina of another kind, but it led to rebuilding that was an exercise in self-confidence. It had steel-framed buildings ahead of their time, a forest of the first skyscrapers in America, and neoclassical buildings that established an early twentieth-century American style. The fire also had the effect of instilling a particular kind of civic pride – donations from abroad allowed it to set up a free library system, for example – and its notable commitment to public art dates back to the period after the fire when politicians, architects and builders coaxed a handsome urban phoenix into life.

Not far underneath is the scandal. Chicago has always been a rough town. During Prohibition, its bootleggers believed they were the best. The gangsters who congregated there in the 1920s were the nastiest around, despite their homely nicknames, and if you take one of the underworld bus tours – surely there can't be anywhere else on earth that celebrates mobsters with such enthusiasm – you'll be shown the restaurants and the pavements where they were gunned down in regular shoot-outs, because most of them, from John Dillinger to 'Diamond Joe' Esposito, ended up at the wrong end of a gun barrel. Therefore, it was appropriate that the Black Sox Scandal was a Chicago affair.

One of the city's two baseball teams – the Cubs still revel in the knowledge that it was the White Sox who shamed the game – were involved in the World Series of 1919, the seven-game series that produces the world champions, although naturally no one from any other country can compete. The White Sox cheated, throwing the series to the Cincinnati Reds in exchange for bribes from an illegal gambling syndicate. Eight players were banned from the game for life, but not before they had pulled off a distinctly Chicago-esque trick in persuading a jury to acquit all of them of fraud, despite the fact that a former player, 'Sleepy Bill' Burns, told the court in detail how the series was fixed, and where the bribes came from.

In this most romantic of sports (although the Sox play in a stadium that now has the dullest name in the game, Guaranteed Rate Field) the scandal became part of its folklore. In *The Great Gatsby*, F. Scott Fitzgerald has a friend of Gatsby's financing the fix, and the narrator, Nick Carraway, sighing, 'It never occurred to me that one man would start to play with the faith of 50 million people – with the single-mindedness of a burglar blowing a safe.' An attack on faith, and innocence. Even today, you feel that it was bound to have been a Chicago plot, hatched in the city of schemes.

Scheming political bosses are part of the same story. Mayor Daley ran a Democratic Party machine that would be the envy of quite a few autocrats around the world. And in the state capital, Springfield, the story has been consistent. Since the early 1960s, four governors of Illinois (three Democrats and one Republican) have been convicted for various forms of corruption – fraud, racketeering and obstruction of justice – and sentenced to a total of more than thirty years in prison. Political shenanigans elsewhere are seldom as rough, or as brazen, as they are in Illinois.

Whether or not it is the Great American City, for good or ill, Chicago speaks powerfully of the country's urban malaise. People in work in their mid-twenties are now worse off, proportionately, than they were in the 1960s, according to the Great Cities Institute. And, inevitably, there is one particularly bleak statistic. In 2018, the institute says, 7 per cent of white 20- to 24-year-olds in the city were neither in work nor in education. For African Americans the figure was 40 per cent. The city that a century ago was a beacon for blacks fleeing the restrictions of the South to find work in the booming factories is now beset by a modern form of segregation.

Just under a third of the city is black and, as rigidly as in the 1920s and '30s when public housing policy split the city in two, neighbourhoods have their own racial character. In schools, on public transport, in parks, you know where you are. Nearly half a century after the civil rights reforms, Englewood on the South Side is more racially distinct than it was in the 1960s. In those years the population was fairly evenly divided between white and black, but over the next three decades 'white flight' changed everything. In now solidly black Englewood, people are poorer and benefit from worse public services than the rest of the city, apart from the neighbourhoods that are just like it. Chicago has become a boomtown for many of its residents, with numerous corporate headquarters installed in fine new buildings in downtown, and the better-off citizens have benefited hugely. But, partly because lower-paid industrial jobs that used to provide employment for many families have gone away to suburbia or overseas, life has become tougher for those who find themselves in places like Englewood and can't escape.

Even as you sense the sheer vivacity of the city, in business and culture, you're aware that it is troubled. For black youngsters on a difficult treadmill through education into a forbidding work environment where their opportunities will be severely limited by their background, the lure of gang culture and an opt-out from 'the system' is strong. Decades of public policy, enlightened in some cities, sluggish or inadequate in others, have failed to heal the divide. In Chicago it is visible on the streets.

The Corporation for Enterprise Development found that in 2017 just under two-thirds (65 per cent) of black or Hispanic households did not have savings that would last for three months if they became unemployed or had a medical emergency. The figure for white households was 28 per cent. The truth about the city is that most of its citizens are either affluent or impoverished – the middle ground has contracted. Academics and politicians argue about how this has happened. What have been the various influences of historic housing policies, a political system that gives considerable licence to local aldermen who wield enormous power in their wards, outside economic forces, residual racism of the old, raw kind? Whatever the mix of factors that has created today's Chicago, it's impossible to take a bus from the invigorating roar of downtown to a neighbourhood not far from the campus of the University of Chicago on the South Side – one of America's most celebrated academic institutions – and not feel that you've passed from one world to another. That's hardly an unknown experience in London or Paris or any other big city, but in Chicago there seems an entrenched separation that is particularly disturbing, partly because the language of progress and integration has been so consistent over the years. It's hard to spend time in the city and believe that it has worked.

These are facts of urban life that have deep significance for the country, because in a nation of immigrants, the question of integration and relations between ethnic groups stretches back to its foundation, and permeates all its arguments about itself. Americans today listen to a president who talks about race with an abandon that none of his predecessors in living memory could have imagined – whether about a white supremacist march in Charlottesville, police shootings in Ferguson, Missouri, which produced a string of riots, security on the Mexican border, where he says the nation is under threat, or about 'sanctuary cities' (which set themselves up as bulwarks against mass deportation), about which he mused that it might be a good idea to transport illegal immigrants there against their will. Trump's language is new. He argues that with job growth strong – more Americans were indeed in work in mid-2019 than for five years – black and Hispanic employment will inevitably improve. The problem is that in the public discourse there is a strong, deeply conservative attitude – which in frequent instances could be justifiably described as far right – which is directly challenged by those on the liberal side of politics who take the most uncharitable view of Trump, his beliefs and his intentions. In the common culture, understanding is unfashionable. In recent times, politics has never been so fiercely and angrily divided. Historically, wouldn't it be right to expect that to play out on the streets?

Therefore this friendly city, full of life and raucous history and boisterous optimism, also has an edgy air. It is hard, even for a traveller with the warmest feelings about it, not to feel some apprehension.

I walked up South Michigan Avenue, alongside Grant Park, past the Art Institute on the East Side, with the lake beyond. Even in mid-afternoon it felt as if the light was fading fast, under a heavy grey sky. On the other side of the street, above Symphony Hall, Riccardo Muti gazed out of a huge poster (he was conducting the orchestra in Shanghai that night). I had a late flight, so I wondered how to spend the evening. Perhaps our son, Andrew, who'd been a graduate student at the University of Chicago, might direct me to one of the blues bars he used to know. I wondered if I might wake him up in London to ask. My phone rang. It was British Airways. The weather was closing in, and my flight was cancelled. Could I get to O'Hare within two hours to catch an earlier one? I jumped.

Outside the terminal, people had buttoned up long coats against the swirls of wet snow and a slicing wind. It was well below zero. I got on board quickly, and settled. There was time to check the news, and to read two tweets from the president of the United States. One was a retweet from his favourite TV programme, *Fox & Friends* (of which he is the most famous fan). It said, 'The Democrats are playing politics with Border Security.' Another spoke of a 'big Crooked Hillary law firm' involved in 'An Unconstitutional Hoax'. The president reassured everyone that it would be exposed. Business as usual in the Oval Office, but business that meant trouble. I knew I would be back soon. The plane pulled back, with night coming down, and as I settled down I wondered how best to try to capture the spirit of two Americas that seemed certain to pull further apart from each other.

We rose, and about 14 miles away the downtown skyline was picked out in lights, but only for a few moments. The cloud was low, and swallowed us up. The Great City was gone.

CHAPTER 10

From Venus to Mars

Two different pulses were beating among Americans as they prepared for the 2020 presidential election. You could feel them both getting quicker. Trump supporters, although apparently not growing in number, were shouting as loudly as they had in his first campaign, given the opportunity by the rallies that were the running commentary on his presidency. On the other side those opposed to him either mildly or fiercely – who were greater in number – were becoming more confirmed in their view. It was hard to find a neutral, which suited the president just fine.

These two Americas remained in their own orbits, looking at each other across the void with suspicion, and anger. Trump supporters would talk about liberals living in a bubble. But there are bubbles outside New York and California. A conservative in South Carolina might speak of San Francisco with horror, embarrassed that such a liberal (and immoral) city was American. In turn, many New Yorkers would watch a Trump rally in Alabama and think themselves lucky never to have set foot in the state, marooned in a southern bubble of its own. Clearly, it's impossible to understand much about America without making contact with both these states of mind.

Just before the midterm election in 2018 I spent a long evening with conservatives in rural Texas, determined to carry Trump towards a second term. A few months later – with the Democrats once more in control of the House of Representatives after that election – I sat down with Hillary Rodham Clinton in New York, the woman who thought she would be president, still wrestling with the consequences of a defeat that she never thought would come and wondering about the extent of her own responsibility. Were voters justified in identifying a feeling of entitlement underlying the Clinton campaign? Far away, in Texas, I was hearing a view of America that was different in almost every respect. A view in which the Clintons – in the minds of opponents always linked together as a couple – are, quite simply, The Enemy. It was a journey from pole to pole.

She was in her office, sitting quietly above the mayhem of Times Square, with the theatre lights below flickering in a darkening afternoon, talking about contemporary America, and particularly her own past. These are accounts of an era that is seen differently from the two sides, but in each case envisaged as a struggle to recover something that has been lost.

When we spoke in London in late 2017 in front of 3,000 people at the Royal Festival Hall about her book, *What Happened*, Clinton talked at length about Russian interference, and the fatal loss of momentum in her campaign after the intervention of James Comey, the director of the FBI, ten days before election day. She also described her phone call to Trump conceding defeat just after midnight at the end of an evening that had begun with her working on a victory speech. She reflected on the depth of the cultural battle that had defined the campaign, noting that people who put economic concerns at the top of their list of priorities had tended, according to surveys taken after the election, to support her rather than Trump. But after Comey's intervention the campaign wasn't about the economy. It was about her. In Pennsylvania, for example, her campaign team watched the suburbs of Philadelphia turning away – maybe there was something in this email stuff, after all, too many voters said to themselves – and that was the end of Pennsylvania, by a margin of only 0.72 per cent. With Michigan (0.23 per cent) and Wisconsin (1.0 per cent) Trump picked up forty-six electoral votes, and the tiny tilt in those three states brought him the presidency.

In New York in early 2019, I found Clinton in a mood that was sometimes swathed in shadow, and certainly subdued. The reason was obvious. When I asked if she thought Trump would survive in office to fight another election, which I knew she had doubted a year before, she gave a reply I had not expected.

'I think right now it looks like he will. His strategy of denying, and dismissing and diverting, has kept 45 per cent plus of the people in his camp.' Only a few months later, she would support impeachment hearings, having come to believe that the evidence had become overwhelming, but, at the time of our conversation, I realised the depth of her agony – not simply about her own defeat in 2016, but about the failure to complete the journey to a more liberal America of which she'd been so confident five decades earlier. To have Trump as the emblem of it all was almost unbearable for her.

After two years in which his dealings with Congress had often verged on the farcical, his foreign policy had still not settled, the White House was in a state of flux with his staff whizzing round in a perpetually revolving door, and the Russia investigation revealing connections that the president had consistently denied, his old opponent was still reconciled to the likelihood that he would see out his time and, I suspected, although she would never say as much, might stand a good chance of re-election. Why?

When we had spoken in London, her tone had been different. When I asked her if she thought he would survive in office, leaving aside the matter of re-election, she said she couldn't be sure but thought that it was an open question. It was impossible to know, she said, whether the Russia investigation and the chaos evident in the White House – when we spoke, a senior Republican senator had just said that under Trump it resembled 'an adult day-care centre' – might be too much for him to surmount, even in a first term. But now in New York she seemed resigned, not just to the fact that he was likely to complete his term, but to the difficulty Democrats would face in trying to beat him in November 2020.

Here was the candidate who had taken a politically mortal blow in 2016, eight years after she first struggled with Obama for the presidential nomination. Of the people who have never been elected president, hers is the career that has taken the most unexpected turns. So it was natural to look back. Remembering the surprise at her appointment as secretary of state by Obama, after the raw feelings engendered by their contest for the nomination, I asked her how she had responded when the call came.

'Oh, I didn't want to do it. No. And I told him that repeatedly.' But he had worked out what he wanted, and would get it. 'I think it was a reflection of his very analytical mind, trying to figure out what worked for him, what kind of government he wanted to put together. But I couldn't have been more surprised.'

I'd had an insight into that mind from Doris Kearns Goodwin, the historian whose book *Team of Rivals* unravels the political mind of Abraham Lincoln and how, before arriving in Washington in 1860, he understood that his task was to take old rivalries and use them to strengthen his administration. She was surprised and flattered to get a call in Cambridge, Massachusetts, from the freshman senator from Illinois after the book came out asking if she would care to drop by next time she was in Washington. She did, and found that Obama, naturally fascinated by the only other president to come from Illinois, wasn't in search of a precis or a short tutorial as you would expect from most busy political figures, but had read the book closely and wanted to delve into Lincoln's reasoning and his purposes.

The conversation convinced her that even before he declared for the presidency he was thinking about how an outsider like him – a Senate baby, a young candidate, and African American – might cope with the rivalries he would inevitably stir up, as Lincoln had with his opponent from New York, William Seward, who had expected to be the Republican nominee, until he was upended by the beanpole lawyer with the silky tongue from Springfield, Illinois.

It was a natural subject to discuss with Clinton, beaten for the Democratic nomination in 2008 by Obama, who had declared for the presidency in Springfield, on the steps of the same state capitol in which Lincoln had served.

'Seward, of course, was senator from New York,' said the former senator from New York.

By chance, I had overheard a relevant conversation involving Bill Clinton, only two or three days after Obama's election. The former president was expressing frustration verging on disbelief at some

of the names that were being canvassed for the post of secretary
of state (his own former trade secretary, Bill Richardson of New
Mexico, being one whom he mentioned with incredulity). From
what I heard on that occasion, I knew that the Clintons had no ink-
ling of where Obama was going to turn, and perhaps had intended
to go from the beginning. For the Clintons the campaign had been
too painful for that.

But he worked on her when he invited her to Chicago.

Yeah, well, look – he and I had been fierce competitors. But we'd
also been colleagues in the Senate, and he was adamant that he
wanted me in his Cabinet.

At the end, you know, my attitude was – look, if I had been
elected and I wanted him in my Cabinet, I would have expected
him to say yes, because you did face serious problems and you're
glad you did. I mean, it was an incredible opportunity. But, you
know, the work was intense, because we had so much lost ground
to cover, you know, and there were so many problems that we
inherited.

Just to pick one. Iran. You know, it was during the Bush
administration that Iran began its march toward a nuclear
weapon. And so the idea of these Republicans criticising us for
taking on a difficult problem, to try to put it in a box, put a lid
on it, and prevent Iran from getting a nuclear weapon, is just so
ignorant about what actually happened in the prior eight years
before Obama became president and I became secretary of state.

Talking about these years took us back to the period of the financial
crash, a few weeks before Obama took office, and the unravelling of
American policy in the Middle East – a time when the country faced
strategic decisions that would influence a generation.

'Part of the reason that Obama asked me to be secretary of state
is that he thought he faced two major crises. One, obviously, the
economy – but the other, the lack of faith in American leadership.'
The recurring theme.

That's exactly what he said?

'Yes, we had those conversations. Yes. The Bush administration had seemed so hyper-focused on Iraq and Afghanistan, that much of the rest of the world felt neglected. Written off. And he said, "Look, I know I can't both save the economy and reassert American leadership. So you go do the leadership around the world stuff, and I'll save the economy."'

You might describe that as a straightforward brief.

When her turn came to run, four years after the end of her term as secretary of state, she believed she had found the language that Democrats needed. But then came, first, Bernie Sanders from the left, with an assault on 'the system' and then Donald Trump from the right, with the opposite solutions but the same complaint that the economy and society more broadly were rigged against the powerless. An imbalance epitomised in the halls of Congress. For Clinton, the conundrum she'd wrestled with all her adult life: how to distil the liberal case to its essence. We spoke about history, and her own story. I found her anxious about a problem that torments her more than ever before.

> It is a perennial problem on our side of the aisle, because the other side's argument is quite simple. You know – cut government taxes, don't let them take your guns, do everything you can so that the individual rules. Yeah, individualism rules. And it's a very appealing and quite effective argument. And ours is much more like this. We've got to stand up to those interests that are destroying jobs, increasing inequity, trying to roll back civil rights, women's rights, gay rights. I mean, it's not an either-or. It's not either an economic or an identity-politics argument.
>
> And what's frustrating is how the press to a great extent, fed by the Republicans, has characterised so much of what Democrats are doing now as 'identity politics'. And indeed it is, but more importantly part and parcel of the whole social and economic progressive agenda that we've been pushing.

Talking about American contemporary culture, she said she acknowledged that it was hard to make the argument for a collective solution to anything. Forget the New Deal, individualism was everything.

'That's the challenge. And, you know, I'm not sure who is going to be able to come up with the answer. Right?'

For her, a melancholy conclusion. So we explored the background to this change, and talked about her first encounter with social activism. At Wellesley College, a liberal arts college in Massachusetts, Clinton was a mild conservative who found herself turned into a liberal by the civil rights movement and Vietnam, supporting Eugene McCarthy's anti-war campaign for the Democratic presidential nomination in 1968. Later, after leaving Yale Law School, she didn't take the settled path to a law firm on Park Avenue in New York but headed south to work for a civil rights charity, the Children's Defense Fund.

It was just the physical feeling of being right, doing that stuff. That's what I remember.

I mean, my very first legal assignments when I went to work for the Children's Defense Fund, both as an intern and then as a young lawyer, doing things like going to South Carolina and investigating the practice of putting young teenagers into adult jails. And those young teenagers were overwhelmingly black.

Going to Alabama because Nixon was trying to get tax exempt status for segregated academies, and gathering information to make the argument that they were not worthy of being treated as exempt entities. So I was very much in the mix on not just those issues but defending migrant workers and their children in places like Florida, looking out for the rights of children with disabilities. So I was enmeshed in civil rights work.

These are the memories that for liberals in Trump's America are painful, because there was a time when they believed that progress would be in their direction, hard though it had been to get started in the 1960s, was destined to continue and would never be reversed.

In conversation with those who opposed Trump – many of them incredulous until election day that such a political iconoclast could be elected and empowered – these broken hopes are always breaking the surface. For Clinton, and leading Democrats to the right and left of her, it seems as if a river has been diverted, to flow in a different direction. They never believed that it could happen. It is why, when we spoke about presidents through history, she said there was no question but that Lincoln was the giant standing higher than the rest, because at a time when the country could have descended into chaos after the Civil War he argued for healing. She believes that if he had lived longer the healing would have been profound.

That was the battle that, in the 1960s, she thought would eventually be won.

'Yes, I did believe that. I believed that the battle would be fought out in many different places and on many different subjects, but that ultimately the dream of a united country that would honor the goals of the civil rights movement would be achieved.'

She knows that it hasn't come to pass.

'You know, I thought that it would take time and concerted effort by not just leaders but citizens to continue to push against racism and intolerance, but that eventually it would be successful.'

From the perspective of figures like Clinton, there was a failure on the liberal side to understand how much could be undone and how, in the course of a generation, the constitution that had underpinned the fight to establish civil rights in the South would be turned into a weapon to negate so much of what liberals considered proper and inevitable progress.

> I think there was not just an expectation, but perhaps a misplaced reliance on the continuing forward progress of how the constitution would be interpreted. What was not well known – or maybe even, no one knew at all – is how determined the right was to undo legislative and judicial victories. The intellectual right – and the well-funded intellectual right – had an agenda and it was to reverse a lot of the political and social changes that they disagreed with.

The battle between those interpretations of the constitution rolled into the 1990s, and it was after Bill Clinton's victory in 1992 that it turned into the cultural struggle from which, eventually, Trump's populism emerged.

For Hillary Clinton, sitting in the White House at the time that was going to become personally destructive for her family in the Lewinsky affair, the most important figure was indeed Newt Gingrich, with his rough, radical-right victory in that 1994 midterm election in Bill Clinton's first term, which captured the House for the Republicans.

'I think that Gingrich changed politics more than Reagan did.' Quite a thought.

I suggested that Reagan deserved the credit he got from his supporters for changing the whole political landscape.

He did, but he didn't create the viciousness and the take-no-prisoners approach. That was Gingrich. I mean, there were some very tough political combat operations. But Gingrich set out to destroy Democrats personally, not just to defeat them but to destroy them. He was vicious and shameless and never effectively held accountable for his numerous lies and distortions that he trafficked in, and he basically told other Republican House members – 'I will lead you to victory but you have to shut up and sit down and let me do it my way.'

So at the time, and of course I was sitting in the White House at the time as First Lady by the president's side, dealing with all sorts of tumult in that period. But you could see, despite our victory in '92 and despite the big victory in '96, that there was something underneath the landscape that was changing quite fundamentally.

I happened to be very conscious – I can't say that many other people were – because I saw a well-organised co-ordinated partisan operation that utilised all the think-tanks and poured much more money into building an infrastructure than had been there previously. And took no prisoners. I mean it was all rough stuff: it was really rough stuff. And, you know, Gingrich was perhaps the most vocal, visible voice but by no means the only one. And, you know, there were lots of things that were just politics as usual. I was doing healthcare. We were told by the Senate Republicans under Bob Dole that they were going to come up with their own plan, and we would come up with a plan and we even had the parameters, we would have an employee-based healthcare plan. Well, it was being worked out.

And then they pulled out because they didn't want to give Bill or the Democrats that kind of victory. I mean, that's oversimplifying, but basically it's what happened. And then, of course, the hypocrisy and the brutality of their political attacks. You know what – it was just so far over any standard or level that people had seen. So it was well organised, well co-ordinated, well funded – very well funded indeed – with key voices like Gingrich's leading the charge.

She spoke of how she had been criticised for talking of a 'vast right-wing conspiracy' in the 1990s, the phrase with which I'd become familiar at the time, and was well aware of the irony that, as the object of so much conspiracy talk, she is simultaneously accused of having stoked up the very attitude that helped, eventually, to end her political career. Lured into the 1990s culture war between liberals and conservatives, she became for conservatives the object of their own conspiracies. There was almost nothing that they wouldn't lay at the Clintons' door.

What we've got now, with a Republican Party that is craven and cowardly and knows no better, is an unchecked presidency, at least until the House was won back for the Democrats [in November 2018]. But they have been stacking the courts with people who have no experience. They're ideologically pure and judicially inexperienced, and they're counting on getting a free pass from a lot of the decisions they make by the judges that they have actually put into place.

So if that happens and you have no accountability from the Senate Republicans, you have the House trying to exercise the checks and balances against an out-of-control presidency. So I think it's a serious threat to the institutions of the country.

You sense in such encounters the extent to which Trump's victory undermined so many assumptions on the other side. For people schooled in the civil rights movement of the 1960s, reared with an international outlook that took alliances for granted, who wanted to reform the UN to make it stronger, and not weaker, who acknowledged the gaping racial divide and the need to heal it, the explosion of a populism that denied it all was the shock of a lifetime. Consoling themselves with the fact that Clinton won the popular vote in 2016, and a shift of a small number of votes in key states would have given her victory, was not enough. Apart from the fact that she lost, and they had to accept it, there was a question that haunted them as they watched Trump sticking to his attack-dog style, and striding through the wreckage of his White House organisation as if it was no more than a passing impediment.

Was it he who represented the real America? Did the tide he had launched tell the truth that they had denied for a generation, since the South was forced to turn away from its past?

Behind the pain of her own defeat, and the campaign mistakes that were made, which she has found it difficult to accept in public, lies the question that has come back, more insistently than she and others expected, about the drift of a country, particularly in its failure to cope with the political question that first gripped her as a young lawyer – race and its divisive impact, or, as she put it on that afternoon in Manhattan, 'the original sin'.

She spoke about a second civil war that she thought had been won, against Governor George Wallace and his police chief Bull Connor, who fought their own citizens in the streets because they were black. The painful irony for liberals lay in the politics of the constitution. The civil rights arguments that seemed to have prevailed by the 1970s – even Nixon, with his southern strategy to show conservatives that they should no longer think of themselves as Democrats just because of nineteenth-century history – were based on an attachment to the Declaration of Independence and the constitution, whose promise they believed had never been properly fulfilled. Yet that constitutionalism was then captured by the right, turning it into a manifesto for individualistic conservatism that excoriated the federal government that liberals had championed in the 1960s as the engine of change, based on that same constitution.

It's interesting to me, looking back to that period in the '70s, that there was much less talk, curiously, about the Founding Fathers or the constitution and all the rest of it, but of course all connected with the inalienable rights and all the rest of it in the declaration and under the constitution. Now what is odd is that when we look back to the '80s the whole constitutional pillar was taken over, as it were, by the other side.

The constitutional argument was turned into an argument of a right, and whatever we call it they had enormous success over eight years under Reagan.

That conversation in New York was a confession of regret, but, more importantly, an indication of how much liberals know they have to do. Speaking in early 2018, when she was unwilling to be drawn on the merits of any likely Democratic candidates, the argument about Trump's re-election prospects was placed squarely in historical context. She spoke about Lyndon Johnson having been right when he said that his Civil Rights Act would mean the end of the Democratic Party in the South (Bill Clinton, of course, being one of the new breed who would buck the tide), but how even in the days of segregation under Old South Democrats – some of the governors and senators of that time now have an air of pre-history about them – there was a concern, inherited from FDR's New Deal in the 1930s, that gave them a feeling for the downtrodden.

Lyndon Johnson coming out of the hill country of Texas did really identify with the common man. He may have been the mover and shaker, and certainly was the man that Robert Caro portrays. But he did have a commitment to making change that would benefit people that he thought had been disadvantaged. I remember watching his voting rights speech in 1965 on television.

I thought it was the most powerful presidential one he gave, in the way he ended saying, 'We shall overcome.'

For Clinton's generation, that was the promise that has never been properly delivered. The 'original sin' hasn't been expunged. And there's a recognition looking back that for all the youngsters who travelled south – like her – to march and join in the efforts against segregation, much of the rest of the country turned to other things.

With respect to the drama of the civil rights movement, that was all playing out in the South as far as most northerners thought. You know, there was the occasional march that got out of hand, like in Skokie, Illinois, places like that. But by and large it was Bull Connor, it was George Wallace. It was all of the Freedom Riders stuff and the voting registration activities, and that was all playing out on your TV screen so you could think – oh, that's Mississippi, that's Alabama, that's Georgia. It didn't seem like it was really part of the whole country's struggle. But it should have been.

Regret, not just about one election in 2016, but about a turning back that maybe happened long ago. This was one of the tasks for Democrats in the early years of Trump – to realise how far the country had moved. Without that, what could they do to reverse it?

We spoke about the Reagan years, and how the Republican coalition had finally embraced both the evangelicals and the moneyed conservatives.

They came together because the religious right was not sufficient alone. The plutocrats on the right who were basically manipulating politics for their own personal greed were not enough either. But marrying them had a powerful, exaggerated impact. And I remember voting in the 1980 election and literally the people who were lined up where I voted at that time were really motivated by the religious arguments they saw. They saw Reagan as the person who would reverse Roe v Wade on abortion.

But the confluence of all of these forces turned out to be really powerful. And also they didn't just focus on the presidential level, they focused on Congress. They focused on state offices from governor to the state legislatures; they created organisations that were writing legislation for people to promote these points of view. Like I say, Reagan himself was so unthreatening as a person that it was not as clear as it is now in retrospect.

A country that had changed direction long before Trump.

As I stepped into the street, Nixon came to mind. Clinton had recalled being at the 1968 Republican convention in Miami as a young intern and watching Nixon giving a speech that she thought 'dark and disturbing'. She didn't meet him until he visited the White House in the 1990s and they made 'perfunctory' conversation. But the reason he had sprung to mind was different, and concerned the future of Donald Trump. In 1973, the House Judiciary Committee was beginning the impeachment investigation that would bring Nixon down. One of the young lawyers on the staff was asked to do some constitutional research, and come up with a legal explanation of the term that was the trigger for the possible removal of a president, 'high crimes and misdemeanours'. The lawyer took to the library to start work.

She was Hillary Rodham.

That conversation had covered the national story since LBJ, and revealed the depth of liberal regret. But the other America has its own version, the one that Trump has taken up as his own. He was never a social conservative before deciding to run for president, and has fashioned his own populism out of impulses that he picks up by instinct rather than from any ideological conviction that can be discerned, of the Goldwater variety, for example. Yet the power of his appeal to many Americans is obvious, though never to a steady majority since his election, according to every reputable pollster. On my midterm journey to rural Texas, from where New York is sometimes seen as a distant planet, I found that the institutions that Clinton celebrated, and the liberal inheritance of the 1960s, were at the heart of the Trump appeal because he could convince voters that he didn't believe in them. They had waited to hear someone who was not afraid to say so.

Cuero, Texas, is a long way from Times Square. Cattle country and Broadway have only their wildness in common, because culturally and politically, they are distant planets, Texan bravado and New York chutzpah having always been incomprehensible to each other. You might have thought that this gap would have narrowed in modern America, the ease of travel having promised to make the place smaller. But the politics of our era has widened and the cultural divisions are as great as ever. In rural Texas, many people talk of 'the coasts' – by which they mean New York and California – as alien territory. That was why, on visiting the state in the fall of 2018, I found that a political challenge to conservative orthodoxy was more than an irritation, it was an insult and a shock.

Republicans could scarcely credit that in the midterm election campaign Senator Ted Cruz, their blood-red conservative hero, was in a fight to hold his seat. A few months earlier, no one would have expected him to end up with anything less than a double-digit margin of victory. In state-wide elections, Texas had been solidly Republican for more than twenty years, and Cruz represented the kind of conservatism that elected Trump, despite their rocky relationship during the primaries and the personal venom Trump directed at him. If you asked a loyal Republican in 2018 if Cruz might lose his seat, you got a pitying look as if you'd somehow forgotten where you were.

But then, almost from nowhere, came Beto O'Rourke. His story – the rise and decline – is a shiny portrait of the American political game. In El Paso, on the Mexican border, they would rightly object to the idea that their city seemed like nowhere to the rest of Texas, but O'Rourke, despite having been a congressman for six years from that city, was not especially well known across the state when he won the Democratic primary to take on Cruz. Quite soon, however, raising a great deal of funding from small donors and mastering a social media campaign that Cruz didn't try to match (by November O'Rourke had spent more than $7 million on social media and Cruz $250,000), he was being noticed not only across the state, but around the country.

Was this the kind of fight that would show how Trump could be challenged? I went to see him on a university campus south of Austin and was surprised to find a candidate doing something that had long since passed out of fashion. He spoke in paragraphs. In jeans and sneakers, wearing a baseball cap, he talked to a hall full of students with instinctive ease. Of course, it was easier because he was on friendly turf. Hardly anyone in the hall would have walked down the block to hear Cruz, and the senator wouldn't have regarded that campus as a place where he was likely to prosper. However, O'Rourke was still a striking lanky figure, an apparently fresh face. There was nothing particularly radical about his politics – he comes across as a centrist and could never be mistaken for a devotee of Bernie Sanders – but he was skilled in taking on the orthodoxy of the right. He spoke about a revival of community, about finding connections that had once been strong but were severed.

Around that time, there was circulating on social media a video of his encounter with a group of veterans, who were infuriated by the 'taking a knee' protest being staged by many African American football players, led by Colin Kaepernick, demonstrating against police brutality by refusing to stand to attention for the national anthem when it was played before every game. Instead, they knelt. This is the kind of act that among football-mad, patriotic white Texans is considered close to treason. Facing an audience of veterans, O'Rourke was asked where he stood on the question. To that crowd there was going to be only one acceptable answer. O'Rourke's response was interesting for two reasons.

First, he refused to dodge the question, as others had tried to do, and said straightforwardly that he supported the protest. Second, he disarmed the likely critics in front of him with a simple assertion – that there were good and patriotic Americans on both sides of the argument. An obvious point, but one not made often enough. He said it was possible, and important, to have a civilised disagreement about such matters. Indeed, the more difficult the subject, the more important it was to be civil. In a political atmosphere alive with hostility, where absolutist views clashed noisily, this was a welcome cold shower. That audience responded with understanding to his straightforward, patient explanations, and with respect.

There was clearly something happening in this Senate campaign. Texans were being asked to think a little differently about the boasts they made about their state. Here's something O'Rourke wrote in the *Houston Chronicle* a few weeks before polling day.

On Wednesday, I toured the Harris County Jail with Sheriff Ed Gonzalez, and met men from this community who have made a mistake from which they may or may not recover. Men who don't have the resources to post bail. Some of whom got arrested on purpose to get the treatment and care they need, care they won't be able to afford or access on the outside. In fact, the Harris County Jail is the largest provider of mental health services in our state, a state that is the least insured in the nation. Of the 10,000 inmates in the Harris County Jail, one quarter of them are being prescribed at least one psychotropic medication. The jail has more people receiving psychiatric treatment every day than the nine state mental hospitals in Texas combined.

But beyond those who need health care, there are many more languishing behind bars for nonviolent crimes – sixty percent yet to even be convicted. Unable to work, to pay taxes, to raise their kids, to contribute to our society, to realize their full potential. And it's happening at the average cost of $87 per person, per day, and more than $400 per person, per day for prisoners requiring medication or medical treatment. That tab is ultimately picked up by the taxpayers of Harris County.

He struck a chord, perhaps by stating such obvious truths that weren't usually heard, and the campaign began to create excitement. So much so that some of those around him would whisper – but only whisper – that the best result for him might be to run Cruz so close that his name became known everywhere, and then to use that performance as a springboard for the presidential nomination. Were he to do the near-impossible and win in Texas, however, it would be difficult to announce a presidential run barely a year after becoming a senator, because he would look too much like a man in a hurry. Such are the calculations in any campaign that starts to generate unexpected excitement.

When he did declare himself as a candidate a few months later, that gloss dulled over. In the first jousts with Kamala Harris, Elizabeth Warren and Pete Buttigieg to knock Joe Biden off his early perch, O'Rourke struggled. His fund-raising started to dip. He couldn't turn that tide, and only a few months after his declaration, he was gone. But it was still instructive to remember how his Texas campaign had managed to stir up excitement. He reduced Cruz's winning margin to less than 3 per cent, which intrigued Democrats elsewhere who were looking for a way to make inroads into solid Republican territory.

Indeed, a few older Texans may have been reminded of stories from the famous 1948 Senate campaign in the state, when the upstart congressman Lyndon B. Johnson had the gall to challenge the former governor, Coke Stevenson, and produced one of the most melodramatic upsets in Texas political history, eventually settled after a series of wonderful jousts in the Supreme Court in Washington, which had to rule on ballot-stuffing allegations in the polling stations of the Rio Grande Valley, where Johnson got his margin of victory. Johnson's lawyers – one of them a future nominee for the Supreme Court under his presidency (perhaps not surprisingly) – managed to prevent the opening of one particular ballot box, No. 19, which the other side said would demonstrate voter fraud. One of the features of that campaign was Johnson's use of a helicopter – at that time, a newfangled machine hardly seen before in rural Texas – which drew curious crowds as it descended into little town squares and tipped the candidate out, waving his 10-gallon hat with one hand and greeting the first approaching voter with the other.

O'Rourke made much of the fact that by November he had visited all of the 254 counties in Texas and – just like Johnson in 1948 – found that there were little communities where they'd hardly seen a candidate before, because it was thought a waste of time to visit the towns that were only a flyspeck on the map. Having heard O'Rourke, and picked up in Austin the murmur from old-time political types that Cruz was going to have to move smartly, it was time to have a long conversation with Texan conservatives, part of Trump's southern army.

Cuero may have a Spanish name ('leather'), but it is not an overwhelmingly Latino town. The population of around 7,000 is about one-third Spanish-speaking, and when I met with a group of roughly a dozen stalwarts of the DeWitt County Republicans it was an almost entirely white company, and English-speaking to a man and woman. My producer, Kate Collins, and I were given an exceedingly hospitable welcome at the Chisholm Trail Heritage Museum, which tells the story of south-central Texas, 'with its roots in the great cattle drives of the late 19th century, when the cowboy became an American icon, and the Longhorn steer a legend'. It was from these parts that cattle were driven on the long trail north towards Kansas City, and then taken on the railroad to Chicago. We wandered for a while among the saddles and spurs, ropes and boots, surrounded by sepia pictures from the time when Texas could accurately be called wild. You can't visit such places, nor spend any time in San Antonio, at the Alamo, without being aware of the weight of the particular history that Texans treasure – especially the state's time as an independent republic after victory in 1836 over the Mexicans, whose border as a consequence was pushed south beyond the Rio Grande, and stayed there. Texans are born to be bullish outsiders.

So when we settled down in a handsome panelled room upstairs to talk, there was pride around the table. There was also a gun. I noticed that one of our hosts was, as they say in Texas, 'carrying'. There was a holstered handgun on his belt.

I asked why he'd brought a weapon. Surely nobody felt threatened by the BBC (an attempted joke). The answer was deadly serious.

'Because I can.'

There wasn't going to be much give and take in a debate about the Second Amendment in that quarter. For Dwayne, it was the embodiment of freedom. European outsiders often find it difficult to tune in to American gun culture because it is so alien to their tradition, even if they hunt, but in Texas the gun is as natural as a Stetson hat or snakeskin boots. And, as everyone has come to realise, the place of the gun in the lives of frontiersmen in the west has been transformed in recent years into one of the symbols of the culture war that has divided America for a generation. If you talk about gun violence here it turns, in an instant, into an argument about fundamental freedoms. Bizarrely, you whizz from guns to gay marriage in a millisecond.

The United States has less than 5 per cent of the world's population but nearly half of all the guns known to be owned by individuals. For some years, firearms deaths have exceeded 30,000 a year. Since the Sandy Hook massacre of 2012, the database *Gun Violence Archive* estimates that there have been 1,600 mass shootings, defining them as incidents in which four or more people are shot. Campaigns to regulate arms sales have had some success, but have never seriously undermined the power of the National Rifle Association, which can make and break a political candidate with its financial might. It has the power to move the debate, succeeding, for example, in persuading a significant number of Americans that a rational response to any school massacre, after a respectful pause for the funerals, is not to discuss how to make it more difficult for another potential assailant to get a gun, but to allow teachers to have access to a weapon in the classroom. Nothing will enrage an NRA supporter more than hearing a constitutional scholar (probably from Harvard, or at best New York) discussing the notoriously ambiguous wording of the Second Amendment: 'A well-regulated Militia being necessary to the security of a free State, the right of the people to keep and bear Arms, shall not be infringed.'

It's all there, or not, depending on where you stand.

Settled at our table, the gun happily out of sight, we began to talk. I wondered aloud if Ted Cruz might be in a bit of trouble. A chorus of 'No!'; 'You kidding me?'

A lady, who emerged as the evening went on as the toughest of the bunch, fixed me with a glittering eye. 'You're talking about Robert Francis O'Rourke?'

The contempt was obvious. No 'Beto' in this room, the familiar contraction for 'Roberto' in El Paso, which is 80 per cent Spanish-speaking. They reminded me that he had admitted (some years before) that as a student he'd jumped over a fence at the University of Texas with some friends and was originally charged with burglary, a charge that was dropped. Much later, he admitted driving under the influence of alcohol.

Did I get the message? There was no need to waste more time on him.

This was a company that was convinced that Cruz would have an easy victory. It was true, someone said, that he might rub some people up the wrong way – he did have the reputation of being among the two or three most unpopular members of the Senate, on either side of the aisle – but his values were the ones most Texans shared. God, country, family. Enough.

I was reminded of a conversation the previous day with Evan

Smith, founder and editor of the *Texas Tribune*, an online publication that has revived political journalism in Austin, full of fire and resolutely solid reporting. We were sitting across the street from the state capitol, and he reflected on the changes he'd seen in Republican politics since George W. Bush won the governorship from the Democrat Ann Richards in 1994, she being a feisty political operator of the old school, probably celebrated away from Texas for one memorable line at the 1988 Democratic convention, directed at the then vice president, Bush's father. 'Poor George, he can't help it. He was born with a silver foot in his mouth.' The son, George W., ran on a programme of 'compassionate conservatism' as an avowed centrist – a fact often forgotten by critics when he was in the White House – and made a virtue of dealing civilly with Democrats. Evan Smith told me that if you wanted to chart the political changes in Texas over twenty-five years, all you needed to know was that if Bush ran in a state-wide Republican primary for any office twenty years after he became governor, he wouldn't stand a chance of being selected and would probably be bottom of the heap. The party had moved a long way, and his kind of conservatism had been left behind.

Our host at the museum was evidence of the fact. He was a Bushite, but he had been drawn into the Trump ambit. 'I'm from La Salle County, was born and reared there, and everybody is a Democrat. They don't even have a Republican primary. They are all Democrats. I was a conservative Democrat until 1960 or '64 or something like that, until the Democratic Party left me, and left me no choice. We were all born and reared in that way – Lyndon Johnson taught school there for a year.'

His was a familiar journey. But then he made his confession. I fancied he looked a little sheepish at this point. 'I'm probably a moderate Republican. I know these conservative Republicans, they always say you've got to be conservative to be a Republican. But that's not accurate. You can be a good Republican and be moderate. And that's what I am.'

There it was, on the table. But it became clear very quickly that moderate views were not the flavour of the moment, however much he might be liked by his friends. The lady who had speared Beto

O'Rourke told me that the thing about Democrats was that none of them believed in God.

None of them? Across America? I suggested tentatively that many Democrats could walk in here and say, 'I'm a Christian.' After all, they went to church in vast numbers every Sunday morning.

'No. They won't even allow God to be in their platform. What are you talking about?'

No quarter given. We spoke for a while about religious commitment, and the view around the table was unanimous. A typical response: 'Christian ideas are the conservative ideas that match what I believe is right. And so that's why I'm conservative, on my stand for those values, those principles. And it just represents who I am.'

In other words, it's impossible to be a liberal Christian? In reply, I got a dose of the Ten Commandments.

The Bible says I shall not kill. It's part of our Ten Commandments. And that's one thing that I really stand as a Republican saying my Christian beliefs stand, and I stand with these kids also to say when it comes to religious beliefs and Republicanism they fall into line. They don't mind praising God. They don't mind showing that God is in what we do and what we believe and how we stand. And that's just one of the things in the Bible and you can't bend it, twist it, or make it to be any other thing other than what God's word is. And pro-life is just – I mean, it is what it is.

Our moderate, Bush-supporting host said that he couldn't understand how some Americans who were 'pro-choice' (over three decades surveys have tended to show the country fairly evenly split on the question) could support the murder of 60 million children. It was as simple as that. Pro-choice, pro-murder. I toyed with the idea of discussing Margaret Thatcher and her delicacy in avoiding these questions, but the moment passed.

And Democrats? Another lady said, 'There's no moral ground to the Democrats at all. Period. Wouldn't you agree with that?'

I looked around. A number of people did indeed agree. 'I think fundamentally the Democratic Party has very little value of anything. They don't value property rights. They don't value much of anything.'

No values at all, of any kind. We were rolling. Someone else joined in.

'They like lots of chaos, and very little order. There's a big defining difference between these fundamental Republican principles and what the Democrat Party puts forward. And there's a certain amount of sanity that comes in logic, that comes with a conservative viewpoint. And a lot of them lack logical emotion. It's emotionally driven insanity that comes out of the left side of the political spectrum.'

Insanity? I asked people to consider Trump's morality, and suggested that I had never thought of him primarily as a God-fearing figure.

One of the women at the table, African American, with one of her two teenage daughters sitting alongside her, acknowledged that there had been a difficulty when the Billy Bush tape emerged during the 2016 campaign.

'I'm glad you asked me that question.' This usually signals an awkward shuffle on the part of an interviewee.

When the tapes came out, and I had friends that I'd been friends with since high school, who identified as conservatives or Republicans, and who said, 'That's it, I'm done. I'm not voting Republican.' I said, 'What happened?' Oh, Trump made this, you know, horrific remark about women, grabbing them by the you-know-what ...

And I thought, girlfriend – you're gonna vote your feelings over serious policies that really affect our personal lives? You're going to vote your feeling?

Feelings? Who needed them? She went on, in a manner of which the president would certainly approve. Somewhere here there must have been a trick, a hoax.

Do you see the tactic that they're using? Do you see what they're doing to divide us? That to me was a set-up. I recognised it for what it was, and you're not going to convince me otherwise. Do you want to know my personal belief about what person candidate Trump was? And I'm just gonna give it to you straight up. He's a billionaire. And there are women out there who are opportunists, who will compromise their virtue and their principles for the sake of financial gain. So if they put themselves in that position for private citizen Trump to do that, well I think that was just a personal decision.

So it was the fault of the women. The poor man was ensnared.

And I let it go from a Christian perspective on morality issues. What do I think about it? I think that he's a man. I think that we all fall short of God's grace, God's glory. And I feel that everybody makes mistakes. I've made them; I'd be a big hypocrite if I said, 'Oh, I'm appalled, I can't vote for him for that reason.' Who's to say that he hasn't redeemed himself and hasn't said, 'Hey I made a mistake, I don't want to be that way. I'm a changed person.'

It was agreed, unanimously, that Trump deserved forgiveness for groping sundry women. I wondered what would have happened if Clinton had asked for forgiveness for mismanaging an email account, but we moved on fairly quickly to safeguard a conversation that might otherwise boil over. Why should Trump be spared? Because he was their representative on the front line of the culture war – opposing people who were pro-choice on abortion, dismissing swathes of liberal thinking, from climate change to healthcare to restrictive gun laws, although, from this group's perspective, he certainly fell short on the matter of same-sex marriage (saying a few months later, for example, that he was 'fine' with the Democrat Pete Buttigieg, the gay mayor of South Bend, Indiana, when he declared he was running for president). As one of my hosts said, everyone occasionally comes up short. We are all fallen. Perhaps Trump was the emblem.

The importance of Trump to these Republicans is not that they agree with everything he says or does, but that he is a battering ram against what they believe to be an embedded liberal establishment, determined to take God out of schools, to let the hand of government direct everyone's life, take away the people's guns and sneer from their east-coast bastions at distant rural communities and their old-fashioned ways. Donald Trump, a New Yorker to his core, has held, as far as we can tell, broadly liberal social views on matters like abortion and gay rights. But for these Texans he is the instrument of change. Sometimes, we must assume, salvation comes in unexpected ways.

This conversation, like many others along similar lines, had a few sparky moments, but it was overwhelmingly friendly and generous. After it, Kate and I were taken to a home nearby where – having said grace standing up, and all holding hands – we sat round a table heavy with lavish Texas home cooking, ribs and chicken, squashes and beans, vast pies and puddings and all the rest of it. A feast to welcome guests from far away. None of the anger that had been obvious in our political conversation was directed at us, visitors who were treated from start to finish with courtesy and warmth. Dwayne Stovall, the gun-toting member of the group, was generous, although his views were by far the most fundamental. After reminding me that every single phone call in the United States – every one! – was routinely listened to by the government, because that's what governments did (surely I understood that?), he laid out his own principles of democracy, which he said he took straight from Thomas Jefferson himself.

'The biggest division in this country is between the people that are living in the bubble in the big cities in the eastern coast and the west coast, and the rural people. It's a huge, huge divide. And right now we are in the midst, I would say, of a very quiet revolution on our part to change back and to take back power, because we have let these people rule us for so long that we see that we're going to have to change our leaders.'

I protested gently that whatever adjective you might attach to this campaign, 'quiet' didn't seem the appropriate word. But Dwayne, politely but determinedly, was on a roll. The constitution had been corrupted not only by Congress but by the courts, allowing the federal government to grow at the expense of state power.

And as for Trump, despite his usefulness on matters like the wall, Dwayne's Jeffersonian principles were offended by a president who had become like a king, and by a Supreme Court that tried to shape people's lives.

If the people in Connecticut want to pass laws that say Adam can marry Steve, wonderful. What business is it of people in Texas? None. But if people in Texas want to pass a legal, properly executed amendment to their state constitution that says the marriage of one man and one woman is the traditional value of Texans then what business is it of people in Connecticut? Well, nothing. The way federalism works is if people in Connecticut are most offended by those laws they would move to Texas and the people in all of Travis County would move to Connecticut. But what happens instead?

We've fallen under this construct of following our rulers who are nine unelected well-connected lawyers in robes and one of those at the federal level can decide for the citizens of Texas, and what they want doesn't mean anything. And they'll overrule our will.

Anyone who imagines that the arguments underpinning the Civil War have shrivelled away needs to realise that they are still alive. Trump himself has never shown an interest – history not being one of his enthusiasms – but a significant element of his support believes that the 'tyranny of the Union' is still a daily impediment in their lives, even as they sing 'The Star-Spangled Banner' at every baseball or football game. You suspect you know which side they'd have chosen in 1861, and you also feel the surging regret that government in Washington was legitimised in the southern surrender at Appomattox four years later.

Dwayne had run on a conservative ticket in the Texas Senate primary in 2014 to try to unseat Senator John Cornyn, and although he failed (getting 10.71 per cent of the vote) he believed it was an important stand against the system that Cornyn represented, for all his professed conservatism.

'The system itself is self-perpetuating. Congress is basically run by judges and lawyers, who're wannabe judges. Right? And they are in cahoots with the Supreme Court.'

In other words, the battering ram is required. And if Trump has no coherent constitutional view, it hardly matters, because the disruption is what is required. I didn't mention, because it would have taken us on a long detour, that V. I. Lenin would probably have agreed.

On that evening, in the museum and round the dinner table, the Trump coalition was well represented. A fundamentalist like Dwayne, who believes the constitution has been betrayed by self-serving politicians and the courts and simply wants to shake things up as hard as he can to start a social revolution. Conservatives who simply want a warrior to take on liberals without mercy, on every front. Voters motivated above all by religious conviction, based on a fundamentalist reading of the Bible, who are willing to forgive Trump his human frailties as long as he nominates judges to the courts at every level, and especially to the Supreme Court itself, who will try to reverse the liberal trend that prevailed for most of the half-century from the mid-1930s and brought on most contemporary ills.

Collectively, they thought of Trump not so much as a hero, but as a welcome outsider who'd do what he said, sometimes inadequately, sometimes embarrassingly, with his personal lapses revealed for all to see, but always unapologetically.

That was enough.

As one of these DeWitt County Republicans put it: 'There is a value that I stand behind, and I see it in my husband. I saw it in my father too, and that is when you say you're gonna do it, do it. And I think we're there. I think we have a president that has performed in the face of adversity and is doing what he said he was going to do.'

This one conviction, shared by all our Texas hosts, banished any concerns about the policy zigzags, the crude tweets, the random insults to Republicans on the Hill as well as Democrats, the regular embarrassment of seeing a president unable to express himself in a fashion appropriate to his office, the soft-pedalling with Vladimir Putin and with Saudi Arabia. He was speaking as he had done as a candidate, apparently uninhibited by office or that insulting expectation at home and abroad that he would eventually conform in diplomacy and in the way he conducted business. To the movement he had stirred into being and led, he represented authenticity. They wanted him to keep his anger warm in the White House, and he had. What else mattered?

For much of America, however, and according to the most reliable surveys, a clear and increasing majority of the people, this performance is seen quite differently. In the 2018 midterm elections, the Democrats benefited from a surge in support from people who had often voted Republican, and had supported Trump two years earlier. It was most obvious in suburban areas, and particularly among women voters. This was the constituency that gave the Democrats control of the House of Representatives, and therefore handed them control of the federal budget and a number of important committees that began to make Trump's life very difficult indeed. They were the voters whom Hillary Clinton had expected to help her to power but who, in a handful of key states, drifted away from her at the last.

These were the two poles of contemporary America: liberal regret laced with a good deal of guilt, and a feeling of loss; conservative anger and a determination to fight the culture war at every turn. Underneath it all, on one side a seeping alarm among those who had taken the same journey as Clinton that the country might not be longing for the liberal future they'd always cherished, but might instead be more unforgiving, and sympathetic to the darker impulses of American history than they'd ever liked to imagine. On the other side, a determination that Making America Great Again was bound to involve rage, and a feeling that despite all those Sunday school lessons, that was a good thing.

On both those visits, to Texas in the sunny fall and to New York on a wet spring afternoon, I was reminded of words that had lodged in my mind decades earlier. At the end of his majestic series for BBC Television in the early 1970s, *America*, Alistair Cooke, who as a writer and broadcaster introduced three generations of people in Britain to the mysteries of the place and its allure, looked to the camera to deliver his concluding thoughts, having explored the history of the country he loved, from the *Mayflower* to Vietnam, and of which he'd become a citizen. Through the years his words seemed to have taken on greater weight.

'In this land of the most persistent idealism, and the blandest cynicism, the race is on between its decadence and its vitality.'

CHAPTER 11

DECADENCE AND VITALITY

On a grey November day, late in the afternoon, I set sail from New York. There was a heavy sky, the temperature was dropping towards zero, and the light was fading fast. The Manhattan skyline behind us was alive with evening lights and as we swung south towards the Verrazano-Narrows Bridge we looked from the stern towards the illuminated Statue of Liberty on our starboard side, and, about half a mile north of it, Ellis Island, where so many of the immigrants who built and sustained the city had first set foot in the New World.

I had never made an Atlantic crossing before, so the chance to take *Queen Mary* 2 only a few weeks before the coming of election year, 2020, was an exhilarating one. New York harbour holds so many memories, as the gateway to a new life for many generations, and it is a cradle of history. Steaming slowly towards the ocean, the waters turning dark as the last light disappeared, the ship gave us some final glimpses of the city. The top of the Chrysler building, now about 6 miles behind us, the Staten Island ferry passing us by, the non-stop bustle under the floodlights in the docks on the Jersey shore, and then, just as we turned towards the bridge, a solitary flag on some warehouse in Brooklyn, picked out by a stray light and bright for a moment in the gloom.

In America, there is always a flag somewhere close by, and it was the right image to carry off to sea. At that moment, with public hearings on the impeachment of a president scheduled to begin two days later, and the country profoundly divided over the character and conduct of Donald Trump, the republic represented by that flag was as troubled as at any time since I first caught sight of the harbour in 1970. Impeachment and a subsequent Senate trial of the president had seemed, as late as in the summer just gone, unlikely. Many Democrats were still reluctant to turn accusation into a legal assault. But the scales had shifted in recent weeks, his Ukrainian machinations having been revealed by public servants who could no longer stay silent, and another act in the Trump drama promised more fire, and more division.

Sailing away, the sight of that flag for a few moments in the darkness stayed with me. It had given the perfect farewell. As the night got colder, and we felt a gentle swell from the ocean, the memory of it swept me back almost exactly a year to my expedition in Texas just before the midterm elections of 2018. I was on the campus of the University of Texas in Austin, in search of some constitutional wisdom. I found there a collection of flags stranger than any I had ever seen.

Old Glory was everywhere. Hanging from the ceiling, draped over bookcases, painted on model cars, stitched on underwear and swimsuits, springing out of photographs covering the walls, showing flags 50 yards wide hanging from the ceilings at conventions, flying from the cabooses of campaign trains of long ago, waving from a capsule in space and from the conning tower of a submarine, even hung behind the platform at an American Nazi Party rally in New Jersey in the 1930s where the slogan was, eerily, America First. Yet this wasn't a museum or a souvenir shop, nor the collection of some eccentric who couldn't resist buying anything that showed the Stars and Stripes. I was in the jumbled study of one of the country's leading constitutional scholars, who peered out from a backdrop of red, white and blue.

Sanford Levinson teaches law and government in Austin, and he admits a lifelong affair with the flag, which he says is quite natural. 'No country has quite the same obsession with the flag as America.' It has always intrigued him. So when students come to his room for a tutorial, after they've navigated towers of volumes of history and law that make the place like the poky backroom of a second-hand bookshop, as likely as not they will find themselves crouching under a plane strung from the ceiling painted with the Stars and Stripes, or maybe sitting on a flag in the shape of a butterfly. Levinson has spent years charting and studying the relationship between citizens and the most obvious symbol of their country, because the constitutional settlement that the flag represents has been his lifelong intellectual interest.

These days he finds the constitution more interesting than ever, because he thinks it is broken.

He talks of how the Founding Fathers would be astonished by the way the political parties have turned it into a weapon. 'The framers simply didn't anticipate how deeply partisanship would hollow out Congress's willingness to hold a president accountable. They hated political parties – George Washington bemoaned "the demon of party spirit".'

But, above all, he thinks that the constitution – notoriously difficult to amend, because it needs the approval of the legislatures of three-quarters of the fifty states – is inadequate in confronting the problems of a modern society, and has become a barrier to good government. But the flag itself, saluted in every sports ground and every schoolyard, is the sacred symbol that makes questioning the constitution seem heretical. And presidential power, Levinson argues, has spread too far, giving sweeping executive authority to the White House with oversight that isn't tough enough to keep up.

He turns to the question that, after our conversation, soon began to become more serious in Washington. 'In Britain you can get rid of a prime minister more easily than we can get rid of a president. And that's a problem.'

Even then, in the fall of 2018, before the publication of the report of the special counsel Robert Mueller, into Russian interference in the 2016 election, conversations like this tended to turn to one question. Could he last? Since Trump had set out to challenge, with pride, any orthodoxy that stood in his way, he was mounting a challenge to his opponents. He thought he could get away with it – and could speak in a new language of confrontation from the White House. Could they stop him? Would they dare? With each week, he believed that he was changing the country, and he was. If America was going to be 'Great Again' by his rule book, it would be more divided, too.

During the contentious hearings on the nomination of Brett Kavanaugh to the Supreme Court in 2018, I spoke in Washington to Ilya Shapiro of the conservative Cato Institute about the divided country. He summed it up neatly.

You do have this polarisation of the country geographically. People live around people who vote like they do more than any time in American history. And the parties are more separated and ideologically coherent than they've ever been. And so the natural effect of that is gridlock. There's no way to compromise. There's no compromise position.

So that's an understandable but unfortunate political dynamic. And similarly with votes on judges. If one judge has a radically different vision of the constitution from another, and those constitutional theories map out onto the separated parties, then in effect you do have a zero-sum game on judicial appointments as well.

The conservative Federalist Society provides Trump with a regularly updated list of judges at all levels in the system whom they deem right-minded on constitutional questions – that is, that the judicial system, above all the Supreme Court itself, should concern itself with setting limits on government power, rather than with being an instrument for modernity and change. It is resulting in a significant shift of ideology in the judiciary. In late 2019, Trump gave a telling answer to a reporter who asked him for his response to a defeat that the administration had suffered in the courts.

Instead of dealing with the question at issue, Trump said simply, 'I've had a great track record. Within a couple of months, we'll have 182 federal judges.'

In other words, he was fixing it, just as he'd promised.

The divided country is, of course, emphasised further by an electoral system that is creaking. When the Founding Fathers established a Senate that would have two members from each state, their reasoning, to balance the interests of competing states at the federal level, was obvious. But in modern times it throws up glaring anomalies.

In the west, for example, the thinly populated mountain states of Wyoming, North and South Dakota, Montana and Idaho have a combined population of around 7 million. Between them they send ten senators to Washington. California, with a population of around 40 million, sends two. In a chamber with only 100 members, this builds in a huge tilt to rural (and mostly conservative) states.

There are other problems with the electoral system. Across the South – there were glaring examples in North Carolina during the midterm election in 2018 – there have been determined efforts by Republicans to find ways of disqualifying voters (by state legislatures seeking registration procedures to try to decrease the number of African American voters, in order to deny Democrat candidates support they would expect in most cases to get). Even without the growing alarm about security in the counting process – hand-held ballots that can mysteriously disappear – electronic voting machines, now used in many states, are vulnerable to attack. No one who glances at the evidence that has accumulated since the 2016 election can seriously doubt the strength of efforts to disrupt the campaign (notably by Russian interference which was clearly designed to tilt the balance towards Trump). Applying the lessons of that experience to the question of integrity at polling stations is obviously an urgent task. But it has barely begun.

So entangled did the issue of interference in 2016 become with the very survival of Trump's presidency that it became a very unpopular issue with Republicans. The 'hanging chads' presidential vote in Florida in 2000, which may well have swung the result thanks to a combination of faulty machines, rough-and-ready supervision, and of course the vagaries of the electoral college system, was an event many Americans tried to forget afterwards. It was surely, though, a forerunner of much more trouble to come, in a form that will be much more difficult to police and eradicate.

And don't forget the gerrymandering of congressional districts, practised by both parties in states where they control the legislature and can use the pretence of 'redistricting' to manufacture boundaries for congressional seats that are designed simply to protect one party's interest by herding sympathetic voters together. There are congressional districts that have no geographical heart, but spread themselves here and there as if they have the arms of an octopus, because one party or the other has manipulated the boundaries to its own advantage. Reprehensible in itself no doubt, but with one damaging wider consequence. With the increase in the number of ultra-safe districts, polarisation in the House of Representatives gets worse. Gerrymandering has an atrophying effect on the system.

So American democracy has practical problems. But the challenge, thanks to Trump, is now a cultural one, too.

His strategy has been to create a distinction between 'real' Americans and others. It is, of course, a denial of the country's history, but if you go to one of his huge rallies for 'the base' – they were becoming ever more fervent affairs in the run-up to 2020 – you are left in no doubt you're being invited to consider a significant part of the population as evidence of an external threat. There was a good deal of outrage when he said that four Democratic congresswomen of colour – three of them born in the United States – should go back to where they came from. 'Send them back!' the crowd chanted. He did not see any reason to apologise.

And when many Americans expressed horror at the sight of children being removed from their parents, or forced to choose between them, before being taken to crude detention centres on the Mexican border – most of them from families seeking asylum from Central America and prepared to go through the system to apply for it – he simply cited the 'bad people' crossing the border, where he still insisted that he would build his wall.

There were also the youngsters who had been protected by the Obama-era DACA programme – the so-called 'Dreamers' – designed to offer a path to American citizenship to young people who had entered the country illegally but wanted to stay. I met a young woman called Palloma Jovita on a balmy evening in 2018 in a Boston suburb. She had become one of the public voices for the 'Dreamers' campaign against Trump who was railing against DACA and associating the Dreamers with the 'bad people' sneaking across the southern border.

Palloma was twenty-two. She'd been brought illegally to the US by her parents when she was five, in an effort – embedded in the American story – to find a better life. Since then, her parents had become citizens, and her sister too. She was working her way through college, seeing herself as an ordinary American looking forward to a world of work, where she'd pay her taxes and eventually get citizenship. But if Trump's effort to rescind the programme was upheld in the courts, she and three-quarters of a million others would be deported, to a 'home' they'd never known.

I woke up when it came on the news that morning that he'd ended DACA. My mum was crying in the kitchen. It was devastating. I didn't even know if I was going to be able to graduate. I was in my senior year in college and I didn't even know if I was going to be able to finish.

People are always saying that it's okay, you can just get married. But at the same time people don't understand that I don't want to do that. Immigration, my status, has touched every aspect of my life, and this is the one thing I didn't want it to affect.

On DACA, the courts blocked Trump, but the episode illustrated the way that division had become the political language of his time. Them and us, friends and enemies.

And, behind it all, race. The 'original sin'. Watching demonstrations in the streets after a police shooting in Charlotte, North Carolina, listening to a pastor leading a crowd in hymns on a street corner near the scene, I was reminded that in many communities across the country a tiny spark can start a bonfire. The reason is that building trust is difficult, and history means that it takes a long time. It can be broken in an instant. When that happens, as it has in many communities, it is hard to get back.

If this is 'making America great again', the evidence is escaping many Americans. They see problems of old being exacerbated rather than solved – urban poverty and decay, low educational standards in many parts of the country, social segregation in many of the best universities, a health system that mostly works for the better-off but fails the rest, a tax regime that gives rewards at the top and penalises many in the middle and at the bottom. On top of it all they see a presidency mired in murky dealings. If they take an interest in the wider world, they see a president regularly humiliated by allies as well as old adversaries.

When Robert Mueller, the special counsel, published his report in spring 2019, the second paragraph began, 'The Russian government interfered in the 2016 Presidential election in sweeping and systematic fashion.' As bald and simple as that.

But Trump declared that the report exploded the 'myths' about which he'd been complaining for two years – that he colluded with Russians in the run-up to the election and that he subsequently tried to obstruct a proper investigation into what happened (an investigation, of course, which he tried to have closed down because his Department of Justice, in his mind infested with Democrats, had become the headquarters of a 'witch-hunt'). There were two pieces of moderately good news for him – that Mueller could not conclusively prove 'collusion' in the many contacts between Trump's campaign and Russians, and that he was not willing to say outright that the president was guilty of obstruction. But Trump's assertion that he had been exonerated was simply not true, as subsequent events would show.

Mueller deliberately left it to Congress to take the next step. Towards the end of 2019, it did.

The Democratic majority in the House, elected in the 2018 midterms, now controlled all the committees and early in the year it began to dig, and to take evidence in a way that their Republican predecessors had not.

This process began to produce revelations and indictments about contacts between Trump associates and Russia, and particularly with Russian interests in Ukraine, which had already led to the conviction and imprisonment of Paul Manafort, who was a campaign chairman for Trump in 2016, on charges of fraud, money-laundering and perjury. His old associate Roger Stone, whom I'd met in such bullish mood at the Republican convention in 2016, was convicted on seven counts of making false statements, witness tampering and obstruction of justice. Others were awaiting trial or sentence. No president had seen more members of his staff and personal circle taking the long walk to the courtroom dock.

Looking back to Trump's election itself, Mueller said that in

2016 a torrent of fake information was pumped into the social media stratosphere by the Russian Internet Research Agency (IRA), which increasingly began to favour one candidate against another, Trump rather than Clinton. He says that accounts controlled by IRA even helped to bring about pro-Trump rallies and encourage all those who went to them ('Thank you for your support MIAMI! My team just shared photos from your TRUMP SIGN WAVING DAY yesterday!'). It was the kind of thing of which any mainstream political campaign, operating out of dingy rooms in New York or Chicago or Atlanta, would be proud. Except it was coming from St Petersburg – at least 123 million Facebook posts – and, with the help of WikiLeaks, it was directed, secretly, at achieving one outcome, the disruptive one that would most please the man who could then deal with Trump: Vladimir Putin.

That campaign cry – 'I love WikiLeaks!' from Trump – rolled down the years. There is no doubt about where Julian Assange of WikiLeaks stood on this question. In a 2015 Twitter comment he confirmed that they believed it would be better for their purpose – widespread disruption, the aim he shared with Putin – if the Republican candidate were to win. For good measure he described Clinton as 'a bright, well-connected, sadistic sociopath', thereby prefiguring dozens of Trump rallies.

By the time Trump came to take American troops out of northern Syria in late 2019, thereby encouraging a Turkish invasion against Kurds who'd thought America was their ally, and simultaneously the escape of ISIS fighters whom Trump had boasted about 'beating', the commentary in Washington focused increasingly on the way American foreign policy was working solidly in the interests of Putin.

That was the background to the impeachment inquiry, which, like so many good investigations, was chasing the money. How did his interests in Saudi Arabia and Turkey impact on decision-making? Why was the family business now preoccupying his daughter and son-in-law, although they were working in the White House? Had the accepted separation between private and public business as a matter of propriety now been jettisoned? All the while, Trump's lawyers were in court trying to keep his tax returns secret.

In the congressional hearings on impeachment, two worlds

collided. Trump told his rallies – and his Twitter followers – that the whole proceeding was either a witch-hunt or a hoax (for him, the words were interchangeable). In one tweet, he called the chairman of the House Intelligence Committee, Adam Schiff, 'human scum'. And his supporters, egged on by the likes of the Fox News anchors Sean Hannity and Tucker Carlson, attacked the character and motives of those who testified against the president, particularly Dr Fiona Hill and Lt Col Alexander Vindman.

She had worked at the heart of American intelligence and security, and he (Ukrainian-born) was the head of European affairs at the National Security Council. Americans watching the televised hearings were treated to the unusual sight of Republicans – led by the acerbic California congressman Devin Nunes – attacking them as political stooges and untrustworthy characters, their public service notwithstanding. Despite Col Vindman testifying in uniform, displaying a chestful of medals including a Purple Heart for bravery, he was accused of playing a game orchestrated by leftist Democrats, and Dr Hill (British-born, and still with a strong trace of her native Durham accent) was painted as part of an anti-Trump conspiracy promoted by enemies of the country.

They told a simple story of how the president has sought favours from the Ukrainian government for domestic purposes, and used public money as the inducement. And they expressed their dismay at the pressure put on public servants to act as political conduits for Trump, and his lawyer Rudy Giuliani, who emerged as a figure trying to run a parallel foreign policy in Ukraine, earning large sums as he did so.

Outside the hearing rooms on Capitol Hill, Americans were also aware of a criminal investigation that was gathering pace. In early October, two businessmen, Lev Parnas and Igor Fruman, were arrested at Dulles airport outside Washington on their way out of the country, with one-way tickets in their pockets. They'd been hired the previous year by Giuliani to try to dig up some political dirt on Hunter Biden, son of the former vice president Joe Biden, who was evidently a potential Democratic candidate that Trump feared. Biden Jr had been a director of a Ukrainian company, Burisma, which Trump was convinced could be shown to be part of endemic corruption in that country. But, as the House hearings were told, that effort involved putting pressure on the Ukrainian president to help by withholding military aid that had been voted by Congress. That quid pro quo, which Trump continued to deny, became the engine of the impeachment inquiry, leading to the charge that the president had solicited the interference of a foreign government in the affairs of the United States, an act which Democrats claimed was as blatant an impeachable offence as you could find.

Trump continued to stir up feeling against the House and its committees, while others speculated who of those already convicted or indicted or under serious investigation would be the first to decide to try to save himself by turning on Trump. That in the end one of them would, no one doubted.

The approach to election year became an argument not just about the survival of Trump but about the strength of America's democratic institutions, the Congress and the courts. As always with Trump, the stakes kept rising.

A time of decadence? For many Americans, certainly.

They could remember him tweeting before 2016, criticising Obama for playing a round of golf, which he did exceedingly rarely. It was calculated that as Trump approached 1,000 days in office, he had visited one of his golf courses or one of his other properties on 389 of his 997 days in office (this from White House records), 223 of which were day trips to play golf. An unkind analyst could interpret that as meaning that 39 per cent of his presidency so far had been spent at Trump properties, and he even proposed that the 2020 G7 summit should be held at one of his Florida commercial estates. He expressed surprise at the hostile reaction, which forced him to abandon the plan, but offered no apology.

Go to a Trump rally and you'll find faith, excitement and anger. They are believers who will never desert him. But by the time the election was looming, it was not hard to find squeamish Republican voters who had overcome their early distaste for Trump and voted him in, but who found their queasiness had come back. It began to look like an election that would turn in the 'rust belt' and in the suburbs across the country. In those suburbs, Trump's fate will surely be decided.

Taking the election as the end point of this story, it would be easy to look back on the journey that began for me in 1970 and conclude that America has been on a downward path and, in a sense, that Trump voters were right when they felt a sense of loss, and wanted to believe in 'great' America again, presumably a greatness threatened above all by his impeachment.

But to predict continuing decline would be to deny the greatest American gift – optimism. The decadence of the Trump era – characterised by chaotic government, an angry public discourse, shameless self-promotion and financial ambition – has forced many Americans to think of another part of their inheritance: the vitality of the place. For inventiveness, determination, a willingness to change course quickly and self-belief, there is nowhere quite like it. On long journeys, with favourite books, I have not been allowed to forget that these characteristics have been embedded from the beginning. The identification of America with the urge to explore and press on flows through its whole culture, from the struggle with the elements and hostile nature in *Moby-Dick* to Steinbeck in the California dust bowl and Mailer in the meltdown of the 1960s.

Think of *Hamilton*, Lin-Manuel Miranda's musical, for many the most original score for the stage since *West Side Story* and the most unlikely adaptation of the extraordinary life of a man who became, from nothing, one of the principal architects and leaders of a collection of colonies that would turn themselves into the most powerful country in the world.

Hamilton begins:

How does a bastard, orphan, son of a whore and a
Scotsman, dropped in the middle of a forgotten
Spot in the Caribbean by providence, impoverished,
    in squalor
Grow up to be a hero and a scholar?
The ten-dollar Founding Father without a father
Got a lot farther by working a lot harder
By being a lot smarter
By fourteen, they placed him in charge of a trading charter

How indeed? It's all there. Speaking one evening in New York to crowds of young African Americans who'd just come out of a performance of the musical in the Richard Rodgers Theatre on 46th Street, it was exhilarating to realise that, for all the doubts about the persistence of the American Dream in recent times, they associated the story – told in a hip-hop score that spoke directly to their ears and minds – with their own prospects and hopes. They were, you might say, 'drawn ceaselessly back into the past' in thinking about America.

Trump has been drawn back too, in a different way. Instead of the endless pursuit of the dream that those last words in *The Great Gatsby* represent, his posture has been defiantly divisive about the here-and-now. Things have to be settled. His pride in identifying winners and losers, friends and enemies, has been the most obvious badge of his presidency, and by the start of 2020, with the campaign road opening up before him, that bullish exercise of power reached a new high. Impeached by the House, facing a Senate trial and mired, Nixon-like, in a struggle to defy subpoenas and lock away documents that Congress wanted to see, and witnesses it wanted to hear, he struck out with the killing of Qasem Soleimani, the Iranian general and strategist-in-chief who'd waged a violent struggle against the Western coalition and its troops for years across the Middle East. But in claiming victory, Trump was challenging the weight of foreign policy and defence thinking in both parties and official Washington, where it seemed a strategic misstep of huge proportions. He was breaking away – again.

Approaching the election in the frame of mind that he found most comforting, he pitted his instincts against those among his advisers and the vast majority of diplomatic, defence and intelligence professionals who had been trying to reign him in from the start. It was Trump alone, using the twin crises of impeachment and self-engineered Middle East turmoil to portray himself, more than ever, as the president who would always go his own way, whatever the cost. Pride, hurt, anxiety and anger, fear of humiliation – they were all on display to everyone in those fevered days as he struggled to disperse the cloud of alarm that wasn't only rising from Democrats but from a troubling number of Republicans too.

As he prepared for the annual State of the Union message in the New Year and then the campaign, Trump's re-election was clearly not going to depend on his economic record, as Republicans had expected and hoped in 2016. Whoever the Democrats nominated, the fight would be about Trump himself, and at the start of 2020 his style, personality and outlook were distilled to an essence with an unmistakable flavour. Nectar to 'the base'; a toxic brew to most others. There would be no muddle in this election, but a choice clearer than any most Americans had known in their lifetimes.

In the midst of the turn-of-the-year drama I spoke to the director Aaron Sorkin, writer of the best episodes of *The West Wing*, and when I asked him whether he could write a drama about the Trump White House he surprised me by saying no, for the following intriguing reason.

I have a prediction, which is that you're never going to see Donald Trump as a character on screen or on the stage. He'll always be offstage, and the reason is that whether it's a hero or an anti-hero, protagonist or an antagonist, there is no such thing as an interesting character who has no conscience. You can't do anything with the character.

The story will be about the senator or the congressman who's up for re-election and is selling their soul ... because even if they're a bad person, even if they're doing the wrong thing, the fact that they're aware that they are making some kind of bargain here, that's enough to get drama. From Trump, you're not going to get a Richard III moment or Richard Nixon moment. So, can I imagine what's going on in the White House? Yeah, he's ranting and raving about something. He's being incoherent. He is not listening. He is not having any kind of attention span. He's eating something from McDonald's and he's raging, tweeting.

Yet if you went to a presidential rally at the time Sorkin was speaking, you would have recognised in the crowd belief, expectation, faith undimmed. Trump's divided America was ready for a fight.

How far it seemed from much of the dreamy rhetoric that has always characterised election years, despite the grubby deals, the money and the street fights. Trump was proud that he had no interest in bridging the gulf between his supporters and the rest. He believed he would prevail, and that was all. Democrats who had refused to believe that he could win in 2016 had to confront that confidence with seriousness and caution. They couldn't know as 2020 began whether they were right or wrong in thinking that the country wanted to turn away from the Trump era, and they faced a fierce battle for the soul of America in which every weapon would be unsheathed. As at all the most troubled moments in the country's past, people were asking in their favourite refrain, 'Who are we?' Trump had sharpened that question for another generation, and it was cutting deep.

This would be no sleepy campaign. There would be vitality on both sides, bubbling up from the depths. Trumpists would burnish their vision of 'America First'; their opponents would talk of a lost public culture, in politics and in communities, and conjure a vision of a different kind of country. As Trump himself had always argued, there could be no escape from the choice.

For an outsider approaching another campaign, with the memories flooding back, many of the problems seemed familiar – social division, poverty, racial tension and the loss of faith among many people in the promise of progress they were given. But in response after 2016, Trump had offered a different kind of leadership, and self-consciously looked back, not forward. His stated intention was to dismantle much of the America that had been shaped over five or six decades. It was therefore inevitable that his appeal would be couched in apocalyptic and hostile terms, and by the beginning of 2020 he had reached some kind of climax in his warlike rhetoric and high-octane defiance against those who would continue to delve into his deals, his family, his business, and pursue his friends.

As he faced the consequences of the impeachment vote, and the world wondered where his foreign policy was bound, no one could know whether it would all end in defeat or whether Americans would have to prepare, in that most familiar of campaign cries, for four more years.

Leaving New York harbour in November 2019, the coming contest was on my mind. You can't really head into the Atlantic from the city without thinking of Herman Melville's hero – 'Call me Ishmael' – who found himself drawn back to sea because he felt 'a damp, drizzly November in my soul', there to confront hostile nature and pursue a great whale in a fight to survive. *Moby-Dick* is a novel about the American spirit – persistent, raw, bold and danger-loving.

Away from the city, on the ocean in the dark, a week and 3,000 miles away from home, I wondered where Trump would take his country in his effort to survive in office and win re-election, and how Americans would respond. The president's approval ratings had remained stubbornly low, but no one underestimated his reserve of raw street-fighting guile and Democrats still feared that if he were able to fashion an election about the economy he would be hard to depose.

How innocent we were. There can be no certainty about the date, but within a few days of that sailing from New York, 7500 miles away in the city of Wuhan in Hubei Province in China, a newly configured virus was starting to puzzle doctors, and then alarm them. But when I returned to the United States in February for the curtain-raising primary election in New Hampshire, no one yet knew how profoundly Covid-19 was going to reshape the campaign, every political and cultural argument, and the lives of all Americans.

I spent a while in Scranton, Pennsylvania, one of the gateways to the rust belt that might still be the route back to the White House for Trump, and the territory that any conqueror would have to win. While there, I visited 2446 North Washington Avenue, the grey-painted three-storey wooden house that was the childhood home of Joe Biden. Who could tell? Maybe the old soldier had one more battle in him.

Then I drove across New York State, passing not far from the corner of the Catskills where my American journey had begun fifty years earlier, and north through the Berkshire Mountains in Massachusetts towards the quirky Granite State, whose motto is 'Live Free or Die!', where the Democrats would start the messy business of organising themselves to take on Trump or, maybe, begin to fall apart.

There was snow on the mountains and the New England spring was still some way off. Everything was cold, bright, familiar. But we were launched on the strangest election campaign in any American's lifetime.

CHAPTER 12

ALONE

In November, after it was all done, the jumbled images from that fevered campaign, unquestionably the most expensive in American history and perhaps the most strangely shaped, seemed to settle into two sharp pictures that told the story from start to finish.

One was of a weary and slightly tetchy Joe Biden in late winter in New Hampshire, before he had to wear a mask and fashion a campaign from semi-isolation, contemplating the steep climb that lay ahead if he was to rescue his third bid for the presidency. The other, from the White House briefing room nine months later, was of a president stamping to the podium without the usual phalanx of aides, nor a vice-president nor even a chief of staff by his side, and repeating, in case anyone hadn't got the message, that he had no intention of accepting the election result. His lawyers would besiege the courts to try to reverse it because of nameless but innumerable crimes.

Each man in his different way was alone in that moment.

The noise disappears. From the Trump rallies, for which so many thousands queued for hours in their Make America Great Again hats for a glimpse of him, the Black Lives Matter protests that were such a part of the soundtrack of the year, the chatter in the long lines of citizens among the 100 million who voted early before election day, the scrambling of both parties to reach voters in the last days in the half-dozen states where they knew it would be decided, the ring of countless phones when hapless 'undecideds' got that fusillade of calls to tell them how to vote. And the sight, on an election night that stretched to four days and more, of the spiralling numbers that showed more Americans had voted in 2020 than in any election before.

When all that is swept aside, you see the men for what they are. Where they come from, what they represent, what they might or might not offer their country. And you're forced to contemplate the wild course of a campaign like no other, in a year that broke the rules.

Biden won just before his 78th birthday, which meant his inauguration in January would make him the oldest man to sit in the White House. Trump, whose unorthodoxy had divided the country, was the first president to have lost the popular vote twice, by around 3 million in 2016 and by over 7 million four years later. The first, too, to threaten to try to block certification of the vote by the states and to try to turn the pro forma vote of the Electoral College in December into a fight for legitimacy.

Afterwards, Democrats spoke of victory as if it had seldom been in doubt. That was not the feeling on election night as they watched the first returns. In mid-evening, I visited a friend who had been preparing a celebration (albeit socially distanced for Covid reasons) which would expunge the memory of the 'victory' party for Clinton in 2016, which he had abandoned before any of the soon-to-be shaken guests had arrived. On the fourth anniversary of that night, I came upon another gloomy scene.

Trump was doing even better than they had feared. In Florida, Biden's support among Latino voters lagged well behind Clinton's, and Trump took the state when, even in the last days, Democrats believed they could snatch it from him. In the house that I visited, I found four friends gripped by something close to horror. Surely, after everything, he couldn't win again? Through those first hours, everyone knew that he could. Democrats were indeed confident that their voters were disproportionately using mail-in ballots – which in most states would be counted in the days to come – but those Trump totals on the night were still a shock.

Could a president who his opponents believed was unqualified for office, and whose conduct over four years had seemed to them to prove the point, yet claim to speak for Americans for four more years? For them, it was a fear as great as the elation I'd seen a few days earlier at a Trump rally in North Carolina, where the mere mention of a gloomy opinion poll – let alone some financial reve-lation about the Trumps in the *New York Times* – was enough to provoke hoots of laughter and disbelief. I asked one woman in the queue of thousands waiting to be bussed to the airport hanger where he was to speak how she could be so confident that he would win. Her God was behind him, she told me, and that was enough. It was what the Almighty wanted.

Another told me, to my surprise, that even defeat, unlikely though she thought it to be, wouldn't be defeat. I was puzzled. She was qui-etly spoken, not a shouter, but with piercing eyes. 'He has a plan,' she said. I asked, with an air of genuine interest, what that might be. She replied, 'The big military.'

This was not the kind of support that was going to melt away before election day. I left her happy to wait hours for the man to arrive.

On the day after the polls closed, as the long wait for the final tallies began, a few of us were talking about what it must be like at Biden headquarters in Wilmington, Delaware, two hours north of Washington. There they were expressing optimism but had to deal with the sight of Trump totals that might soon exceed his 2016 vote, and were beginning to accept that their hopes of increasing the number of Democrats in the House and winning the Senate by a clear margin were slipping away. Just before 2.30 am, they watched the early declaration of victory by Trump, which his campaign had signalled days before as a tactic they'd use if they had an early lead, before the later counting. 'As far as I'm concerned, we already have won this,' he said. Even Fox News disagreed.

Vice President Mike Pence, whose face seldom reveals his emotions, did seem a touch embarrassed when he came to the micro-phone in the East Room to express optimism about the final result, and thereby to contradict Trump's assertion a moment earlier that it was already over.

We knew we should prepare for a long wait.

My mind went back to New Hampshire in the cold in the second week of February. Biden was in trouble in the Democratic primary. In the Iowa caucuses the week before, he'd been pushed easily into third place by Pete Buttigieg and Bernie Sanders. Buttigieg, until recently mayor of South Bend, Indiana, and the first declared gay candidate to make a serious run for the presidency, headed for New Hampshire as a shooting star. Sanders, ageing darling of the Democratic left and Senator from next-door Vermont, was confident that he'd repeat his 2016 victory there.

'The Rip van Winkle of Vermont,' a Biden person said to me, managing to insult in one go both Sanders and his state, which has a reputation as a sleepy hideaway populated by the Yankee equivalents of hillbillies and ageing hippies. The trouble was that, with Biden at 77, the insult had something of a reverse sting.

Buttigieg, who had just turned 38, was pulling in big crowds. His appeal was evidently fresh, and his quick intelligence was giving his audiences performances to savour. At one meeting someone asked him what he'd say to Trump in debate if the president raised the question of his marriage to a man, when so many Americans were said to think such a union unnatural. Buttigieg said he'd point out that, unlike Trump, he hadn't had to pay off any porn stars to try to save his marriage.

A nice way to bring the house down.

And Sanders, with his rasping voice and his sermons against Wall Street, was still leading the pack, his audiences overwhelmingly young and happy to be believers. Like the substantial number of Democrats who were supporting Senator Elizabeth Warren of Massachusetts, it was clear that they wanted the election to be a crusade.

Biden is not a crusader by instinct. He likes a fight, can stir up a crowd, but enjoys his reputation as a Washington fixer as much as a man-of-the-people. Both are appropriate tags. In nearly fifty years in Washington politics he's mastered the business of deal-making; but he revels in the portrait of the young Senator who took the Amtrak train home to Wilmington every night to be with his two children, his wife having been killed in a Christmas car crash just before he took his seat in the Senate in 1972. He has never pretended to be a fresh face and prefers familiarity as his calling card.

He appealed to Democrats in New Hampshire not to swing left-wards – for example, on Bernie Sanders' healthcare plan that would eliminate private insurance – to a position that would make it difficult to capture the middle ground. But it didn't work. On the weekend before the primary vote, it was obvious that the Sanders-Warren vote and the Buttigieg insurgency would probably see him off. So he decided to leave for South Carolina, there to try to salvage his campaign in the next primary.

My producer, Jess Quayle, and I noticed that on the Saturday afternoon he was due to make a brief stop to greet volunteers at one of his campaign offices in Manchester, the old mill town that is always the focal point of the primary. Expecting nothing more than a bit of handshaking and a photocall, we turned up to the usual sight of a few trestle tables, soft drinks and sandwiches and some modest piles of Biden campaign hats. The place didn't tremble with expectation of victory. It was a downbeat scene.

When his bus drew up – The Soul of the Nation painted on the side – we were told that the candidate had decided to say a few words. Not only that, but he was going to take questions. The press contingent (apart from photographers) was modest in size, so it was clear we were going to have the chance of a close(ish) encounter. Biden, taking off the dark glasses he was wearing against the low winter sun, stood on a cross that had been quickly marked out with duct tape for him on the floor. We gathered round.

We had a fascinating insight into a man preparing for the fight of his life. He knew at that moment that he was losing. Sanders was going to win on Tuesday; Buttigieg was pressing; Warren's vote was holding. Biden gave us his pitch, now and again revealing the strain. 'I'd LOVE to debate Donald Trump!' he said, bending down to repeat himself, 'LOVE to!' The point was that he thought none of the others could do it as well as he could, a veteran of dozens of campaigns.

Someone mentioned Buttigieg and his time as mayor in South Bend, only the fourth biggest town in Indiana, and probably best known as the site of Notre Dame University and its famous college football team. 'South Bend!' said Biden, stopping himself just before he made an injudicious remark about the Hoosier State. Buttigieg had boasted about spending $70 million. Where had he got it? By the intervention of Vice President Biden's office, that's where. 'Mayor Pete. Please! C'mon.' We knew what he was saying. The boy just wasn't ready.

He was getting into his stride. I suggested that he seemed a little angry. 'Angry? I'm not angry ...!

Maybe not, but he was agitated. 'Feisty, then,' I suggested.

He accepted the word as a fair description. There was a fight going on and, given time, he'd win it. His stalwarts gathered round. A rotund Irishman – I guessed as much because of the droopy shamrock sprouting from his lapel – grabbed Biden by the shoulders and they had a bearhug, although I gathered they'd never met before. 'I drove from Cape Cod to be here,' the man said, and pressed some kind of Catholic talisman into Biden's hand. 'We'll win.' There was a lot of God-bless-you, some talk about the Massachusetts firefighters' union, and Biden was in his close-up element, reassured by the old gang that was still rooting for him, somewhere. I couldn't help thinking of that hoary classic of Boston politics from the fifties, *The Last Hurrah*.

He left the hall and walked to the bus, zipping up a leather jacket. We knew he'd soon be gone, and that if he were defeated in South Carolina less than three weeks later, his campaign, already short of cash, might quickly run out of steam.

By chance I ran into an acquaintance that afternoon, who materialised after the Biden bus had arrived. I asked him what he was doing there, and was a touch surprised at the answer – helping Biden on national security and intelligence matters. We had a conversation, and he laid out for me the plan that they still believed could deliver the nomination to Biden. A big bounce from South Carolina before the fifteen primaries on Super Tuesday, when he'd show his strength across the south and midwest, knowing that Bernie would romp home in California. I remained sceptical, a wariness that was strengthened three days later when the New Hampshire result turned out to be worse for Biden than he probably expected. He came fifth. The comeback seemed improbable.

Buttigieg almost overtook Sanders and Warren underperformed. It's part of the tradition in New Hampshire that someone does something surprising, usually with short-lived effect. This time it was Senator Amy Klobuchar of Minnesota who made a run. Her supporters, with the absurdity that attends these events, chanted 'Klomentum'. But it didn't last long.

The morning after, I had to find a spot to fix up a live link to London to speak to *The World At One* on Radio 4, and found myself alone in the cavernous space where various media outlets had been anchoring their broadcasts the night before. The moving men had been in and the place was empty, except for one piece of BBC equipment that I'd managed to save from the derigging operation, and a couple of cameras on a little platform behind. I was banging away on my laptop, trying to organise my thoughts, when I heard someone talking quite loudly behind me.

I turned. It was Pete Buttigieg, alone except for a young press aide. He was doing a series of interviews into one camera, which was being patched through every four minutes or so to different local stations across the country. His aide would say, 'Dallas' and the give name of the breakfast presenter he was talking to, and he'd insert a remark about Texas into his spiel. 'Minneapolis' – a couple of mentions of midwest farmers. 'Sacramento' – a reference to looking forward to the California primary. And so on.

A candidate without a crowd, nearly on his own in a draughty hall, looking like a young man in his twenties, talking to hundreds of thousands of people he couldn't see about being President of the United States. Truly, a New Hampshire scene. We had a few words, and that was all. Someone pointed out to me later in the morning that if Buttigieg were to run for president in 2054 he would still be younger than Bernie Sanders, Joe Biden or Elizabeth Warren or Donald Trump were at that moment.

But Old Joe was still full of fight. In South Carolina he had the gift of the support of James Clyburn, a veteran African-American Congressman, whose endorsement gave Biden the lift he needed. He got nearly 50 per cent, sweeping up the African-American vote and leaving his rivals far behind. He'd been counted out too soon, he told his victory rally. 'Just days ago the press and the pundits had declared this candidacy dead. Now, thanks to all of you – the heart of the Democratic Party – we just won, and we've won big.'

The question was what that 'heart' really wanted. On Super Tuesday we might find out. Like many others, I'd made my way to Burlington, Vermont, because it seemed that, one way or another, the story would revolve around Sanders. He was all-but-certain to win in California, with more delegates to the nominating convention than any other state, and even with modest performances in the

South he remained favourite for the nomination. But he was about to slide away.

By the end of the night, Biden had the nomination in his grasp. Buttigieg had helped by dropping out, throwing his support behind him at a Texas rally the night before, and Biden surpassed every expectation. He won ten of the fifteen primaries. At breakfast the next morning I met an old American friend whom I knew to have impeccable contacts in the Sanders camp. The message filtering through from them was clear. Their fight would continue, because the cause demanded it, but the game was over.

No one doubted after that night that Biden would be the nominee, and attention turned to the means by which he would accommodate those in the party who wanted to move leftwards and who were the self-styled progressives. He would be able to summon unity for the campaign against a bogeyman president – only on the diehard fringe would there be opposition to any Democrat fighting Trump. But the power of the progressive campaign had revealed to everyone that, if Biden won, he would face a testing struggle in defining a new Democratic coalition that could bind middle-of-the-road voters, some of whom had voted for Trump, with those who yearned for more radical leadership.

Politics, however, was about to change in a different way.

From the White House, the coming crisis was still being denied. In late February, Trump had said of Covid-19, 'It's going to disappear. One day – it's like a miracle! – it will disappear.' Three days after Super Tuesday, he said, 'The United States has, as of now, only 129 cases and 11 deaths. We are working very hard to keep these numbers as low as possible!'

In his ubiquitous Tweets, he predicted the quick arrival of a vaccine, praised his medical advisers – who, a few months later after 200,000 Americans had died, he called 'idiots' – and said that a combination of the Chinese authorities, the media and 'Sleepy Joe' had so exaggerated the threat of the virus that it had become a political hoax.

Warming to one of the themes that his strongest supporters had come to expect at every rally, he railed against the tyranny of 'experts' who blinded the public with science. As with climate change, about which he insisted the scientific consensus was simply wrong, he presented himself once more as the man of common sense who knew more about viruses than the virologists, just as he had once said that he knew more about ISIS than the generals, more about intelligence than the CIA, and more about how money worked than anyone. On 6 March, he revealed his medical gifts. 'I really get it. People are surprised that I understand it. Every one of these doctors said, "How do you know so much about this?" Maybe I have a natural ability. Maybe I should have done that instead of running for president.'

Throughout the spring, the virus, even as it spread, seemed to become less of a public health challenge to the White House than a new front in the culture war. For Trump it represented the divide between left and right, them and us. Democratic governors were shutting down their states; he would open them up. People were wearing masks when he said it was unnecessary. They were trying to stop you going to church. The economy was hurting.

With the inexorable rise in cases, Trump was obliged, from April onwards, to accept that the crisis which he had predicted would disappear 'like a miracle' was still there. But in scrambling to explain his earlier insistence – against 'expert' advice – that it would be short-lived and a minor episode, and that he 'knew' that a vaccine was on its way, he found himself on familiar ground. Where most political leaders would have found it hard, perhaps impossible, to reconcile the contradictory statements made over the months, Trump did what he enjoyed most, and organised a festival of denial.

Anything that contradicted him was not only a confection by a hostile media, led by 'the failing *New York Times*' and the rest of them, or the 'far left', or the dark forces of the kind that many of his supporters believed to be part of a global conspiracy against America. He turned the debate about how far and how fast suppression measures should go, and what the best advice to the public should be, into a campaign in which 'rationality' was a code word for deceit and in which doctors' warnings of 'danger' was an exaggeration, probably designed to undermine his administration and certainly to assist the Democrats who, it was well known, hated America and feared its success.

In normal times, the exaggerations and about-turns from the

White House at such a time of crisis would be devastating for a sitting president. But Trump had so fashioned the political landscape to his purposes, and changed the rhetorical tone to such a degree, that turning the pandemic into another revelation of life as a matter of 'them against us' seemed to fit naturally. Bizarre though it might appear to outsiders, such an interpretation to 'the base' did not only sit easily with the Trumpist view of the world, but, as a consequence, appeared reassuring. It was simply, on a grand scale, evidence of what he had always told them. Big government and its experts – the people against whom he'd taken up arms on the people's behalf – were simply trying to have their way again. And the Chinese were helping them along.

This election was replete with ironies. This was one of them, that a public health crisis of immense proportions – a quarter of a million dead by Christmas – would allow Trump to stir up more of the resentment that had brought him such political strength, and to talk with even more gusto about a country divided, between those who were part of 'the greatest political movement in the history of the United States' and those who wanted to destroy it.

There was another irony, of course. If Covid-19 allowed Democrats to focus on Trump's style of government and what they believed were his incapacities in office, the national crisis also delivered them from the kind of election they most feared. From early on in Trump's term of office, they had realised that an election fought on the economy would be hard to win. If ordinary Americans saw signs of growth, unemployment rates falling and felt that he was winning in trade wars with China and others, they realised that the extra effort that's required to remove a sitting president might be beyond them. However much they might rail against his crudity, the mystery over his debts and tax returns, the exploits of his family in and around the White House, the economic numbers might help him home. What they needed, by contrast, was an election that was not about the economy, but Donald Trump himself.

Covid-19 allowed them to focus on the man, and the way he led the country. And they could be sure that he would play into their hands: at a moment of crisis, he would certainly ensure that the whole story turned around him. He would give briefings in person from the White House; offer reassurance; lead from the front. In short, he would stick his own label on the whole affair, turning it into another conquest.

The struggle between Trump's appeal to his base – telling them that at this moment they needed him more than ever – and the Democrats' critique of his zigzag handling of the pandemic became the story of the election. It ended with evidence that was less of a revelation than a restatement of what we already knew: that the country was evenly divided and that for all Joe Biden's efforts to portray Trump as an incompetent and dangerous president, he retained enough support to suggest strongly that Democrats were right in suspecting that if it had been a contest on the economy he would have been re-elected.

Through the summer, it was odd to watch the campaign from far away without the milestones of the conventions and then the beginning of a run-up to polling day that looked like every other election. Instead, Biden was emerging intermittently from isolation – popping up like the Loch Ness Monster, said Donald Trump Jr, although how many voters in Wisconsin or Nevada knew what he was talking about is open to question – and the procession of rallies was missing. On the Democratic side, it was understood quietly that that might not be a bad thing. Biden's propensity for verbal infelicity and malapropism has been an obvious (though sometimes endearing) characteristic of his whole public life and a locked-down campaign certainly helped to reduce the chances of a gaffe or misstatement that would set off a Trump riff about 'Sleepy Joe' or some public musing about the signs of dementia.

As it turned out, by far his most important announcement in that period was the choice of Senator Kamala Harris as his running mate who, despite some frostiness from those in the Sanders camp who thought her dangerously centrist, was able to satisfy the natural question attached to any campaign by someone who would turn 80 in office if he were elected. Was she fit to take over? As a former public official – district attorney for San Francisco then Attorney General for the biggest state in the land – she was an experienced executive. Harris was safe. No one tried seriously to advance the argument that she wasn't qualified. Biden killed the question with her appointment, and guaranteed that if he won, she might well be propelled, one way or another – the first woman to sit in the White House as vice president – to the Oval Office.

If the Covid-19 crisis tended to highlight American divisions and the arguments about public policy, and helped to cement them, perhaps the other most significant public event of election year did the same.

On 25 May in Minneapolis, an employee in a convenience store rang 911 at around 8pm to report to the police that a man had paid for some cigarettes with what appeared to be a counterfeit $20 note. Less than twenty minutes later, George Floyd, a 46-year-old African-American, was pinned down by four police officers and soon showed no signs of life. Video footage showed one officer's knee pressing on his neck for more than eight minutes, while he was handcuffed and on the ground. Paramedics couldn't revive him, and he was pronounced dead in hospital.

Because smartphone footage of these events was broadcast on every news channel, the reaction was instant and fierce. There were huge demonstrations across the country. One poll suggested that 20 million people of all races may have taken part. In a year when demonstrations by Black Lives Matter were already a prominent feature of the political landscape, provoking fierce argument and causing Trump to adopt a law-and-order theme in the early months of his campaign, Floyd's death was an incendiary event. Third-degree murder and manslaughter charges were laid against one officer. Three others also faced charges. In the black community, it was seen as the latest in a series stretching back years in which they argued that police forces had regularly used tactics that wouldn't be used against white suspects. In the Minneapolis case, millions of Americans had seen what happened, and watched the officer whose knee was on Floyd's neck refuse not only the appeals of bystanders to let him breathe, but a desperate request from paramedics who feared for his life.

The public shock was palpable and trouble in the streets inevitable. Some demonstrations turned violent, and even at the end of the year many Washington shops and restaurants were still boarded up because they feared trouble and especially – though they were diplomatic in the way they explained it – if Trump were to win the election.

There was a familiar battle of voices. In the African-American community, a recitation of similar fatal incidents – in Louisiana, Florida, Maryland, Missouri – and from the right an assault on those demonstrators who'd turned violent during protests, or looted shops and businesses. Floyd's killing became the most notorious episode since the beating by four police officers of Rodney King, a black man arrested in Los Angeles on suspicion of drunk driving in 1991. The officers were charged, but none found guilty by a jury. Since the beating had been filmed, and broadcast, there were nationwide protests and campaigns in King's support. Floyd's death, nearly thirty years later, provoked even more anger and another bout of introspection about the conduct of some police forces across the country.

In response, Trump called Floyd's death 'a terrible thing', but he reacted angrily to a CBS television interviewer who asked him about the number of black people killed by police, saying 'so are white people ... many more white people'. Protesters were 'thugs', he said, and he also employed a phrase made notorious by a Miami police chief in 1968, 'when the looting starts, the shooting starts'. The effect was to fan the flames.

As before, when many public figures began to follow athletes in 'taking the knee', as some football players had done a few years before, the public split into two camps. For or against?

Throughout the summer, a familiar atmosphere of distrust grew, often laced with hatred. At the end of September, in the first of the candidates' scheduled televised debates, a notably ill-tempered series of exchanges produced one remark from the president that touched one of the most sensitive political questions of all, one that all but the few political figures who still take succour from the history of Southern demagoguery take care to avoid. Asked if he would condemn white supremacists, Trump talked of his loathing of the left and especially 'Antifa' (the protest group that styles itself Anti-Fascist and who'd had become the target of most antagonism from the right) and went on to say that groups like the Proud Boys should 'stand back and stand by'.

Now, most Americans watching had probably never heard of the

Proud Boys, a group that describes itself as committed to 'reinstating the spirit of Western chauvinism', which has been labelled by US intelligence agencies as extremist and dangerous. Some of its members are happy to describe themselves as neo-fascist, and it's admired by militia groups that have had less success in getting supporters onto the streets. After Trump's comments, it proudly took his words as an endorsement – indicating that they should prepare themselves for action – and although he later said under pressure that he disliked all white supremacists, including that group, the damage was done.

For the many attracted to far-right rhetoric – let alone those who associated with the subterranean network of avowedly racist groups and organisations that style themselves militias – his words, in a debate about the future of the presidency, were electric.

The effect was to polarise further the views on race, crime and social justice. Even Trump supporters who were happy to be critical of some of his pronouncements, and would never give the time of day to the likes of the Proud Boys, found themselves forced to take sides. As always with Trump, the middle ground was out of bounds. Make your choice: it's us or them. In this case, 'they' encompassed everyone from mainstream Democrats to groups like Antifa willing to contemplate violence and 'we' meant everyone from the mildest Republican to people who were willing to take up arms in defence of a white nationalist America.

Long before the election, Trump had made clear that the campaign would be a reflection of his personality, and of his conviction that politics is like business. There is a winner and a loser, and that's all.

Anyone with a political memory was likely to have had a sense of shock in the course of this campaign at moments when it became clear how much had changed, and what was deemed acceptable in the Trump era. The idea that a presidential candidate could offer even a sliver of support or sympathy to a white supremacist group would once have seemed unthinkable, and the kiss of political death (at least since the days of segregation in the Deep South). Yet Trump's success, built on the argument that convention is an impediment and decorum a sham, has allowed the public discourse to darken.

In any reasonably sized town you can find a radio station that will pump out inflammatory commentary as a matter of course, and in the vast echo chamber where these voices dominate, it now seems as if anything goes. Think of a commentator like Laura Ingraham on Fox News, who is one of Trump's favourites. Take her conversation in 2019 with a conservative lawyer, Joseph di Genova, who offered the following prediction about the American future, to her evident approval: 'The suggestion that there's ever going to be civil discourse in this country for the foreseeable future is over ... it's going to be total war,' he said. 'I do two things; I vote and I buy guns.'

Remarkably, you can hear sentiments of that kind if you spend only a few minutes with one of the shock-jock shows. They used to be kept private, or only uttered to kindred spirits. I remember during the Obama's 2012 re-election campaign being shaken to be told in Pennsylvania by a woman who'd been a Republican party official in the state that if he got a second term it might be necessary for 'a Second Amendment solution', in other words a recourse to the gun. I was later told that she was regarded by the party as a wild card and on the nutty side. By 2020 I think she would have had no problem in making her voice heard.

She swam back into my mind soon after election day in 2020 when Donald Trump Jr told a Pennsylvania rally that it was going to be 'total war' in arguing that massive fraud had been perpetrated against his father.

There's an oddity in this cacophony of antagonism. Trump supporters who're most determined that he will deliver his MAGA promise, and sing along at his rallies to Lee Greenwood singing 'I'm Proud To Be An American' ('where at least I know I'm free . . .'), seem simultaneously pessimistic about how it will all turn out. Despite their hero's relentless optimism – his insistence that nothing can stop him and the country – there is often an apocalyptic flavour. It's been well-described by the writer Anne Applebaum, a Reagan Republican who saw the end of the Cold War as the potential start of an era in which her preferred kind of inclusive conservatism, internationalist in tone, might prevail in a world where liberal democracy would advance. She became disturbed and then appalled by the Trump ascendancy and she notes that Ingraham, as an exemplar of an army of apocalyptic commentators, has said that not only is Western civilisation at risk, but it may have already 'fallen over the cliff'.

This cataclysmic view is the stuff of firebrand preachers here and there, but only in the last few years has it found its way into the daily language of high politics. I've heard Senator Ted Cruz talking about the 'end of days', after which the moment of rapture is meant to raise all true believers to salvation, leaving all the rest to destruction. For Trump, the wilder fringes of religious fervour proved a happy hunting ground, although there is no evidence that he went on the expedition with any conviction of his own, save that there are votes to be won there. Michael Cohen, his lawyer jailed on eight counts of fraud, quotes the president in his memoir *Disloyal* as saying after a meeting with southern evangelical preachers, who circled round him to pray for his success, 'Can you believe that bullshit?'

This did not stop him appointing a White House 'spiritual adviser', Paula White, who takes a lot of beating, even in a crowded field. Soon after the election she told followers at her 'megachurch' in Florida that 'angels from Africa' were on their way to reverse the election result and save America. Banging her pulpit, she cried, 'The Lord says it is done. The Lord says it is done. The Lord says it is done. For I hear victory, victory, victory, victory. In the corners of heaven. In the corners of heaven. Victory, victory, victory, victory, victory, victory.'

Unfortunately for her congregation, who are used to hearing her speaking in tongues and going into a trance to receive the latest divine message, election counters across the country were telling a different story even as she yelled.

Looking back from November to the summer, it was hard not to conclude that Trump's extraordinary refusal to say that he would accept the result – 'We'll have to see,' he told Chris Wallace on Fox News – and his regular assaults on mail-in ballots (which were likely to be the preference of many voters who wanted to stay at home during the pandemic) were a preparation for defeat. Opinion polls were sending him the same message as the Democrats were getting: his approval rating was stuck in the low forties and, although Biden's lead fluctuated week by week, it never disappeared.

The moment when defeat began to seem real to him may well have been at a rally that was billed as his comeback in the last week of June, after the pandemic had effectively closed down the campaign he wanted. Rallies gave him oxygen and energy. He needed them.

Unfortunately for him, the experience in Tulsa, Oklahoma, was a public relations disaster, and therefore a humiliation for a man who has shown that one of his deepest fears is public ridicule.

His campaign manager, Brad Parscale, assured him that the 19,000-seat arena would be full, despite a recent slight increase in Covid cases in the state in the preceding days. But on the night, it was three-quarters empty. They had to cancel an overflow event for the many thousands Parscale had told him would be clamouring to get in (despite the fact that the speaker was to be the less-than-inspiring Mike Pence, with Nigel Farage as a warm-up act) because he had assured the president, according to the *Washington Times*, that the campaign had received 800,000 requests for tickets. Whether or not Trump believed that, he could hardly argue with the Tulsa Fire Department's estimate that 6200 turned up, because everyone who was there could see how sparsely populated the stadium was.

From the Trump camp came word that he was livid. News footage showed vast swathes of empty seats, and – as we know from his near-obsessive concern about the size of his inauguration audience in 2016 – crowds matter to him. Parscale was dismissed two weeks later and assigned to a subsidiary role in the campaign. By the end of September he was gone, citing 'overwhelming stress'.

There may have been a contributory factor in Parscale's downfall. Throughout election year, Trump was tormented by TV ads produced by a group called the Lincoln Project, established by seasoned Republicans who had broken with him and had decided to campaign against him. The ads were razor-sharp and deadly in their focus. The campaign purchased advertising time on some of the Fox News programmes that were known to be part of the president's daily routine, and the videos amounted to a careful psychological assault. Sometimes it seemed as if they had been constructed to be watched by one individual alone. In early July, the project published an ad – Whispers – in which a quiet voice addressed the president directly. 'They're whispering about you, Donald . . .'

A series of shots of his aides, Cabinet members and even his family suggested that he was mired in treachery. 'Why do you think you're losing, Donald? They're in your campaign, the White House, Congress, even your own family . . .' said the quiet voice. A series of shots showed figures close to him, sometimes talking behind their hands, all of those with black-outs over the eyes to suggest that they were hiding their identities. One of the figures who appeared several times in the ad was Parscale. He was dismissed two days later.

So, in the summer, Trump began to prepare for the fight that he eventually launched on election night, arguing that defeat wouldn't be defeat at all. For loyalists, it was easy to understand. In a world of conspiracies, didn't it make sense to believe that his enemies would stop at nothing, and fix the election? It is hard to resist the conclusion that behind the bluster he knew this was how it would end, and prepared the way.

The frustration of watching events from home for me came to an end in October, when I was granted permission by the US authorities to enter the country despite the severe Covid restrictions on travel. New York was a ghostly place, the streets quieter than I had ever known them. The city that never sleeps was in a long slumber. I walked past Trump Tower on Fifth Avenue, where the usual crowds of the curious were missing. There was hardly a jogger to be seen in Central Park, and even the cabs seemed to have stopped honking as they rattled down Broadway. It was a relief to get away, in a melancholy morning mist, and hit the road.

Scranton, Pennsylvania. Why not? If Biden were elected, ten days later, it would be good to have touched base with 2446 North Washington Avenue. There was now a little paper sign on the gate confirming that this was indeed his childhood home, and announcing that visitors were welcome to take photographs from the outside. Wisely, the occupants seemed to have decamped. That quiet tree-lined street, with 'Scranton loves Joe' signs on most of the porches, amid the Halloween pumpkins, was likely to get busy.

Outside the house, a noisy bus drew up. It had 'Faith, Hope and Love' written on the side. A cheery band of people got out, and we spoke. The leaders of the gang turned out to be two evangelical pastors, one from Minneapolis and one from Arkansas, who'd been touring the country since January – and not with the usual purpose. They were meeting faith groups to argue that if they were supporting Trump they should think again. For them, he represented everything a person of faith should reject.

I asked one of them, a woman who ministered in rural Arkansas, why it was that so many voters who said they cherished decency, a traditional morality at home and humility, should be among his strongest supporters.

'You tell me!' she said.

With my producer, Tom Smithard, I found a coffee shop where we encountered two voters, sixty years apart in age, one voting for Trump and one against him. The 83-year-old retired maths professor was a reluctant voter for the president. He was a Republican who wanted a return to 'the common ground' in politics. Did he have much hope that it would happen if Trump won? He didn't seem to me to answer with much conviction. At another table, a 23-year old newly graduated woman was worried about climate change. Who would take up the fight? Her conclusion was that it was time for her generation to take charge: the others had failed.

Our encounter – with political passions expressed politely, quietly, reasonably – was an antidote to the raucous attack ads running on every TV and radio station, giving the last days of the campaign a frenzied air. Everyone knew Pennsylvania would be close, and possibly decisive on election day, so it was reassuring to be reminded that in coming to their decision they wanted less noise, fewer insults, more civility.

In the next few days that became a theme. In Jacksonville, Florida, Siottus Jackson was helping an effort run by the charitable First Coast Leadership Foundation called My Vote, and he told us that the pandemic meant that more voters were having to spend more time at home and were therefore listening to argument. We were sitting outside a polling place where he said there was a steady stream of early voters, and he thought he knew what they wanted.

'No one wants that much bickering from both candidates. You know, people want to see a country unite. They want to see that soft tone. They want to see leaders bring folks together and not fight, because ultimately America's that country where we don't really want to fight. We want to try to resolve it before fighting. And that's how average folks are.'

This was optimism of a kind that we didn't often hear in those days. For example, a few miles north we passed into South Carolina where Senator Lindsey Graham was in a rough fight to hold on to his seat – and, he hoped, his chairmanship of the judiciary committee. His opponent, the Democrat Jaime Harrison, had raised more money than any Senate candidate anywhere in any election – $109 million. The result? War on the airwaves. Graham's seat was such a prize for Democrats that they were determined to throw everything at it, and Harrison, who'd been the first African-American chairman of the South Carolina Democrats, was certainly giving him a scare. But it was a reminder of the relentless inflation in election spending. One estimate in November put the total spent by candidates for every office up and down the ballot in every state at more than $14 billion. Given the Supreme Court's decision in the Citizens United case, it seems as if decades of congressional effort to limit spending have come to nothing. The merry-go-round is bound to whirl faster and faster.

The lack of effective legislative control is one reason, but the explanation for the depth of the anger in this election was also the fundamental nature of the argument. This wasn't a discussion about whether a particular tax rate should go up or down a little, or a piece of environmental regulation should be weakened or strengthened. In Columbia, South Carolina, the Republican state chairman, Drew McKissick, put it to me like this.

'Now we're talking about fundamental American principles, things that relate directly back to the Constitution, Bill of Rights, the structure of the Supreme Court. And, when one side begins to question actual fundamentals that we really just took for granted, and never argued about before, it moves the window of argument just further afield.

'I attribute that largely to what we would define as the left in this country, which increasingly has taken control of the modern-day Democrat party, and the Democrat party today is not the Democrat party of your grandfather or your father. I mean, it's not the party of Jimmy Carter. It's not even the Democrat party of Bill Clinton or Barack Obama anymore. I mean, just within the last six to eight years, it has taken a radical move even further to the left and that has awakened a response from the other side. And it has made things much more argumentative.'

When the question is asked – especially outside the United States – why so many voters who seem to have little in common with the over-the-top figure of Trump, continue to support him, this is the answer. Putting aside for a moment the fact that Biden won the Democratic nomination precisely because he didn't represent the Sanders left, McKissick's point has some weight. Many Republican-leaning voters who wouldn't waste a moment defending Trump in private – and might be contemptuous of aspects of his behaviour in office – would nonetheless argue that they sense a fundamental debate about America's direction. And if Trump happens to be the spokesman for the more conservative view – however strange his public performance may seem – then so be it.

When he nominated Amy Comey Barrett for the Supreme Court in September, after the death of the liberal icon Ruth Bader Ginsburg – and the Senate majority leader Mitch McConnell and Lindsey Graham expedited her confirmation – Trump established a secure majority on the court that conservatives could rely on to oppose many liberal social reforms and to act as a brake on the federal government. When Republicans like Drew McKissick talk of fundamental principles, this is what they mean. And you will often hear them say privately that if the price is a president whose behaviour crosses many of the red lines they draw in their own lives – or breaches standards that they'd demand in politicians of another stripe – then it is worth paying.

However, to attribute the ferocity of contemporary politics to left-leaning Democrats is to ignore the capture of the Republican Party first by Tea Party conservatives a decade ago and then by Trump. Radicalism on the left is more of a response to that than a home-grown movement.

In the days before polling day, 3 November, Tom and I spent some time in the north-west corner of North Carolina, a place of high mountains and deep woods near the Tennessee border, where a particular congressional race seemed a microcosm of the election. The seat, with the city of Asheville at its centre, is largely rural and it was the domain of Mark Meadows until he was appointed Trump's chief of staff in the White House in the spring of election year. The Republican candidate to replace him was Madison Cawthorne – a name that might spring from a Mark Twain story – who had dabbled enough in far-right politics to be accused of supporting white supremacists, which he fervently denied.

He was embarrassed, however, when enthusiastic social media messages were revealed about his excitement at visiting the site of Hitler's 'Eagle's Nest' retreat in Berchtesgaden, saying it had been on his 'bucket list' of attractive sites for a long time. Cawthorne, who was only 25, was given a hard run by Democrats who thought he was vulnerable – but sailed home on the night. After his victory he tweeted 'cry again, lib' – a favourite refrain of Republicans, in enjoying the memory of Hillary Clinton's tears after her defeat in 2016. A woman in North Carolina told me that she wanted Trump to win again, most of all 'to see these liberals cry some more'.

Cawthorne, who's one of the youngest congressmen ever elected, says he is the face of the next generation of Republicans. It is figures like him that pro-Trumpers will champion in the future, when Republicans face the inevitable struggle about where their ideological compass will point them.

Before we left North Carolina, Trump did us a favour with a final rally near the town of Hickory. The state was a swinger, as it had been in 2016, and he wanted to pump up his support. He did so without difficulty. Arriving hours before he touched down for a short airport rally, we found thousands of MAGA-hatted supporters streaming across the fields to get there. A fearsome biker zoomed past us on the road, with 'Trump 45' emblazoned on his leathers. Everywhere there were signs: 'The silent majority – The Sound of Freedom' (though Trump rallies are not known for their silence), 'Jesus is my Saviour, Trump is my President', 'Cry Some More, Liberals' and with a picture of a gun centre 'Heavily Armed, Easily Pissed'.

At that rally, standing in front of the helicopter that was ready to take him to his next stop, he inserted into the familiar lines – 'I will fight for you' – the lyrics of a song called 'The Snake' by a 60s civil rights activist, Oscar Brown Jr. His daughters have expressed outrage at Trump's use of the words, which tell the story of a tender-hearted woman who takes pity on a snake, which then attacks her. Trump used the song in 2016 as part of his anti-immigrant message. The moral was meant to be simple – if you're lax at the border this is what these people will do to you.

So, two days before polling day, he was reaching for old favourites. In the course of remarks about immigration, he said. 'Has anyone heard of "The Snake?" Should I do it?' The crowd cheered. 'This has to do with this subject. It's been a long time since I've done this one, but so many people are asking ...' It was a performance that an entertainer might give on a farewell tour to remind the audience of his great hits. Trump believed that the fable of the snake – which ends with the line 'You knew damn well I was a snake before you took me in' – was the perfect motif for his immigration policy, and it kept his people happy.

Two days later he did win North Carolina, though the margin was narrow enough for it to take some days for that to be confirmed. No one was surprised that it was not one of the states where Rudy Giuliani and his team of lawyers turned up to challenge the result and demand a recount.

Election day seemed to give the president and his staff more hope than they might have expected, but they must have known that when the huge volume of mail-in ballots were counted the picture would change. Since Trump had spent months telling Republicans not to vote by mail, it was obvious to everyone that a preponderance of that vote in states like Pennsylvania was likely to be for Biden. But, as the Axios website had reported two days earlier, Trump was determined to declare early victory as a tactic to sow seeds of doubt.

At just before 2.30 am he claimed that he had won, and went on to make what the *Washington Post* called the next morning 'a remarkable assault on the integrity of the US election system'. The pollsters, he said, had been part of a deliberate campaign of voter suppression, and the media had joined them. He then made one of the most extraordinary statements by any presidential candidate – let alone one who was standing in the East Room of the White House at the time – in which he not only suggested that the valid counting of votes should be stopped forthwith, but that he would try to force the authorities to do his bidding.

He said, 'We'll be going to the U.S. Supreme Court. We want all voting to stop. We don't want them to find any ballots at four o'clock in the morning and add them to the list, OK? We will win this. And as far as I'm concerned, we already have won.'

The implication that any votes counted after he had declared 'victory' would be somehow fraudulent was, of course, false. Giuliani was soon out of the traps with claims of a massive conspiracy and promising lawsuits by the dozen, which in the course of the next few days, would start to fall away in court after court when they were shown to be based overwhelmingly on gossip, falsehood and wishful thinking.

But the President of the United States had declared, surrounded by flags and speaking from the White House, that his country's electoral system, could not be trusted. So much for the crowds with whom he sang 'I'm Proud to be an American . . . God Bless the USA.' In pursuit of a second term in office, he was happy to tell them after all that their faith was misplaced. The electoral authorities – some of them in states with Republican legislatures – were engaged in fraud and deceit on a grand scale.

However, the truth soon dawned. Twenty-four hours later, the tide had turned against him in Pennsylvania, Nevada and Arizona. Georgia was clearly going to be desperately close. Wisconsin and Michigan, where he had squeaked home in 2016 (and Democrats hadn't asked for recounts) were looking safe for Biden. Everyone settled down, in the expectation that nothing would be settled for sure until the weekend.

In a Washington unusually quiet, there was still noisy gossip – most of it about the president's performance. Placing his own future against the integrity of the election was, even for Trump, a giant leap. Filtering out of the White House – the president's circle was leaking like an old colander – came news that despair was seeping through the building. Meadows, the chief of staff, had tested positive for Covid. Others hadn't turned up for work. Jared Kushner was said to be the one who would confront Trump with the truth, but no one knew whether or not to believe that.

We went to Georgia three days after election day, and spoke there to the commissioner for elections, Mary Carole Cooney, chair of the Registration and Elections Board in Fulton County, which includes most of the city of Atlanta, and she was robust in her faith in the system her bipartisan board administered. There would almost certainly be a recount, because state law mandated one if the margin was less than 0.5 per cent between the candidates, and that would be by hand, meticulous, and inevitably a lengthy process. We sat in her living room and talked about the public's faith in the process. She believed, absolutely, that it would hold. There was no reason to doubt the way the count was being conducted, nor the intent of those who were counters and poll watchers.

Meanwhile, Trump was assailing the authorities in all the states where it looked as if he might eventually lose in the votes counted after Tuesday. Oblivious to the irony of calling his win in 2016 'a massive landslide' when Biden seemed on course for a popular vote win of around 7 million (compared with Trump's loss by 3 million against Clinton) and to have a higher electoral college vote than Trump achieved in that contest (306 compared to Trump's 304). By that stage, however, the language had parted company with reality. He was sending Giuliani into battle with threadbare arguments that usually fell at the first hurdle in court. By the eve of the formal certification of the result in Pennsylvania, for example, 30 out of 31 legal challenges across the country had already been dismissed and Giuliani was told by the judge that the case he had put together was a 'Frankenstein's monster'.

He was disappointed, Giuliani said, but claimed that he was encouraged that the judge's words gave him a better argument to take to the Supreme Court. This was not a statement that seemed to attract any serious legal opinion in its support. Shortly afterwards, Pennsylvania's Republican senator, Pat Toomey, announced that he thought it was time to accept that Trump had lost, and he congratulated Biden on being elected. Giuliani was appearing by then as a desperate figure, a fact highlighted in one cruelly humiliating moment on television when his sweat-drenched state produced rivulets of hair dye that dribbled down his cheeks, provoking ridicule at the very moment when he was struggling to keep alive some embers of respect for his legal argument.

Embarrassment, unlike the hair dye, did not show on his face. Nor on that of Sidney Powell, one of Trump's other lawyers, who engaged in an unlikely row with Tucker Carlson – one of the Fox News commentators whom some Republicans would adore to see as a candidate in 2024 – when Carlson said she had produced no evidence to back up her claim that social media companies had conspired to defeat Trump. In a comment that revealed pain, he said: 'If Sidney Powell can prove that technology companies switched millions of votes and stole the presidential election, she will have almost single-handedly uncovered the greatest crime in the history of this country and no one will be more grateful for that than us.'

But sadly for Trump loyalists, even Carlson said he had seen no such evidence, and Powell – who took to social media to denounce him for apostasy – had to fall back for support on the followers of various conspiracy-based websites.

Trump was now in public denial about the state of the entire American electoral process. On the evening after election day, in his appearance alone in the White House briefing room, he had attacked the system for which, as president, he was ultimately responsible.

'I've been talking about mail-in voting for a long time. It's really destroyed our system.

'It's a corrupt system. And it makes people corrupt even if they aren't by nature, but they become corrupt; it's too easy. They want to find out how many votes they need, and then they seem to be able to find them. They wait and wait, and then they find them.'

So he approached the moment when defeat was certain with a last complaint about corruption in America. Not even Nixon had gone that far.

The end, for most of America, came on Saturday. All the TV networks, which had been cautious about declaring a winner in Pennsylvania until the published voting tallies county-by-county showed that it was impossible for Trump to catch up, came to their conclusion. The numbers rose, Philadelphia and Pittsburgh giving Biden an unassailable lead, and at 11.24 am, eastern time, CNN declared that the election was decided. Sixteen minutes later, Fox joined the rush, the last of the networks to agree.

There were a few demonstrations of delight in the streets, but it was hard not to believe that across the city, and much of the country, the overwhelming feeling – perhaps, for once, crossing party lines – was one of relief.

Back in Washington I sat down with my old friend Dan Balz of the *Washington Post* in his back garden. Over a pot of tea we talked about this strangest of election years and the uncertainty that remained, after everything. Trump had lost, but what would he do? I asked if he thought Trump would turn up for Biden's inauguration on 20 January, to participate in the passage of power.

Dan shook his head. 'I just don't know.'

Neither of us had thought we would ever have that conversation.

Walking the next morning through Lafayette Square, the Black Lives Matter banners and slogans were still decorating the steel fences that had sealed off the White House from demonstrators for weeks, a lockdown that had nothing to do with the virus. There were a few musicians, some people writing new anti-Trump slogans to hang up, and a few peering through the wire to see if there was any sign of coming and going from the West Wing a couple of hundred yards away. Later, I went to see Tom Countryman, whom I talked to two years earlier, after his removal from the upper echelons of the State Department, where he was under-secretary for arms control and nuclear non-proliferation, when Trump took office. I asked him what he thought the atmosphere must be in his old building. 'I think there is an audible sigh, shriek, scream of relief from those who are still working in the State Department. It's not because they are inherently Democratic. It's because the mismanagement and the distrust that's been promulgated by the White House since day one will come to an end.'

But I found him troubled about the future of the public service. 'I think most Americans would like to see a competent government, and one of the few saving graces of the Trump administration has been that the president and most of his appointees are so spectacularly incompetent.

'If they had had a modicum of knowledge about how to do their job, he would have done far greater damage, not only in foreign policy, but in environmental policy, in economic policy and in many other ways. It is difficult to convince half of the American people that government can be competent. Since the Reagan days, public trust, not just in politicians, but in the civil service, has declined rapidly. And it's not going to be easy to rebuild that. And even the best efforts of the best people that Joe Biden can appoint will not immediately fix the economy and the coronavirus, restore America's standing in the world. And so all of that, I fear, is unlikely to change the opinion of most Americans that they don't trust the expertise of people whose job it is to serve the American people.'

Everywhere you turned, you heard another warning about how uncertain the near future was bound to be – even if we assumed that Trump's legal efforts would not throw the election result into doubt. I had a pessimistic conversation with David Remnick, editor of the *New Yorker*.

'The origins of Trumpism have to do with a lot of things – race, income inequality and all kinds of things that have been rehearsed over and over. But the fact of the matter is, in my view, what we've seen in the last four years is an authoritarian bigot who is anti-democratic, and who is in sync with a lot of authoritarians all over the world, whether it's in Hungary or Russia or Poland or anywhere you can name. It's both a global phenomenon and an American phenomenon. And if Joe Biden becomes the next President of the United States, those divisions will persist, this dream of a return to immediate normalcy is, I think, a fantasy.

'So much has been stripped and laid bare by the Trump experience and the pandemic, whether it has to do with race or inequality or many other issues, that Joe Biden, who's a rather ordinary politician, will have to become extraordinary in a hurry.'

In the evening I went to record some script on Capitol Hill, a place that breathes continuity. It was dusk, a cloudless sky darkening from bright blue. The lamps were lit outside the Senate and the House, there was a glow from the rotunda, and the Supreme Court building picked up on its columns some of the last of the light as darkness came down. Everything was quiet – there was hardly a car to be seen and you could even hear birds in the trees. The scene was tranquil. Washington at rest.

But next day, from the train leaving Union Station bound eventually for home, I watched from the window until the Capitol dome disappeared and knew that peace, even in a city at rest after tumultuous days, was an illusion.

There was too much anger.

CHAPTER 13

AFTERWARDS

Most presidencies, whether happy or sad, end simply. Even Nixon's, with the melodramatic flourish of his resignation, provoked so much relief that his successor was swathed in good will and was allowed, for a while, to get on with the job. But Trump's America, challenged by its own president to doubt its democratic institutions, was denied a natural transition to something new. He initiated legal challenges that would explore every byway in the hope of political salvation, and no doubt would target any sympathetic judge he could find, and even in the event that everything failed his parting gift would be a guarantee that he wouldn't let the anger die.

A new era is supposed to bring hope, because some debris is cleared away. But two decades into the new century, any optimism is matched by a feeling of fragility. Reconciliation between the tribes who clashed in 2020 seems a long way off. One side gained the presidency but saw the balance in the Supreme Court tilt decisively the other way. Even if the January run-off for two Senate seats in Georgia went their way, Democrats knew that the kinds of social reforms they wanted – notably on healthcare, but on issues like gun control too – were facing a long struggle in the courts.

Divisions have deepened to a degree that makes it difficult to see an easy way through. The people at Trump rallies to whom I've spoken in recent years are resolute, and however much politeness they have summoned up for a foreign visitor (for whom it is often refreshing to find such a warm response at any mention of the BBC), they are not about to abandon the way of thinking that has become second nature, and which will certainly be encouraged by a successor. As one Democrat put it to me, their nightmare is 'a clever Trump'. And on the Democratic side, there is trouble ahead.

Republicans call it 'identity politics' which is a phrase hated on the liberal left, but both sides know what they're talking about. The anger that was obvious after George Floyd's killing is no less likely to subside than rage among the Trumpists who are convinced that they are victims of 'the deep state'. Moving from the temporary truce that was fashioned to support Biden in 2020 will be neither quick nor easy.

The political challenges don't spring from nowhere. They are the evidence of a nation, confused and angry. The right are convinced that 'socialism' in some form is about to be foisted on them in defiance of everything they've been brought up to believe, and their opponents determined that the social reforms of the last half-century that have been their cause shouldn't be weakened or reversed. This is a potent cocktail.

But each side will press on. The American mood is seldom given to calm – to the 'normalcy' that Warren G. Harding (a weak president, to put it kindly) once used as a campaign slogan, believe it or not. The idea of progress is embedded in the national spirit, because that's how it's been nurtured for two-and-a-half centuries.

Alistair Cooke's reference to 'persistent idealism' is accurate, but since I first set foot among them I have not known Americans so uncertain about where that belief is taking them. They see a long road ahead with many turnings, without being able to agree which of them lead in a hopeful direction and which will take them to disaster.

Anyone of roughly my age has watched the pendulum swing and has become used to the idea that some law of nature means that it will always correct itself. But the country has tilted, and one of the reasons for the anger on both sides of politics is that no one can be sure when and how the next shift will come. With a controversial Supreme Court in place, and a defiant Trump vote that was greater in numbers than in 2016, despite everything, liberals wonder whether their belief in perpetual progress sixties-style was misplaced and whether the *real* America is not what they thought it to be, but a different place. Conservatives believe that the reshaping of the state that Trump, despite all his blunders, delivered for them in the courts may be the beginning of a counter-revolution against the tide that they watched run the other way for so long, even after Reagan's intervention.

For a journalist, of course, this is naturally fascinating, even exciting. But the story I have told is more personal than professional. It's impossible for someone with so many American friends, such vivid memories of people and places and such a cataract of experiences in every corner of the country, not to share some of the despair that's flowing so strongly through the public discourse from coast to coast.

Anyone looking for hope, and trying to put aside for a moment the obvious fragility in parts of American society, will surely look to the next generation – or perhaps the one after that – who watched an election in which both candidates, and the likely leaders of both the House and Senate were all deep into their seventies, or, in the case of Nancy Pelosi, already leaving them behind. Washington these days does not feel like the distillation of a young country. And America has always been at its best and most inventive when it has looked and felt young.

Only when the present turmoil passes away will that be possible, and it can't happen without a period of painful introspection. In that conversation with David Remnick just before leaving Washington for home after the election, I found myself carried along by his dark upsum of the last four years.

'In many ways, these are divisions that have been with us from the very start, from the very start of this country, and if Hillary Clinton had won seventy thousand more votes in the now famous counties in 2016, it's possible that we wouldn't have been quite as aware of the volcano on which we live. And it is a volcano. But I do think that if anything good comes out of the Trump experience, it is that we will become much more aware of who we are, what we are and what we have to contend with.'

Who are we? The oldest question of all, and one that I realised on my first visit fifty years ago was somehow more important to Americans than to most Europeans. History is always with you, whether in pilgrim-settled New England or the far West or the old South. But learning from it has proved difficult. They're still arguing in parts of the south about whether the confederate flag should fly above public buildings (in memory of battles fought against the United States) and in trying to decide how an eighteenth-century constitution conceived for a vanished society should apply to today's world where there are disagreements so deep that they can't be settled by a quick, rational argument.

One of America's allures is its fascination with its own story, a remarkable series of triumphs as well as disasters. At best, that affection, sometimes turning into obsession, is uplifting. But you can't visit the country today – and this will be true when the pandemic is over as much as it was in 2020 – without feeling that the course of this century for Americans may be set irrevocably by decisions they make in the next twenty years or so. Race, social inequality, the balance between individual and corporate power, the institutions of the state themselves, not forgetting the electoral system – they are all in need of urgent attention. Every historian, on the right or the left knows it and says so, as do thoughtful political people on both sides. But the public debate – a genuine, open and inclusive argument that spreads far and wide – has hardly begun.

Until it does, all the hope will be fragile.

Those of us who have experienced so much of America at its best, as well as witnessing some of its worst, will watch that debate with much more attention even than we give to the theatrical events brought on by the 2020 election. Fifty years of watching and experiencing the place has convinced me that out of the fire it has always found it possible to pluck something that hasn't been despoiled, but cleansed instead.

Most Americans know in their hearts that the challenge to reinvent themselves is facing them once again, and they know that the time is now.

ACKNOWLEDGEMENTS

Writing this book has depended on the generosity of many friends. I have been fortunate to travel with so many journalistic colleagues – writers and producers, scribblers of every kind – that I would not try to name them all here, particularly so many colleagues at the BBC (they know who they are). I hope their memories are as precious as mine. Like successive editors at the BBC, they have shared comradeship on the road, the excitement of discovery, the moments none of us will forget. Particular American friends have been sustaining over the years – Helen Hershkoff and Stephen Loffredo, Sidney and Jackie Blumenthal, Ted Smyth and Mary Breasted, my extended family in Oregon and a host of fraternal colleagues on the *Washington Post*, one of the longest-standing of whom, Dan Balz, even gets a picture credit in this book. In Washington, a rolling cast of editors and correspondents in the BBC bureau on M Street have been a part of my life for decades, and unfailingly generous, even on some of the chaotic nights that we have shared at moments of drama.

But at home, with the last chapter of this story still to be written, it was a wrenching sadness for me that my agent Felicity Bryan, who wanted me to write this book and saw the original text to fruition, died in the summer of 2020. She was loved by a horde of friends that spread far beyond the publishing world in which she was such a shining star. We all miss her. I first knew Felicity through the Laurence M. Stern Fellowship at the *Post*, of which she was the driving force in the UK for all of forty years, and it has been renamed the Stern-Bryan Fellowship in her memory. Iain MacGregor and then Ian Marshall at Simon & Schuster were patient and wise editors, and my family ever-stalwart in support – our son Andrew using his razor-sharp editing skills to improve the text significantly. Ellie has, as ever, my profound gratitude and love.

INDEX

Aaron, Hank, 105
ABC, 102
Abedin, Huma, 188
Abernathy, Ralph, 155
abortion, 119, 175, 176, 203–4, 204, 265, 274, 276–7
Abourezk, James, 80
Abramsky, Jenny, 110
Accidental American, The, 143
Afghanistan, 112, 132, 159, 258
Agnew, Spiro, 44, 49, 51
al-Qaeda, 132
Alda, Alan, 45
Alexander, Bobby and Gloria, 175, 176
All the President's Men, 57
Allen, Gavin, 155
Allen, Woody, 16
Amash, Justin, 199
America, vi, 280
American Conservative Union (ACU), 146, 197
American Enterprise Institute, 98
American Spectator, 120
America's Crisis of Leadership, 111, 113, 114
Ames, Aldrich, 93
Andy (student), 24
Annan, Kofi, 131
anthrax scare, 139
anti-communism, 38, 98, 145
anti-Semitism, 14, 16, 216

Apprentice, The, 177
Arafat, Yasser, 115
Assange, Julian, 290
assassination, 49, 71, 72, 78, 82, 198, 202, 219
assimilation, 9–10, 15
Associated Press (AP), 34
Atlanta Constitution, 56
The Atlantic, 81–2, 202
Audacity of Hope (Obama), 154
automaticity, 141

Baker, Howard, 42
Baker, James, 126
Baltimore Sun, 56
Balz, Dan, 82
Barenboim, Daniel, 95
Barnum & Bailey, 62
BBC, 38, 50, 63, 106–12 *passim*, 115, 122, 154, 155, 169, 183, 241, 271, 280
    M Street offices of, 116, 191–2, 299
    Naughtie joins, 5
    Radio 4, 5, 75, 95, 110, 111–12, 125, 153
    Radio 5 Live, 111, 154
    World Service, 50, 241
Beach Boys, 78, 79
Beame, Abe, 32
Bear Stearns, 158–9
Beck, Glenn, 176

Becker, Daniel, 104–5
Begin, Menachem, 69
Benenson, Joel, 190
Benn, Tony, 84
Berkowitz, Mr and Mrs, 16
Berle, Milton, 15
Berlin Wall, 95–6
Bernstein, Carl, 38, 57, 80
Bernstein, Leonard, 31
Bess (dog), 207
Biden, Hunter, 291
Biden, Joe, 168, 269, 291
Bingham, Joan, 83
Birch, John, 98
Black Lives Matter, 216
Blair House, 84, 122
Blair, Tony, 120, 121, 122, 129–
    33, 141–3, 147–51
Blitzer, Wolf, 121
Bluestone, Irving, 89
Blumenthal, Sidney, 120, 124
Bobbitt, Phil, 215–16
Bolton, John, 143, 144, 146
Borscht Belt, 9, 14, 15, 20
Boston Globe, 56
Bradlee, Ben, 79, 80–1
Breasted, Mary, 134, 299
Brexit, 197, 242
Broder, David, 42, 87–8, 120
Brooks, Mel, 15
Brown, Gordon, 120
Brown, Jerry, 88, 205–7, 208–9
Brunson, Doyle, 173–4
Buckley, William F., 98
BUNAC, 6, 10–11
Bureau of International Security
    and Nonproliferation, 203
Burke, James Lee, 6
busboys, 12, 13
Bush, Barbara, 108, 181
Bush, Billy, 275
Bush, George H. W., 85, 95, 103,
    104, 108, 110, 119, 183, 215,
    273
  becomes POTUS, 96–7
  Tokyo banquet incident
    involving, 114
Bush, George W., 129, 132–3,
    141–2, 146, 147–52, 153–4,

158, 165, 169, 177, 183, 207,
    219, 257, 273–4
  becomes POTUS, 125–8
Bush, Jeb, 126, 177, 178, 181
'Bush v. Gore', 127
Butterfield, Alexander, 39
Buttigieg, Pete, 269, 276

cable news, growth of, 109
Calusa (dog), 207
Camp David, 69, 122, 132, 147–8
Campbell, Alastair, 142–3, 149
Cannon, Lou, 79
Carlson, Tucker, 291
Caro, Robert A., 6
Carrington, Lord, 84
Carter, Jimmy, 61–2, 64, 65, 67,
    79, 81, 85, 88, 202
  becomes POTUS, 69–70, 90, 105
  Iranian hostage crisis affects,
    71, 86
  Kennedy challenges, 72, 73–5,
    76
Carter, Miz Lillian, 74–5
Carville, James, 101
Casey, William, 86–7
Cato Institute, 285
CBS, 72, 102
censorship, 38, 111
Chadderdon, Liz, 192
Chappaquiddick, 72–3, 77
charitable endeavour, 36, 183, 194,
    236, 238, 259
Chaucer, Geoffrey, 38
Checkpoint Charlie, 95
Cheney, Dick, 129, 143, 147–8
Chicago Tribune, 55
Children's Defense Fund, 259
Chirac, Jacques, 149
Christie, Chris, 179, 181, 182
CIA, 38, 86, 93, 183, 203
civil rights, 24, 26, 40–2, 54, 90,
    249, 258–65
Clark, Gen. Wesley, 153
climate change, 196, 208–9, 214,
    220, 276
Clinton, Bill, 101–6, 109, 113, 119,
    123, 128, 130, 131, 162, 165,
    166, 168, 169, 177, 182, 185,

190, 214, 215, 254, 256–7,
    262, 264
becomes POTUS, 97, 114, 260–1
Bush W.'s battles with, 125
as 'the comeback kid', 102
and government shutdown, 119
healthcare reform pursued by, 116
impeachment trial of, 119–20,
    124
infidelities surrounding, 102,
    119–24
as Rhodes scholar, 104
sexual harassment claims against,
    102, 119
Clinton, Chelsea, 131, 214
Clinton, Hillary Rodham, 102,
    103, 120, 157, 161, 162–8, 181,
    182, 185–92, 197, 208, 209,
    214, 231, 241, 276, 280, 290
healthcare reform pursued by,
    116
Naughtie interviews, 253–66
popular vote won by, 263
as Secretary of State, 255–8
2016 election campaign, 183,
    210–11, 255–6
CNN, 121
Cohen, Michael, 197
Cold War, 4, 84, 92–8, 113, 150
Cole, Thomas, 14
Collins, Kate, 270, 277
Comey, James, 188–9, 190, 209, 254
compassionate conservatism, 125,
    273
Condon, Alexis, 113, 172
Condon, Eddie, 75
Connally, John B., 48–9
Connery, Sean, 49
Connor, Bull, 265
Conscience of a Conservative, The
    (Goldwater), 97
Conservative Political Action
    Conference (2019), 195
conspiracy theory, 184–5, 215, 219,
    262, 291
'Contract with America', 118, 119
Cook County Jail, 80
Cook Library, 135
Cooke, Alistair, vi, 26, 280–1

Corbett, Jasper, 175
Corera, Gordon, 122
Cornyn, John, 278
Country Club Republicanism, 54,
    119
Countryman, Tom, 203–4
Cox, Archibald, 35, 52
CPAC, 197–8
CREEP, 57
Crouse, Tim, 87
Cruz, Rafael, 179
Cruz, Ted, 178, 179, 197, 198,
    267, 269–70, 272
culture wars, 104, 119, 176, 262,
    271, 276, 280
cummings, e. e., 139
Cummings, Elijah, 123
Cuomo, Mario, 91
Custor, Peg, 137

DACA programme, 287–8
Daley, Richard, 65, 66–7, 124,
    130, 248
Daniels, Stormy, 198
Dave (student), 24
Day, Robin, 75
Dean, Howard, 152
Dean, John, 39, 51, 52
Declaration of Independence, 64,
    263
Deep Throat, 57–8
deficit reduction, 114
Democrats for Nixon, 49
Desert Storm, Operation, 110
determination, 35, 57, 96, 141,
    280, 293
Detroit Free Press, 55–6
Dickinson, Jim, 247
Dillinger, John, 248
Dobson, Kevin, 68–9
Dole, Bob, 119
Drucker, Nancy, 74
Duncan, Rudy, 46
Dylan, Bob, 64

editorial comment, 55, 80
'Education of David Stockman,
    The' (Greider), 82
Edwards, John, 163–4

Ehrlichman, John, 42, 52
Eisenhower, Dwight D., 40, 98,
    121, 219
embedding reporters, 111
Ervin, Sam, 40, 41–2
espionage, 92–3, 93, 96
Esposito, 'Diamond Joe', 248
exit polls, 114, 125, 153
'expletive deleted', 53, 54

fairness doctrine, 99
fake news, 54, 185, 196, 198, 214,
    251–2
Falk, Peter, 46
Falklands War, 84–5
Fallows, James, 202–3
Falwell, Jerry, 99
Farage, Nigel, 197
fascism, 35, 216, 217, 283
FBI, 58, 161, 181, 182, 188–9, 190,
    194, 254
Felt, Mark, 58
financial crashes, 29, 49, 109,
    158–9, 257
First World War, 110, 163
Fisher, Ken, 46
Fitzgerald, F. Scott, 3, 159–60, 248
Flagler, The, 14, 17, 18, 20, 23
Flanders, Ned, 144
Fleischer, Ari, 142
Flowers, Gennifer, 102
Flynn, Mike, 181
Foot, Michael, 90
Ford, Gerald, 32, 51, 54, 58, 61,
    67, 69, 70
Ford, Richard, 237, 239–40
Foreback, Caroline, 209
forty-niners, 3
Foster, Don, 162
Fountains of Rome, 20
Fourth of July, 62–4, 78–80, 199
Fox & Friends, 179, 219, 251
Fox News, 100, 176, 187, 198
freedom of speech, 55, 99
Frost, Robert, 6, 140
Fruman, Igor, 291

Gaffney, Frank, 145, 146
Galbraith, John Kenneth, 109

Gale, Bob, 180
gang culture, 249–50
gangsterism, 32, 222–3, 225, 248
gay rights, 175, 176, 186, 258, 271,
    276, 277, 278
Gephardt, Dick, 219
German reunification, 95–6
gerrymandering, 128, 286–7
Gershwin, George and Ira, 28
Gettysburg Address, 2–3
Gill, Jat, 165
Gingrich, Newt, 118, 119, 181,
    261, 262
Giuliani, Rudy, 167, 291
Glenn, John, 67
Glienicke Bridge, 96
Goldwater, Barry, 58, 97–8, 99,
    146, 183
Gonzalez, Ed, 268
Goodman, Steve, 224
Goodwin, Doris Kearns, 256
Goodwin, Fred, 49
Gorbachev, Mikhail, 92, 95–6,
    97
Gordievsky, Oleg, 92–3
Gore, Al, 104, 106, 107, 124–8,
    169
Gould, Joe, 29
Graceland, 243, 244
Graham, Katharine, 52, 83
Graham, Lindsey, 201
Gramm, Phil, 117
Great Depression, 33, 62, 159
Great Fire (1871), 247
Greenstock, Sir Jeremy, 141, 150,
    151
Greider, William, 81–2
Gromyko, Andrei, 150
Guardian, The, 5, 56, 57, 237
Gulf FM, 111
Gulf War (1991), 97, 110, 143
Gun Violence Archive, 271
Guthrie, Arlo, 224, 226, 228–9
Guthrie, Woody, 65

Haig, Alexander, 58, 85, 218–19
Haldeman, Rob, 42, 52, 53
Hamilton, 193, 293
Hamilton, Alexander, 193

Hancock, Colin, 106
hanging chads, 127, 154, 286
Hannity, Sean, 291
Harris, Emmylou, 103
Harris, Kamala, 269
Harris, Katherine, 126
Harrison, William Henry, 195
Hart, Gary, 90, 219
Harvey, Jonathan, 191
Harwood, Dick, 82
Healey, Denis, 90
healthcare, 103, 116, 146, 159, 163, 164, 175, 176, 178, 201, 205, 241, 245, 246, 261, 276
Heath, Edward, 50
Henderson, Sir Nicholas ('Nico'), 84
Herald Tribune, 29
Heritage Foundation, 98, 214
Hermiston, Roger, 95
Hersh, Seymour, 38
Hill, Fiona, 291
Hoagland, Jim, 82
hockey moms, 170, 171
Hodgson, Godfrey, 78
Honegger, Barbara, 86
Hook, Andrew, 37
Houston Chronicle, 268
Humphrey, Hubert, 65, 66, 67, 75, 89
Hurricane Katrina, 170, 235–41, 247

'I Have a Dream' speech, 176
'I Have a Scream' speech, 152
immigration, 3–4, 7, 28, 154, 163, 166, 200, 206–7, 213, 220, 250–1, 282, 288
impeachment, 5, 34, 39–40, 56–8, 119–24, 218, 255, 266, 282–3, 290–7
Independence Day, 62–4, 78–80, 199
industrialisation, 4, 49, 89, 91, 166, 225, 249
Internet, arrival of, 113
Internet Research Agency (IRA), 289
interstate network, 232–5
Iran, 71, 86, 131, 294

Iran–Contra, 87, 91, 95
Iraq, 97, 110, 132
Iraq War, 132, 141–4, 147–52, 159, 202, 258
Irving, Washington, 14
ISIS, 203, 290
Israel, 69, 80, 114–15

Jackson, Andrew, 181
Jackson, Henry 'Scoop', 145
Jackson, Rev. Jesse, 91, 155
James, Henry, 139
Jaworski, Leon, 51, 52
jazz, 1, 25, 27, 75, 160, 222–5, 240–1
Jeff (student), 18–19
Jefferson, Thomas, 240, 277, 278
Jerry (mechanic), 136
John, Elton, 121
John (salad chef), 11, 12, 14, 24
Johnson, Gary, 241
Johnson, Haynes, 82
Johnson, Lyndon B. ('LBJ'), 6, 40, 54, 97, 174, 200, 215, 264, 266, 270, 273
Johnson, Peggy, 134, 135, 137, 138, 140
Jolson, Al, 18
Jones, Alex, 184–5
Jones, Paula, 119, 123
Jordan, Barbara, 67
Jordan, Hamilton, 70–1
Jovita, Palloma, 287–8

Kaepernick, Colin, 268
Kaiser, Bob, 82
Kasich, John, 181
Katz, Diane, 214
Kavanaugh, Brett, 120, 285
Kaye, Danny, 45, 46
Kemp, Jack, 219
Kennedy, Caroline, 167
Kennedy, Christopher, 76
Kennedy, Edward ('Ted'), 71–5, 76, 154, 167–8, 200
Kennedy, Ethel, 76
Kennedy, John F. ('JFK'), 38, 40, 49, 72, 74, 77, 121, 124, 167, 168, 179, 198, 200, 202, 219

Kennedy, Robert F. ('RFK'), 32, 38, 65, 71, 72, 76
Kennedy, Rose, 76–7
Kerouac, Jack, 6
Kerry, John, 152–3, 154, 163
KGB, 93
Khatami, Mohammad, 131
Khomeini, Ayatollah, 71
Kim Jong-un, 195
King, Carole, 154
King, Martin Luther, 24, 65, 122, 155, 169, 176, 202
Kirkpatrick, Jeane, 85
Kissinger, Henry, 57, 59, 64
Klein, Joe, 162
Koch brothers, 120
Kohl, Helmut, 95–6, 97
Kopechne, Mary Jo, 71–2
Kornblum, John, 96
Krauthammer, Charles, 182
Ku Klux Klan, 216

Lavrov, Sergey, 150
Lee, Christopher, 110
Lee, Robert E., 172, 216
Lenin, Vladimir, 279
Leubsdorf, Carl, 34–6, 51
Levinson, Sanford, 283–4
Lewinsky, Monica, 119, 120, 121, 123, 261
Lewis, Jerry, 12, 15
Lieberman, Joe, 170
Life, 73
Lincoln, Abraham, 2–3, 41, 66, 120, 134, 194, 256, 260
Lincoln Memorial, 78, 169
Loeb, William, 180
Los Angeles Times, 55, 76
Louisiana Purchase, 240
Lowell, Robert, 6

McBain, Ed, 6
McCain, John, 167, 169–74, 181, 200–1
McCarthy, Eugene, 259
McCarthy, Joe, 38
McGovern, George, 54, 64, 180, 212
McHutchon, Graham, 116–17

Macintyre, Ben, 93
McPherson, James, 6
McQuaid, Joe, 180–1
Mailer, Norman, 6, 42, 293
Major, John, 117, 121
Making of the President (White), 74
Manafort, Paul, 183
Manchester Union-Leader, 180, 195
Marcia (cousin), 46–7
M*A*S*H, 45
Mason, Jackie, 15
Meadows, Chris, 209
Medina Ridge, Battle of, 111
Meese, Ed, 83
Melville, Herman, 297
mental health, 124, 269
Meyer, Christopher, 132
Milosevic, Slobodan, 130, 203–4
Miranda, Lin-Manuel, 293
MI6, 93
Mitchell, John, 52
Mitchell, Joseph, 29–31
Mondale, Walter, 67, 68, 88–9, 90–1
Mosey, Roger, 109
Mudd, Roger, 72, 73
Mueller, Robert, 184, 188, 195, 205, 221, 284, 289–90
Murdoch, Rupert, 100
Muskie, Ed, 180
Muti, Riccardo, 251

Nagin, Ray, 236
National Enquirer, 179, 198
National Governors Association, 87
National Press Building, 55
National Review, 98, 150
Naughtie, Andrew (son), 251, 300
Naughtie, Ellie (wife), 110–11, 300
Naughtie, Flora (daughter), 111
Naughtie, James:
    in Chicago, 80, 155, 158, 220, 221–52, 222
    education of, 36–8
    first arrives in US, 7, 9–33
    first Thanksgiving of, 47

Greyhound travel of, 6–7, 11, 23, 34, 50
indentures of, 63
Leadership series of, *see America's Crisis of Leadership*
literary nature of, 6, 37, 52
in New Orleans, 23, 25, 222, 222–42
as Stern Fellow, 78–80
taco incident involving, 68–9
NBC, 74, 177
Negroponte, John, 151
neoconservatism, 129–31, 144, 149, 182
New York Post, 32
New York Times (NYT), 38, 54, 55, 76, 94, 104, 107, 176, 211
New Yorker, 29, 42, 120
Newhouse School of Communications, 42, 45
Newsday, 55
Newsome, Hawk, 216, 217
Newsweek, 162
Nichopoulos, George ('Dr Nick'), 244, 245
Nightline, 102
Nixon, Richard, 5, 34, 35, 38–41, 43–4, 49–58, 65, 69, 79, 103, 124–5, 164, 183, 200, 294, 295
Ford pardons, 61
impeachment trial of, 265–6
resigns as US president, 59, 218
Watergate scandal, *see main entry*
Norquist, Grover, 145–6
Novak, Phil, 45
Nunes, Devin, 291

Obama, Barack, 154–6, 160, 162–76, 183, 190–1, 193, 196, 199, 217, 231, 255, 287
becomes POTUS, 157–8, 168, 256–8
Obama, Michelle, 166, 193
Obamacare, 175, 178, 201, 205, 241
Observer, The, 76

'October Surprise', 86
oil crises, 50, 69–70
Oklahoma bombing, 185
O'Neill, Terry, 183, 184
O'Neill, Tip, 94
optimism, 3, 4, 33, 60–1, 67, 154, 159, 168, 172, 251, 293
O'Rourke, Beto, 267–70, 272, 274
Oslo Accords, 114–15
Osnos, Peter, 82
Oswald, Lee Harvey, 179, 219

Palestine, 80, 114–15, 146
Palin, Sarah, 170–1, 175
Parker, Dorothy, 29
Parnas, Lev, 291
PBS, 38
Peel, John, 155
Perle, Richard, 144–5
Perot, Ross, 114
Pew Research Center, 237
philanthropy, 36, 183, 194, 236, 238, 259
Pick, Hella, 57
Pilgrim Fathers, 27, 133–4, 280
Plain Dealer, 55
Poirier, Dan, 135, 136
populism, 4, 118, 119, 152, 175, 180, 185, 193, 211–12, 260, 263, 266, 283, 296
Posner, Richard, 135
Powell, Gen. Colin, 143, 149, 151
Presley, Elvis, 155, 243–6
Press and Journal (P&J), 63
Primary Colors (Klein), 162
Pringle, Peter, 75, 76
Prohibition, 248
Project for the New American Century, 129
Public Broadcasting Service (PBS), 38
Putin, Vladimir, 150, 183, 201, 205, 217, 247, 279, 290

Qasem Soleimani, 294
Quai d'Orsay, 110, 150

Rabin, Yitzhak, 115

racism, 14, 16, 193–4, 199, 206,
    207, 216, 249–50 (see also
    segregation)
railroad, 15, 42, 66, 207, 209–10,
    222–34, 271
Ramsbotham, Sir Peter, 50
Randolph, Eleanor, 75–6
Reagan, Nancy, 78, 82
Reagan, Ronald, 67, 73, 81–2,
    90–6, 104, 105, 109, 114, 116,
    118, 121, 145, 165, 261, 265
  acting career of, 79, 100, 105
  assassination attempt on, 78, 82
  becomes POTUS, 75, 77, 85–6
  blue-collar support for, 88–9
  leaves office, 98
  political spell cast by, 83–5, 97,
    98–9
  'Star Wars' proposed by, 92
  Thatcher's view of, 84–5
Redford, Robert, 57
Reid, John, 192
Reston, James, 94
Reynolds, Paul, 115
Ribicoff, Abraham, 65
Rice, Condoleezza, 142, 148
Richards, Ann, 273
Richardson, Bill, 257
Richardson, Elliot, 35
Rickles, Don, 16
Rivers, Joan, 16
Robinson, Eugene, 197
Robinson, Leonard, 42
Rockefeller, Nelson, 183
Rockwell, Norman, 79
Rodino, Peter, 57
'Roe v. Wade', 265
rolling news, 110, 111
Rolling Stone, 82
Romney, Mitt, 176, 177, 181, 216,
    218
Roosevelt, Franklin D. ('FDR'), 41,
    92, 104, 132, 145, 175, 200,
    219, 264
Rostropovich, Mstislav, 95
Rothkopf, David, 195
Rove, Karl, 142, 154
Rubio, Marco, 179
Rumsfeld, Donald, 143

Runyon, Damon, 2
Ruth, Babe, 105

Sablière, Jean- Marc de la, 150
Sadat, Anwar, 69
Saddam Hussein, 110, 141, 142,
    144, 147, 149, 151
St Andrew's Society of New York,
    36, 37, 48–9, 63
Sanders, Bernie, 185, 258, 268
Sandy Hook massacre, 185, 271
Saturday Night Massacre, 34, 51
Saudi Arabia, 279, 290
Savalas, George, 68
Savalas, Telly, 68
Scalia, Justice Antonin, 127
Scaramucci, Anthony ('The
    Mooch'), 177, 178, 189–90, 192
Schiff, Adam, 208, 291
Schlicke, Paul, 37
Schwartzwalder, Ben, 45
Scotsman, The, 5, 80
Scott, Hugh, 54
Scowcroft, Brent, 97
Seattle Post-Intelligencer, 55
Second World War, 14, 35, 95,
    109, 131, 132, 139, 176, 194,
    208, 237
segregation, 14, 24, 26, 40–2, 216,
    249, 264, 288
Seinfeld, Jerry, 15
Sergeant, John, 117
Serpico, Frank, 32
Sessions, Jeff, 197
Seward, William, 256
Shapiro, Ilya, 285
Sharp, Rhod, 63, 154
Sheen, Martin, 152
Shrum, Bob, 74
Sick, Gary, 86
Simon, Neil, 139
Sinatra, Frank, 16, 44, 78
Sirica, Judge, 53
Six-Day War, 114
Sky, 111
Sloman, Anne, 112
Smith, Evan, 272–3
Smyth, Ted, 134
Solomon, Mr and Mrs, 16

Sorensen, Theodore, 168, 169
Sorkin, Aaron, 295
Stalin, Joseph, 92
Starr, Ken, 120
Stennis, John C., 52
Stephanopoulos, George, 103
Stern, Larry, 78–9
Stevenson, Coke, 270
Stewart, Sir Iain Maxwell, 49
Stockman, David, 81, 82
Stone, Roger, 182–4, 289
Stovall, Dwayne, 271, 277–9
Straw, Jack, 143, 149
Streisand, Barbra, 16, 121
Sunday Telegraph, 50
Sunday Times, 37, 76
supply-side economics, 81–2
Swift Boat Veterans for Truth, 153

'taking a knee' protest, 268
Talese, Gay, 42
Talmadge, Herman, 42
taxation, 81, 104, 114, 119, 146,
    182, 183, 200, 202, 218, 290
Tea Party movement, 146, 170,
    175, 176
Texas Tribune, 273
Thanksgiving, 47, 133–41
Thatcher, Margaret, 81, 83–5, 90,
    92, 93, 117, 175, 274
Thomson Regional Newspapers, 37
Thorpe, Jeremy, 50
Times, The, 37, 93
Times-Picayune, 56
Today, 5, 95, 113, 116, 117, 122,
    125, 191
Toledo Blade, 56
trickle-down economics, 81–2
Tripp, Linda, 119
Truman, Harry S., 40, 126
Trump, Donald, 1, 31, 51, 88, 120,
    127, 143, 144, 146, 160, 167,
    170, 171, 175, 176–92
  Achilles' heel of, 213
  becomes POTUS, 157, 158, 192,
    193–6, 262, 267
  'currency of contempt' of, 220
  'draining the swamp' rhetoric,
    230–1

federal regulations despised by,
    245–6
foreign policy of, 217, 255, 294
and government shutdown, 230,
    232
Huntington rally of, 211
impeachment trial of, 5, 218,
    266, 282–3, 291–3, 294
inauguration of, 193–7, 202,
    203, 221
lack of knowledge of, 4–5
McCain opposes, 200–1
MAGA slogan of, 180, 211–12
Mexican border wall promise
    of, 188, 200, 206, 211, 244,
    250, 267, 287
moral compass of, 274–7
presidency of 'self' created by,
    218
presidential power excesses of,
    284
stream-of-consciousness style of,
    187
tweets of, 4, 161, 189–90, 193,
    199–200, 205, 208, 217,
    251
unorthodox approach of, 197–
    206, 213–16, 250–1, 287
Trump, Fred, 211
Tsongas, Paul, 104

Ukraine, 183, 217, 283, 289, 291
'Unite the Right' rally, 216–17, 250
United Automobile Workers
    (UAW), 88–9
United Nations (UN), 112, 131,
    133, 141–2, 144, 147–51, 203,
    220, 262
United States (US):
  'blue wall', 190, 192
  Charlottesville rally, 216–17, 250
  Civil War, 3, 6, 40, 41, 134,
    172, 202, 207, 212, 231,
    260, 278
  coal-mining, 209–10
  constitution, 40, 51–2, 55–6,
    99, 193, 206, 212, 218, 260,
    263–4, 266, 271, 272, 277–9,
    283–5

United States (US) – *continued*
  counting regime discredited in,
      126–7
  culture war within, 104, 119,
      176, 262, 271, 276, 280
  Declaration of Independence, 64,
      263
  'Dreamers' 287–8
  Founding Fathers, 27, 193, 263,
      284, 285, 293
  Gettysburg Address, 2–3
  Green Deal, 197
  labour relations in, 88–9
  middle-income, 114, 159, 222–3
  midterm elections, 116, 122,
      175, 205, 208–10, 253–4,
      261, 266–7, 280, 283, 286,
      289
  Naughtie first arrives in, 7,
      9–33
  New Deal, 145, 258, 264
  New Frontier, 71, 75
  opioid addiction in, 209, 230,
      244–5
  'pathway to citizenship', 200
  post-Reagan, 104
  President of (POTUS), *see by
      name*
  rainbow coalition, 91
  religion within, 118–19
  Russian interference in, 184,
      188–9, 197, 201, 205, 217,
      221, 247, 254, 255, 279, 284,
      286, 289–90
  sanctuary cities, 207, 250
  Second Amendment, 271, 272
  Supreme Court, 39, 58, 117,
      120, 127, 178, 270, 278–9,
      285
  TV culture informs, 100, 110,
      111, 241–2, 243, 265
  'white flight', 249
'United States v. Nixon', 58
Up All Night, 154
Up in the Old Hotel, 29
Updale, Eleanor, 75

Veterans For Peace, 139
Vidal, Gore, 6, 42

Vietnam War, 1, 2, 4, 21–3, 34, 45,
      54, 61, 64–5, 102, 139, 152–3,
      195, 200–1, 202, 208–10, 212,
      215, 259, 280
Villepin, Dominique de, 151
Vindman, Lt Col Alexander, 291
voodoo economics, 82, 85

Waco massacre, 148
Walker, Scott, 177
Wall Street, 29, 30, 109, 159, 167,
      177
Wallace, Chris, 187
Wallace, George, 26, 263, 265
Warren, Elizabeth, 269
Washington, George, 284
Washington Post, 6, 38, 42, 52,
      54, 55, 59, 78–9, 80–1, 82,
      83, 87, 182, 193, 197, 247,
      299
Watergate, 1–2, 5, 34–6, 38–9, 41,
      42, 49, 50–8, 61, 64, 69, 79,
      80, 183
Watkins, John, 138
Waxman, Murray, 17, 18
Weinberger, Caspar, 85
Weiner, Anthony, 188
West Wing, The, 152, 295
Weymouth, ADM Ralph, 139
What Happened (Clinton), 254
Wheeler, Charles, 38
Whipple, Chris, 73
White, E. B., 28
White, Theodore H., 74–5
WikiLeaks, 182, 189, 290
Williams, Tennessee, 237
Wilson, Harold, 50
Winchester, Simon, 56–7
Wolfe, Tom, 42
Wolfowitz, Paul, 143
Wonder, Stevie, 121, 169
Woods, Rose Mary, 53
Woodward, Bob, 38, 57, 58, 80
Wordsworth, Dorothy, 38
'Wordsworth, Pornography and
      Mr Nixon' (Naughtie), 38
World, The, 29
World at One, The, 5, 75, 106,
      109

World-Telegram, 29
World Trade Center (WTC), 33,
   63, 137
Worsthorne, Claudie, 50
Worsthorne, Peregrine, 50
WVNS, 209
Wynette, Tammy, 102, 103

xenophobia, 186, 206

Yasgur, Max, 19
Yearling Row Ranch, 100
YMCA, 43, 51
Yom Kippur War, 45, 69
Young, Andy, 155
Young Republicans, 154

Ziad Abu Ein, 78–80
Ziegler, Ron, 56